CW01217736

British Rail
Designed 1948-97
—
David Lawrence

Crécy

www.crecy.co.uk

This book is for Leila.

Crécy

Published by **Crécy Publishing Ltd**
1a Ringway Trading Estate,
Shadowmoss Rd, Manchester M22 5LH
www.crecy.co.uk

First published 2016
Reprinted 2017
Reprinted 2018

© David Lawrence 2016.

ISBN: 978-0-7110-3837-0

Designed by Theo Inglis.

Typeset in Rail Alphabet
and Monotype Grotesque.

Printed in Bulgaria by Multiprint.

Copyright
Illegal copying and selling of publications deprives authors, publishers and booksellers of income, without which there would be no investment in new publications. Unauthorised versions of publications are also likely to be inferior in quality and contain incorrect information. You can help by reporting copyright infringements and acts of piracy to the Publisher or the UK Copyright Service.

Picture Credits
Every effort has been made to identify and correctly attribute photographic credits. Should any error have occurred this is entirely unintentional. A list of picture credits is given at the back of this book.

Table of contents

Chapter One →   4
Introduction

Chapter Two →   8
Britain buys a railway:
Branding the network and
making trains 1948–55

Chapter Three →   56
Where people meet trains:
British Railways' station
architecture 1948–85

Chapter Four →   104
Prime movers:
The Design Panel 1956–60

Chapter Five →   156
Design researched
1960–81

Chapter Six →   218
The new look:
Design diversity
and privatisation
1982–97

Notes to the text   254

Glossary of design terms   261
and abbreviations

Glossary of colours   262

Reference sources and   265
further reading

Index   268

Picture credits   272

Chapter 1 →
Introduction

British Rail Designed 1948–97 is about the design successes, and failures, of Britain's most extensive state-sponsored industry. It is a story of people and ideas, movement and design, speed and colour; it is a comprehensive celebration of the crafting, operation and marketing of a national railway system, by which four main-line companies with steam-powered empires were transformed into a modern transport system.

British Railways, operating from 1964 as British Rail, was a public organisation providing a national transport network. Many of Britain's influential and talented twentieth century designers were drawn into this complex project to create a positive travel experience, leaving an extraordinary legacy of two- and three-dimensional design icons. Experts from the Royal College of Art, from Design Research Unit and Pentagram are discussed here. Perhaps surprisingly, but importantly, the story also takes in motor car stylists, fashion designers and silversmiths, all leaders in the theory and practice of design. Moving railway aesthetics from the consequences of engineering decisions, to an expression of the purpose and culture of a nation, British railway design has been both synchronised with, and has led, world design trends. It paralleled design developments in the former nationally owned airlines British Overseas Airways Corporation and British European Airways, and the former General Post Office; it set the standard for the rebranding of Danish State Railways, and for changes to railway identity across Europe. Every aspect of the British railway system, from printed materials to vehicles and buildings, was in a few years reconceived and re-branded by the individuals and teams who styled much of modern Britain's environment and consumer goods. After the radical developments of the 1960s, British Rail continued to receive the attention of leading professionals, culminating in the heading of the Directorate of Architecture, Design and Environment by Jane Priestman from 1986 to 1991. With this appointment the role of design on Britain's national rail system was reinvigorated once more, albeit as a precursor to the eventual full privatisation of the system in 1997. The effects of this design programme are manifested today in good, clear communication and product design, from the international *Eurostar* network to contemporary revivals of letterforms conceived in the early 1960s.

Design ideas and practices are intended to both solve problems for travellers and staff, and to further improve on previous designs; they may be concerned with a ticket lasting for a single journey, or a vehicle operating for many years. As an idiom – a flexible, pervasive, unifying, orderly and contemporary visual appearance – design should produce an effortless and efficient environment, whilst itself being invisible or unobtrusive. British Rail design encompasses brand, service, two- and three-dimensional objects and products from badges to buildings, posters and trains. Design is about why things look like they do, to do what they do, and it is about things looking aesthetically right: with good proportions, and parts in good relation to one another. Designers work with two-dimensional shapes: symbols, lettering, outlines, and three-dimensional forms: vehicles, buildings, uniforms. Each of these qualities is equally valid for a powerful locomotive or a tailored garment; all are present in design for British railways. The design process has resulted in both successes – the environment around us when we travel – and rejected or abandoned projects which demonstrate how design ideas might have developed, had the context been different. With railways once again topical, as *Crossrail, Crossrail 2*, the *HS2 'Y' network*[1] and other projects serve as a means of developing or regenerating regions, so it is timely to consider the creation of the modern, nationally-owned railway system, which forms the basis for these initiatives.

Most accounts of railway development have focussed on the technical achievements of engineers largely, if not exclusively, in the field of steam locomotive design. Other volumes have considered railway station buildings from the perspective of industrial heritage, and the colourful history of poster design has featured in association with everything from tourist merchandise to artists' monographs. Styling of internal combustion and electrically powered vehicles, of tickets, and of spaces for travellers has been considered in a limited number of publications, of which those by the late Brian Haresnape are outstanding.[2] Practically, Haresnape's work was constrained by the cost of colour printing, so that key aspects of the subjects in his books - colour and pattern particularly - could not be fully represented. Haresnape documented the period he lived through as a professional artist and writer; the resulting publications covered the period up to the mid-1980s. Since then, the rich architectural, graphical, engineering and technological innovation in British Rail design has been covered only in fragments.

Themes and Structure

The principal subjects of this book are the railway system as an entity; the means of encouraging and facilitating travel (printed publicity, graphics, tickets, holiday packages); the vehicles themselves (locomotives, passenger and freight vehicles); the places where trains stop (station architecture and interiors, lettering design); the people who operate the system (uniformed staff). This is also a study of how politics and the civil service, geography and urbanisation were manifested in the design processes and products.

The book is structured chronologically, with a thematic subsidiary structure, to show elements of design development which correspond to the changing character of the organisation. Chapter Two: Britain buys a railway: branding the network and making trains, 1948–55 surveys the period when the railways were combined as a state-owned business. The origins of British Railways' design in the private rail transport operators are considered here. London Transport's influence and that of overseas operators is introduced. The chapter discusses the creation of the first brands (symbol, lettering, livery) used by British Railways, and the extension of these brands into signs, publicity and staff uniforms. We see the growth in design practice of the publicly-owned organisation, with the problems and solutions it encounters along the way. Locomotives, vehicles and industrial design realised up to and including the 1955 British Railways *Modernisation Plan*, are included in this chapter.

The British Transport Commission Design Panel had no direct influence over architecture, although its efforts in industrial design would impact on the built environment of the railway. This aspect of the system was much slower in finding a coherent visual language, so it is possible to focus on the architecture of British Railways stations and ancillary buildings over a longer period. Chapter Three: Where people meet trains – British Railways' station architecture 1948–85, describes the station as urban focus and social place, as shelter and container of services both commercial and retail, and as shop front for the organisation. It examines colour schemes for stations, interior designs, and the production of ancillary passenger spaces including travel centres, restaurants and cafeterias.

Chapter Four: Prime movers: the Design Panel introduces the special British Transport Commission design management group formed as a reaction to the visual results across the network of the *Modernisation Plan*. It explains the need for the panel, lists the panel's first members and the personnel responsible for engendering a better quality of industrial design for the railway and associated transport activities. The design consultancies are presented together with their projects, across locomotives, diesel and electric multiple-units, passenger vehicle décor and upholstery, lettering, and publicity. We observe the use of the Council of Industrial Design's *Design Centre* in London as a showcase for British railway developments.

In the shadow of system curtailment proceeding from publication of *The Reshaping of British Railways* in 1963 (the 'Beeching Report'), all aspects of the British Rail network were transformed by the radical influence of Europe. Chapter Five: Design researched 1960–81 brings together many elements of the design programme implemented thorough the network, examining how they flourished, making British Rail a corporate monolith during the 1970s. By the early 1980s the rail system was in design stasis, a serious impediment to the unwavering expectation that it generate enough revenue to be mostly self-sufficient. Organisational change was allied with design as an important tool for obtaining more passenger and freight business: this is the topic of Chapter Six: The new look: design diversity and privatisation: 1982–97. Harnessed with considerable energy to make a better public railway, design would finally carry it into privatisation. Completion of privatisation during 1994–97, following the *Railways Act* 1993, created disparate elements from the former organisation, with rapid dilution of the extensive achievements which had been gained.

The main text is supported by notes, a glossary of design terms, a glossary of colours used in livery schemes, and an extensive list of sources.

Acknowledgements

Particular appreciation is due to Michael Walton for thinking of this book; to Nick Grant, Kevin Robertson, Alan Butcher and Sue Frost at Ian Allan for leading the project; Theo Inglis for the book design; at the former Wilkes & Ashmore: Jill Coombs, David Higgins, Perry King, Kenneth G Sadler, Don Tustin, Jack Ward; Gerry Barney; Andrew Barron; Brian Boddy; John Bonnington; Simon Bradley; Dave Brennand; Ben Brooksbank; Joe Brumwell; Tim Brown; David Burnicle; Margaret Calvert; Professor Dugald Cameron; David Christie; Max Clendinning; Piers Connor; Harvey Coppock; Godfrey Croughton; Helen Dann; Department for Transport: Julie Okpa; Mary de Saulles; Alan Drewett; Mike Denny; Val and Stan Friedman; Sir Kenneth Grange; Chris Green; Bob Haresnape; Ged Haresnape; Anne Haring; Tony Howard; W R Headley; Graham Higgins; Anthony Hill; Sasha and Atholl Hill; Tony Hillman; Mike Howarth; Bernard Kaukas; John Kennet; Rob Latham; Chris Leigh; Roger Marsh; Joy and William Mitchell; Jennie Moncur; Roy Moorcroft; Bruce Morgan; The National Archives; Brendan Neiland; Michael Papps; David Pearson; Bruce Peter; Dr John Prideaux; Dr Jane Priestman OBE; Railway Lines (www.gloucesterrailwayana.com): Paul Workman; Peter Raybould; Chris Ridley; Michael Rodber; Ab Rogers; Su Rogers; Trevor Saunders; Search Engine, the National Railway Museum library and archive centre; Anthony Stephen; Richard Taylor; Travelling Art Gallery/Greg Norden; Roy Turner; Peter Trewin; the Victoria & Albert Museum Archive of Art and Design; Pete Waterman OBE; Nigel Wikeley; 'Barking' Bill Wright; Sean Wyatt; Alan Young.

Attribution

Designers work in teams and singly; they work with clients, manufacturers, and customers. Most projects in this book represent the work of more than one individual or group, acting as authors of ideas and facilitators of concepts, right through to advisers on production processes. Only where a designer has been identified with a particular project, is their name featured in the text to give fuller details of attribution.

Chapter 2 →

Britain buys a railway: Branding the network and making trains 1948–55

We will start our design journey by considering the intriguing means by which a socialist government applied aspects of commercial branding practice to fashion a national railway system from private companies. Not just the making of a recognisable identifying symbol – although in fact there were several – but the wholesale shaping of a massive business made up of machinery, buildings, printed materials and people. This chapter first discusses the inception of British Railways as a corporate entity, and the quest for a contemporary symbol and sign under which it could press forward. Next, we note how the railway system was changed visually – today we would say 'rebranded' – by the introduction of signs, publicity and uniform insignia based on new emblems. The final part of this chapter is concerned with the locomotives and passenger vehicles built by British Railways before the British Transport Commission made the decision to create a Design Panel, for better management of how it presented itself to the public, government, and the international transport industry. The project had to be effected in the face of powerful loyalties to former railway operators, and to traditional aesthetic practices like locomotive colour schemes. It was influenced by the great success of the 'house style' which brought London Transport a distinctive, world-leading image; what the Commission produced was a rather home-spun and fragmented approach to corporate design.

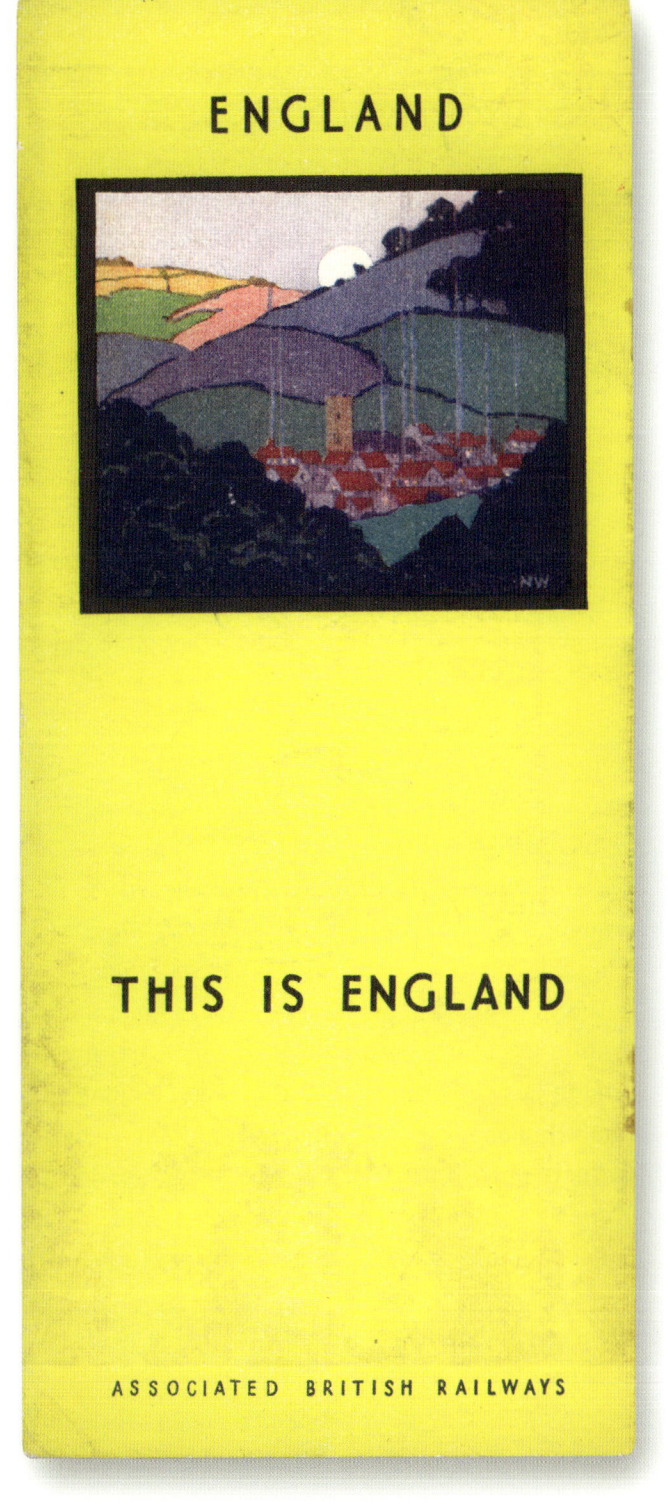

From the 1930s, the private main line railways advertised themselves collectively in North America as 'British Railways' (1936).

Building the organisation

The main line Great Western, London, Midland and Scottish, London and North Eastern and Southern railways of the United Kingdom had been marketed collectively overseas as 'British Railways' since the 1930s. During the Second World War they were controlled by the Railway Executive Committee, who used the inclusive term 'British Railways' for national cohesion and propaganda purposes. In peacetime, the private operators all planned to restore and improve their networks. In the face of impending transfer to national ownership, they lobbied parliament, industry and the public to gain support.[1] Whatever their ambitions, the private railway companies were unsuccessful in resisting acquisition by the State. The *Transport Act* passed on 6 August 1947 was intended to bring integration across the rail, road and waterborne transport system in Britain. On 1 January 1948 the British Transport Commission (BTC) came into being, chaired by Lord Hurcombe 1948–53. Subordinate to the Commission, the Railway, Docks and Inland Waterways (ports, railway-owned canals), Hotels (and railway catering), Road Transport (renamed Road Haulage from June 1949), Road Passenger (without operating responsibilities), and London Transport executives, worked the majority of passenger and freight systems. Each executive expressed itself through design; the largest and most evident was the Railway Executive. Its members were directly appointed by the Minister of Transport, so they were not directly answerable to the Commission. From the start, this confused matters. The Railway Executive controlled several regions: Eastern, London Midland, North Eastern (merging with the Eastern in 1967), Scottish, Southern and Western (a North Western Region was considered but not adopted). Because the regions represented the railway to the public, and historical allegiances were hard to suppress, it proved difficult to give public impression of a truly national network.

The railway was still struggling with the effects of the recent war organisationally, the private railway companies had not fully accomplished their own assimilation of independent operators when they were themselves nationalised. This context made unification under the Railway Executive more pressing, and yet more difficult.

To effect the partial reverse of the 1947 Act, and improve profitability, a further *Transport Act* followed in 1953. The Railway Executive, which had done much to ignore the Commission's direction, was abolished. Railway management was decentralised to Area Boards, whilst the emphasis on a system with a single national identity was reduced. The effect of this was not immediately evident, but in time it would see the regions attempt to revert to an impression of their pre-nationalisation owners, encouraged by a Conservative government. Able to move forward without the complication of consulting the Executive, the Commission could embark on a project to modernise traction and rolling stock, and later to form a Design Panel to promote a consistent visual appearance to all aspects of the railway organisation.[2]

A house style

London Transport, with a considerable reputation for excellence in design for public travel environments, had also been nationalised when the Railway Executive was created. Wherever its services were present, the London Transport Executive displayed a bar and circle, or bulls-eye symbol. This had originated in 1908, was drawn to precise specifications by calligrapher Edward Johnston during 1916–19, and gradually evolved as typographical trends changed. London Transport had shown that a symbol and logotype was exceptionally useful for uniting an organisation, in its public relations, and in its advertising. From 1929 the London and North Eastern Railway (LNER) developed a house style for all publicity, posters, and lettering on signs at stations and on vehicles, based around the sans serif lettering drawn by Eric Gill for the Monotype Corporation. When the British Transport Commission and its subsidiary executives came into being at the start of 1948, the rush began to find a suitable symbol with which to unify assets of the nationalised railway companies, and support the restructuring of the industry into six regions with standard operating practices. LNER practice would form a major component of how the Commission and its subsidiaries communicated with the public.

The historian Michael Bonavia[3] has suggested that Lord Hurcomb made it a personal project to procure a symbol for his organisation.[4] Medallist, coin and seal designer Cecil Thomas produced a formal device for the Commission in February and March 1948.[5] It was described as 'a lion bestriding a composite symbol which includes a [locomotive] wheel; a winged arrow superimposed on a pattern of wavy lines, symbolising the activities of the Docks & Inland Waterways; and a pair of torches emitting flashes of lightning, symbolising modern forms of power.'[6] In this book the symbol is identified by the nomenclature from British Rail

Official seal of the British Transport Commission in its original, ornate form, 1948.

Director of Industrial Design - James Cousins: lion & wheel. Lacking the authority of a grant of arms - heraldic emblems would perhaps not have been appropriate for an organisation transferred into state ownership by a socialist government - Thomas's seal for the Commission presented little visual appeal. Extracted from the fussy assemblage of antiquated elements, the lion standing on a bar superimposed on a wheel formed the basis for crests identifying three transport entities with the trading names British Transport, British Railways, and British Road Services. Ignoring the somewhat distorted lion, it can be seen that the wheel crossed by a bar is not dissimilar to London Transport's own, brilliant, bar and circle logo. Michael Bonavia remarked that the lion & wheel was: 'so generally disliked…the Railway Executive agreed to use it on locomotives but not much elsewhere.'[7]

Too complex for effective use on signs, the lion & wheel derived from the Commission's insignia also represented administrative control from above, which the Executive preferred not to promote. Some alternative symbol was needed, to use across publicity, signs and uniform badges. As the largest section of the British Transport Commission, and with a century of independent heritage shared amongst its many predecessor companies, the Railway Executive was determined to establish its own image.

The Railway Executive asked London Transport's advice, but it was not given because a dispute over selection of an appropriate logo was perceived and London Transport did not wish to be involved.[8] A J White had held various roles for the London and North Eastern Railway since 1933, ultimately becoming Advertising Manager in 1945 when he succeeded C G G Dandridge.[9] Dandridge had been instrumental in adopting the typographical work of Eric Gill for the LNER, and White would have been very familiar with this pioneering work on branding by a railway operator. Michael Bonavia was Assistant (Public Liaison) to the Chief General Manager, LNER 1945–47, at which time he worked with A J White; his interest in branding of transport services quite likely informed these developments.[10] At nationalisation White was made Advertising Officer for the Railway Executive, bringing with him the belief of his former employer that the LNER lozenge totem and Gill Sans typeface was as good as, or better than, the corporate identity used by London Transport.[11] With this background and view, and with professional links to officers responsible for publicity and signs across the regions, White was well placed to devise a trading symbol and house style. It was to London Transport that he looked for inspiration. The Railway Executive asked the London Transport Executive to advise on a symbol in January 1948: London Transport avoided the question to keep out of any conflict with their managers at the Commission. White found his own solution: compressing the ring of the London Transport into a lozenge, he enlarged the bar and followed the contemporary vogue for streamlining by rounding off the bar ends. The result, whilst lacking the elegance of the symbol from which it was derived, provided a clean, effective brand mark suitable for use on publicity and uniforms.

Free of historical or imperial references, White's totem was redolent of the socialist government's aspirations for equality which had brought the Railway Executive into being. Each geographical region of British Railways was to be colour-coded: it is likely these colours were selected by White in discussion with his Advertising department colleagues across the regions. They were confirmed at a meeting between British Railways and London Transport in February 1948, when the proposed totem was also shown: Southern - white on green, likely derived from the green signs and passenger vehicles of the Southern Railway; Western - cream on chocolate, part of the livery of the former Great Western Railway; Eastern - white on blue, an association with Great Eastern Railway locomotives; North Eastern - tangerine, not a good colour for signs, and probably included because it was the only distinctive hue not allocated to another region; Midland - white on crimson lake, a colour which had been used for London, Midland and Scottish Railway (LMSR) rolling stock; Scottish - white on pale blue, a reference to the livery of former Caledonian Railway locomotives.[12] Even here, at the inception of nationalisation, we can see the regions attempting to hold on to some distinguishing attribute. White's totem was published April 1948. Excluding the North Eastern Region, these colours were a clever way of respecting railway heritage whilst

A J White, designer of the 'British Railways' totem, in 1954.

applying a high degree of consistency to the appearance of signs and publicity. Objectively, beyond the use of consistent colour schemes within the regions this was no great innovation: the white on green of Southern Region signs copied Southern Railway practice, changing only the letterform and shade of green; the London & North Eastern Railway had adopted Gill Sans in white on deep blue for new signs in the early 1930s; from 1946 the London, Midland & Scottish Railway made similar items using Gill Sans letters on a dark red background.

British Transport Commission seal adapted as the lion & wheel crest for use by British Railways on vehicles and printed material.

The totem devised by A J White proved more useful and popular than the lion & wheel, and was adapted in various ways for marketing purposes.

13

Other bar and circle symbols

Perhaps the lion & wheel and totem logos could be carefully allocated to different functions and complete the styling of the nationally owned networks, but in fact there was a third symbol to truly complicate matters. The British Transport Commission included the Docks and Inland Waterways and Hotels executives. Employees of the latter subsidiary were mainly employed in buildings, but dock and canal workers wore outdoor uniforms. Having no more affection for the Commission's crest than did the Railway Executive, and an equally determined leadership team, some other badge was sought by the Docks and Inland Waterways Executive (D&IWE). It approached the Commission's Works Development Office, where a Leslie Marson had made direct copies of the London Transport bar and circle, adapted to show a locomotive wheel (for Railways), a lorry wheel (for Road Haulage) and a lifebelt for water-related activities.[13] This last design was adopted by the chairman of the D&IWE Sir Reginald Hill, who had worked with Lord Hurcomb during the Second World War. Various derivatives were made as cap badges and reproduced on publicity until 1953 when the D&IWE was abolished.

The availability of two distinct operating symbols for British Railways inevitably caused confusion. The 'British Transport' lion & wheel was rarely used because it was too generic to have meaning; 'British Road Services' formed part of the livery applied to nationalised road freight-carrying fleets; the British Railways crest emerged as part of the livery for locomotives, and on official printed material for staff use. A series of uniform cap badges (see pages 32–35) was also produced for wear by supervisory staff in contact with the public as part of their duties. A J White's design work formed the template for British Railways signs used comprehensively until the early 1970s: these are discussed in Chapter Three. The totem also formed the basis for branding on printed publicity material and uniform insignia issued to lower staff grades until 1956.

Lion & crown crest

Following the *Transport Act* 1953, British Transport Commission Chairman Sir Brian Robertson worked to suppress the totem, which was seen as a legacy of nationalisation. A grant of heraldic arms was requested; it was not unusual for civic organisations to make such a move, and here it was a strategy for distancing the Commission from its politically left-leaning origins. Correctly described as a demi-lion rampant, holding a spoked railway wheel and issuant from a crown decorated with the rose (England), thistle (Scotland), leek (Wales) and oak leaf (Great Britain), the crest would be used for locomotives, passenger coaches and uniform cap badges from 1956. Most publicity, however, continued to feature the totem until about 1963. The lion & crown did not add any modernity to the image of the railway. In the form applied to locomotives it was not an outstanding success, *Design* magazine describing it as 'a variation on the original clear, crisp outline of the London Transport sign; while it certainly avoids the jelly-like curves...in the British Railways "totem", the unduly extended "ears" have debased the original fine shape of the London Transport symbol without allowing comfortable space for the lettering. At the same time the rounding of the corners makes a bad foil to the circle.'[14]

Opposite page top: Little-used lion & wheel crest identifying the British Transport Commission.

Opposite page middle and bottom: Adaptations of the London Transport bar and circle symbol used to mark the Commission's dock and waterway activities.

This page top: British Railways lion & crown crest in the form applied to locomotives from 1956. Middle: Lion & crown roundel made for passenger vehicles and some locomotives, based on an LMSR motif. Bottom: A similar roundel carried by the vehicles of Britain's nationalised freight carrier.

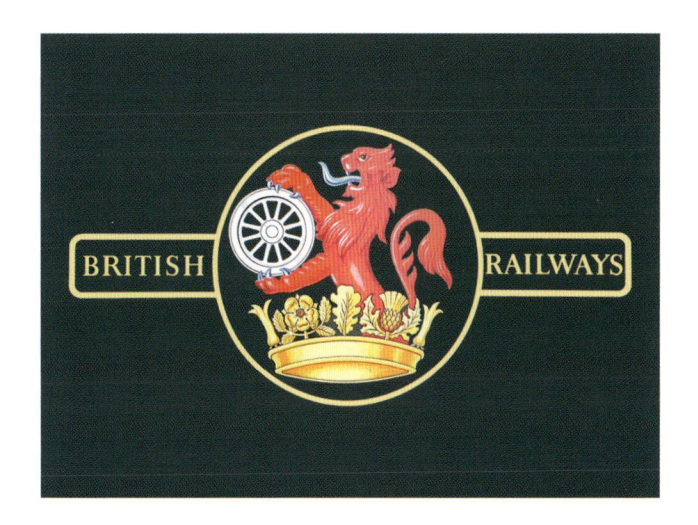

Publicity

Countless cheap paper handbills could be printed quickly to advertise anything from a football match or firework display to a carnival. Each was identified by a regional totem symbol marked with 'British Railways', or an abbreviation of the region name. Gill Sans comprised the majority of lettering used for handbills.

British Railways took on an extraordinary heritage of publicity material from the private companies which preceded it. The practice of commissioning new and established artists to enhance promotional material continued largely as before until the late 1950s, when graphic devices and photography began to compete with pictorial images.[15] Besides the large posters for platforms and public billboards manufactured by letterpress, lithographic and silk-screen techniques, artists contributed illustrations for the holiday guides which were issued each year, in each region. Their subject matter tended towards glamorous interpretations of sunny beach activities. On a seasonal basis, lithographed folder leaflets specified areas of particular appeal for recreation; some of these featured artworks which also appeared as prints in railway carriages. The totem took many forms. On glossy leaflets it was frequently reproduced in black, whist for cheaper handbills, or timetables, it would often take the regional colour, or the colour of the main text. In this context, styles of lettering varied considerably.

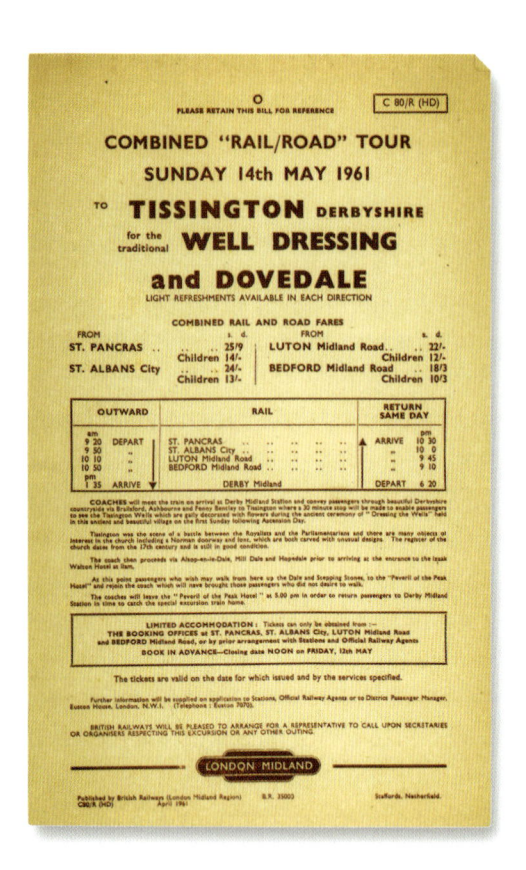

Above and below: Millions of cheap handbills, made to advertise regular services and special events, featured the totem symbol in various forms.

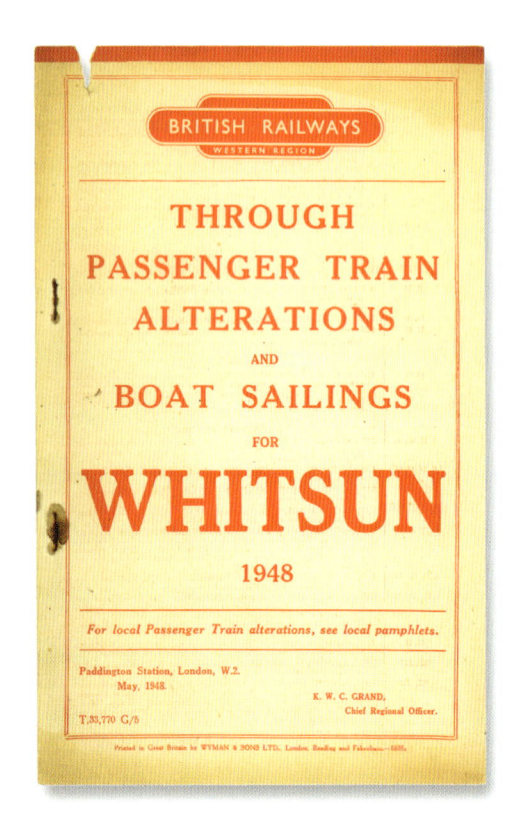

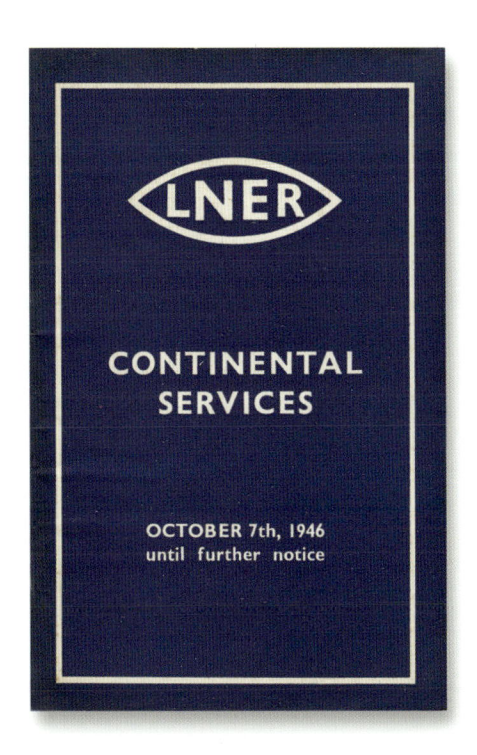

Top left: Private main-line railway companies operating before 1948 established a near-standard format for the passenger timetable book.

Top right: When British Railways began to publish its own timetable books from 1948, it used the existing format with minor variations.

Above left and right: Where possible, British Railways' regions continued the identifying colours introduced by its predecessors. The Southern Region took the Southern Railway's green, and the Scottish Region was branded with a light blue which made indirect reference to earlier Scottish railway operators.

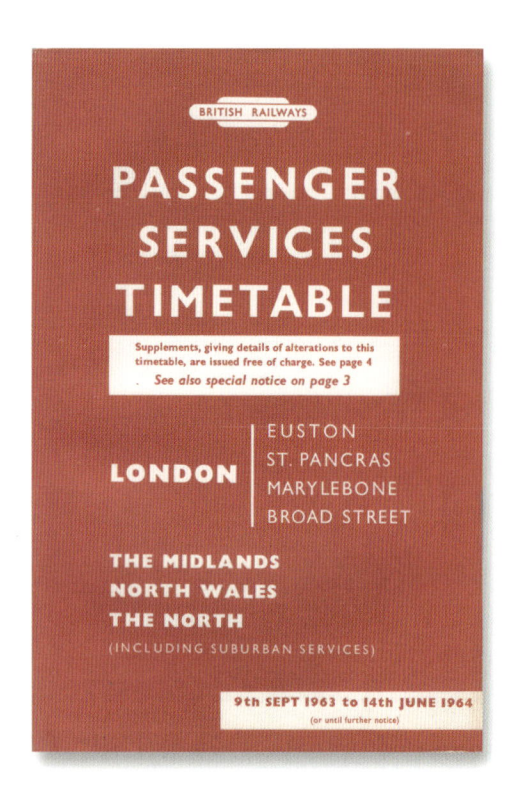

Design of covers for timetable books evolved quickly in the early 1960s. Regions retained their specific colour-coding alongside variations in typography. The totem symbol began to disappear from publicity in the early 1960s, to be replaced by a simple 'British Railways' logotype. Cover formats were varied with each issue to distinguish them from the superseded edition.

18

In an attempt to move away from the monolithic identity conceived for British Railways in 1948, the regions exercised sometimes considerable licence to devise their own symbols. Left top: The Southern Region applied a quasi-modernist feel to some printed publicity. Left middle: For a few months in 1962 the London Midland Region tried to reprise the name of its forerunner, the London, Midland (and Scottish) Railway. Left bottom: In 1960, Eastern Region routes were marketed by adapted totem symbols. Above: in 1962 the Western Region also tried to break away from its parent organisation by crafting a name based on its heritage - (Great) Western Railway.

Timetable books had barely changed in design since the 1920s: British Railways merely added their totem symbol to the existing cover format, and colour-coded the books according to region.[16] Timetables of the early 1960s reveal a search for modern graphic character which predates the full British Rail corporate image programme. From 1963 the convention of a standard timetable cover layout began to unravel. With the familiar totem mark gone, a logotype of plain text now showed the trading name 'British Railways', sometimes paired with the regional title as a subsidiary detail. Regions employed various graphical devices to enhance timetable book covers: arrows for the Western Region, the silhouette of a rail for the Southern, bold bars of colour for the Eastern and London Midland. The North Eastern Region advertised the 'Deltic' locomotive, honoured hauler of trains on the East Coast Main Line. Regions deliberately did not adhere to one style of branding. More ephemeral than timetables, publicity leaflets showed experiments in visual identity. The Eastern Region began to market its lines as individual services, with handbills of 1960 carrying totems lettered 'Great Northern', 'Great Eastern' and 'L. T. & S.' (for the London, Tilbury and Southend route). The Southern Region often used a symbol labelled 'Southern' and the same practice applied for 'London Midland'. This latter region advertised itself as 'London Midland Railway' in 1962; the Western Region briefly renamed itself 'Western Railway'.

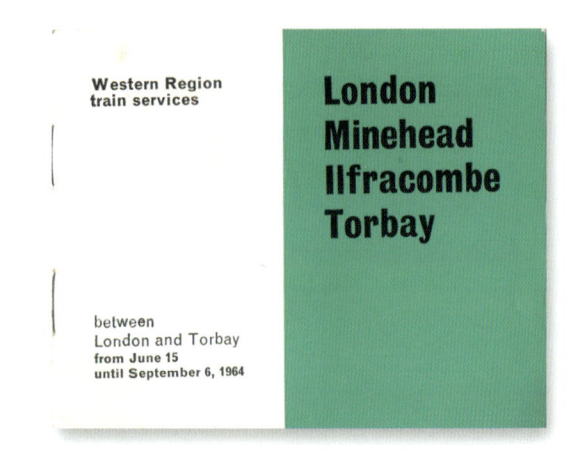

As the 1960s progressed, typographers devised new forms of timetable that were more convenient.

The idea of using non-regional colours to identify specific routes, a concept which would be taken up fully from 1965, began with these small timetable booklets.

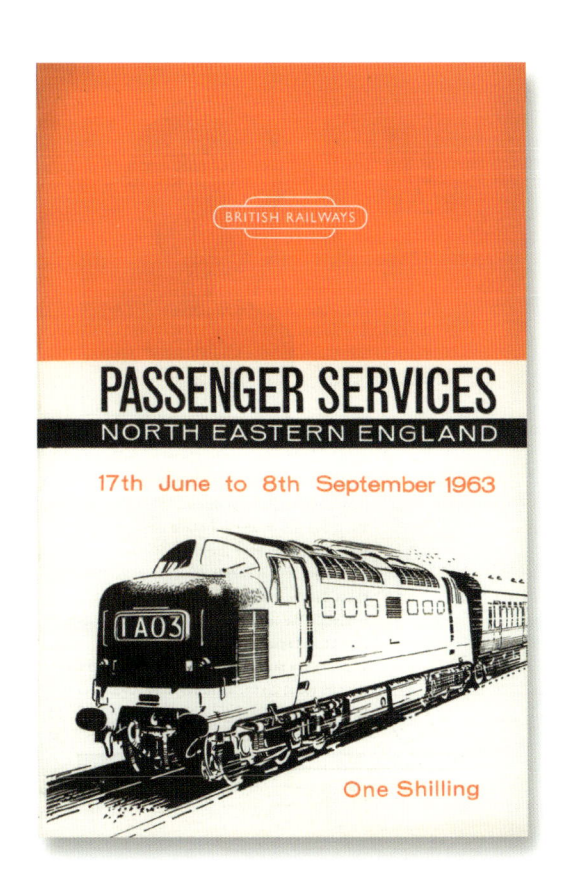

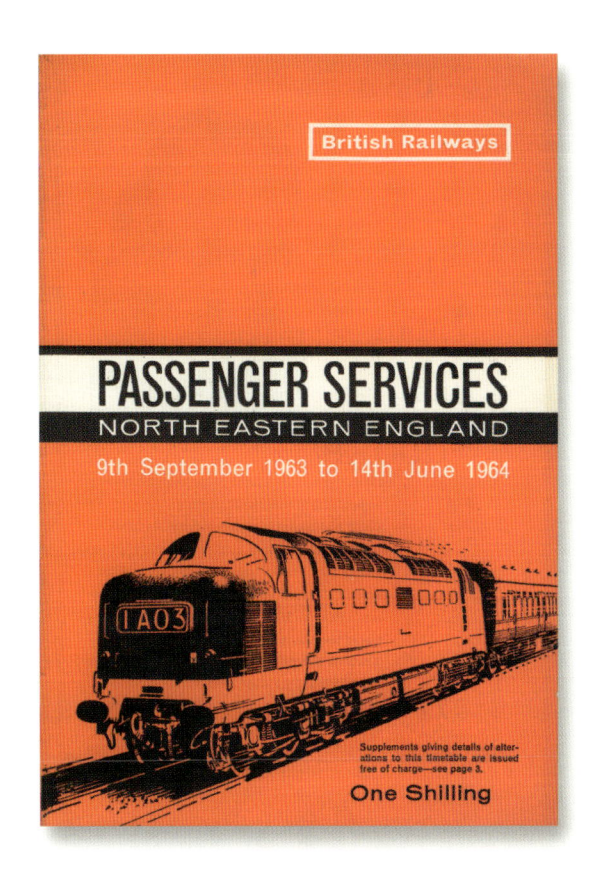

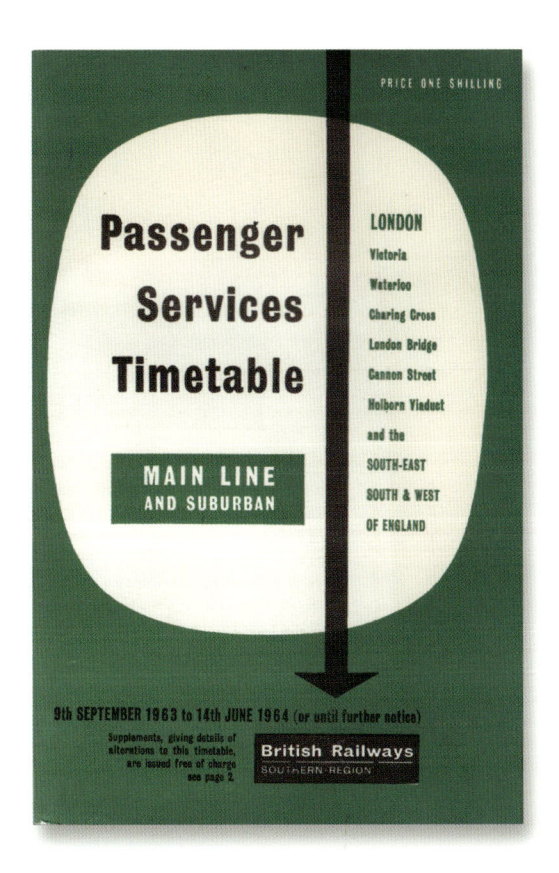

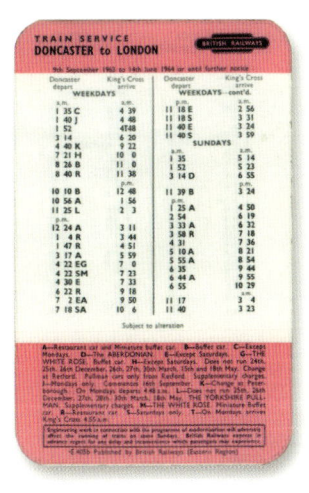

It is evident from these books that timetable design was not consistent, but took several routes through modernisation in the early 1960s. The North Eastern Region retained its orange colour scheme, and included an image of its prestige D9000 (class 55) 'Deltic' express locomotive. The Southern Region seems to have tried various 'pop' graphic devices. Small, attractively coloured cards of train times indicated a move away from the bulky books.

Pages 22–23: Continuing a theme established by the main line railways, comprehensive guides to regional seaside resorts made reference to the idyll of sun, beach and youth. Occasionally graphic designers like Tom Eckersley produced more abstract variations on the subject.

BRITISH RAILWAYS
HOLIDAY
GUIDE
1954
WALES & NORTH WEST
including the Isle of Man
1/-

BRITISH RAILWAYS
HOLIDAY GUIDE
1955
EASTERN
ENGLAND
1/-

BRITISH RAILWAYS
Holiday Haunts
1958
SOUTHERN ENGLAND
(KENT TO CORNWALL)
& THE CHANNEL ISLANDS
1/6

1959 Holiday Haunts
BY BRITISH RAILWAYS
SOUTHERN ENGLAND
(KENT TO CORNWALL)
& THE CHANNEL ISLANDS
1/6

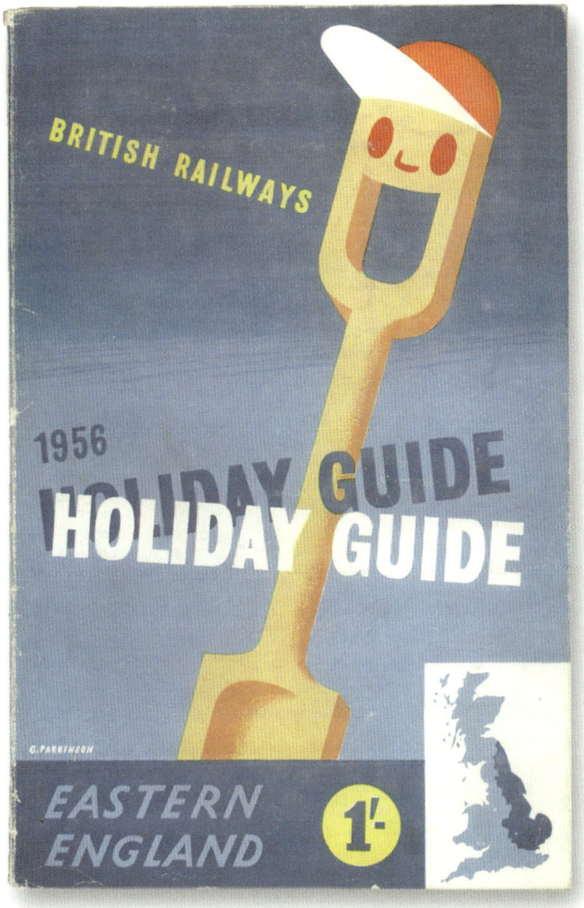
BRITISH RAILWAYS
1956
HOLIDAY GUIDE
HOLIDAY GUIDE
EASTERN ENGLAND
1/-

BRITISH RAILWAYS
Holiday Guide
1957
1/-
SOUTH & SOUTH EAST
INCLUDING THE CHANNEL ISLANDS

Eastern and North-Eastern England 1961
holiday haunts
BRITISH RAILWAYS
PRICE 2/-
ECKERSLEY

1962
Holiday Haunts
BY BRITISH RAILWAYS
SCOTLAND
2/-

DEVON
BRITISH RAILWAYS
JACK MERRIOTT

SCOTLAND
BRITISH RAILWAYS

THE WEST COUNTRY
BRITISH RAILWAYS

SOMERSET
BRITISH RAILWAYS
JACK MERRIOTT

ESSEX
BRITISH RAILWAYS

THE GLORIOUS THAMES
BRITISH RAILWAYS
JACK MERRIOTT

25

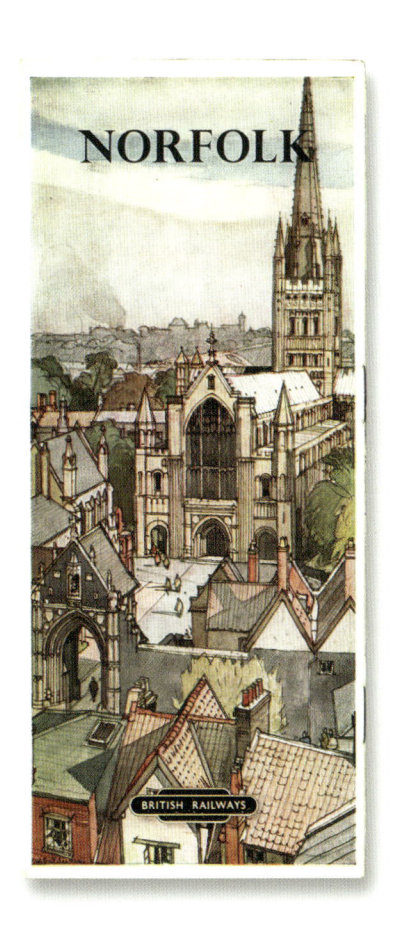

26

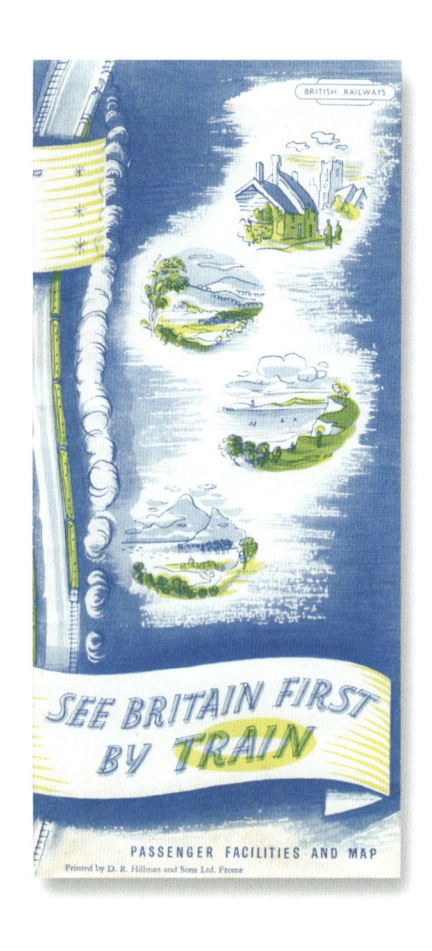

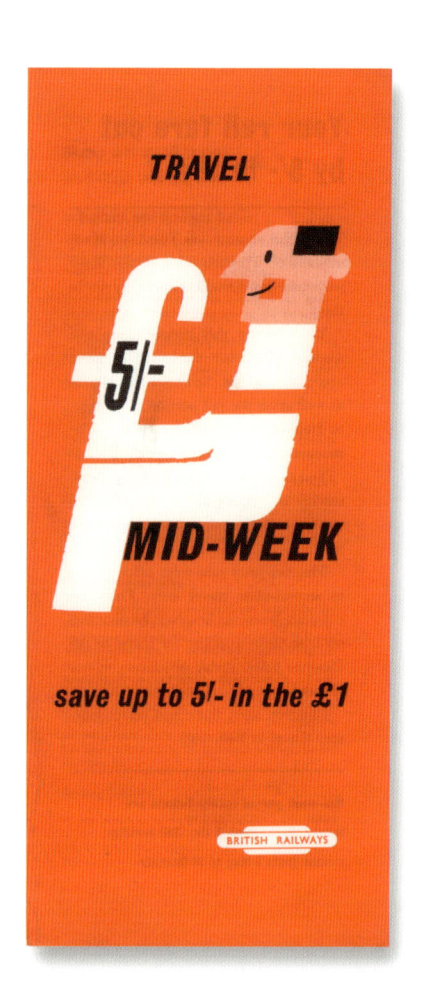

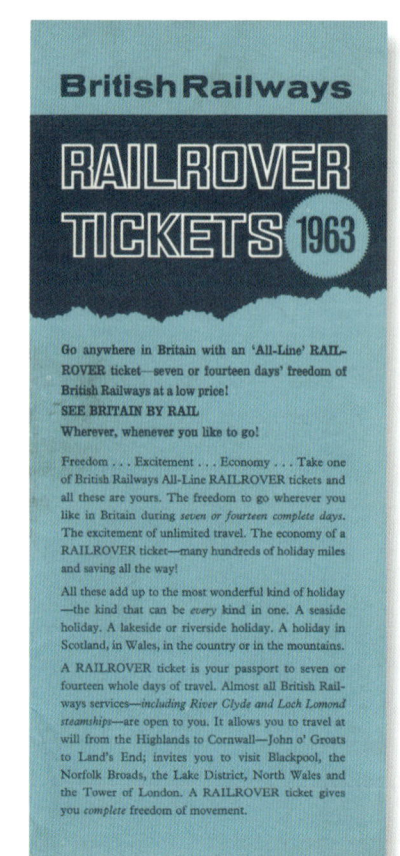

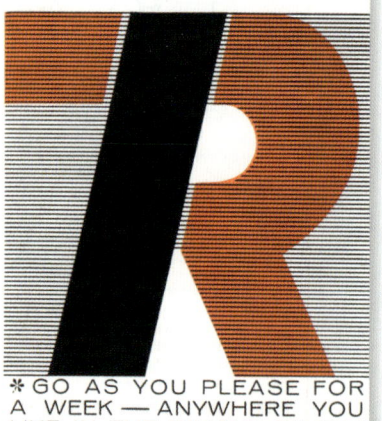

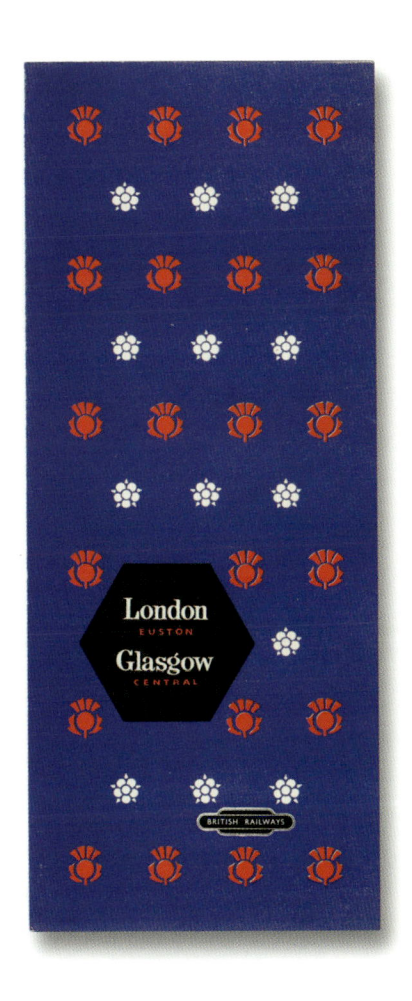

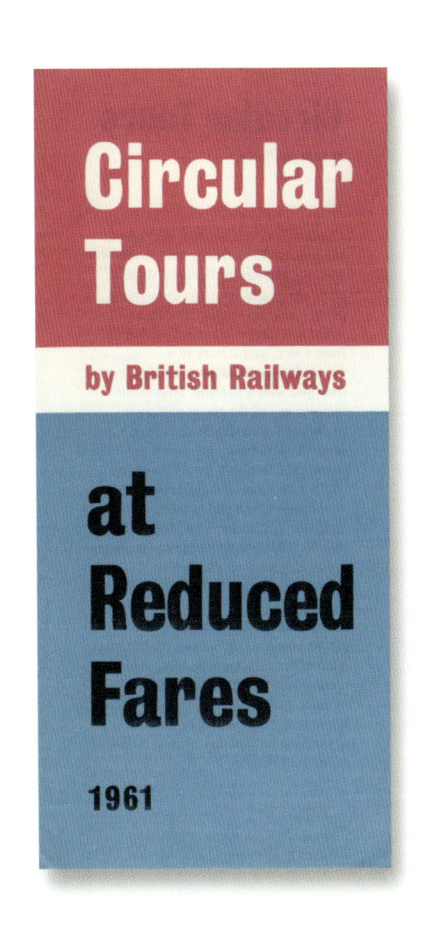

Pages 24–25: Artists painting stylised scenes for British Railways posters also produced images for display in passenger carriages, and for high-quality leaflets advertising leisure resorts. Of these, Jack Merriott was prolific. Upper row left to right: Jack Merriott 1950; anon. 1950; Hodgkinson 1950; Merriott 1950; Merriott 1950; Dobson Broadhead 1950. Lower row left to right: Jack Merriott 1950; Raymond Teague Cowern 1950; Merriott 1950; Frederick William Baldwin 1952; anon. 1953; Roselman 1953.

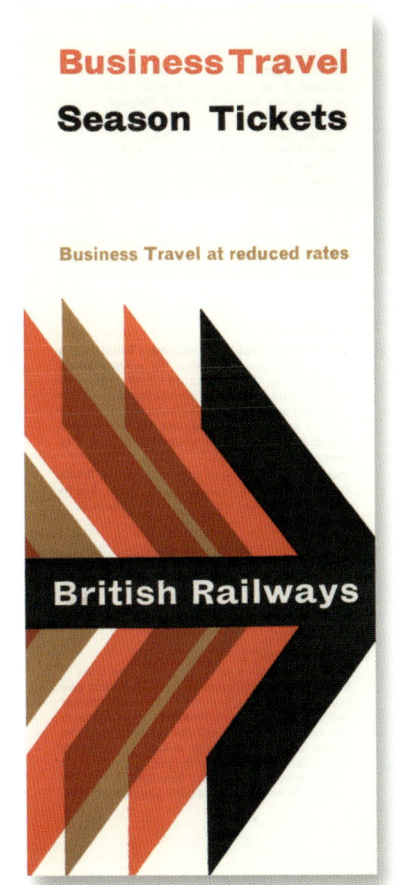

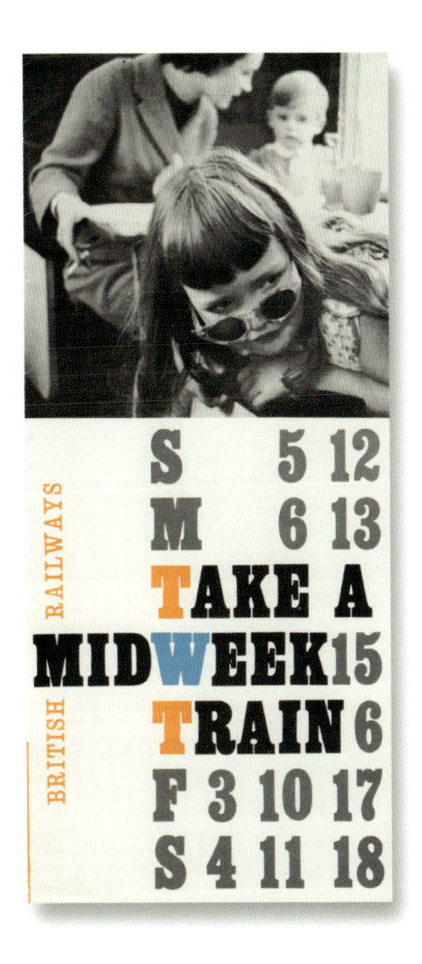

Opposite page and this page: British Railways publicity was procured by the regional commercial departments, meaning that much of the design varied considerably according to subject, budget, changing graphic styles and the taste of the civil servants buying the print work. This is a small selection of leaflets from 1950 to 1964, chosen to illustrate variations in approach.

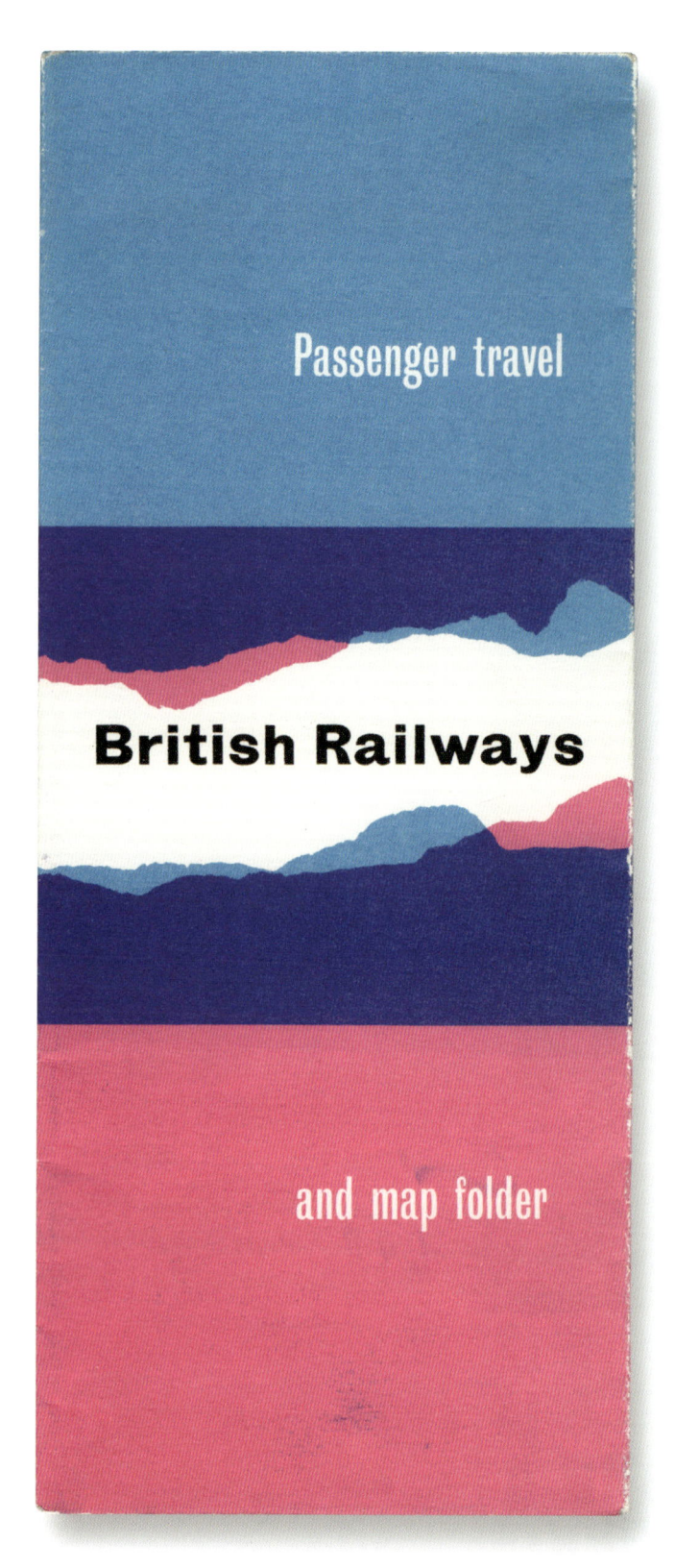

Graphic design innovation for British Railways utilised every technique available to the artist and the printer. The potential of four-colour lithography to create a third hue from two overlaid colours is used well here to enliven a simple layout.

Small, succinct, anthropomorphic drawings have frequently been employed for railway subjects aimed at adults as well as children. They are quick to communicate a service or concept, making it seem friendly and familiar.

Developments in illustrated popular magazines encouraged British Railways to explore the use of colour photography to compete with other visual communication media. Items like this folder map are now useful historical documents, long outliving their ephemeral purpose.

If photography could promote the railway's comforts, it could also look deep into the landscape served by the system, affording travellers views of fauna characteristic of the area (1965).

The railway handbill - a disposable means of quick advertising - prompted artists like Tom Eckersley to use attractive artworks which exploited this cheapest of mediums.

ECKERSLEY

FROM 29 APRIL   **TO 27 OCTOBER 1962**

Holiday Runabout Tickets
in all the popular holiday areas

With a Holiday Runabout Ticket you can travel **as much as you like** throughout the Area, **every day** while the ticket is valid.
With a Holiday Runabout Ticket you can see – conveniently, cheaply – all there is to be seen within a wide radius of your chosen holiday centre.
You can get your Holiday Runabout Ticket on demand at a principal station, or on 48 hours' notice at any other station, in an Area (12 hours' notice in Scotland).
Children aged 3 and under 14 travel at half-price in most cases. (Please note that prices of tickets remain the same where, in certain Areas, there are no services on Sundays.)

BRITISH RAILWAYS   **Ask for full details when you arrive at your holiday centre**

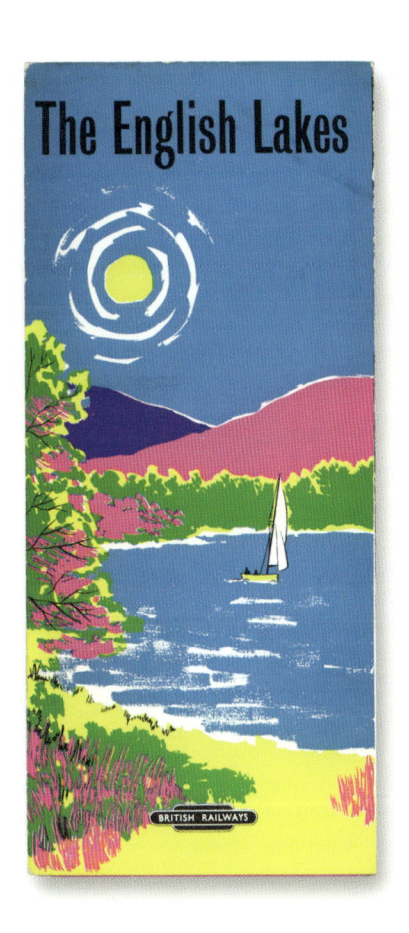

In contrast to the highly-worked artists' depictions of British topography presented on pages 24–25, the anonymous artists who created these two pairs of folder leaflets preferred a compelling, abstracted, scenery made possible by fluorescent colours.

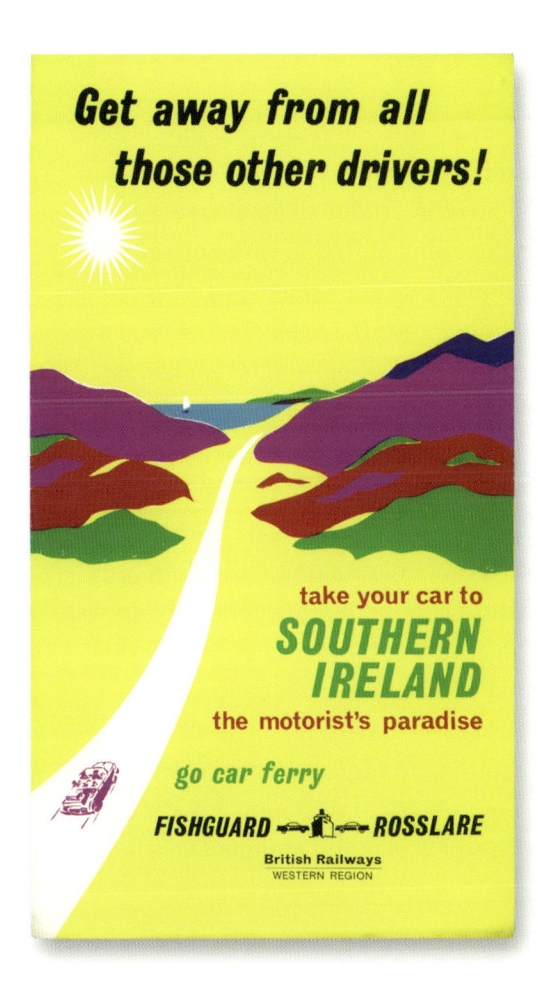

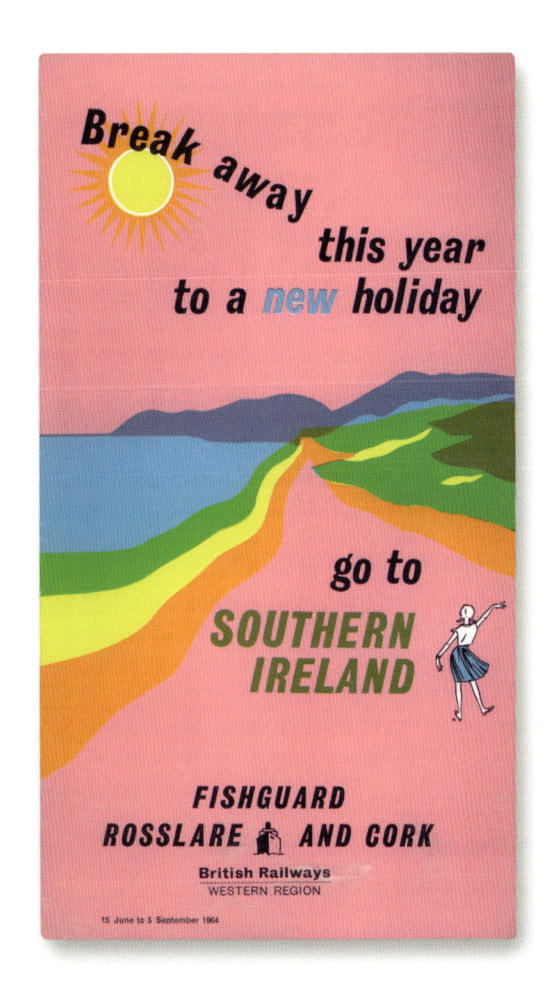

Uniforms: 1948 and 1956

Alongside the station as shop-front of the railway, the staff is the most important interface between the operator and its travellers. Those workers coming into direct contact with the public have been issued with uniforms of some description almost as long as there have been passenger trains. Uniforms have two main elements: the garments, and the insignia by which these garments and their wearers are identified with the organisation. In 1948 British Railways had more than 641,000 employees. Many were employed in administrative roles, but the substantial operating staff required appropriate uniform insignia. Adoption of the new dress was not universally welcomed: staff were shown in official photographs wearing pre-1948 uniforms, carefully preserved out of allegiance to their former employers, into the early 1950s.

Public-facing railway uniforms were of vaguely Victorian military design, familiar to many men who had served in one of the world wars. Jackets and trousers were cut for manual work, to fit all sizes and shapes, be adaptable to indoor/outdoor work from ticket offices to engineering depots and out on the lines themselves, and to suit all climates from western Cornwall to the far north of Scotland. Made from a heavy wool cloth of black or very dark grey hue, clothing was economical and hard-wearing, necessary in an environment close to steam motive power. Male staff hats were of military type, with a widened circular crown above the hat band, and a peak over the eyes. Supervisory staff wore caps with stiffened crowns; for other grades the crowns were soft. Insignia was limited to a metal badge attached to the hat, manufactured by regalia companies located in the 'jewellery quarter' of central Birmingham.[17] In this context the confusion over management of the railways was particularly manifest. Workers across the system simultaneously received badges variously featuring the lion & wheel *or* the totem. The regional colour coding applied to all badges.

Badges were plated in nickel or yellow metal to indicate rank. Totem badges were issued in all regions from 1949. Public-facing employees received a dedicated badge: 'Porter', 'Excess Luggage' [clerk], 'Ticket Collector', 'Guard' or 'Foreman'. A generic 'British Railways' version would be worn by drivers, firemen and signalmen.[18] In the scheme of insignia based on the totem, Station Masters and Inspectors were provided with headwear showing their titles embroidered in gold bullion wire on the hat band: no separate badge was provided. The tension between the British Transport Commission and its Railway Executive gave rise to a second series of insignia for headwear. Lion & wheel badges were issued to supervisory grade employees (with some overlap of the grades covered by the totem badges) and female platform staff in all regions from 1950. This seems partly to have been an attempt by the BTC to override the prevalence of the totem in the public eye.[19]

In order to feature the lion & crown crest derived from the heraldic arms of 1956, two badges would be issued to several grades of employee. All would wear the crest, plated in white or yellow metal. Additionally an anonymous artist drafted new hat insignia for staff, to replace the mixed distributions of lion & wheel and totem badges. A ribbon-shaped strip lettered with the grade title or the generic 'British Railways', would be enamelled in the regional colour.[20] The use of white or yellow metal to identify gender was set aside, the different colours now indicating rank. Station Masters and Inspectors continued to wear hats with the grade embroidered on the band, with a smaller lion & crown crest surrounded by a wreath of laurel leaves, all on a felt pad coloured according to region. Subsequently the bullion embroidery of the laurel wreath was replaced with a yellow metal stamped version.

Variations in uniform dress can be observed by reading the magazines produced to promote staff news and social activities. Top row, left to right: Senior Porter C Barber, St. Ives, 1954; Passenger Guard E Norris, St. Ives, 1954; Foreman F W Barber, Sleaford, 1961; Station Master M J Rich, St. Ives, 1954; Station Master G R Rowell, Helmdon for Sulgrave, 1954. Middle row, left to right: Leading Porter W C Coman, Wroxham, 1961; Ticket Collector J Camp, Hertford East, 1961; Foreman W Brunning, Hunstanton, 1961; Signalwoman Dorothy Palmer, Althorne, 1961; Station Master J G H Hull, Burnham-on-Crouch, 1961.

Above: Ticket Collectors, with their Foreman in the background, prepare for an unidentified occasion at Paddington, London, in the early 1960s.

TICKET COLLECTOR
BRITISH
35
FOREMAN
PORTER
GUARD
INSPECTOR
PORTER
GUARD
PORTER

PORTER
PORTER
FOREMAN
PORTER
GUARD
PORTER
BRITISH RAILWAYS
PORTER
FOREMAN
TICKET COLLECTOR
BRITISH RAILWAYS
BRITISH
FOREMAN
RAILWAYS

Rolling Stock

Thousands of steam locomotives, a significant proportion of them several decades old, made to many different designs and needing a multitude of components, presented the Railway Executive with a major renewal programme if it were to maintain services. It would be very costly. Modernisation meant the replacement of steam by internal combustion and electrically-powered trains. But the technology for replacing steam in Britain was not ready in 1948, beyond a few forays which had been made by the private companies. Consequently Robert A 'Robin' Riddles, Member of the Railway Executive for Mechanical and Electrical Engineering, with assistants Roland Bond and E S Cox, determined that twelve standard types of steam locomotives be designed. They would draw on the best practice of existing examples from all the main constituents of the Executive, but with the particular influence of Riddles' former employer the London, Midland and Scottish Railway, and locomotives shipped to England from North American manufacturers during the Second World War. A total of 999 locomotives were manufactured, the last example being '9F' freight locomotive number 92220. In tribute to the Great Western Railway, it was named *Evening Star* in a televised ceremony on 18 March 1960.

Pages 34–5: A selection of British Railways badges made in enamelled metal and embroidered cloth, worn as current insignia by different grades of uniformed operating staff from Porter to Station Master in the period 1949–1965.

Standard class 2MT, 2-6-2T, 84006. Series introduced 1953.

Standard class 2, 2-6-0, 78000 when new in December 1952.

Standard class 3MT, 2-6-2T, 82000, new in April 1952.

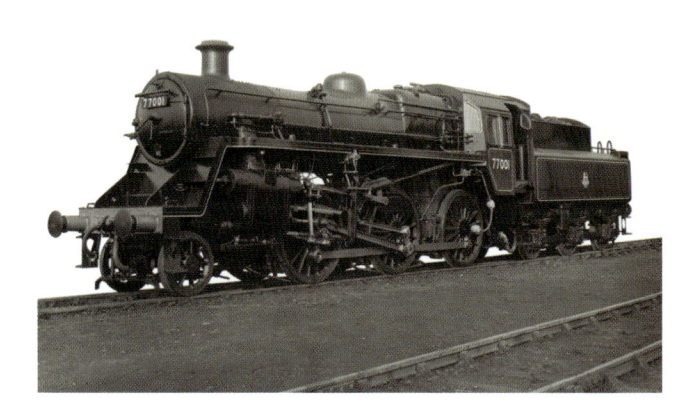

Standard class 3MT, 2-6-0, 77001. Series introduced 1954.

Standard class 4MT, 2-6-4T, 80118. Series introduced 1951.

Standard class 6P5F 'Clan' series, 4-6-2, 72003 *Clan Fraser*. Series introduced 1952.

Standard class 4MT, 2-6-0, 76000, new in December 1952.

Standard class 7P6F 'Britannia', 4-6-2, 70015 *Apollo*. Series introduced 1951.

Standard class 4MT, 4-6-0, 75019. Series introduced 1951.

Standard class 8P, 4-6-2, 71000 *Duke of Gloucester*, a one-off example introduced in 1954.

Standard class 5MT, 4-6-0, 73108. Series introduced 1951.

Standard class 9F, 2-10-0, 92000. Series introduced 1954.

37

The standard British Railways green livery with black and orange lining is carried by class A4, 4-6-2, 60034 *Lord Faringdon*, Perth, Scotland, July 1966.

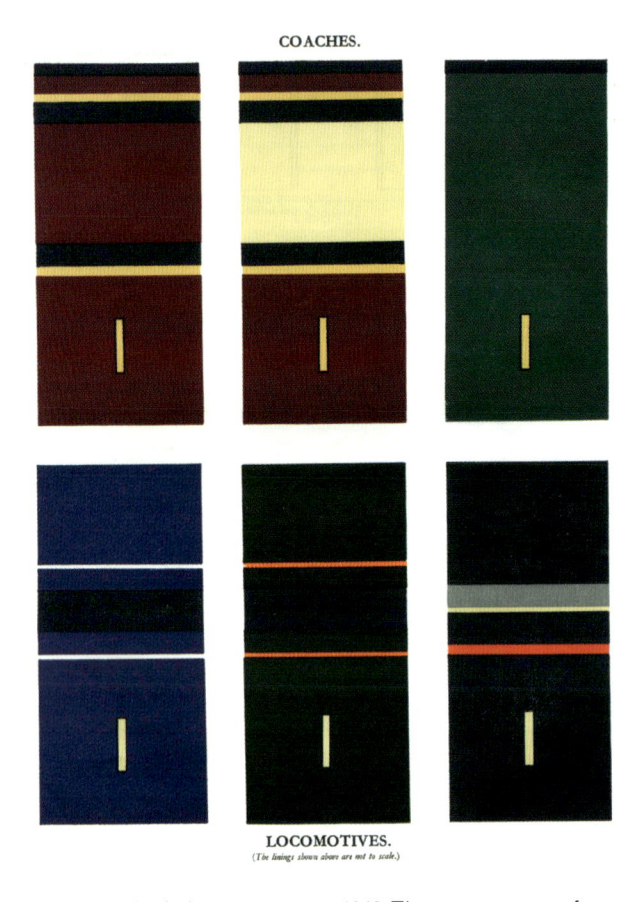

Proposed vehicle livery patterns, 1948. The upper row are for passenger coaches, and the lower row for locomotives.

New uniforms for vehicles

Livery is a pattern of colour or colours used to identify three-dimensional moving objects. It has its origins in the distinguishing of military and civilian groups by arrangements of colour, often with accompanying symbols. Livery is also derived from the colours used in heraldic coats of arms. In Britain, it has been used by people of power and wealth, governmental departments, civic and commercial organisations. Transport vehicles are essentially boxes with a particular form, and a series of windows and openings which enable them to function and to be operated. Lining is used to highlight forms and details. British Railways experimented with vehicle liveries when it was first formed in 1948, again in 1956, in 1964–65, and from the late 1970s until privatisation. Suitable colours must weather well in different climates, must suit both urban and country conditions, not clash with the livery of passenger vehicles, and communicate the unity of the organisation. Some colours work better on some forms more than others. Colours, and particularly patterns of colour, can emphasise mass or lightness, power or speed. Some suggest the reliability of tradition, others the exciting potential of innovation. Finally, the painting scheme can unite or conceal physical features which might otherwise be in visual conflict. Railway companies, conceived in a period of fierce and relentless competition for funding and custom, resorted to liveries in continuation of the custom seen in road coach operation. Observers of steam locomotive history and heritage railways will know that railway companies selected colours from across the spectrum so that their services would be recognisable: every hue from deep blackberry black through light blue to salmon pink would be encountered by a traveller crossing Britain by train in the late nineteenth century. Many railway companies painted their vehicles and details of their buildings in shades of green. Green was cheap and relatively durable: it bore the dirt of an open, industrial environment well; it was innocuous in city or country surroundings. Shades of red, from crimson to maroon, allowed a railway company to advertise itself as powerful and dominant. Variations of white mixed with red, yellow or black produced pinks, creams and greys to brighten or highlight parts of vehicles. Requiring more fastidious cleaning than darker paints, they were less popular with operators.

British Railways wished to announce itself as new and progressive: what colours should it choose for locomotives and passenger coaches? Four ex-LMS class 5 steam locomotives painted in potential colour schemes were exhibited at Kensington Olympia station, London, on 30 January 1948. Reluctant to stray far from tradition, officials had the engines liveried in Great Western Railway dark green, London and North Eastern Railway apple green lined with red, cream and grey, Southern Railway Malachite green, and a pre-1923 London and North Western Railway (LNWR) black, lined in red, cream and grey. One ex-Southern Railway electric locomotive carried blue paint with silver lining. Coaching stock present was painted maroon or brown and cream, with variations in lining colours. No decision was made. In April/May of the same year, British Railways managers viewed an express passenger locomotive livery of royal-deep ultramarine blue with red, cream and grey lining, and a general passenger livery of light apple green with red, cream and grey lining, at London's Marylebone station. They saw too coaches finished in maroon, and light maroon or 'plum' with off white or 'spilt milk', all lined with black and old gold/golden yellow.[21]

What seemed to be final standard colours for locomotives were published in 1949. Express passenger steam and electric locomotives would be bright blue, lined with black and white.[22] This scheme for express passenger locomotives did not remain in use for very long; from about 1951, blue engines were repainted into dark green, lined black and orange, with other selected express passenger steam locomotives.[23] Passenger and mixed traffic steam and mixed traffic electric locomotives which were not blue or green were painted in a version of the LNWR scheme: black lined in red, cream and grey. This last pattern - the oldest - continued until the end of steam operation. Diesel main line locomotives took a livery of black with aluminium lining and bogies. By early 1949 it had been decided that main line coaches with corridor connections would be bright crimson lake/carmine red and off-white lined black and gold, with plain crimson for non-corridor coaches. Southern Region electric trains and diesel multiple-units across the regions operated in plain shades of green. The explanation for this last colour was given in 1961 by the first Chairman of the British Transport Commission Design Panel T H Summerson: 'it is a pleasant colour: it does not show the dirt so much. It has been tried out with success in various other applications, principally on the Southern Region. We wanted something which was distinctive and different from the livery which was normally used on the normal British standard coaching stock, and we also had to obtain something which would be accepted without too much trouble by the Regional General Managers; and as a result green was a compromise.'[24]
From 1956 passenger coaches on most regions except the Southern and Western appeared in a darker maroon colour, lined in black and gold. Some Western Region coaching stock reverted to a non-corporate scheme of chocolate and cream in homage to the Great Western Railway.

First agents of modernity: multiple-unit trains

This section discusses the advent of self-propelled trains in the British Railways' passenger fleet. It is included here because the determination to construct diesel mechanical-unit (DMU) and electric multiple-unit (EMU) stock arose before the mass programme of vehicle changes which has come to be called the *Modernisation Plan*. This chronology also means that beyond some details of interior décor, the British Transport Commission Design Panel had very limited input into the appearance of the first batches of multiple-unit trains.

In our present time many trains take the form of multiple-units: sets of passenger cars with on board power generation and/or transmission equipment. Multiple-units are considered to be cheaper to operate, and more flexible, than locomotive-hauled trains. By the 1930s, the biggest threat to railway transport was the internal combustion engine, as the middle classes discovered the convenience and pleasure of motor coaches and private cars. Rural railways fared badly in competition with bus services. Family saloons were mass-manufactured by Ford, Vauxhall, Austin, Morris and the Rootes Group on production lines giving potentially continuous outputs of units. Railway companies tried to make economies and improve convenience for passengers. Engineers explored alternative forms of propulsion, including internal combustion engines connected to the wheels electrically, mechanically or hydraulically, and electric motors fitted to the trains but deriving power from external sources: typically overhead catenary wires or additional rails fixed in parallel to the railway tracks. Purpose-built diesel mechanical railcars, usually self-contained vehicles with a driving position at one or both ends, were tested in Britain as a successor to the steam railcars which had been designed for use on routes with low passenger numbers. Most distinctive of the British railcars were those used by the Great Western Railway from 1933, with innovative technology and streamlined bodies. These demonstrated that railway travel could be clean and contemporary, indicating a future beyond Victorian steam-powered transport. The railcar/railbus concept would continue to evolve, and develop into the diesel multiple-unit. Some decades later, seeking even cheaper rolling stock solutions, British Rail would return to the idea of mixing road and rail vehicle units.

The Southern Railway was one operator which chose to use electric multiple-units, inheriting various examples from its constituent companies. Other operators, notably the London and North Eastern and London, Midland and Scottish railways, also had sections of electrified lines. Early electric multiple-units were not purpose-built, but fabricated from former passenger coaches with stylised ends. Realising the value of these trains, railway companies did produce new units to their own designs. Some versions continued to be manufactured by British Railways after 1948 because they were good designs, or because the Second World War and its consequences delayed more development. As a quick means of replacing steam traction the Railway Executive wished to build diesel mechanical units for branch lines. Capitalising on its experience with electric traction technology, the Southern Region preferred to develop diesel electric mechanical units (DEMUs) for operation on routes not served by its extensive fleet of electric multiple-units. This section discusses diesel and electric multiple-units built for all regions before the British Transport Commission Design Panel became involved in their external look. Similar trains built after this time are discussed in a subsequent section.

Multiple-unit appearance

Traditionally railway historians have considered the output of diesel and electric multiple-units separately. An understanding of the development of multiple-unit styling, however, invites a survey of diesel and electric multiple-units *together*. Manufacture of the entire first phases of DMU and EMU fleets was rapid: 4–5 DMU classes were allocated for production each year through 1951–63. This meant innovation time was limited. Most British Railway multiple-units were styled by engineering draftspeople trained to design in plan, section and elevation views as steam locomotive drawing conventions had dictated. They relied on coach-building techniques, road vehicle styling, or at best looked at aviation production methods for any new references. Pre-war examples of internal combustion or electrically powered trains, such as the Great Western Railway's railcars, were largely ignored by British Railways. For ease of construction, simpler designs were preferable. Most vehicles were fabricated from sheet steel, stamped with openings and fixed into shape over frames. Before the adoption of glass reinforced polyester (fibreglass) to create softer, more rounded forms, cab fronts were made by welding different sections together to make enclosures for the train control desks and operating crew. Priority was given to function and safety. Some manufacturers introduced combinations of radiusing and tapering panel junctions to improve the vehicle contours. These assembly processes gave acceptable but unremarkable results.

With a few exceptions, the units had identical cab fronts at each end. The basic form of cab front design varied only marginally from one British Railways' region to another. British Railways' first multiple-units were electrically-powered vehicles for the Southern Region. O V S Bulleid (1882–1970) Southern Railway/British Railways Southern Region Chief Mechanical Engineer 1937-49, and his chief draughtsman Lionel

A 4SUB multiple-unit, at Coulsdon North, Surrey, August 1982.

Lynes had designed the 4SUB family of electric multiple-units built for the Southern Railway in 1945-6, specifying coaches with elliptical body sides for increased capacity. 4SUB unit fronts reflected the vehicle profile, styled as three vertical panels with two folded back from the central section; Southern Railway electric locomotives CC1–CC3 (20001–20003) and experimental steam locomotive 'Leader' shared this feature.[25] This was a well tried solution to creating a characteristic, standardised appearance. Lynes had worked for the Great Western Railway, which built steam railmotors from 1908, their driving cabs also fashioned as three angled planes. When the Great Western created 'push-pull' auto trailers and autocoaches from 1912 - an efficiency in which a driving cab was included at the opposite end of a passenger coach to the locomotive which hauled or propelled it - the same chamfered end form was continued. What is also likely to have informed Bulleid and Lynes' work was the styling of the electric multiple-units used by the Southern's predecessor the London and South Western Railway from about 1915.

Two classes of diesel multiple-unit made for the Western Region had cab fronts built up from four planes, arranged to meet at both horizontal and vertical fold lines: a way for the Region to reflect its Great Western Railway heritage in national ownership. Those for the London Midland and Eastern regions had fronts made with two planes, joined at a horizontal crease below the windows. Diesel multiple-units of most classes adapted the three-part form of Southern Region EMUs, many with an additional horizontal fold below the windows, creating cab fronts with six planes. This pattern was most neatly handled by Metro-Cammell. Inclusion of three front windows gave a way of achieving more shape to cab ends; it also gave the driver a better view of the route.

British Railways continued a practice of coding its multiple-units according to the number of vehicles, purpose and/or sequence of manufacture. Whilst the individual codes can be interpreted in order to identify distinct units, the logic of their application followed various systems which are too complex to discuss here.

Eastleigh builds for the Southern, Eastern, London Midland and North Eastern regions

From 1948 to 1960, multiple-unit building was concentrated at Eastleigh, Hampshire, the British Railways works which had most experience of this train type because it served the extensive network of Southern Region electrified railway lines. Guidance on requirements for new EMUs was given by chief mechanical engineer R A Riddles, a steam locomotive designer who strongly favoured electrification as a replacement for steam. The priority was to produce utilitarian passenger stock quickly at a time when government restrictions on public spending limited investment for design innovation.
In autumn 1951 the 4EPB (class 415/1) was introduced, made to a profile used by Southern Railway for its 4SUB (class 405) multiple-units of 1945–6. There were a few visual detail differences, most obviously the addition of a headcode window in the cab fronts, and the revised proportions of the cab windows. Rain strips over cab windows and all doors broke up the smooth lines of the 4SUB form. This first EPB design was regarded as perfectly serviceable in the period of post-war austerity, when labour and materials were too scarce to expend on much innovation. Through to 1957, 213 units were built. In spite of later developments, the template was used again for 2HAP (class 414) trains built in 1957–59, and 2EPB (class 416/1) units of 1959.

The 2EPB (class 416/2) of 1953–58 saw the design revised slightly, when the central section was widened so that the creases were moved to the inner edges of the cab windows, all beneath a forward projection of the roof. Units produced at Eastleigh for the North Eastern Region Tyneside system in 1954–55 copied the 1953 2EPB appearance, substituting marker lights for the headcode panel. They returned to the Southern Region in 1963. Two further builds of 2HAP (414/1) stock through to 1962–63 also used the 2EPB (416/2) template. Built by British Railways at York/Doncaster in 1958–60 for the Eastern Region Fenchurch Street–Shoeburyness line, AM2 (class 302) trains adopted the Eastleigh 2EPB (416/2) styling. Eastleigh also made four-car AM7 (class 307) units in 1956 for the Eastern Region's Liverpool Street–Shenfield outer suburban service. Their fronts, based on the 2EPB (416/2) form, were characterised by five marker lights and a small horizontal destination indicator. From 1960 the class was rebuilt. For the London Midland Region north London electric services, Eastleigh made three-car class 501 units in 1957, combining the standard Mk1 carriage body with the 1953 EPB (416/2) style cab ends. An extra destination indicator window was fitted above the headcode display, an electric tail light was included in the cab fronts, and an air whistle replaced the usual air horns. The handrail layout varied from the Southern Region's 2EPB.

Southern Region 4EPB multiple-unit, new in November 1951.

Eastern Region AM7 (class 307) unit, introduced 1956.

Southern Region 4EFB multiple-unit of class 415/1, at Victoria, London, in 1978.

Eastern Region AM2 (class 302) train, introduced in 1958, and photographed at Roydon, Essex in 1975.

Units built for the Tyneside suburban system during 1954–55 followed the 2EPB design of 1953.

A class 501 unit, built for the London Midland Region in 1957.

43

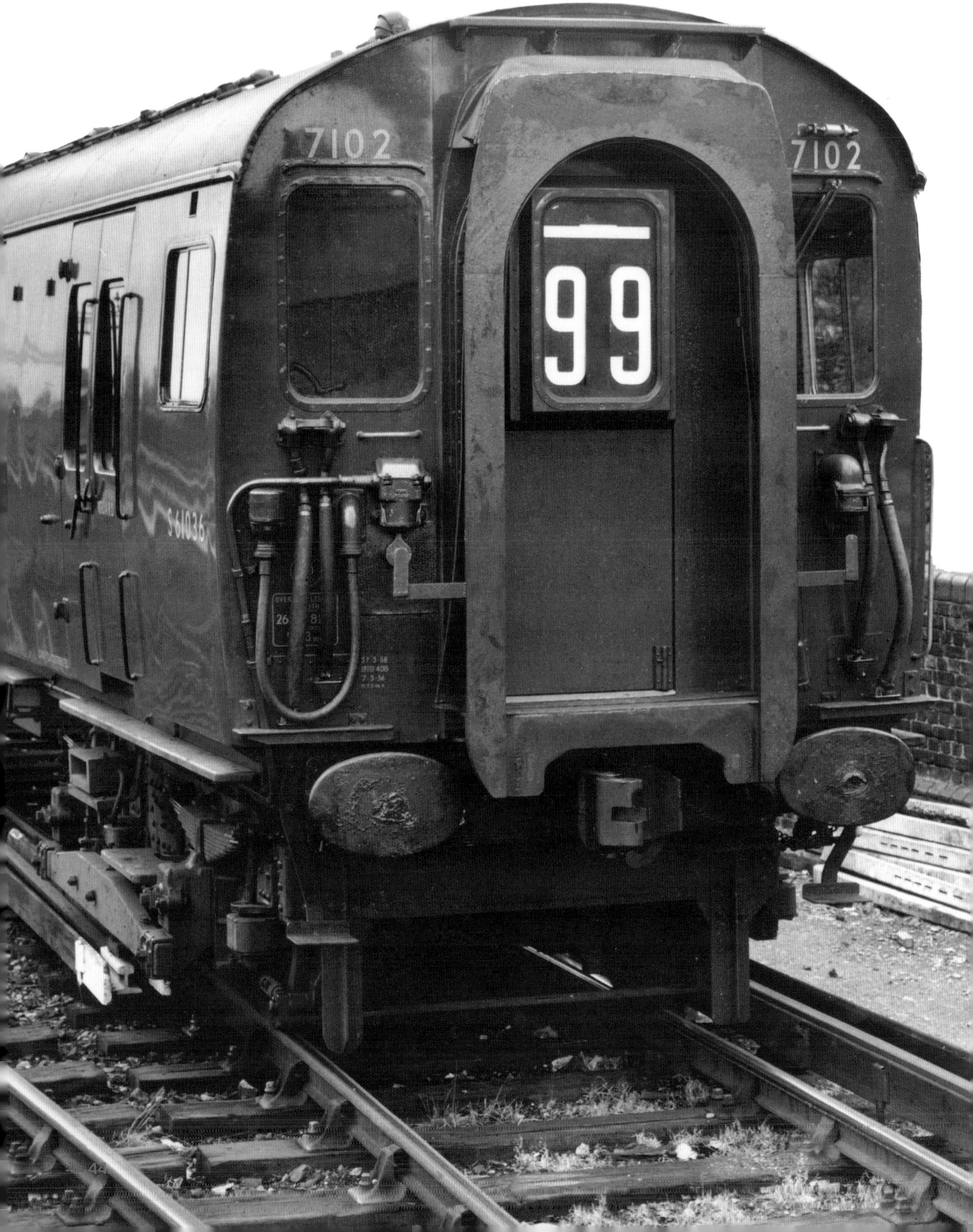
7102
7102
99
S61036

Opposite page: For electric services to the Kent coast inaugurated during 1959–62, 111 4CEP (class 411) and 22 4BEP (class 410/412) trains were produced. Their style was based on the standard British Railways Mark I carriage with fronts as the 2EPB (416/2) of 1953, to which were added a gangway connection and headcode box on the gangway door.

This page above and left: Both first class compartments and second class open saloons featured in the passenger coaches. Architect Trevor Dannatt designed the interiors, specifying sycamore or ash wood veneer panelling, and grey-blue, light grey, pale pink, yellow, green and white laminates. Curtains were green or orange-gold. The seat upholstery in Second class areas was called 'Trojan', a dark grey moquette with stripes of small square motifs coloured white, red, blue and yellow.

AM4/class 304 when new in 1957.

AM5/class 305 at Liverpool Street, London, circa 1959.

AM8/class 308 at Wickford, Essex, circa 1960.

Class 504 when new in 1959.

Interior of a class 504 passenger saloon, 1959. Decor for the second class saloons included walnut veneer panelling, stardust blue *Warerite* laminate doors in yellow *Warerite* partitions, a pigeon grey linoleum floor and seats upholstered in dark green uncut moquette. First class compartments had walnut veneer throughout, seats of blue/black moquette and a charcoal/gold patterned carpet.

This page: British Railways' Wolverton works created a standard appearance for the cab ends of electric multiple-units. The design, comprising two rectangular planes meeting at a horizontal fold, and angled away from the centre by vertical folds, was based on the class 101 diesel multiple-units built by Metro-Cammell 1956–59. Once the general form had been evaluated by building a full size mock-up, the cab form was used for several classes built at the Wolverton and Doncaster manufacturing sites: AM4/class 304 (1957, for London Midland Region main line stopping services); class 504 (1959, for the London Midland Region Manchester–Bury line in Lancashire); AM5/class 305 (1959, for Eastern Region North East London suburban Liverpool Street–Chingford and Enfield 'Chenford' routes);[26] AM8/class 308 (1959, for the Eastern Region main line between Liverpool Street, and Shenfield, Walton-on-the-Naze and Clacton in Essex).

Opposite page: AM4/class 304 at Birmingham New Street in 1980, with modified front design after the headcode boxes were taken out of use.

47

Diesel mechanical units

British Railways' Southern Region also built DEMUs in the period 1957–62, using the 2EPB (class 416/2) front styling and Mark I coach body, with variations to suit the restricted width necessary to negotiate trackside objects on certain routes. In these trains the engine was fitted in a compartment behind one driving cab, resulting in ventilator grilles mounted in the bodysides.

Type 6S/class 201 'Hastings' diesel multiple-unit at Hastings, 1983.

Interior of a type 6S/class 201 diesel multiple-unit when new.

The 6S/6L/5L (class 201/202/203) 'Hastings units' operated from 1957 on the London–Hastings main line via Tonbridge. To clear restrictions along the route, their vertical sides were built to a narrow (9 feet) width. This made them appear somewhat mean in proportions. Cab end design continued the Eastleigh 1953 2EPB (416/2) pattern.

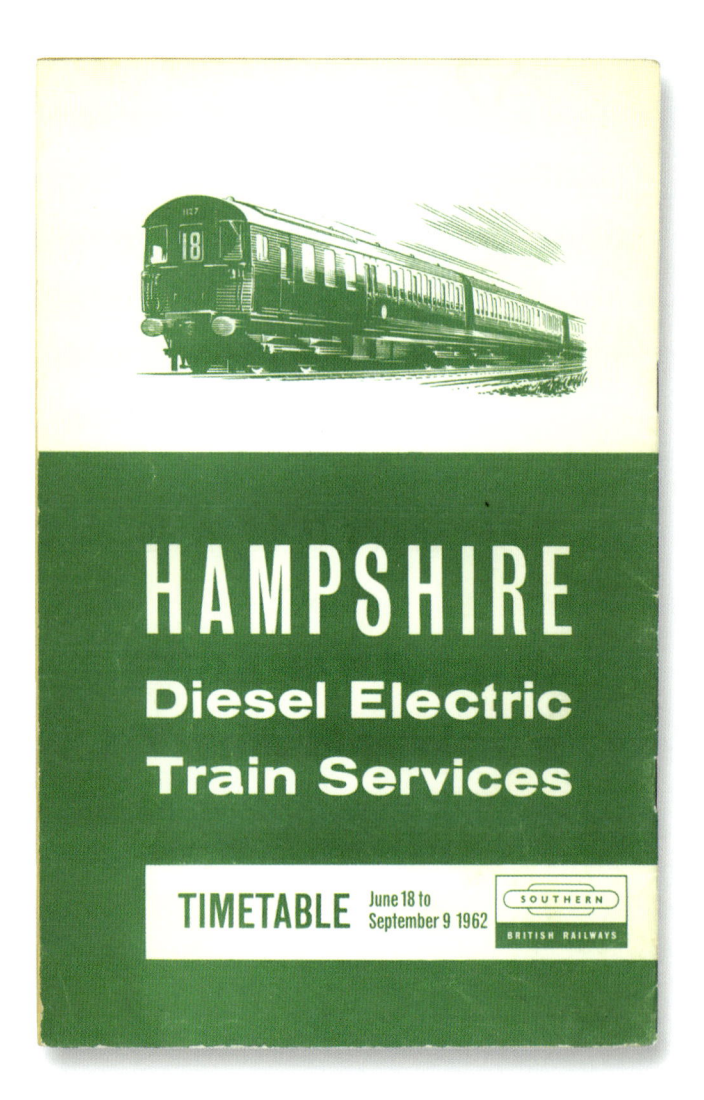

For general branch line and local services on non-electrified routes in Hampshire and East Sussex areas, the 3H (class 205) 'Hampshire units' were introduced in 1957. Their appearance was similar to classes 6S/6L/5L, but with full-width coach bodies. Interiors followed the standard Mark I coach décor schemes.

British Railways' Derby, Swindon, Wolverton and York works, and private contractors, built other diesel and electric multiple-units. An initial series of DMUs comprised some 28 classes built between 1954 and 1963. This short span of production, with the need to make many units quickly to replace steam locomotives, meant that body styling varied little from one class to the next. Units made to repeat orders inevitably also repeated the formal features of previous classes from the same manufacturers. Derby works commenced DMU production in 1954; when production ceased in

1960 it had constructed nine classes of unit. Swindon works made four classes. Private manufacturers Metropolitan-Cammell Carriage & Wagon (Metro-Cammell) and Gloucester Railway Carriage & Wagon companies built three classes each during 1955–57 and 1957–8 respectively. The Birmingham Railway Carriage & Wagon Company (BRC&W) contributed three classes 1957–61, Cravens and Pressed Steel both supplied two classes: Cravens in 1956 and Pressed Steel 1959–60, with one class each from D Wickham and Park Royal Vehicles - both in 1957.[27,28,29]

The very first units produced by Derby for introduction in 1954 borrowed from Southern Region practice, having cab fronts of three planes angled vertically, with the creases carried up into the roof domes. A large two-part window in each side plane had its upper margin angled downwards towards the sides, with all corners radiused. Front and sides met at rounded corners, these points following the curved profile of the Mark I coach body. Passengers enjoyed a new innovation: the provision of glazed screens behind the driving compartment affording them a view of the route ahead. Derby continued to built DMU trains of similar appearance, all having unit fronts of six panels joined to give a convex form. Disposition of destination indicators, doors and quality of interior fittings was modified according to each classes' original purpose. Several classes emerged from Derby in a very few years: 114 (introduced 1956), 116 (1957), 108 (1958), 125 (1958), 127 (1959), 107 and 115 (1960).

Gloucester Railway Carriage & Wagon provided British Railways with three classes of diesel multiple-unit. Class 100 (1956–58) emulated the appearance of British Railways' 1954 'Derby Lightweight stock', with two main detail differences in the unit fronts. Firstly, each of the class 100 windows was of the same height, with only the outer corners of the outer windows radiused. Secondly, the tumblehome of the carriage sides was expressed in the fronts as a pronounced s-shaped curve. The class 119 three-car and 122 single-car trains, both of 1958, were similar in appearance to Derby's 114 and 116 units.[30]

Metro-Cammell built DMU trains during 1955–57, producing an unclassified two-car unit, classes 101/102 (introduced 1956) and 111 (1957). A clean, simple appearance was used consistently across the four examples: a raked back plane containing the cab windows rising from a flat lower front and meeting the roof at a sharp crease following the roof profile. All window corners were radiused. Unit fronts and carriage sides met at rounded corners.

Park Royal Vehicles class 103 (introduced 1957) emulated the British Railways' Derby works design, with the difference of a domed, rather than segmented, roof over the driving cabs.

Birmingham Railway Carriage & Wagon Company's class 104 (built 1957–59) was one of the most visually austere units of the 1950s, having cab fronts made of three equal panels with vertical creases and deep windows. As designed, these trains carried both destination indicators and headcode displays. Class 118 (1960) three-car sets, were similar in appearance to British Railways' Derby-built units. Class 110 (1961–62) represented a third version by BRC&W, combining the three-part front of class 104 with the unequal window profile of the 1954 'Derby Lightweight' trains.

Class 100 by the Gloucester Railway Carriage & Wagon company, built 1956–58.

Metro-Cammell-built class 101 unit in original green livery with cream stripes, circa 1957.

Park Royal Vehicles assembled the class 103 units in 1957.

Class 104 diesel multiple-unit produced by Birmingham Railway Carriage & Wagon Company during 1957–59, seen here at Shrewsbury.

Class 108 made by British Railways' Derby workshops in 1958, in service at Gateacre, Merseyside, 1964.

Birmingham Railway Carriage & Wagon Company-built class 110, new in 1961–62.

Opposite page above: Class 101, made by Metro-Cammell and introduced in 1956, at Dovey Junction, Powys, during the summer heatwave of 1976.

Opposite page below: Built by British Railways at Derby works in 1959, this class 127 diesel multiple-unit is working on a service from St. Pancras, London, in 1983.

Class 119, built by Gloucester Railway Carriage & Wagon Company, operating at Weymouth, Dorset, 1979.

51

As with its other products built for the Great Western Railway and British Railways, Swindon works DMU designs did not conform to the output of other in-house factories or external contractors. The three- or six-car class 120 trains (introduced 1957) and three-car class 126 'Inter–City' trains (introduced 1956, second batch 1959) varied the Derby type unit front of the standard Mk 1 coach bodyshell by having one central vertical crease instead of two bisecting the single horizontal crease. Carried up into the roof dome, the vertical crease required the use of two cab windows. This styling was severe, especially for class 126 where one end was simply a flattened version of the coach profile, fitted with a gangway connection between the half-width cabs. The addition of two headcode windows in the cab fronts of the later class 126 batch did not improve the appearance. Swindon cross-country units often included buffet cars, decorated with abstract murals procured by the Design Panel. Some class 120 units were later sold to Liberia.

Above: A class 120 diesel multiple-unit when new, painted in dark green with cream stripes. The so-called 'speed whiskers' were an attempt to improve sighting of the trains by track workers, but they also emulated an outdated form of streamlining device.

Opposite page: Class 120 unit in later British Rail livery. The uncompromising four-part form of the cab front is evident in the raking winter light.

52

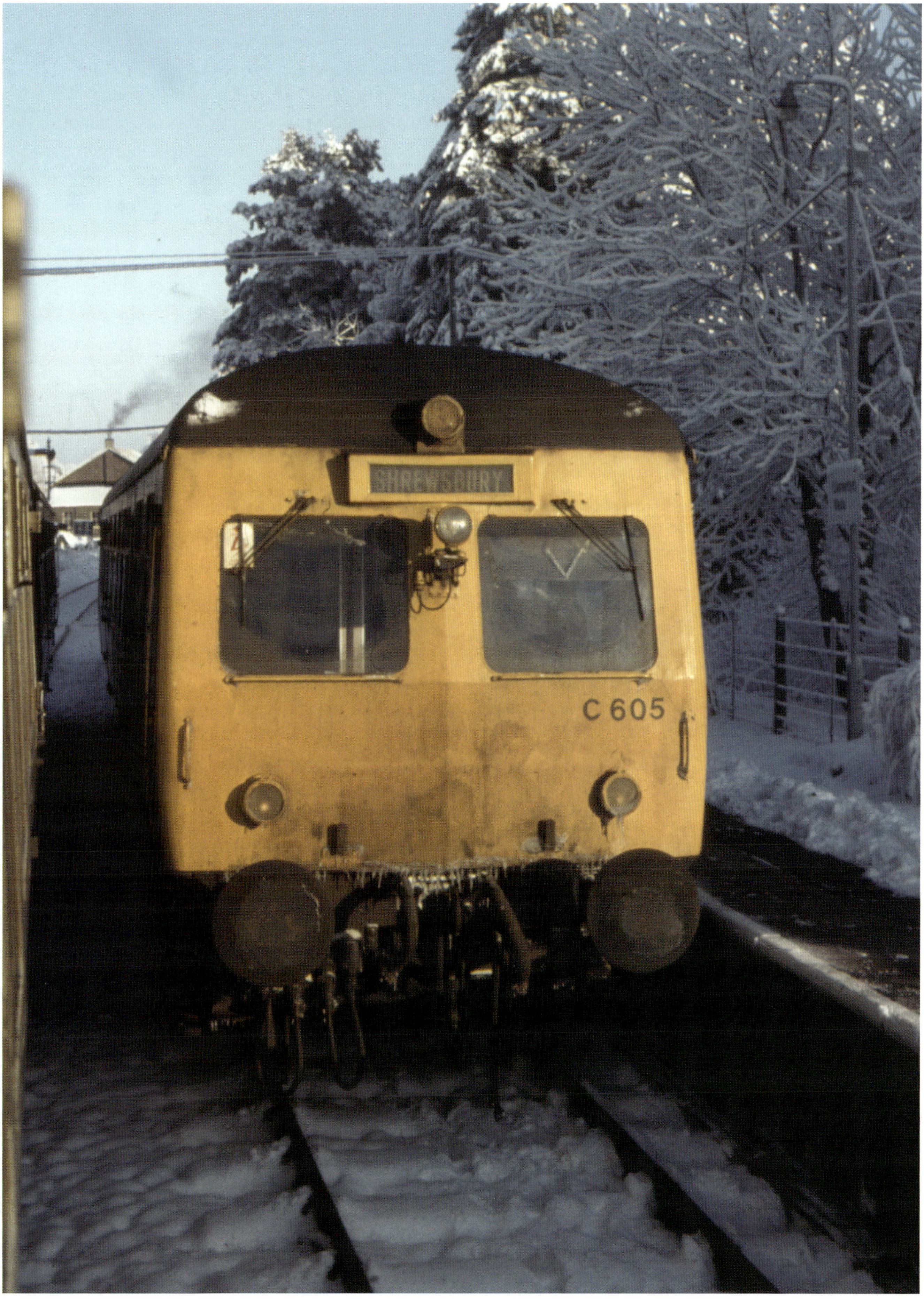
SHREWSBURY
C 605

The Mark I coach

Built from 1951, the Mark I coach amalgamated the best design features of vehicles operated by the main-line companies which preceded British Railways. It was to be standard for locomotive-hauled trains on most routes, and used a standard all-steel body shell with common, interchangeable components. Several workshops and external contractors built versions of the Mark I coach until it was replaced by the Mark II from 1964. Many permutations of layout were possible with this design: it was produced with first class compartments, a second class open saloon, a catering or sleeping car, and as a Travelling Post Office vehicle, parcels van, horse box, fruit van or car transporter. A series of liveries were carried by passenger coaches: these are discussed above on pages 38–39. The Design Panel had some limited opportunities to influence the interior of the Mark I coach, specifying colour schemes for walls and textiles, including upholstery fabrics by Marianne Straub.

We conclude this chapter with a brief look at the *Modernisation and Re-equipment of British Railways* published by the British Transport Commission on 24 January 1955, and commonly referred to as the *Modernisation Plan*. Proclaiming 'a transformation of virtually all the forms of service now offered by British Railways', it promoted electrification, diesel haulage of main-line trains prior to electrification, diesel multiple-units for secondary services, re-signalling technology, and withdrawal of passenger services and station closures.[31] Because electrification would take many years, the Plan resulted in the *Pilot Scheme*, whereby 174 non-steam locomotives of several power capabilities would be purchased from a number of manufacturers, and built by British Railways in its own works. Hopefully, the best performing equipment could be selected for bulk production. The British Transport Commission studied the form of London Midland & Scottish Railway engines 10000, 10001 and 10800, Great Western Railway engine 18100, and Southern Railway machines 10201, 10202 and 10203. Designed by George Ivatt of the London, Midland and Scottish Railway with manufacturers English Electric, locomotives 10000 and 10001 of 1947 copied the North American practice of having a 'nose' in front of the driving cab. Doors in this nose allowed the passage of railway staff from one locomotive to another during long-distance main-line journeys. The side panels included a number of small and large openings, placed according to the equipment inside rather than to appear as a co-ordinated pattern. The English Electric 'nose' style would characterise the appearance of locomotives used wherever Britain and the United States influenced vehicle design. Locomotive 10800 of 1950 was for passenger or freight services. It also emulated a transatlantic design, this time that of the 'hood' or 'switcher' type, where the superstructure was dominated by the bulk of the equipment housing, with a cab at one end or partway along the hood.

Most *Pilot Scheme* locomotives *did* receive some attention from the Design Panel and its consultant industrial designers: these are discussed in Chapter Four. The Design Panel made only minor adjustments to the form and colour of superstructures for the D200 (class 40), D5900 (class 23), D6700 (class 37), and D8400 (class 16) engines built for the *Modernisation Plan*.

Conclusion

In this chapter we have seen how the British Transport Commission and the Railway Executive made considerable efforts to produce a unified public image across printed material, staff uniforms and vehicles. If not always of consistently good quality, the achievement was nevertheless extraordinary in the context of changing politics and a complex industrial legacy. Here we have focussed on corporate identity and rolling stock; in the next chapter, we review developments in architecture for the railways.

Above: Great Western Railway-designed and British Railways-built gas turbine-electric locomotive 18100 of 1951, seen after conversion to electrically-powered locomotive E1000 (later E2001), when used for training drivers on electrified routes.

Below: Southern Railway-designed diesel-electric locomotive 10202 of 1950, at Derby in 1956. The livery is the same as that used for contemporary steam locomotives operating passenger services.

Chapter 3 →

Where people meet trains: British Railways' station architecture 1948–85

This chapter discusses British Railways' station design up to 1985. For further detail of the way in which stations were designed and decorated after 1985, please see Chapter Six: The new look: design diversity and privatisation 1982–97.

The railway station began as a simple dwelling for a railway worker and family. It adapted to sell tickets for travel. In city or small village, it evolved as a civic focus and social space for the transaction of business and news. It was an outpost of centralised time and organisation in settlements where only the church had previously regulated daily life. Produce and goods departed from the station; men and women left for work or war; new communities arrived. Knowledge of the world beyond came by mail and newspaper. Railways pioneered telegraphy: soon the station became a point for public communications too. Changing practice in railway architecture depended on the finances of the operator, its aspirations for presenting itself to the public, availability of building materials, and the architectural style considered appropriate for the location and function. Each railway company had its own style of building, which might be that of the local contractor or of a professionally trained architect. The model could be local domestic buildings or, to impress investors and passengers, a fantastical essay on some or other influence from Gothic to 'Mooresque'. Recognising the potential for expressing the ambitions and reliability of the organisation, a number of operators commissioned series of similar buildings, and adopted particular paint colours as part of the company image.

British Railways' substantial railway building estate makes it inevitable that this chapter is a survey of significant architectural developments. It is possible to gain a better understanding of the thinking behind British Railways stations, and the buildings themselves, by assuming distinct phases. Firstly, in order to understand the state of building design inherited by the nationalised organisation, the stations made by the private railway companies in the years immediately prior to 1948 are useful to note. The intervention of the Second World War inevitably halted building work associated with expansion or modernisation, and the economic difficulties after 1945 meant that new architecture in Britain was produced at a relatively slow rate until the mid-1950s.

In the post–1945 reconstruction of Britain, much of the work was in government or local authority departments. Secondly then, we look at the first steps to finding a modern, efficient form of railway passenger structure. Architects were professionally regulated, so that their ability to advertise services was limited. This meant that several of the most influential designers of twentieth century Britain worked for the railway early in their careers. Aspiring architects had the opportunity to make plans for the future, exploring their vision of creating a new world from pre-war utopian ideas, focussed on pubic buildings such as the railway station. London presented a range of case studies built during the 1930s for the Underground railway. Examples were to be found across Northern Europe. The Western Region Architect's Office, for example, closed entirely for a week each year to make a study tour of overseas buildings. There they saw new forms and materials, and therefore new possibilities for advancing station design.

Several innovative and aesthetically successful projects were completed from the late-1950s to the mid-1960s: this is our third period. Produced as modernisation gained speed alongside projects to electrify routes, these stations introduced the prefabrication which had been proposed in the late 1940s, and made use of reinforced concrete and timber construction techniques to make carefully considered modern buildings which won awards in their time and remain as exemplars of modern design today. New work was contingent upon a number of factors: locations scheduled for closure might be overlooked in all but necessary maintenance; sites to be rebuilt in future programmes would not warrant interim cosmetic improvements. If an entire new-build or reconstruction project was available - as was the case to service new town developments or replace worn out infrastructure - then the scale, form and material of the building could be considered together. Some stations and hotels were treated in this way. Smaller, but more plentiful prospects came with the redevelopment of station facilities as ticket issue was mechanised, and routes were converted from steam-hauled trains to electrified services. Our final phase is the period 1975–84, when investment in station building coincided with increasing large-scale development at and over station sites, as the British Rail Property Board exploited the 'air rights' by selling space above platforms and tracks.

As a continuation of traditional civil engineering hierarchies, British Railways architects worked in departments which were subsidiaries of the chief civil engineer. Within the architectural teams, there was also a clear structure of authority: the British Transport Commission chief architect supervised the activities of the regional architects, who themselves managed principal assistant architects, senior assistant architects, assistant architects and finally a group of designers and drafts-people. Building projects were always credited to the regional architect and his senior assistants, although the real design work may have been authored by a much more junior member of the team who brought the real design flair. Railway architects occupied studios dedicated to the almost exclusively manual production of drawings; besides stations they designed hotels and ferry terminals, travel and left luggage offices, restaurants and cafés, ticket collectors' booths and platform shelters, sign systems, seating and litter bins.

Frederick Curtis, formerly an architect for the Southern Railway, and Chief Architect to the Great Western Railway, was the first Chief Architect to the British Transport Commission.[1] Curtis is an important figure because he had also worked on London Underground stations with Adams, Holden and Pearson before 1939, and he had a good knowledge of European practice. Bernard Kaukas succeeded Curtis in 1968, and was Environment Director of British Rail from 1974 until his retirement in 1982.[2] The regional architects included: Eastern Region: H H Powell (in 1959); London Midland Region: W R 'Bob' Headley (in 1959); North Eastern Region: A N Thorpe (until December 1960; Sydney Hardy 1961–74); Scottish Region: J A Arthur (in 1961); Southern Region: H H Pittaway (in 1961; later Nigel Wikeley); Western Region: Howard Cavanagh until July 1960, and Roy Moorcroft from December 1960.[3]

Opposite page: Artist's rendering of Banbury station, Oxfordshire, rebuilt to a design by British Railways' Western Region architects during 1956–58.

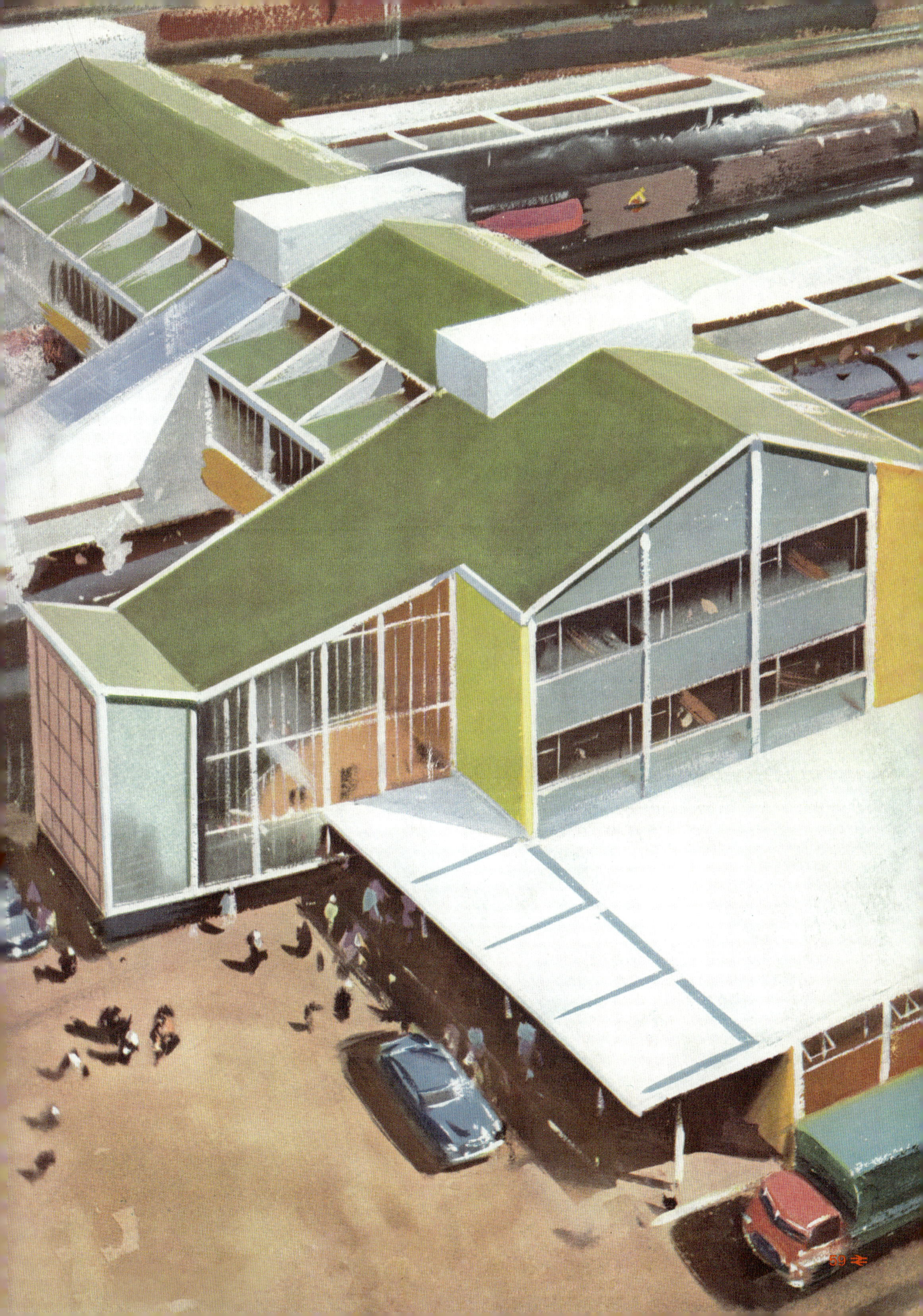

Before 1946

Britain had begun to adopt modern styles of building in the 1920s. Art Deco, a mainly superficial aesthetic of form and colour originating in Europe and North America, became popular with commercial developers of cinemas, shops and hotels, and there were some railway buildings designed by Britain's main line railways using Art Deco features. Railway companies had derived the basic form of their buildings from domestic architecture, modestly adapted to suit the particular needs of the railway. Guided by consultant Charles Holden (1875–1960) of Adams, Holden and Pearson, the London Underground adapted international modernism in architecture to reconceive the form of the railway station. Holden tried to avoid overt stylistic trends, choosing instead to craft an architectural idiom inspired by Northern European public buildings made in brick, stone, glass and concrete. Once this first step had been made, new ways of specifying of materials was a positive consequence; finally new colours could be selected to complement the natural hues of the building fabric. Main line railways working alongside the Underground were inspired to essay their own versions of the modern railway station.[4] The Southern Railway, which included in its architectural design team future British Railways' Chief Architect Frederick Curtis, directly emulated London Transport for a number of stations including Bishopstone, Tolworth, Malden Manor, Chessington North and Chessington South. To a lesser extent, the London, Midland and Scottish Railway (LMS) adopted London Underground design ideas for its stations built under Chief Architect W H Hamlyn during improvements to the London, Tilbury and Southend line in 1932–35.[5]

By 1938, London Underground brick and concrete aesthetics were being employed by the LMS for Apsley, Hertfordshire.[6] Most attractive was the street building at Hoylake, Merseyside, formed as a double-height cylindrical ticket hall, with adjoining lower level round kiosk, linked by a curving cantilevered concrete roof. Innovative too were the pre-war Great Western Railway buildings designed by its Chief Architect Brian Lewis to give modern facilities for the projection of London Transport's Central line. These were West Acton (1940), and Hanger Lane, Perivale and Greenford, all completed by British Railways Western Region architect Peter MacIver in 1949. In connection with the eastern extension of the Central line, the London and North Eastern Railway produced one notable station at Loughton (1940), designed by consultants John Murray Easton and Howard Robertson.

Perivale, London, station designed circa 1940 by Brian B Lewis for the Great Western Railway and the London Passenger Transport Board. Illustration by Alan Sorrell.

The Southern Railway station at Bishopstone, Sussex of 1938, shares features with the London Underground stations designed by Adams, Holden and Pearson in the period 1930–39.

Hoylake, Merseyside (1938) demonstrated the modernist architecture of the London, Midland and Scottish Railway. Made using extensive areas of reinforced concrete, it was an appropriate solution for electric train services to this seaside town.

1946-48: System building

A desire for good, economical railway stations of consistent form and appearance encouraged architects to look at making buildings with processes and materials conventionally applied to the motor industry: prefinished metal and glass units which could be connected using common components. From 1939 these same architects found themselves accelerating development of such techniques for the mass production of military vehicles and prefabricated structures. W H Hamlyn had experimented with enamelled steel sheet as a facing material for the streamlined platform building at South Kenton (1935). Having seen the benefits of this method, the LMS made plans for prefabricated buildings in 1940, projected to be realised from 1946. Engaged on the programme were Leslie (later Sir Leslie) Martin and Richard (later Lord) Llewelyn-Davies. Martin would soon become known for his design of the Royal Festival Hall, London, opened 1951; Llewelyn-Davies excelled in hospital design and urban planning.

Martin and Llewelyn-Davies made their first system-built platform waiting room at Queen's Park, London, in 1946. A second was installed at Stonebridge Park, also in London. Marsh Lane and Strand Road (now called Bootle New Strand), Merseyside, demonstrated how this innovative design could be applied to an island platform situation, with some refinement of details following the Queen's Park project. Steel columns and beams acted as the framework, onto which were bolted precast concrete, enamelled steel and glass panels. The canopies represented an experiment in cantilever structures, having no vertical support beyond their fixings at the long edges of the building. An idea adapted from Charles Holden's London Underground stations was the feature of high level, or clerestory windows, making the canopies seem almost weightless. Below the clerestories the station name was repeated along a 'frieze' panel, another London Underground feature. Bright vitreous enamelled panels in grids provided a low-maintenance, durable wall surface. Rainwater was drained through slender tubular steel columns designed specially to match the aesthetic.

Having proved the usefulness of new architectural approaches to railway building, Leslie Martin and Richard Llewelyn-Davies extended their proposals to encompass all sizes of station. Their studies became a comprehensive manual for the design of passenger stations, including guidelines for every aspect of planning and architecture from the relationship of the station in the town, to the design of equipment and colours to be used for buildings[7] (these colours are given on page 262). Standards could be applied to complete station reconstructions, or minor improvements. Government plans for 'new towns' - new settlements for decentralised urban populations - informed the report too, contextualising the station as a 'point of transhipment' which would be an essential component of the many post-war reconstruction programmes.[8] As a first example of architecture guided by the standards, images of Marsh Lane and Strand Road, and Queen's Park, demonstrated the principles of building platform shelters using components. Larger stations were represented by models, and resembled variations on the box form of ticket hall tower - with all passenger facilities grouped around a central concourse - established by Charles Holden for London's Underground/London Transport. The scale of traffic could be used to plan station size. Volumes of departing and arriving passengers would determine the facilities needed at the station.

London, Midland and Scottish Railway prototype prefabricated passenger building at Queens Park, London, 1946. The design combined enamelled steel panels over a base of concrete blocks. Moved to West Hampstead circa 1950; demolished 1980s.

Fully prefabricated station made for Marsh Lane & Strand Road, Merseyside, in 1947.

Left and above right: Materials specified for station interior décor by the Martin and Llewelyn-Davies report of 1948, reflected tastes of the time: pale paint colours were matched to complement wood veneer panelling and terrazzo floors. Technology such as train service and arrival indicators, and public address systems, would make the stations truly modern. Station name signs were to be plain rectangles of enamelled steel, showing white letters on a background of the regional colour.[9] Had this specification been adopted, the 'totem' station nameplate might never have been created.

In 1948 there were some 6685 passenger stations, with a further 1674 goods stations. With this massive real estate portfolio to repair and improve or replace, standardisation of railway buildings would not be easy to obtain. Through the early 1950s architectural innovation and building maintenance was 'reduced to a minimum, due to the war and the continuing shortages and restrictions after it.'[10] British Railways did not have sufficient budgets to expend on making the best of Martin and Llewelyn-Davies' ideas, but it did recognise the value in creating standard guidelines for the superficial appearance of its buildings. These would determine colour schemes - mostly carried over unchanged from the private companies - and the use of signs.

Long before British Railways tried to bring visual unity to its system, railway companies had used standardised paint and sign colours on their buildings to indicate ownership and authority. Livery schemes were commonly based on vernacular building traditions, rather than the more commercially-oriented colours of a company's locomotives or rolling stock. Alongside the natural shades of weather-resistant brick or stone, paint used to protect wood, iron and steel from deterioration was predominantly white or cream. A few contrasting colours - green, brown or blue - completed the palette for doors and frames around doors and windows, and the dado or lower sections of exterior and interior painted walls. Where decoration was incorporated into cast iron work such as brackets or seat supports, this naturalistic, heraldic or typographic detail might be emphasised by more varied and intricate application of hues. The economies of maintenance, and regional attachment to the former private companies, saw established colour schemes being perpetuated after 1948. The Great Western colours of chocolate and cream persisted, even being applied to stations transferred into the Western Region when routes were reallocated. London Midland Region favoured cream with maroon or green; the Eastern cream with pale 'verdite' blue-green; North Eastern cream with green or red-brown or dark brown; Scottish: cream with brown or pale green; Southern: green and cream.[11] It would only be from 1955 that the liveries for stations changed markedly and then often mainly where a larger project of reconstruction was in progress.

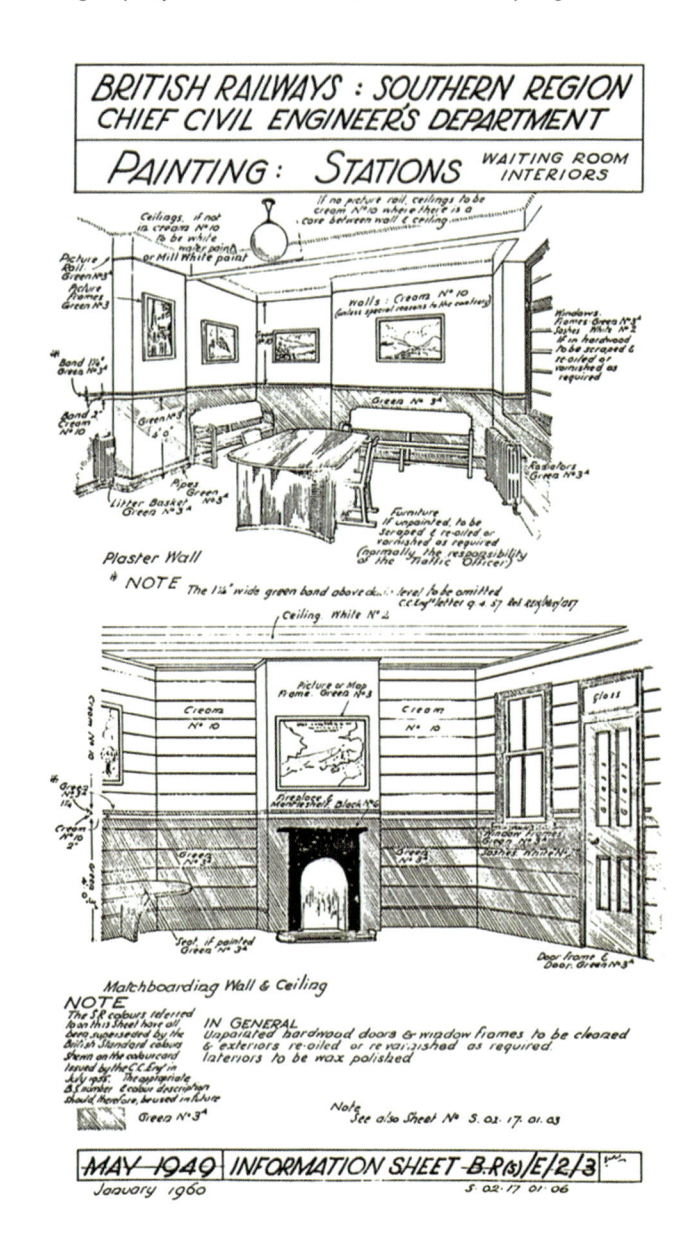

Railway companies produced detailed specifications for standard colour schemes to be applied to their buildings.

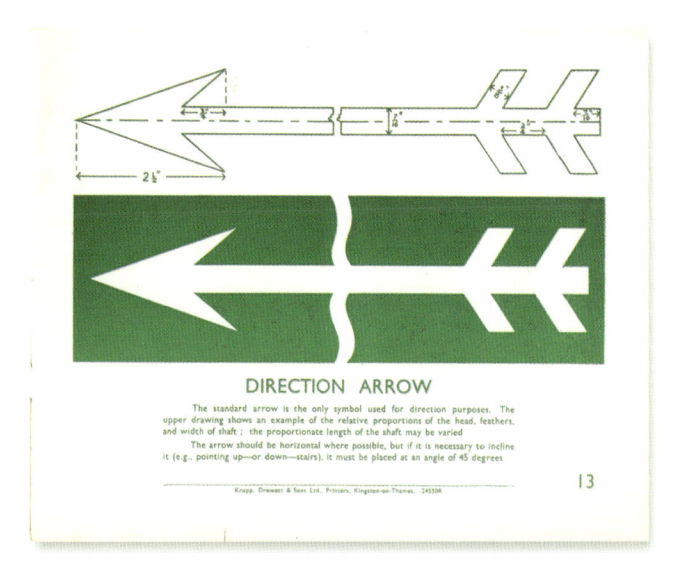

Very quickly after nationalisation, British Railways published a manual of typographic rules for its visual communications at stations. Based on the 'totem' symbol devised by A J White, and the Gill Sans letterform, the manual outlined all the likely signs which would be needed outside and inside buildings. Application of these guidelines varied from region to region, and station to station, according to the local circumstances and available space. All signs were in the regional colours, with totem symbols in the regional colour or white.

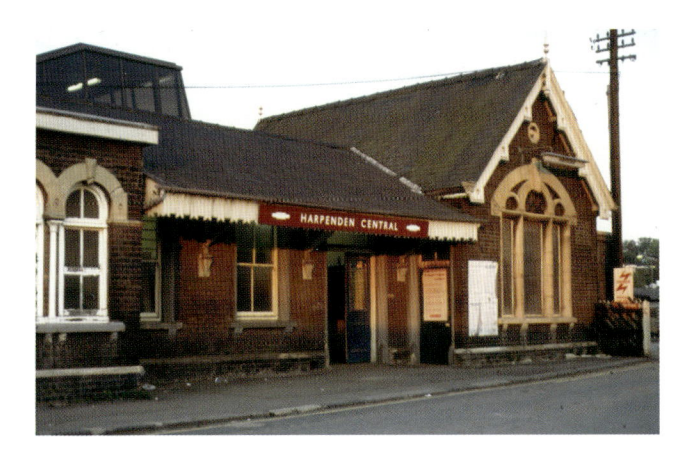

Harpenden Central, London Midland Region, photographed 1982.

Edinburgh Haymarket station, Scotland, 1978.

Station signs

Besides antiquated painting schemes, many railway stations still featured the signs which had been made for them when built in the nineteenth century.[12] Fabricated using cast metal or wood letters secured to wood boards, and painted in the house colours of the owning company, these signs tended to be large and heavy, meaning they were used sparingly except at the larger stations. Cheaper versions had letters painted onto the backing by a signwriter. For smaller applications such as doors, cast metal or enamelled steel plates followed the colour scheme. Of British Railways' immediate predecessors, the Great Western Railway identified even its smallest wayside stopping places with wood nameboards carrying a recognisably regular grotesque letter form. The best British Railways could do in communicating its ownership in an architectural context, was to mark each site with its corporate identity. A *Sign Standards* manual was issued in April 1948 and the *Code of Instructions for Station Name and Direction Signs* in September 1948.[13] These documents proposed a regulated system of signs - made in the regional colours and with Gill Sans as the typeface - for station buildings, offices for the reception and delivery of freight, signal boxes and travel bureaux. Railway managers, sign manufacturers and staff installing the signs on site referred to these guides. Given the need to unify the system through its signs, this needed to happen quickly, meaning there was little time to consider exactly how the British Railways brand might best be displayed. Even with printed visual standards, the application fluctuated from place to place. Walking to and through a station, the passenger would first encounter a large rectangular plate fixed to the entrance canopy or wall. This indicated the station name, supplemented in many, but not all, cases by the totem in full, outline or silhouette form. Smaller stations might only have a modest name sign. Conversely, the exterior of a large terminus was often treated with a substantial totem made in three dimensions, and individual, illuminated,

The 'running-in' board on the station platform at Gleneagles, Scotland, 1964, in Scottish Region colours.

Scottish Region enamel signs at Corrour, Inverness-shire, 1978.

Stone Crossing Halt, Southern Region, 1979.

Gill Sans letters for the name. Signing within rooms was limited, because most locations faced onto platform or concourse areas. Most obvious on the platform were the large rectangular 'running in boards' at one or both ends of the platform, displaying the name and additional information for junction point. A number of totem lamp tablets repeated the name along the platform, fixed to posts or walls. The amount varied according to the level of passenger traffic and size of the station. Signs hanging at right angles to the buildings indicated facilities for public use; doors for both the public and staff had smaller identifying plates.

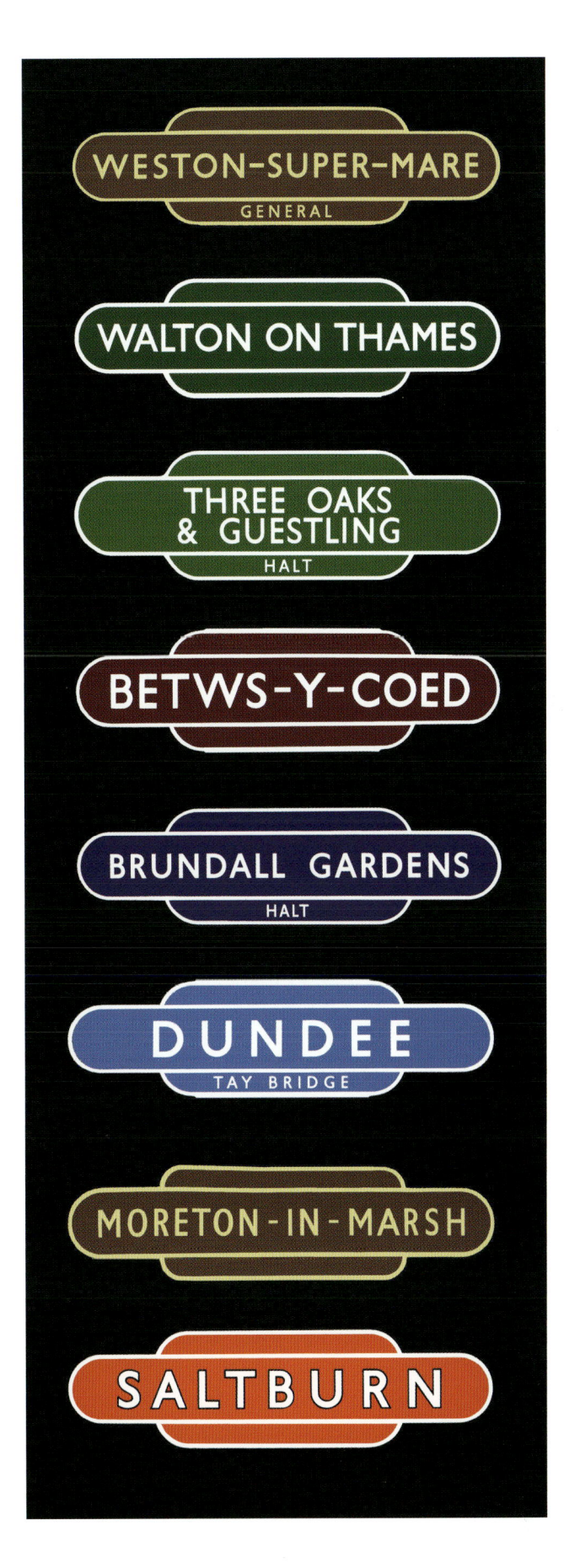

The totem symbol devised by A J White proved a useful solution to creating a family of station name signs across Britain. This followed the practice of the London, Midland and Scottish Railway, who installed 'hawk(s)eye' nameboards at stations across its system during the 1930s, and the Southern Railway, whose publicity officer John Elliot knew London Transport's Lord Ashfield, created a 'target' station nameboard adapting the form of the London Underground bar and circle.[14] Produced in a limited range of sizes, and colour-coded according to region, the signs were officially known as 'lamp tablets' because they were frequently fitted below the lights which would illuminate them. In line with established railway practice, the tablets were made by screen-printing a liquid vitreous enamel frit onto a previously enamelled steel form. Station names required the letterer to make decisions about font size and the position of words. In general, if the station name words all related to the location, then they would be accommodated in the bar of the symbol by reducing the lettering size, varying the spacing of letters, and adding further lines of words. If a name including the qualification 'halt', 'junction' or 'platform', or even a part name to distinguish one station from another in the same town, this would be placed in the area below the bar, known as a counter. Sometimes the sign maker split the name between bar and lower counter to distinguish between main and secondary parts of the name, or for no apparent reason other than ease of working. Conversely there are examples of totem signs where the subsidiary part of the name is placed below the main part, with a consequent reduction in letter size and legibility (see Dundee Tay Bridge). The use of 'and' or '&' also varied, sometimes to make the name more readable where space was limited; there was often no obvious rationale for the choice.

Inevitably there were variations to the standards. The tangerine colour of North Eastern Region signs, which made white lettering difficult to discern in a bright environment, caused later examples to be manufactured with a black outline to each letter (see Saltburn). One station - Besses o' th' Barn north of Manchester - featured lower case Gill Sans lettering. The 'Transport' alphabet designed for British motorway signs by Jock Kinneir and Margaret Calvert was offered to British Railways too, resulting in its use on some totem and other signs manufactured in the late 1950s.[15] Whilst regional colours were fixed, manufacturers inadvertently varied the precise shades according to available materials supplies. This was especially evident for the Southern Region, where the green varied considerably.

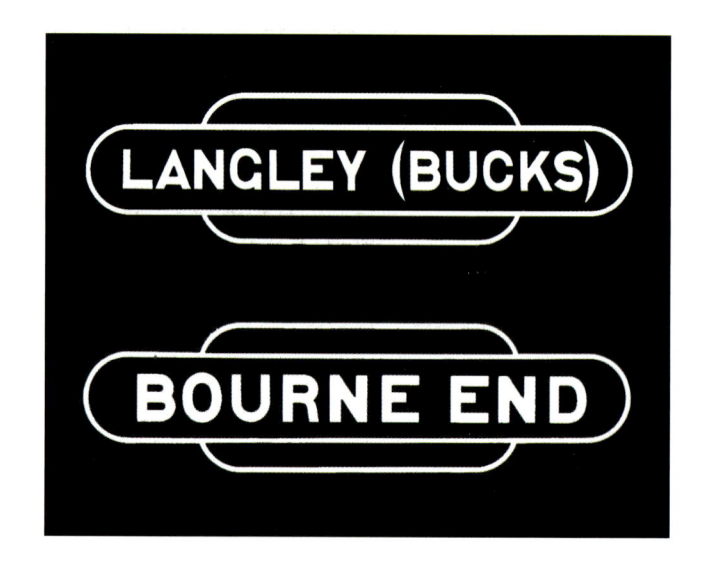

Top: The 'Transport' lettering designed 1957–63 for Britain's road signs, was used for some totem nameplates and other passenger information.

Middle: Station nameplates almost exclusively used the Gill Sans font in capital letters only. One exception was Besses o' th' Barn, Lancashire, where the two abbreviated words required lower case letters, prompting upper and lower case for the whole name.

Above: In the early 1960s, British Railways Western Region explored returning some traditional features to its stations, to break away from the standard visual identity. At a very few stations, totem name signs were made using the Great Western Railway idiom of white grotesque block lettering on a black background.[16]

1948-59

Prefabrication was not developed immediately, architects preferring to use familiar structural practices and materials. New building remained limited in this period, but interior alteration and modernisation gathered pace.

South Ruislip, Ruislip Gardens and West Ruislip, all west of London, were designed in 1948, by Howard Cavanagh and R H Jones of the Western Region. There was no money to complete them until late 1961, by which time they were in the charge of architects John Kennett and Roy Turner. Potters Bar (1955) was the first of the rebuilt Eastern Region stations. Designed by J Wyatt, it was a simple brick box with clerestory ticket hall windows, and a cantilevered concrete entrance canopy. The public spaces were lined with tiles, and platform waiting rooms were furnished with bench seats designed for British Railways by Robin Day. In east London, Barking, completed in 1961, served as a combined station for British Railways and the London Transport Executive. Eastern Region architects began to show the design flair for which they would become highly respected in the 1960s: the open concourse at this small suburban station was located beneath cantilevered and canted concrete beams modelled on the *Statione Termini* at Rome, Italy of 1948–51.[17]

Barrow Central, renamed Barrow-in-Furness on rebuilding in 1959, also followed European railway architecture styles, being a brick ticket hall tower with cantilevered concrete canopy over the passenger entrance. The wall-mounted clock was a civic feature common at European railway stations. The building still stood in 2014, but the entrance canopy had been demolished and the clock removed.

Southern Region architects looked to immediate post-war design styles for Chichester, West Sussex. Adopting the by then standard practice of a brick box with glazed front wall for the ticket hall, the interior decorations included one entire wall of powder blue *Warerite* plastic laminate. When opened in 1961, Chichester was regarded by critics to be already outdated in its styling.

South Ruislip, Middlesex, designed in 1948; formally completed 1961.

A cantilevered concrete structure brought Italian styling to east London: this is Barking, opened September 1961.

Barrow-in-Furness, Cumbria, when new in 1959. this project is attributed to architect Derrick Shorten.

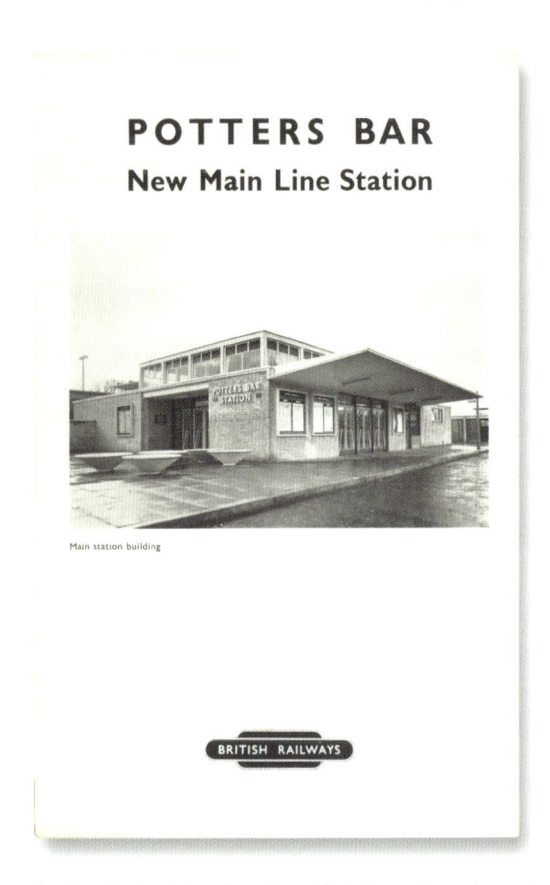

Pages from the booklet celebrating the official opening of new buildings at Potters Bar, Hertfordshire, in 1955.

70

Opposite page bottom left and right; this page: At Chichester, West Sussex, the ticket hall was designed as a tall brick box, with lower buildings faced in green stone. Inside the ticket hall, an electric chandelier hung from a ceiling moulded with a hexagonal pattern - features derived from styling used at the *Festival of Britain* a decade earlier. A large clock set into a wall of blue and white plastic laminate dominated the circulation space.

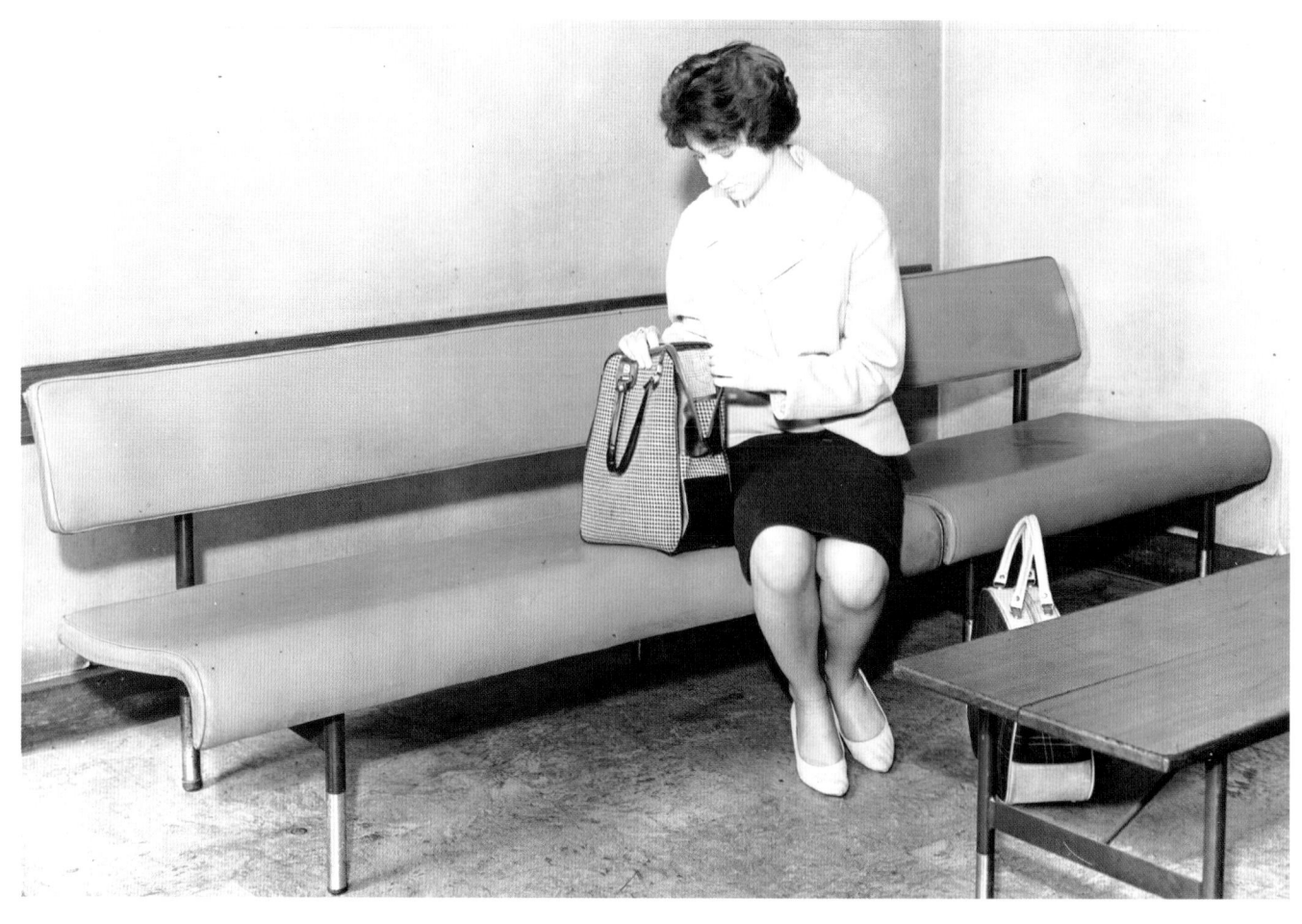

Above and below left: The refurbished ladies waiting room at Liverpool Street, London, with award-winning furniture designed in 1957 for British Railways' Eastern Region by Robin Day.

Above: Colchester, Essex, station refreshment room in 1962. The front of the bar counter is faced with a specially-commissioned panel in *Warerite* plastic laminate, showing military figures in various costumes.

Where funds for rebuilding remained limited, focussing new work on catering spaces ensured passengers would see positive improvements at close hand. British Railways' architects could treat these small projects as experiments in using new materials and trends in decoration which might have seemed out of place or too vogue-ish at a larger scale. Born out of *Bakelite* plastic technology, laminate boards were selected for interior design from the early 1950s as a cheap, colourful and durable surfacing material. *Formica* and *Warerite* brands both experienced great popularity with the rise of the 'do-it-yourself' home improvement craze. British Railways followed this wider trend by adopting laminates for passenger coaches and public rooms at stations. Laminates suited the design of new rolling stock being built in a period of restricted budgets, and their simplicity in use made them effective in the repair of damaged surface linings. Many ready-made patterns were available. For custom applications, the paper sheet just below the clear surface of the board which normally carried a pattern or plain colour, could be printed with any design: a unique artwork, or a repeating brand mark. Buffets and waiting rooms featured laminates as wall-height murals and counter tops; booking offices and signal boxes installed with mechanised equipment could be made to look more efficient by application of plain colours which needed no repainting. The Eastern Region produced several examples of attractive dining spaces. At Sheffield Victoria (1957), old passenger rooms and dividing walls were stripped out, to be replaced by bright spaces lined with mosaic and wood panelling, and an abstract mural, sparkling under arrays of spotlights. Waiting areas at London's Kings Cross and Liverpool Street, and at Southend on Sea Central were refurbished with Robin Day sofas, chairs and tables during 1957; this furniture won Day a *Design of the Year* award in 1962. The Liverpool Street to Clacton and Walton-on-the-Naze lines were completed in spring 1962, bringing new stations, ancillary buildings, and new trains. Colchester station was rebuilt internally, the wood-lined refreshment room being fitted with a counter front of plastic laminate with a bespoke decoration of stylised soldiers in coloured *Warerite*.

Sheffield Victoria refreshment buffet, 1957. At the rear of this view is a large abstract mural formed in plastic laminate.

Sheffield Victoria general waiting room, 1957. At the rear of this view is a large abstract mural formed in plastic laminate.

1960-85

As British Railways entered the 1960s, a number of projects planned late in the previous decade were realised. Some borrowed from more general building practice; several benefitted from the contributions of talented young architects passing through the civil service on their way to major roles in the modernising of Britain. This section looks at selected one-off station redevelopments to indicate the scale of architectural change with which British Rail hoped to renew its building stock. We also review smaller buildings produced in numerous examples of a common type.

The British Transport Commission Design Panel did not have direct influence over architecture - this was still under the control of senior civil engineers in each region - but it did create the subsidiary Architects' Study Group to share ideas. This Group produced the *Code of Practice for minor station improvements* around 1960, detailing ways in which low cost works could be implemented to a consistent pattern using standard furniture and other small details. A list was compiled of items which were of standardised appearance and to an approved quality. Station colours had begun to change in the mid-1950s. The adjustments were not consistent across the network, but showed some improvement on the essentially pre-war schemes. On the Eastern Region the dark champagne and verdite green house colours were replaced by a range of pastel shades including blue and grey with black at Liverpool Street; for the North Eastern Region a subtle pairing of ivory (actually a pale silver grey), black and sky blue was applied to many stations to positively transform their appearance.[18] Southern Region redecoration included the blue and grey used for Chatham.[19]

Folkestone Central opened in 1961 for the Kent Coast Electrification programme. Like its contemporary Chichester, it implied a confusion of architectural styles as though the architects, given a reasonable budget after years of pecuniary constraint, wanted to explore several styles simultaneously. Below the main entrance canopy, two smaller canopies projected in line with the doors forming the access to passenger facilities within the railway viaduct. The soffit of the canopy had a patterned surface, and the wall in which the doors were set was clad in coloured ceramic tiles. A tall brick and concrete tower based on European examples, and without any decoration, incorporated the station clock and advertised the position of the station in a side road. Folkestone Central's ticket hall mixed the lighting and lettering of a post-1951 *Festival of Britain* aesthetic with exposed concrete and brick. Polished wood panelling and terrazzo tiles completed the interior scheme.

The Eastern and London Midland regions electrified a number of routes in the early 1960s. Stations to complement the works were designed by future architectural luminaries including Charlotte Baden-Powell, John Bicknell, Michael Brawne, Max Clendinning, Roger Cunliffe, Patrick de Saulles, David Goldhill, Paul Hamilton, Derrick Shorten, Paul Taylor and Maurice Wheeler.

Broxbourne, Hertfordshire, of 1960 was designed for the Eastern Region as a bridge building, here with yellow brick walls between concrete slabs for much of the span so that the footbridge was the dominant element. The double height circulation area integrated with one end of the bridge contained cantilevered stairs, and the concrete deck supporting the bridge was exposed in the circulation area to reveal the structure. Glazing was limited, but carefully designed to make good use of proportion.

Folkestone Central, Kent, rebuilding completed 1961.

Broxbourne, Hertfordshire, 1960, by Peter Reyniers and John Ward for British Railways Eastern Region. Now a Grade II listed building.

Interior of passenger concourse, Folkestone Central, 1961.

Stairwell tower at Broxbourne, 2011. The stair itself is original, but has been painted and fitted with additional handrails.

Made to handle the massive increase in traffic resulting from a new settlement, the Harlow Town, Essex, station designed by Paul Hamilton can be compared to transport structures influenced by the ideas of architect Ludwig Mies van der Rohe, built around Chicago, USA in the late 1950s.[20] A similar formal approach would be used for early motorway service areas in Britain. Opened in July 1960, Harlow Town featured a glazed bridge with a deep roof punctuated by three lift towers, appearing to float over the platforms. The entrance area was an abstract composition of three roof units emerging from the glazed façade, the central part forming a canopy extended out over the entrance. Structural beams were enclosed within the clean, minimal forms of the roofs. To emphasise the apparent lightness of the building and the interior space, walls were made as free-standing panels, with the train departure board and poster panels shown as subsidiary layers within the design. Exterior walls at ground level were of light coloured brick, and interior walls faced in white tiles, with mosaic for columns, balustrades and the departure board. Pine strips lined the ceilings. All signs were integrated into the overall design.

Planning for Coventry began in 1961. Various delays set the opening back to May 1962, by which time the station had been completely redeveloped. Designed by London Midland Region architects W R Headley, Derrick Shorten, John Collins, M J C Edwards and Keith Rawson, it was planned as two rectangles arranged as a cross. The new station had as its central feature a passenger concourse two storeys-high under reinforced concrete beams, forming the principal structural system and the unifying factor of the design. Curtain walling, a technique common to the development of tall office and residential buildings, was suspended from these beams using aluminium and glass. A fascia of brown-grey Derbydene limestone slabs around the roof gave the visual impression of a clean, uncomplicated and purposeful place for people and trains to meet.

Above and opposite page: Exterior of Harlow Town, circa 1960–1961. The station formed a hub for the 'New Town' being developed nearby.

Left: Harlow Town passenger concourse. Timber, ceramic tiles and glass mosaic are used to create ordered variety and durability. The various elements clustered around the stairwell are arranged as an abstract sculptural relief.

Coventry station exterior.

To form a porte-cochère over the entrance and forecourt waiting area, the main roof projected forwards on two columns. Adjoining the concourse a single storey structure contained the offices, with a flat above to accommodate female catering staff. This was furnished with Swedish rugs and floral wallpapers. Waiting and refreshment rooms were combined and, like some of the best office designs of the period, given the special feature of a patio courtyard with water pool and mature tree. External walls were of dark blue facing bricks – the type normally used only for engineering purposes – and the glazed areas framed by bright aluminium, with black anodised aluminium for openable windows. Interior walls were surfaced with white ceramic mosaics, beneath ceilings of varnished pale African hardwood. Fluorescent lighting throughout completed the functional aesthetic of the spaces; a heating system beneath the Genoa marble terrazzo floor tiles, and passenger announcement loudspeakers set into the ceiling, were other technical innovations. Internal partitions were of glass wherever possible, with signs in white on black, using an adapted form of Jock Kinneir and Margaret Calvert's newly-developed Ministry of Transport typeface for motorway signs. To minimize visual distraction, the only bright colour was a tangerine red for platform ticket and Post Office stamp machines, and pepper red for interior passenger seats. Continuing the emphasis on cuboid forms, lift towers were plain white blocks, ticket hall seats were square, and cubes with wide bright aluminium frames contained poster and publicity units.

Max Clendinning, who would later become known for his interior design and furniture work, spent some five years on the architecture of Oxford Road, Manchester.[21] This awkward triangular site suggested a novel approach for the new building. With experience in his family's furniture manufacturing business, Clendinning looked beyond any standard form of building to imagine Oxford Road as 'a giant piece of furniture.'[22] Realising a lightweight solution was needed for the location on a viaduct, he drafted a scheme

Coventry station waiting area, 1966.

expressing the possibilities of laminated wood, with three conoid shell roofs - each made smaller than the one before by the wedge-shaped ground plan, and canopies formed on curved supports.[23] Inspiration came from Oscar Niemeyer's work in Brasilia, and vernacular buildings seen in the French countryside. The designed was realised by close co-operation with Hugh Tottenham of the Timber Development Association. Individual wood pieces were fixed at angles to emphasise the method of construction. Inside the tapering ticket hall, the interest in folded and intersecting planes which would characterise Clendinning's later furniture design was evident. Most surfaces were of exposed, varnished wood. There were very few right-angle corners in any of the woodwork, because radiused corners were easier to cut. An island unit containing the booking office, staff, waiting and refreshment rooms was enclosed by a wrap-around timber and glass wall in which the framing was crafted with tapers and facets. In the refreshment room, oval tables and patterned terrazzo floors were influenced by the abstract art of Jean Arp.

Model for Oxford Road, Manchester, 1959.

Detail of buffet and kiosk at Oxford Road, 2006.

79

Manchester London Road, shared by the London Midland and Eastern regions, underwent redevelopment from 1959. To replace the Eastern Region (north) section of the Victorian station frontage a glass-fronted hall containing 'luxury passenger facilities' was proposed, with a sweeping roof borne on concrete pylons at either end.[24] The London Midland (south) part of the frontage was replaced by a nine storey office tower for railway and private office use. Spending cuts produced a somewhat less exuberant development in front of the existing train shed. Adjacent to the office tower, a low-rise brick and concrete block housed the passenger facilities and concourse.[25] Renamed Manchester Piccadilly, the finished development had none of the exuberant ambition of the contemporary Oxford Road station nearby. Beneath a functional steel and glass roof, much use was made of wood and melamine laminate surfaces. Services included a ladies' waiting room, cafeteria, small bar and shops, all lined in the same austere ceramic tiles.

Platform and track alterations completed the works. Over time, the 1962 building has largely been subsumed beneath other developments.

Artist's impression by Claude Buckle of a design for Manchester Piccadilly.

Opened in November 1961, St. Helens Shaw Street, Lancashire, made much use of steel and glass units, a tribute to nearby manufacturers Pilkington's and a demonstration of how factory-

Manchester Piccadilly main entrance as built, a much-reduced version of the initial proposal.

made architectural elements could usefully make pre-fabricated, standardised buildings. Its form was an interpretation of Charles Holden's stations for the London Underground, and its appearance was not dissimilar to the petrol filling station kiosks developed by Dennis Birchett for Shell-Mex and BP in 1951–57, being a regular grid of clear and grey glass walls, in white frames with black divisions. Below a raised clerestory roof with central valley, the ticket office was faced in red glass panels, and other walls were made of *Vitrolite*, a coloured glass product which had been popular with architects since the 1930s. A platform canopy was made as a projection of the building's main roof, and of simple rectangular form painted grey.[26] The station was replaced from 2007.

St Helen's, Merseyside, built using a system of enamelled metal panels and glass sheets.

The new ladies waiting room at Manchester Piccadilly, 1962.

From the mid-1950s onwards, new architectural work at almost sixty stations was associated with the introduction of electric services. Many stations between London, Birmingham, Manchester and Liverpool, and around those cities, had to be replaced as a result of the engineering works.[27] Large terminals were redeveloped as one-off projects. Construction of train sheds - London's Kings Cross being an example much cited - suggested the utility of making stations from components. Railways were of course well experienced in the manufacture of many thousands of parts for their vehicles, so why not make buildings too? By 1960, prefabrication was once more an important theme for new works. Based on the principle of highly engineered building elements made in factories, then deployed on site by train, prefabrication seemed the answer to creating a quick and economic uniform architectural style in suburban areas. South of Manchester the Styal line - through Mauldeth Road, Burnage, East Didsbury, Gatley, and Heald Green - was given a series of prefabricated stations developed by London Midland Region architects J S Wyatt, David Goldhill, Patrick deSaulles, Peter Newton, Cosimo Pacitti, T A Snow and M Wheeler.[28]

East Didsbury and Burnage used a building prefabrication system developed by the London Midland Region architects' department called 'Mod-X'. Around a steel frame wood, glass, vitreous enamelled metal and board were assembled to form a regular grid of wall units. The canopy used lightweight plywood formed into triangular elements to act as cantilevering beams, to avoid the need for supporting columns. Station names were printed onto the back of glass panels fitted into the wall panelling. After this a 'Mark II' system based on an aluminium structural frame was developed. In the resulting design canopies were omitted entirely from the flat roofed, single storey buildings. It would be adopted for new works at stations including Sandbach, Chelford, Handforth, Holmes Chapel and Mossley Hill. The main building at Heald Green was of Victorian origin, but partially demolished and then clad in new materials to appear entirely rebuilt. Cosimo Pacitti made Heald Green distinctive by specifying walls of three-dimensional metal panels swaged, or impressed, with a pyramid pattern, below a deep fascia of profiled metal sheeting.[29] Macclesfield (1960) and Perry Barr (1962) also employed prefabrication techniques.

Profiled and pressed metal elements were used by Cosimo Pacitti to modernise and extend the old buildings at Heald Green.

Above and opposite page lower: Passenger shelters at Mossley Hill, Liverpool, and Handforth, Cheshire, built with the the London Midland Region's aluminium and glass 'Mark II' prefabrication system.

'Mod-X' building system at East Didsbury, south Manchester.

Kidsgrove and Congleton, stations were provided with single-storey structures in which the defining detail was the projecting beams beneath the flat roofs. Other stations remade during this period using bricks and concrete included Tamworth (1962), Stafford (1963), Hemel Hempstead (1964), Wolverhampton High Level (circa 1965), and Bletchley (1966), the last site in the renewal programme for London Midland Region stations.

At other stations, new platform structures gave architects the chance to make perfect small buildings. Sawbridgeworth, Hertfordshire (1961), and Hadley Wood, Greater London, are good examples; Leytonstone High Road, Essex, (1960–61) obtained a prefabricated platform shelter with a canopy of the same box form used at Harlow.

Above: Designers of new platform structures utilised steel and timber to make clean, rational groups of canopies and spaces for passengers and staff. Sawbridgeworth, top left, Leytonstone High Road, top right, Hadley Wood, above, and Sunderland, opposite page, are good examples of such work, and reveal the enduring influence of German architect Mies van der Rohe.

Right: As an extreme opposite to the reconstruction of stations with modern architecture, locations of lower priority saw their passenger buildings replaced by basic metal and glass shelters. This is Dalston Junction in the early 1970s, with the type of structure installed along the North London Line (now part of the London Overground network) as stations were run down and de-staffed.

New ways of building: station architecture of the 1960s-70s

Chairman of the British Railways Board Dr Richard Beeching supported a rapid improvement in the appearance and condition of BR stations. Critics who had been impressed by Design Research Unit's work on graphics and vehicles turned to the un-modernised bulk of the railway estate and saw it filled with bookstalls, flower kiosks and groups of vending machines or left luggage lockers, none of which were integrated into the design.[30] Urban areas which had been damaged by aerial raids during the Second World War retained tracts of derelict land right through the 1950s. Canny speculators acquired large and small plots at low prices when no-one else saw their potential for future rebuilding. Architects wanted to imbue their railway work with the continuing flow of ideas from Europe and North America: an angular, often anodyne aesthetic of steel, glass and concrete: they imagined cities of towers containing offices and shopping precincts. By the early 1960s, public organisations lacking the resources to enable extensive urban renewal on their own, partnered the now-powerful private developers who, compared with state bodies, had seemingly limitless resources. A balance between public and commercial agendas could not always be reached, and in any case the developer often had a more focussed idea of what they wanted from a deal. The space over stations became a valuable asset that the railway had hardly imagined, and could not resist selling in the pursuit of modernity and revenue. Excepting the case of London's St Pancras station and other successful preservation campaigns staged by the emerging Victorian Society, little thought was given to heritage until it became apparent that the public might appreciate new facilities in conserved older buildings. As funding receded towards the end of the decade, new buildings of lesser quality replaced existing stations, simply because the existing structures cost more to staff and maintain, or were redolent of a past age. 'Paytrain' services - where the guard sold and checked tickets on the multiple-unit - resulted in the widespread replacement of station buildings by extremely basic wood, metal and glass enclosures. Some redundant structures became private houses or offices, and many were demolished to pre-empt the vandalism which was a constant problem for British Rail in the 1970s. Urban land values and powerful development companies forced a fresh approach to the status of large stations. 'Air rights' enabled British Rail to sell space over its facilities, for retail and office development.

The New Euston

Several London major termini were reviewed for rebuilding potential. Holborn Viaduct (now replaced by City Thameslink), Fenchurch Street, Cannon Street, and Blackfriars (demolished) experienced varying degrees of development. Euston, a metropolitan terminus of the London Midland Region, retained features of being one of the world's oldest stations. British Railways architect W R 'Bob' Headley engaged Taylor Woodrow on the process of completely renewing the Euston site in advance of the West Coast Main Line being converted to electric train services. Bob Headley was succeeded as British Rail's representative during the Euston project by Roy Moorcroft. Within the Taylor Woodrow drawing office, young architects conceived a scheme for transforming the station into a multi-level retail and cultural complex, something like London's Barbican Arts Centre in permanent festival-mode. Retail units and offices would pay for the development; passengers would move through a visionary gateway which embedded the railway at the centre of modern urban life. The men who made this proposal would become the Archigram group, respected internationally for their speculative theories of fluid, exciting future cities. British Railways trimmed its budget and took the project in-house; for the first stage of Euston's renewal there would be a replacement passenger terminal and limited office building.

Planning of the station was based on the flow of travellers between street, Underground and main line trains. Retaining the original strategy for a multi-level facility, a main line passenger station was placed partly beneath a parcels depot, and above a car and taxi circulation/parking area with the Underground station beneath it. This segregation of cars and people followed contemporary ideas of urban design. Euston's new architecture served as a sober enclosure for the necessary offices, catering and retail facilities. Central to the new station was a rectangular concourse three storeys high, glazed on four sides just below the flat roof. Like other railway stations built 1920–1939 and 1945–70, this arrangement is analogous to London Underground stations designed by Charles Holden. Over a floor of green stone, the concourse roof structure of deep concrete beams was supported on columns faced with black marble. Architects intended this dull colour scheme to be a backdrop for the large illuminated advertisement hoardings around the space.

Brochure to announce the official opening of the redeveloped Euston, London, terminus of British Rail's London Midland Region.

Euston Station model, 1962.

Artist impressions of the new Euston ticket hall (left) and travel centre (above).

Adjacent to the concourse, British Rail explored the concept of a Travel Centre, in which all aspects of journey planning and booking could be serviced in one place. Across the circulation space, the *Sprig Buffet* was designed to segregate passengers and staff: the public sat at booth tables, overlooked by the Statue of Britannia, rescued from the former Great Hall in the old station. Beside them special gangways were used to take orders and deliver food. Brown, dark blue and black dominated the interior colour scheme. A waiting lounge, concourse tea and coffee bar, 24-hour *Railbar*, toilets and retail kiosks augmented the amenities. On the first floor a second waiting lounge was placed adjacent to the *Lancastrian Snack Bar, Lancastrian Grill* room, and *Pennine Bar*. Unusually, Euston also offered a party catering room. Terence (later Sir Terence) Conran's contract business supplied the furniture. Externally, the station appeared as a flat roof building with double-height colonnade to the front comprising polished black granite piers against a white mosaic fascia. Along the colonnade a series of shops included a tailors, camera store, bank, book and stationery seller, hairdresser, holiday and travel service, and pharmacy. Work started in 1961, with demolition of the old structures, including the Doric propylaeum or 'Euston Arch'.[31] The project was troubled by British Rail's relations with the planning authorities, so much so that the original vision was significantly compromised. Opened by HM the Queen 14 October 1968, the new Euston was widely criticised for its mediocre design. This was due in part to the widespread protests over the British Transport Commission's refusal to preserve the Doric propylaeum. During 2014–15, following similar developments at other London termini, a mezzanine deck has been installed in the concourse area over the main station entrance.

An aspect of the old Euston which modernisation was to clear away: the *Continental Restaurant* opened in September 1958, as an attempt to bring post-war European gaiety to an odd corner of the old station.

Artist's impression of the new Euston Grill Room, 1967.

The *Lancastrian Grill Room* at Euston in use, 1969.

The *Sprig Buffet* at Euston, 1969, with the passenger concourse beyond.

Ladies' *Superloo* at Euston, 1969.

Many stations where total redevelopment was unnecessary or unviable, underwent partial renewal of those areas most used by passengers and which generated income. British Rail published a five-year modernisation programme for new cafes and bars in October 1970. Hulme Chadwick & Partners, known for their interior design work in aeroplanes, on ships, and in buildings, designed several catering spaces for British Rail, using the best contemporary practice in retail design. *The Toreador* restaurant and bar at Birmingham New Street, featured highly stylised ceiling gold and white units suspended over the dining bays, and an abstract mural along one wall. Waiting staff took orders and dispensed food from segregated runways. Customers sat in booths lined with white plastic and upholstered in orange imitation leather. Call buttons could be used to order food or wine. Set behind smoked glass within the Edwardian terminus, *The Drum*, opened at London's Waterloo in January 1972, had as a defining feature cylindrical modules descending an entire storey from the ceiling to illuminate circular tables. Intimations of a future newly-arrived at Waterloo were emphasised by the specially-made plastic trays used by customers at *The Drum*: six together completed a circle around the communal ashtray centrepieces. At *The Centre* Bar and Buffet in London's Charing Cross a moulded concrete fascia incorporating stylised lettering and circular windows.[32] In Scotland, *The Hebridean* Restaurant at Glasgow Queen Street offered intimate luxury for city dwellers and travellers. Examples like these, where canteens were transformed into boutiques, made good ways to communicate modernity to passengers and their companions; they also made for entertaining places to encounter other travellers, in spite of the criticism often applied to the standard of food and drink.

Exterior and interior of *The Drum*, at London's Waterloo, 1970.

Left and above: *The Toreador* Restaurant, New Street, Birmingham. Diners sat in booths served by staff using special runways and equipment.

Below: *The Hebridean* Restaurant at Glasgow Queen Street, 1973, provided a more restful atmosphere than catering spaces developed during the 1960s.

wine service | food service

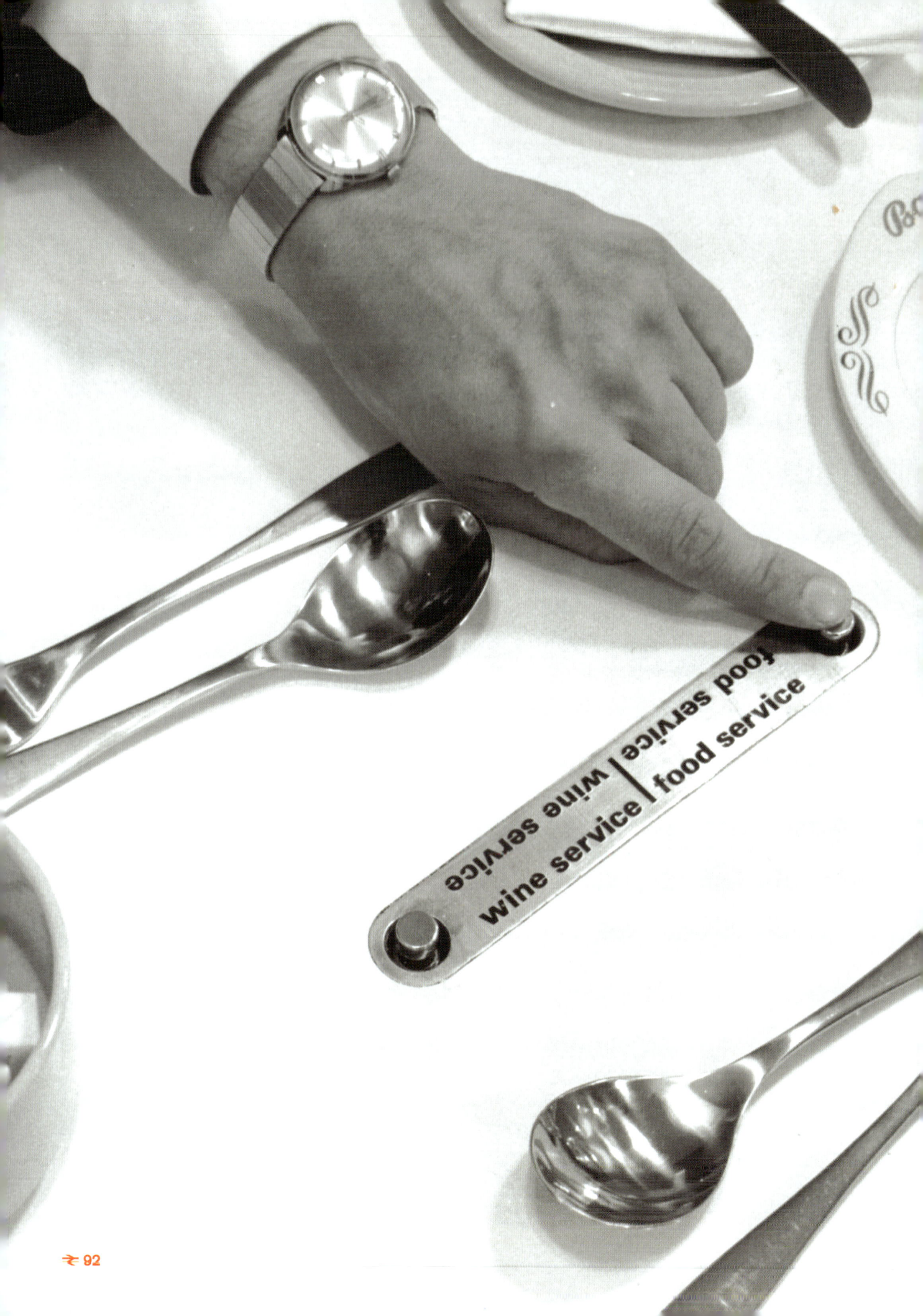

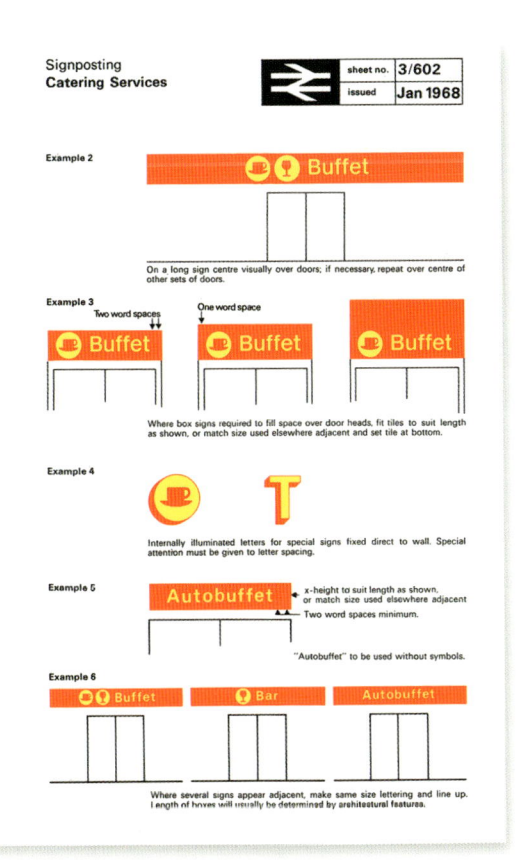

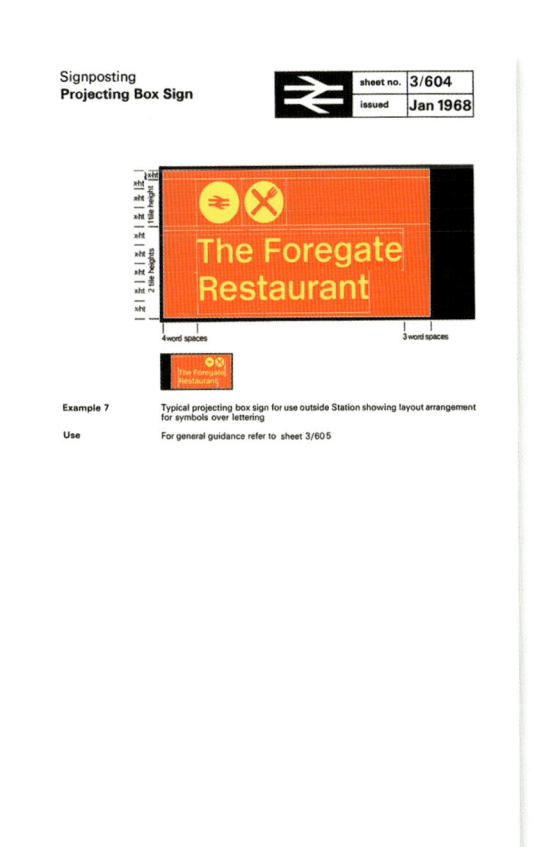

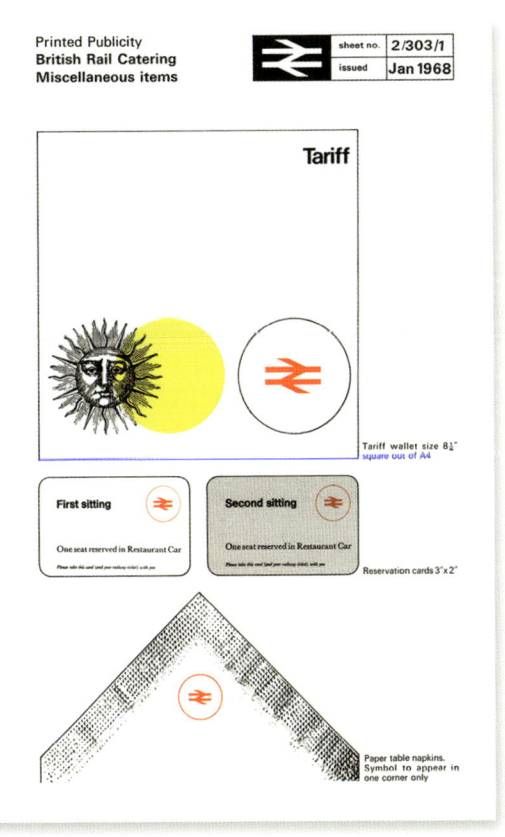

This page: Specifications compiled in 1965 for the signing of British Rail refreshment facilities, with an example of their application. From this branding came the trading name 'Travellers-Fare', a feature of the passenger environment until the mid-1980s.

Opposite page: With railway electrification came automation, of a sort: press buttons to call waiting staff at *The Toreador* Restaurant, Birmingham New Street station.

Architect's drawing of a CLASP structure for Belvedere, Kent, 1967. A similar building was provided at Forest Hill, south London.

Detail of the ticket hall entrance area at Fleet, Hampshire, 1967.

System-building for the Southern Region

The Great Western Railway had employed prefabricated parts for its 'pagoda' platform shelters from about 1904. Leslie Martin and Richard Llewelyn-Davies of the London, Midland and Scottish Railway (LMS) experimented with prefabrication after its efficacy had been demonstrated during the Second World War for quick, consistent, assembly of aircraft and structures. Historic buildings have acquired a status since the 1970s which invites their protection and continued use, but in the period when British Rail focussed primarily on the need to rapidly modernise its public image, it was thought that old railway stations were best cleared away entirely. This attitude was especially evident on the Southern Region of British Rail, where regional architect Nigel Wikeley led the programme to quickly displace vintage stations with an award-winning form of system building called CLASP, originally developed for new Nottinghamshire school projects in the 1950s.[33] Writing in *Modern Railways* in 1967, Wikeley observed how CLASP would see 'soot-grimed brick and brake dust-grained timber... superseded by vitreous enamelled steel, pre-cast concrete panels, plate glass and neoprene.'[34] Now it would be for the Southern Region to implement a comprehensive scheme of new stations made from ready-made components produced industrially.

Unlike the LMS examples, CLASP was not specially designed for railways: Wikeley noted its successful application for 'computer buildings, community buildings, old people's homes, libraries, police and fire stations', commenting that it 'required no design work before it appeared on site'.[35] Redevelopment using the CLASP system of more than a hundred stations was projected; twenty nine were eventually completed. Sunbury (Middlesex) was the pilot site, then Fleet (Hampshire), more locations in the London suburbs, and beyond.[36] Three Western Region sites also received CLASP stations, and one of the last examples of CLASP on British Rail opened at Alfreton & Mansfield Parkway in 1973.[37] It is perhaps an odd notion that architects chose a form of making structures which did not so evidently invite their design flair, but during this period there was a fascination with the idea that the most modern edifices - stations and houses no less than trains or cars - must inevitably be manufactured by machines. The flexibility, speed of assembly, visual order and cheapness of CLASP made it a very attractive proposition. Commonly single-storey, steel-framed and faced with concrete slabs of standard dimensions, CLASP stations had flat roofs with rows of shallow windows at high-level. Made as a lightweight kit of parts, no extensive foundation work was necessary. The unitary form of assembly was evident in the vertical pillars between panels, or as free-standing supports to platform canopies and cycle stores. Only the station name and British Rail symbol indicated the building's function. Interiors were planned as simple boxes - ticket office, waiting room, toilets - standard CLASP partitions of glass and plastic laminate linings, or plasterboard and tiling. A basic colour scheme of pale grey or cream walls, black doors and metalwork, and white frames to doors and windows introduced at this time remained standard until the mid-1980s. In reviewing the programme, and effectively confirming its legacy, Nigel Wikeley stated 'the end result...may mean that reconstructed stations are only shadows of their former selves. But we are confident that they will be more efficient from the point of view of both passengers and railway staff'.[38]

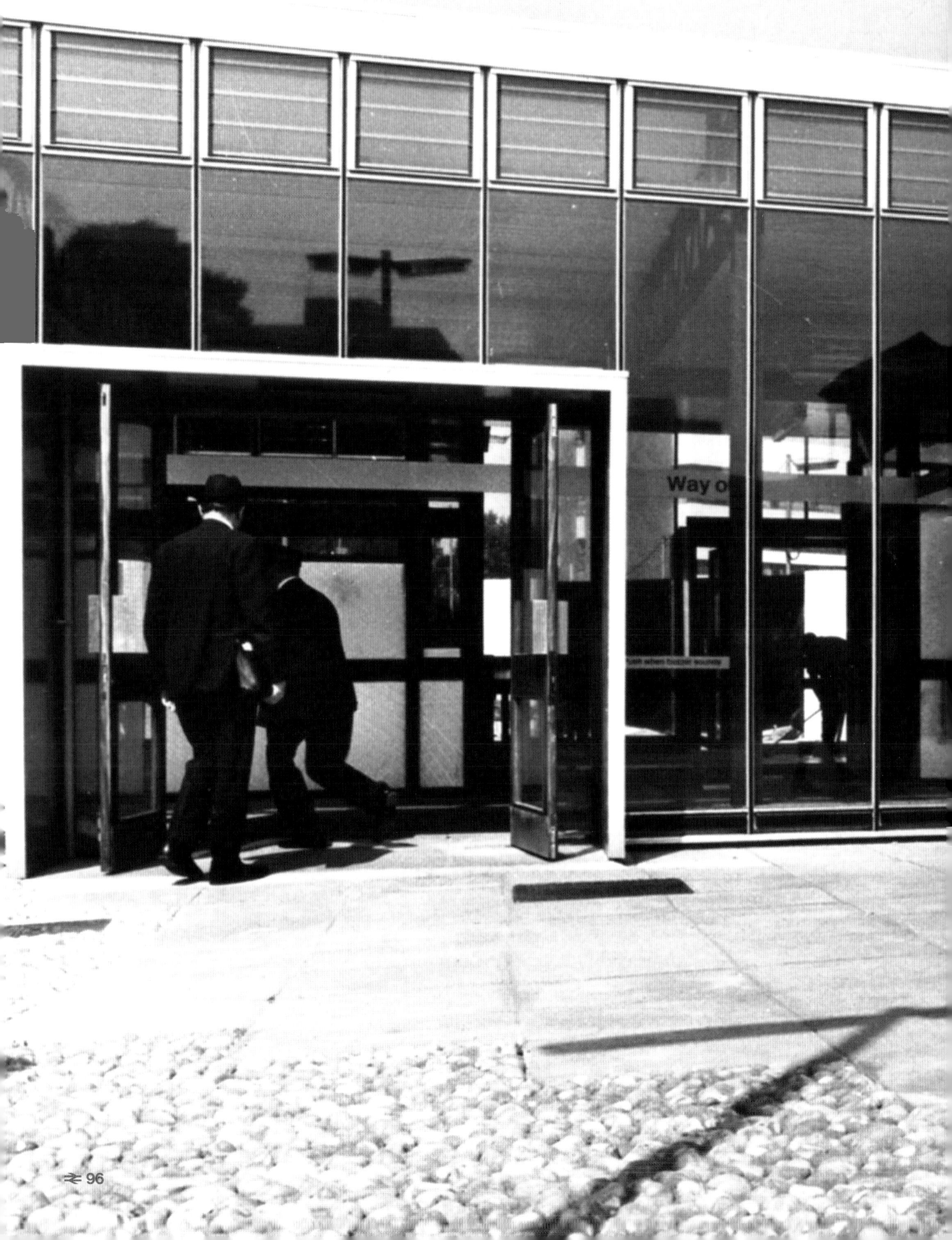

97

Maze Hill, Liss, Camberley, New Cross, Stoke Newington, Hadley Wood, Wood Street and Rye House

The style of German-American architect Mies van der Rohe again influenced some small stations towards the end of the 1960s. From Summer 1971 the south-east London suburb Maze Hill had a prefabricated station prototype designed by Nigel Wikeley and described as the 'D70 - or "Design for the 70s"- style.'[39] D70 was a truly modern adventure in station design, advancing the building type from a derivation of Charles Holden's pre-1939 work to a fresh, bright and functional architecture. Based on a steel column and beam structure enclosed by a glass box, with entry points defined by simple architraves, the D70 could be operated by one person from the central ticket office using remote control ticket barriers. Colour was limited to black, grey, brown and the natural hues of materials. Similar structures were provided on the Southern Region at Camberley, Liss (Liss attributed to project architect R Owen) and Southampton, and the Eastern Region at Rye House and Stoke Newington (both by E J Fletcher, 1974–75; Rye House now demolished), Hadley Wood and Wood Street. Back on the Southern Region, New Cross - opened August 1985 - represented a late, adapted version of the D70 idea.

Pages 98–99: The prototype D70 station building at Maze Hill, London, 1972.

A D70 building at Liss, Hampshire.

Eastern Region version of the D70 type at Rye House, Hertfordshire.

Southampton ticket hall interior, 1986 - a variation on the D70 type.

A further variation of the D70 building at Hadley Wood, Enfield, London.

D70 station building at Camberley, Surrey.

Wood Street station, Walthamstow, London.

New Cross station interior and exterior, 1985.

Bishop's Stortford, Gatwick Airport and King's Cross

Evolving construction systems continued to be reflected in railway station design. The space frame - a structure requiring support only at its perimeter - facilitated open-plan spaces which could be arranged, and rearranged, according to operational needs. Eastern Region architects adapted their glass box station type to incorporate a space frame at Bishop's Stortford, Hertfordshire, circa 1965, and the London Midland Region used one at Bedford (opened October 1978) and a smaller version at Radlett. The structural device was used again for the extension of the passenger concourse at London's King's Cross during 1972–3. Here, architects Sydney Hardy and H E Green used space frame technology to provide shelter for travel office, shops and concourse without imposing undue weight on the Underground railway below. For the interior a limited selection of materials included extensive use of aluminium finishes, with white tiles for the walls. The site has now been redeveloped.[40] On the Southern Region, Gatwick Airport station was rebuilt in 1980–81 with a space frame making it possible to create an extensive rail to air circulation area above and beside the platforms.

An exemplary use of the space frame within a glazed block ticket hall at Radlett, Hertfordshire.

Gatwick Airport station concourse, 1981: brown and white tiled walls below an extensive space frame.

Beyond the passenger spaces, some infrastructure projects were of outstanding quality. At Birmingham New Street John Bicknell and Paul Hamilton, assisted by John Hoile and Diana P. Quin, demonstrated the potential for concrete to be used with strength and delicacy, a poetic interpretation of the centralised control of train movements for which the building was made.[41] Pre-cast concrete panels with a serrated surface enclosed the several stories of the box, giving it a distinction among the indeterminate towers appearing in the second city at this time - 1966. Above the control room windows, 'sunbreakers' were a practical way of introducing contrasting form and details. Hamilton was responsible for several British Rail power signal boxes which transformed the appearance of this previously traditional, utilitarian structure.[42]

The New Town of Milton Keynes, Buckinghamshire, obtained a Central station in 1982. Set in front of an extensive plaza, with a prospect up the Midsummer Boulevard, this station suggests a combination of expressionist early European glass architecture in the setting of a classical city plan. Over three decades, British Railways/British Rail architects worked through most contemporary styles of building, and used a wide range of construction techniques to produce the best passenger spaces possible on the budgets available. In the next chapter we will see how the need for design to be part of the modernisation of British Railways prompted the formation of a specialist Design Panel, engaged in all aspects of British Railways visual appearance except for architecture. We will return to station design in Chapter Six: The new look.

Architect's model of Milton Keynes Central, circa 1980.

Exterior of Milton Keynes Central station and office block, 1986.

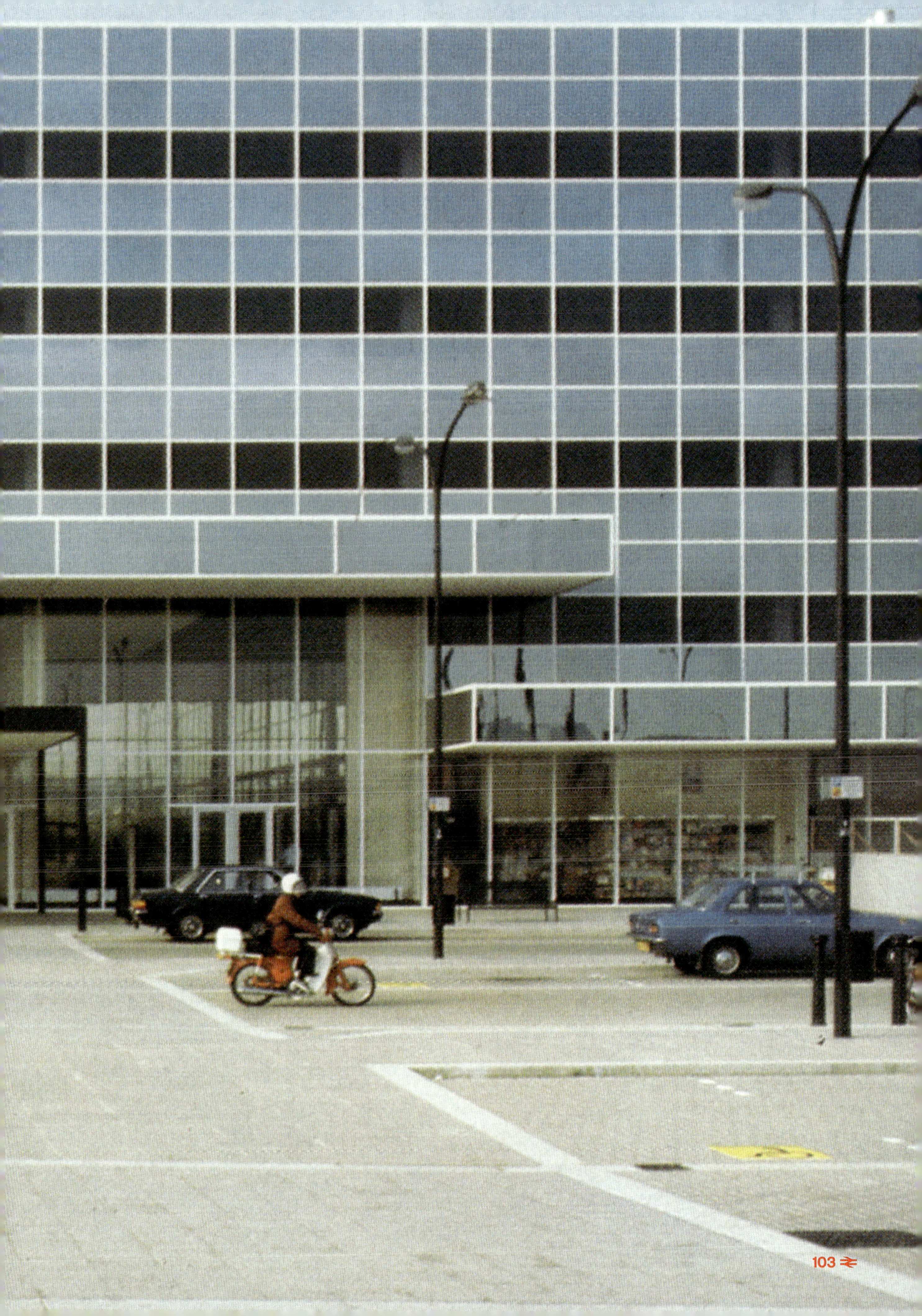

Chapter 4 →

Prime Movers:
The Design Panel
1965–60

'An organisation is required which, using the professional advice available within and outside the Commission, will secure the following objectives for the aesthetic design of the Commission's fixed and moveable equipment, especially equipment the technical design of which is centrally reserved: -

a) The appearance of the equipment must invest it with a character appropriate to a great public service and in keeping with the prestige of the Commission.

b) The liveliness and vitality of the appearance of the equipment must project the idea of a keen and progressive management.

c) The attractiveness of the equipment must promote the commercial development of the Commission's activities, and engender pride among those who use it.'[1]

British Railways' *Modernisation Plan* of 1955 was to have been the instrument by which the railway moved out of its serious financial deficit. Continuing economic difficulties accompanying the Plan's *Pilot Scheme* for new locomotives accelerated the production of vehicles without significant design intervention. Ernest Marples, Minister of Transport 1959–64 and a supporter of road transport, argued that the *Modernisation Plan* had evidently not brought the promised improvement in British Railways' viability. This concern, aggravated by the ruling Conservative Party agenda to turn the national system into a profitable business, culminated in the *Transport Act* of 1962. The British Railways Board replaced the British Transport Commission from 1 January 1963. Dr Richard Beeching had become Chairman of the Commission in June 1961, and continued in the same role for the new Board until 1 June 1965.

This chapter first discusses the conception and composition of the British Transport Commission Design Panel. It then introduces the consultants who worked to create the body/superstructure designs for products which emerged under Design Panel supervision. As the consultancy period overlaps the *Modernisation Plan*, those locomotives from the Plan which were subject to design advice are included here. To maintain thematic continuity in this chapter, rather than a strict chronology, we will look at work by industrial designers R D Russell[2] and John Barnes,[3] and the architect Jack Howe.[4] We then examine the projects of Wilkes & Ashmore for the full period of their tenure as consultants, 1956–68. When rationalisation of the railways gained further momentum in the early 1960s, good design formed an essential tool for imparting a coherent modern image. Consultants then began to provide the Design Panel with ideas and proposals from the scale of individual projects, up to strategies for the unification of a complex network comprising disparate vehicles, buildings and graphic systems. A second practice - Design Research Unit (DRU) - contributed some work on vehicles, and would become much better known for creating the British Rail corporate image. DRU work up to 1962 is covered in this chapter, and their projects visible on the railway network from 1964 are considered in Chapter Five: Design researched 1963–81.

Industrial design in Britain after the Second World War comprised a community of individuals who knew each other as a small network engaged in this emerging discipline, working together on British projects and with increasingly international influence. Britain's culture of design had been founded in the industrial revolution, given new impetus by the Arts & Crafts movement, and invigorated once more by the contributions of Europe and émigré designers during the 1920s and 1930s. The main centres of industrial design were Birmingham - centred on the teachers and students of the Birmingham Art School and the city's extensive industrial culture - and London, focussed on the Royal College of Art's staff and students. Birmingham and Midlands-related designers included E G M Wilkes, Peter Ashmore and Jack Ward of Wilkes & Ashmore, John Barnes of Allen-Bowden, Roger Jones of Jones Garrard and David Carter of DCA Design. London designers included Misha Black and John Beresford-Evans of Design Research Unit. Smaller centres of design existed in Glasgow - the base for J P 'Joe' McCrum - Edinburgh, and Dundee - location of Athol Hill.

Many early industrial designers trained as architects, a convention arising from centuries of architects being required to draw every part of a building project in order for it to be made to their specifications. Modernism in design, covering the period from approximately 1890 well into the twentieth century, perpetuated the idea that architects were best equipped to make form which was fit for purpose. War, and then commerce, changed this assumption, leading to the formation of the government's Council of Industrial Design (CoID, later the Design Council) in 1944. Briefed expressly with using the creative arts to improve the appearance of British products, the CoID became a considerable asset to the design professions. After the Second World War had shown the benefits of collaboration between engineers and designers, and brought motor manufacturing to prominence, so in peacetime the car industry began to produce adept individuals with a fresh understanding of how technology and three-dimensional form could be crafted together. The 1951 *Festival of Britain*, which convened design for business, leisure, and for export, gave further impetus to design as a key tool in fashioning a forward-looking nation. Every aspect of design practice was present at the Festival, acting as a forum for established and aspiring architects, industrial and graphic designers to be exhibited to potential clients: politicians, industry, and the public.

The relative flexibility of private industry, and the variety of routes through which training and employment was available, facilitated growth in independent consultancy. Design teams attached only to their own private practice were better placed to follow contemporary trends, making them attractive to large industries. Two-dimensional design took longer to emerge from the mixed status of commercial art: as the pictorial images which had been in vogue before the war were replaced by typography and abstract devices, graphic design was recognised as an important, effective means of communicating information about advertising products and services to potential customers. By the late 1950s a compromise position had evolved, organisations assembling design teams to work on projects themselves, and more often to write briefs for external consultants.

Opposite page top: E G M Wilkes making a prototype car model for George Williams, early 1950s.

Opposite page bottom: Model of 1958 for the D800 (class 42) series locomotive by John Beresford-Evans and Misha Black of Design Research Unit. Whilst this vehicle was not built, the superstructure style was revived for the D1000 type.

107

The Design Panel

Traditionally, design for the British railway industry was the responsibility of the engineering, publicity and administrative departments of the private operators and nationalised British Railways organisation. There was little formal provision for ensuring that these agencies worked together for the benefit of the railway, its passengers or staff. After it had begun a massive modernisation programme in 1955, producing hundreds of locomotives and thousands of vehicles ordered without visual co-ordination, the British Transport Commission realised that effective sourcing and management of design was essential, to make the plan convincing politically and socially as a real improvement to the image of railways.

In June 1956, the British Transport Commission established a Design Panel, as a way of ensuring that the modernisation programme gained more visual consistency in how it was manifested across the national transport networks.[5] The emphasis would be on railways, and the Panel had the public as its focus, to make better any and every situation in which travellers encountered trains. Facing the Panel - a purely advisory group with no direct power - was the immense task of moving the railways away from a fragmented version of an heroic and romantic, sentimental and picturesque Victorian plurality, away too from the patchy application of regional colours, to a clean and coherent, sober and rational emblem of progress. Although not all parts of such an extensive geographical territory or historically rich system could be changed, there were definite ways in which selected projects would make a considerable and positive difference. The Panel chose to address locomotives and rolling stock first, because of the unsatisfactory design results of the *Modernisation Plan*. T H Summerson, a Member of the British Transport Commission who also headed British Railways' North Eastern Area Board, chaired the Design Panel. He was joined by Commission Members Major-General Llewelyn Wansborough-Jones and John Ratter, who would succeed Summerson as Chairman in October 1963.

E W Arkle, chief commercial officer of the Railway Executive's London Midland Region, and London Transport Executive chief supplies and services officer E C Ottaway, were selected for their expertise. Representing industry were W J Worboys, former director of Imperial Chemical Industries and Chairman of the CoID, and Sir Gordon Russell, furniture designer and the CoID's Director.

Two Panel members are of considerable importance to this account: British Transport Commission Chief Publicity Officer Christian Barman,[6] and Design Officer George Williams. An architect and designer, Barman was of ideal background for the role of advising the Panel and communicating its intentions throughout the organisation. He had worked at London Transport during 1935–41 as publicity officer for Frank Pick, both men motivated by a strong sense of image and identity to maintain a pioneering programme of design patronage which generated much of the visual idiom for London's rail and road passenger systems. After the Second World War Barman joined the Great Western Railway, managing its own vision for modernisation whilst working as a writer on design subjects. In 1949 Christian Barman defined his work: 'transport is a personal service provided by a large group of skilled workers… the pieces of stationary and mobile equipment… are the tools by which [they] perform their work…. the designer's task is narrowed down to the simple problem of producing the best possible tool for a given job.'[7] He advocated the 'unified environment provided by public transport…buildings, rolling stock, and equipment generally, as well as through their posters and many other forms of publicity.'[8] With this ethos, Barman was without equal, and an extraordinary asset to the Commission. George Williams joined the Design Panel in March 1957, working for Christian Barman with two design officers for industrial/graphic design and research, to prepare the briefs for external consultants who would do the bulk of the actual designing.[9] Williams had begun his career designing passenger cars, racing cars and commercial vehicles. He was a senior product designer for Design Research Unit 1946–48, and an industrial officer for the CoID from 1948, dealing with projects related to street furniture and the wider engineering industries. Williams also led the team organising the road, rail, sea and air display for the Transport Pavilion at the *Festival of Britain* 1951. Included by Williams in the 1951 exhibition was the 'Car of the Future', designed by E G M Wilkes, Hugo Poole and Peter Ashmore for automotive manufacturer Borg Warner and the CoID. Williams would later commission Wilkes & Ashmore as consultants for the design of locomotive superstructures.

In its early years the Design Panel tackled the enormous remit of advising on the appearance of locomotives, passenger vehicles, the environment and equipment of public railway spaces (but not the architecture), and sundry equipment along the railway lines. It met only twice each year; it was instructed that costs which might be incurred by evaluating the *Modernisation Plan* locomotives were to be avoided. These two conditions afforded the Panel limited time to suggest improvements to the vehicles planned during 1955–57, beyond painting schemes and superficial adjustments. A new intake of young railway managers was also keen to embrace innovation and let go of the past. Specialist advice came in the form of consultant designers: architects, car stylists, industrial designers, lettering designers. As the Panel guided British Railways into the 1960s, design became a tool to accelerate the modernisation of railways and therefore Britain, to unify the country in an increasingly technological age. There would of course be obstacles. The extraordinary scale of design work required would always challenge financial and human resources. Civil servants administering those resources did not have design training, whilst the Design Panel was too small to effect total change, or to ensure that external contractors always followed its design guidelines. The Design Panel had also to convince its own colleagues at British Railways

that good design would not negate or dissipate tradition, but promised good business in Britain, and national prestige overseas.[10] In spite of these factors, we will see that much was achieved.

Christian Barman inspects the first D5500 locomotive, 1957.

George Williams, 1960.

Designing for movement

This section discusses the general principles of railway vehicle design for British Railways, in order to better appreciate the specific projects which are considered subsequently. We summarise the various aspects of planning locomotives and passenger trains, and talk about the way colour has been used for the liveries of these trains and the environment in which they operate.

Until the era of the ubiquitous multiple-unit the locomotive was an icon of the railway operator, communicating through its design the organisation's public image: at best strong, assured, efficient, clean; at worst ponderous, unreliable, dirty. The appearance of locomotives was therefore critical to the public perception of the transport provider. Steam locomotive forms are expressions of the mechanics of the machinery itself, and the processes used to fabricate it. Any disconnect in design processes had been limited in steam locomotive development because the engineers were the designers. The visual aesthetic of steam locomotives resulted from draughtsmen-designers bringing beauty, often instinctively, to the necessary shapes of the vehicle - its water and coal storage, boiler, cylinders, chimney and moving parts. Most of these elements were a derivation of the essential forms of rectangle and circle; they relied on gentle arcs and precise geometry for visual harmony. The parts could be understood as connected stages of power generation and use, contained by thin sheets of metal, painted in colours not much changed since wheeled road vehicles were first decorated in the liveries of their owners.

The process of designing a new item of rolling stock began with a need being identified - perhaps a new service, or replacement of vehicles. Operating staff, with a brief to match train performance to timetables and passenger volumes, would consider the purpose and use of the project, to determine the required performance. Engineers would then develop a machine which aimed to meet this need. Steam locomotive designers had developed a visual language for the locomotive over several decades, albeit that it varied from country to country. Rarely did they need to depart from general forms established in the mid–nineteenth century. Designers tasked with styling more modern forms of motive power had only a very few years to determine the visual appearance of their subjects. The effects of modernisation in industry included dividing roles into isolated activities, meaning that the designer was increasingly separated from the final product, and had reduced opportunity to ensure that their intentions were followed. Technical considerations remained foremost, because they would ensure a functional outcome. In British diesel and electric locomotive design this was not really recognised as a problem until the late 1950s. Even then, advice from consultants employed for the purpose of improving locomotive designs was resisted - even ignored - by the manufacturers and British Railways' own workshops. Consistent appearance requires co-operation between the engineer and designer throughout the process, with the shared aim of achieving a particular form and related details. If the engineer planned the technical aspects of the vehicle without working with a designer, then seemingly practical decisions like the height of the cab floor could markedly affect the external appearance. This is because the available space for the superstructure, inside the maximum possible dimensions or 'loading gauge' and *outside* the locomotive's equipment, is relatively limited. There are other physical considerations: the vehicle superstructure must remain stable at high speed; it must be resilient to the pressure shocks of entering tunnels, cross winds, or passing other trains; it must give protection to the operating personnel in a collision situation.

Modern machinery - discrete technical modules such as motors, generators or electrical circuits linked together - requires housing to protect it and provide an interface with the user. Equipment needs ventilation and access for repairs; passengers need to observe the passing landscape. Beyond the provision of openings in these boxes, their form is related to the way in which their engineers want them to function and how the engineers and designers establish that they will look. Because the enclosure is separate, the image of the object can be distinct from its function. Motor cars are a notorious example of this distancing between utility and form, but it applied equally to railway vehicles. The design of a locomotive, therefore, aided by the work of consultants, could be manipulated to convey whatever impression that the British Transport Commission - on behalf of the state - wished to give its public. As the 1960s progressed, the influence of Italian and north European design trends - seen by young designers in magazines and at first hand - came to bear on British industrial design.

Aesthetics of diesel and electric locomotives were influenced variously by concepts of demonstrating speed, or power, or a combination of both. Their body shapes often comprise truncated curves and potentially abrupt changes of direction. In selecting form, a guiding principle is to consider either the vehicle cross-section or longitudinal section. Driving cab fronts, the main features of the vehicles, can be curved, flat or angled in horizontal and vertical planes. The choice of profile might be to match the outline of the coaching stock, or to adopt some or other form which was considered redolent of efficiency, strength, or a trend in transport design. Each approach produces different results: the D1000 series is an example of using the vehicle cross section to produce an extruded form terminated by single-plane fronts (see page 152). In the D7000 series, the longitudinal section generates a series of horizontal lines which appear to elongate the cab portions (see page 138). Vertical planes imply height and power, independent of the vehicle sides. Horizontal planes suggest stability in relationship to the track, leading to a focus on the horizontal plane for the body length. Either approach requires a precise relationship between proportions of forms and between windows and solid areas. When planning the disposition and shape of cab windows, another factor is very important - the view given to the vehicle operator who will spend some hours looking out from the cab. Experience showed that windows with gently curved margins were more restful than those with straight edges.[11] Designers work through models and full-size mock-ups to adjust the volume and mass of their project, noting like a sculptor how light shaped the folds, curves and planes to achieve the desired appearance. Body sides and roof can be tapered towards the cab, or finished at edges which are angled or radiused. The precise handling of the sides would indicate actual or potential speed. Straight side panels are easier to fabricate. Introducing curves or tapers into the body sides can make the vehicle seem top-heavy or slow. A better solution is to introduce tapers both up and down, away from the waistline. This enhances the width without seeming bulky, and so infers power.[12]

Conceiving locomotives with the same sensitivity to detail of a much smaller object or a sculpture, brought increased sophistication to superstructure outlines, making planes meet each other in pleasing ways, moving the locomotive beyond a basic metal box containing power-generating equipment. It also brought the railway industry and industrial design together with extraordinary results.

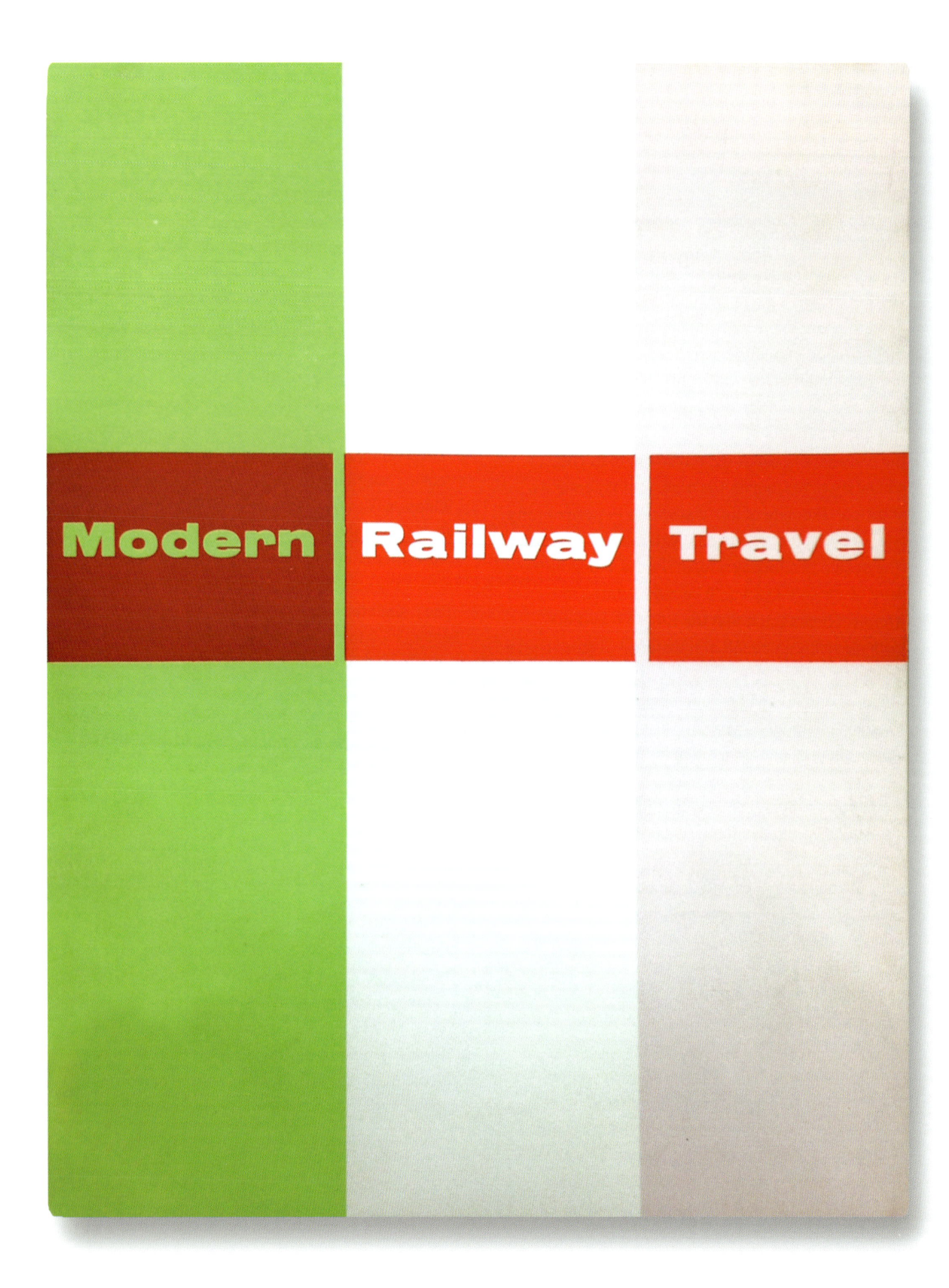

Modern Railway Travel

Exhibition: New Ideas in Rail Transport 1957

In the shadow of the power station, London's Battersea Wharf sidings were utilised for the British Transport Commission exhibition 'Modern Railway Travel', presenting innovation in railway services under the Modernisation Plan. This was the first of a series of promotional exhibitions staged by the Design Panel until the mid-1980s, and it launched the Panel into public awareness. Press announcements stressed that most of the items had been commissioned before the Design Panel had an opportunity to influence the appearance of British Railways, and that none was a standard for the future.[13] Open to the public 28–30 June 1957, the thirty-two exhibits included the prototype 3300hp main-line 'Deltic' locomotive, the first 1000hp mixed traffic locomotive (D8000 series, later class 20), and a 350hp shunting engine. There were also thirteen experimental passenger carriages: six built by British Railways at their Doncaster Works, and seven by four private contractors.[14] Several of the coach interiors were designed by consultant architects: each was to demonstrate how the standard British Railways passenger vehicle could be improved, for example in seating, lighting or heating. It may seem odd that architects were given the job of rethinking train interiors, but after all the train is really a room, or series of rooms, on wheels. Farmer and Dark proposed first and second class open coaches for builders Cravens. Details included reclining seats, folding tables, and a patterned melamine laminate wall finish. Their double-glazed windows of larger than standard dimensions and enclosing adjustable Venetian blinds would be used in diesel multiple-unit trains operating from 1960. Trevor Dannatt's first class open coach comprised revolving seats for flexible business meeting configurations, within walls and ceilings surfaced in Aspen wood veneer, and teak surfaced end screens. Sir Hugh Casson, formerly Director of Architecture for the *Festival of Britain* and head of Interior Design at the Royal College of Art, designed a first class open coach built by the Birmingham Railway Carriage & Wagon Company. Intended to have a club atmosphere, it was lined with Australian walnut veneer, and borrowed from airline innovation to use luggage racks fitted with integral reading lights. Dr F F C Curtis, British Transport Commission Chief Architect, styled interiors for first and second class saloon coaches, working with Trevor Dannatt on compartment accommodation. C P Johnson, the architect for British Transport Catering, designed kitchen-buffet and restaurant-buffet cars. A class 120 'Inter-city' diesel multiple-unit included a buffet area by architect Peter Miller. Further rolling stock on display included catering vehicles, a sleeping car, a diesel-electric multiple-unit of the 6S/6L/5L 'Hastings' type (see page 48), and a range of coaches to be hauled by diesel locomotives on main-line and secondary services. Each had much use of laminated plastic boards in the interiors, to give a bright, economical appearance. A platform refreshment trolley, a train corridor refreshment trolley and a lounge-buffet area represented catering developments. Finally, full-size passenger station facilities included a mocked-up waiting room interior with a range of waiting room furniture designed by Robin Day and made by Hille & Co. for use on the Eastern Region, a ticket office with mechanical ticket issuing machines, and a 'self-help' passenger barrow.[15]

Prototype Buffet kitchen car, 1956. There is extensive use of patterned plastic laminates and highly stylised fittings.

D8000 (class 20) locomotive built by English Electric. A team at London's Royal College of Art handled the superstructure design and specified the livery.

The D8000 series body copied the North American 'switcher locomotive' format. A long hood or bonnet contained the power generation equipment, with an operating cab at one end.

114

D8200 (class 15) type locomotive designed by John Barnes. In this design the cab was partway along the hood. The body was painted dark green, with a lighter shade for the cab front panels.

Mock-up coach interiors shown at Battersea were criticised for being focussed more on fashion than ergonomics or function. In contrast, the locomotives on display would prove to be some of the most long-serving vehicles on the national railway system. English Electric D8000 was the first locomotive made for the British Railways *Modernisation Plan*. Built by Vulcan Foundry and Robert Stephenson & Hawthorn, D8000 was styled by Professor R D 'Dick' Russell at the Royal College of Art, London, with his students Vilhelm Koren (who would become a freelance high-performance automobile designer, styling the *Bentley S2 and S3 Continental Drop Head Coupe* motor cars) and Canadian Frank E Dudas.[16] Their superstructure for D8000 was of the North American 'high hood' type, referring to the bulky equipment enclosure forming the majority of the vehicle's body beyond the cab. It shared similarities with 'switcher' locomotives like those built by the American Locomotive Company of Schenectady, New York, from the 1930s onwards, and by Fairbanks-Morse of Wisconsin from the early 1940s.[17] D8000 began service in June 1957, painted in a clean, confident livery of dark green with a medium grey roof above the cant rail. Also shown was the prototype *Deltic* locomotive, an extremely powerful machine for the period in Britain. In time, twenty two 'Deltic' locomotives would be made for British Railways; the shunting engine (later class 08) continued to be built for ten years, resulting in 996 examples.

John Barnes of Allen-Bowden industrial designers authored the superstructure for the D8200 series (later class 15) British Thomson-Houston locomotive operated from November 1957. A variant on the D8000 body, its shape was developed from London, Midland and Scottish Railway locomotive 10800, again based on the North American 'hood' type 'road switcher'. For D8200 Barnes softened the outline: he made the shorter hood the same height as cab, and the long hood slightly lower to reduce the apparent bulk. The end of the shorter hood comprised two planes meeting at a vertical crease. Ventilation grilles were placed in a tidy line above the cant rail.[18]

In 1961 Barnes styled the D8500 series (later class 17).[19] This was a rethinking of the hood type, with the equipment compartments reduced in height either side of a central cab to give better visibility for the operators. He specified a colour scheme of two greens for the body and cab, with a roof of light grey, later adjusted to suit British Railways paints.

A smaller version of D8500 completed Barnes' work for the British Transport Commission. The D9500 (later class 14) design would be a multi-purpose shunting locomotive. It was ordered in 1963, placed in service from 1964, and the entire fleet had been sold or withdrawn from British Rail use by 1970. With D9500 Barnes proposed a radical colour scheme which is comparable to the thinking of Wilkes & Ashmore in the same period, suggesting a possible new direction in British Railways liveries: the hood units were to be mustard yellow, the cab pale grey, and the roof dark brown.[20]

Jack Howe

Architect and industrial designer Jack Howe handled the D1 series (class 44 locomotive) for British Railways' own manufacturing division, and two projects for Metropolitan-Vickers: the D5700 series (class 28) locomotive, and the high speed diesel electric multiple-units colloquially known as the 'Blue Pullmans'. Howe was asked to look at the D1 series superstructure late in the development process, limiting his ability to amend the design. The body, with short bonnets in front of the driving cabs, was generally similar to London, Midland and Scottish Railway locomotives 10000/10001. Howe rearranged the grilles in the body sides, concealing a series of apertures behind two visually related elements. To give it emphasis the horizontal grille had a polished metal frame; the square grille was painted to appear part of the superstructure. Built at British Railways' Derby Works, the D1 series commenced service in 1959, in the same Wilkes & Ashmore-devised livery as the D5700 series. The former class carried names when new. Jack Howe supervised the nameplate design for D1–10, producing red-painted signs with Gill Sans lettering. British Railways' Derby Works built locomotives D11–D137 (later class 45) during 1960–62. This group was followed by D138–D193 (later class 46) built 1961–63. Both used Howe's body design.

For Metropolitan-Vickers, Howe attempted to avoid North American bonnet-type cab fronts when he worked on the D5700 series (class 28). Looking at the result, a blunt-ended box form with the conventional three windows aligned to the arc of the roof, it seems as if the bonnets were simply removed without assessing the consequences. Howe did give the cabs the distinction of wrap-around windows, and made a neat pattern of body side grilles. Painting the superstructure in dark green with light grey side bands, accentuated the smooth form of the superstructure. The unusual wheel arrangement of a four-wheel and a six-wheel bogie, and the mechanical faults associated with this class, did not endear them to railwaymen. Only twenty were made, in the period 1959–60.

George Williams said in 1962 that British Railways must modernise itself rapidly to compete with the 'young and apparently uncomplicated' public face of the similarly state-owned British European Airways, which was threatening to take away passenger rail traffic. His employer had recently recognised that it needed a modern luxury train to meet this external pressure on passenger numbers, a threat which would continue to challenge main line services for many years. With George Williams, Howe visited several European railways to study best practice. A small fleet of impressive diesel express trains, branded the *Midland Pullman* and *Western Pullman*, was commissioned to transform the image of long-distance rail travel for business customers. Howe later became known for designing the first British ATM machine, and he brought his understanding of form and material to the exterior and interior appearance of these trains.

As a sophisticated, high-speed application of the diesel multiple-unit, the sets had driving cabs in the motor coaches at each end of the six- or eight-car formations. Jack Howe succeeded in

D8500 series (class 17) D8578, in July 1965. The colour scheme of two greens specified by designer John Barnes is shown well.

D11 series (class 45) locomotive D20 at Leeds City, August 1967. Jack Howe made adjustments to the north American body styling selected by British Railways.

D5700 series (class 28) locomotive D5716 in April 1966. Superstructure design by Jack Howe.

combining the crisp aesthetic of Great Western railcars with a unique form based on triangular panels joined by precise, curved, creases. Great Western influence is further evidenced by the ridge carried up into the cab roof dome, shown in early artist's impressions as a definite line but softened in production. Trapezoid windows set in a recessed panel around the cab fronts also suggested the influence of contemporary jet airliners such as the de Havilland *Comet*. The motor coaches and trailer carriages had near-straight sides, a form that would be taken forward for subsequent British Railways standard passenger coach designs.

Conventionally, rolling stock used for *Pullman* services wore a livery of umber (brown) and cream. Artists' impressions - some drawn by Peter Ashmore of Wilkes & Ashmore - suggest that the units were to be green with black window surrounds and a grey roof. But these trains were to evidence British Railways making a leap into modernity: the final colour scheme comprised all-over Nanking Blue (hence the name 'Blue Pullman'), with white panels along the line of the windows.[21] It might be assumed that the blue was selected by Jack Howe; we need to note, however, the presence of Misha Black as another consultant to the British Transport Commission Design Panel. He had a distinct preference for Nanking Blue, adapting it for British Railways electric locomotives, and securing it as the hue to denote London Underground's Victoria line on which he was lead design consultant. In white serifed lettering the title 'Midland Pullman', or simply 'Pullman' for Western Region units, was displayed on power car sides.

Carriage interiors presented the most luxurious environment, to compete with airline comfort. Technically, they were sound-proofed and air-conditioned throughout. A public address system could be used to give journey information. Double-glazed windows contained passenger-operated blinds. Every table had a reading lamp to supplement the overhead lighting. One decorative

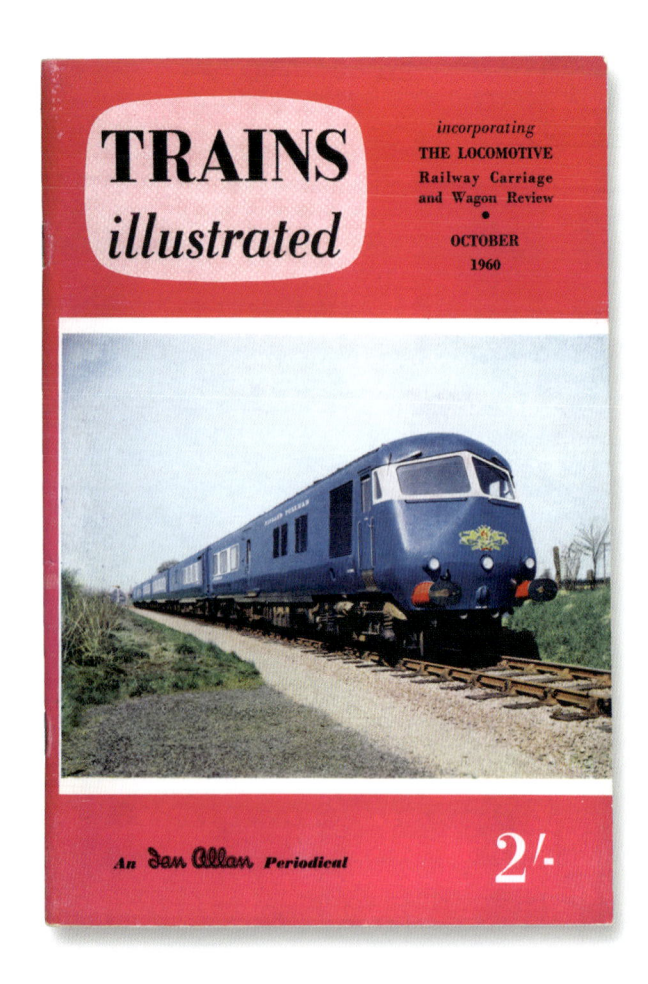

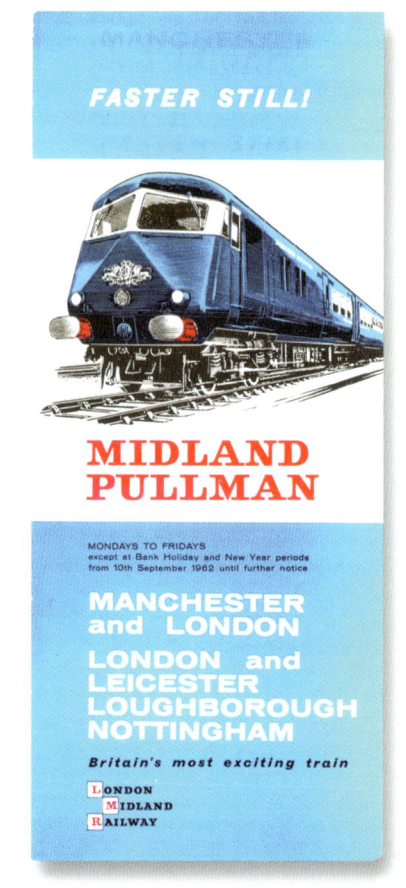

Opposite page: Marketing and promotional material for the High Speed Diesel Trains styled by Jack Howe for British Railways' premier 'Pullman' services to the Midlands and West of England.

This page, top: Illustration of the proposed 'Blue Pullman' train prepared by Peter Ashmore of Wilkes & Ashmore. The cab front features more streamlined styling than the production form of the train.

This page, above: Designer Jack Howe kept the unit ends free from all unnecessary detail and placed the ventilation louvres in an ordered pattern. Cab fronts were taken down around the buffer stocks, concealing the drawgear behind hinged doors. Three lamp units arranged across the front served as tail and head lights by the fitting of red or opaque covers. A redrawn version of the *Pullman* coat of arms, lavishly decorated in gold, replaced the initial plan for a headcode box in the lower part of the cab.

scheme was specified for the Second Class cars, and two for the First class vehicles. Ceilings were panelled in pale grey plastic with a black pinstripe. Second class coaches had walls lined in textured grey *Vynide*, a plastic artificial leathercloth; those in first class were grey *Lanide*. Through George Williams, Jack Howe engaged William Mitchell to create mural decorations of mythical creatures inlaid into the polished Rio Rosewood surfaces in one scheme for First class Parlour Car ends, and for Kitchen Car bulkheads. Mitchell made the murals at his studio in Forest Hill, London, assisted by David Millett.[22] In the second scheme partitions and doors were veneered in polished Macassar Ebony. Much use was made of synthetic materials in the coach saloons, to a colour scheme of greys, with details in black, dark blue or grey, and panels of pastel blue or grey. Patterned grey melamine laminate lined the partition walls in second class areas. Carpets in first class were suitably sober shades of 'Cortina Kingfisher' blue or 'Cortina Cardinal' red on black; second class carpets were red on black 'Devon Weave'. Individual reclining seats were upholstered in red and navy blue, or blue and navy blue striped cloth, all with grey

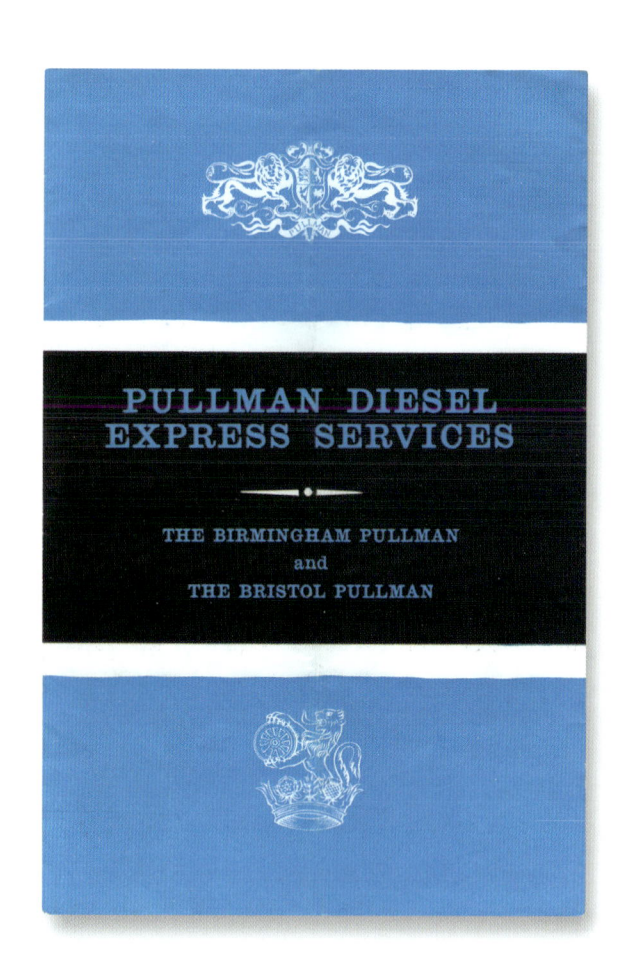

Above: Printed guide to the 'Blue Pullman' services, 1960.

Below: *Bristol* or *Western Pullman* arrives at Paddington, London, in September 1962.

hide arm and headrests. Second class seats were blue with a black stripe. This is likely to be 'shaded stripe', designed by Marianne Straub for Warner Fabrics.[23] In first class the metal parts - window trims, luggage racks, and other details - were aluminium anodised in a satin finish pale gold colour; in Second class they were anodised satin silver. For ease of cleaning, toilet areas were variously lined with melamine laminate in shades of blue, pink and grey. Their position in the corridors was highlighted by panels of red or pale blue (First class) and blue-grey (Second class).[24]

The *Midland Pullman* began passenger service in July 1960; *Pullman* trains followed on the Western Region in September 1960.[25] Midland units were transferred to the Western Region in April 1966 when the West Coast Main Line was electrified. In compliance with transport safety requirements, Pullman units had their cab fronts painted Warning Yellow from 1966. Soon Nanking Blue gave way to a British Rail colour scheme which reversed that used for ordinary passenger coaches: vehicle bodies were finished in Rail Grey with Rail Blue bands at window level. All units had been withdrawn by May 1973.

'Blue Pullman' First class saloon, 1960.

'Blue Pullman' Second class saloon, 1960. While still luxurious, the decorations made more use of synthetic materials in these spaces.

Design consultancy gains ground

E G M 'Ted' Wilkes of the practice Wilkes & Ashmore (W&A), and Misha Black of Design Research Unit (DRU) were appointed as British Transport Commission Design Panel consultants in 1956. It is likely that they were recommended to Christian Barman by George Williams, who knew both men from his involvement in the *Festival of Britain*. John Beresford-Evans came to DRU in 1958 to lead the locomotive design work. Wilkes & Ashmore created the form of locomotive superstructure preferred by British Rail - a refined flat fronted body style - and became the main adviser for the locomotives, multiple-units and passenger vehicles; this practice is discussed first.

Wilkes & Ashmore (later Wilkes & Ward)

E G M Wilkes[26] and Peter J Ashmore[27] met at the motor manufacturers Rootes Group, an English industrial conglomerate building motor cars under the marques Hillman, Humber, Singer and Sunbeam. Wilkes was Rootes' chief stylist from about 1944; he was joined by Ashmore, an expert artist producing seductive renderings of motor vehicles for presentations and sales brochures, after World War Two.

Wilkes left Rootes in 1952 to establish an industrial design business in Horsham, West Sussex. Horsham had a growing artistic community; it was near London and the coast. Ashmore followed him in 1953, having worked in the intervening period with John Barnes at the Allen-Bowden practice. Jack Ward became the third partner at W&A in 1954.[28] Wilkes led the industrial design work, with Ashmore responsible for presentation drawings, and Ward for engineering design, model-making and manufacturing matters. In 1960, as the practice expanded, they commissioned purpose-built offices and workshops where designers worked at drawing boards alongside carpenters making models of the developing ideas.[29] The premises were of sufficient dimensions to produce full-size mock-ups of railway vehicles. Employees of the practice included Jill Coombs, David Higgins, Perry King,[30] Don Tustin (ex-Rootes Group & Ford Motor Company vehicle styling departments), Peter Cambridge (from Ford's styling department) and Kenneth Sadler.

General appearance of W&A designs

In the automobile industry efficiency and good visual design are essential, if the vehicles are to be mass-produced as attractive objects and sold at a profit. Materials must be used to the limit of their performance, formed in ways which expedite assembly by semi-skilled workers (and now robots too). Traditionally locomotives had been designed through engineering conventions - drawn as plans, side and front elevations. The meeting of each elevation at the edges was often left for craftsmen to resolve independently. Industrial designers are trained to understand three-dimensional form. They work with engineers in styling studios, developing products through a staged process of drawing, modelling, prototyping at full-size and testing. With car styling having become so important an aspect of industrial design by the 1950s, the potential for transferring its techniques to the railway industry seemed very attractive. It was an obvious move to choose automotive designers for new locomotive projects, the latter really being a scaled up version of the former: a skin shaped to be visually appealing, its form not fully dependent on its contents or function. Experience in product and car design gave Wilkes the skill to 'go around corners', or understand vehicles as three dimensional forms.[31] W&A worked by sketching ideas for locomotive superstructures to match technical requirements. These would be evaluated by the office team, and then produced as scale drawings and models. Ultimately, full-size drawings would be interpreted by the manufacturers as full-size mock-ups. In parallel, colour schemes would be devised to suit the vehicles, so that discussions with British Railways might be more comprehensive and fruitful.

Jack Ward, F G M 'Tod' Wilkes and Kenneth Sadler, of industrial design practice Wilkes & Ashmore, discussing a project at their Horsham, Sussex studios circa 1962.

D5500 (class 30/31)

Brush Traction prepared a curiously dismal first scheme for what would become the D5500 locomotive. Rejected by the Design Panel, it was given to Wilkes & Ashmore to revise. With the D5500 design the consultants developed what was to become the officially preferred form of cab front - an arrangement of two planes meeting at an obtuse angle level with the waistline of the vehicle body. In plan, the cab fronts had a bowed form to suggest forward motion; in elevation 'a thrust-back below the slight nose contour, and a reverse sweep of the cab windscreen above.'[32] The three-part window arrangement was necessary to fit around the gangway doors in the cab fronts; subsequent W&A jobs - D7000 series (class 35), D0280 *Falcon*, D0260 *Lion*, D1500 series (class 47) - adopted the European practice of giving locomotives two-part windscreens set in near-flat fronts. Another feature repeated in most W&A designs was the roof cowl, used to conceal air horns and visually correct the rounded appearance of the cab dome. W&A were working on the design by February 1956. By July 1956 a full-size test model was made at Brush Traction of Loughborough, England. This intermediate stage between the Brush sketch and final scheme had a short snub nose, not dissimilar to the contemporary D6100 (class 21) locomotive by Joe McCrum (see page 150).[33] In the consultants' words, 'we have always felt justified in introducing some feature which will give a feeling of power and mobility to the locomotive. The short nose and forward slope of the lower panel is the most economical way of achieving this.'[34] With adjustments for manufacturing requirements, this was the final approved superstructure. The first unit was officially handed over to British Railways on 31 October 1957.[35]

Steam engines had their own tradition of coloured liveries. Diesel and electric locomotives and multiple-unit trains, with none of the heat, grease or soot of steam, presented a new opportunity to experiment with colour. As with any form of vehicle, the choice of painting scheme would communicate particular

Brush Traction proposal for the D5500 (class 30/31) locomotive superstructure, 1956.

First full-size mock-up of the D5500 by Wilkes & Ashmore, 1956.

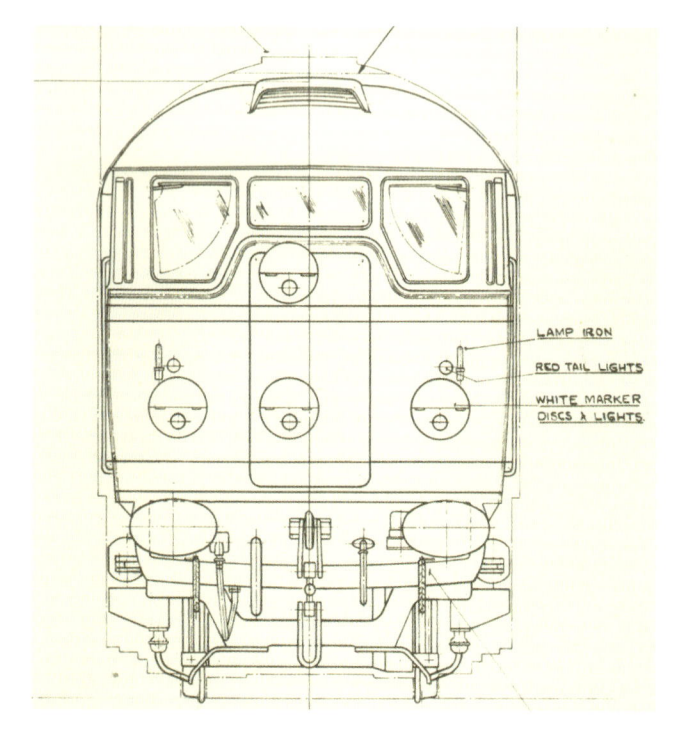

Design drawing of D5500 series cab front.

qualities to observers. A locomotive could appear fast and powerful, or strong and reliable, by the colour applied to its superstructure. Wilkes & Ashmore believed that emphasis on horizontal lines gave an impression of speed with stability. D5500 carried a livery of dark green paint with two horizontal light grey bands added to accentuate the length of the locomotive, counteracting the visual complication caused by the shape of the lower body margins.

On early units the window surrounds were painted light grey; in a later batch this feature was dropped, before the painters resumed highlighting the window area with pale blue, or white. After D5500, D5300 (class 26) and D6500 (class 33), the lower grey line was omitted from livery designs because it showed the dirt and did not suit all superstructure forms.

Illustration by Peter Ashmore of proposed painting and lettering scheme for the D5500 series. The cab front coat of arms, and bodyside italic lettering was not used.

Above: Cab front design for the D5500 series was dictated by the need to include a connecting gangway for operating staff.

Left: Brush Traction marketing brochure for the D5500 series, produced at a time when British engineering had customers across the Commonwealth.

125

D5000 (class 24)

Drafted by the British Railways engineering team at Derby, the D5000 series locomotive preceded any intervention by design consultants. Its cab fronts were an attempt to produce a vehicle with good forward vision for the driver. All three cab windows had upper margins following the curving junction of cab front and roof dome. Cab side windows were set lower than cab front windows, and several large and small grilles made an uncoordinated pattern in each bodyside. The result was a functional, but visually unattractive locomotive, the form of which would be used for one further class - D5151 (later class 25). Wilkes & Ashmore were asked to improve the vehicle. Unable to achieve much, stating that they 'were called in too late and received no co-operation', they made some recommendations.[36] Doors were to be flush with the cab sides, rather than recessed, and a band of dark green taken across the fronts above the windows would reduce the apparent bulk of the roof. The consultants also suggested minor changes to the areas around the windows, reducing their backward slope from 30° to 12°. The joint between this rake and the vertical cab front was to be lowered. The curvature of the cab in plan was reduced. To the livery of plain green was added a horizontal grey waistline to make the body appear as one coherent unit. After the first unit this was moved to skirt level at the request of the Design Panel. The D5000 type locomotives began service in August 1958.

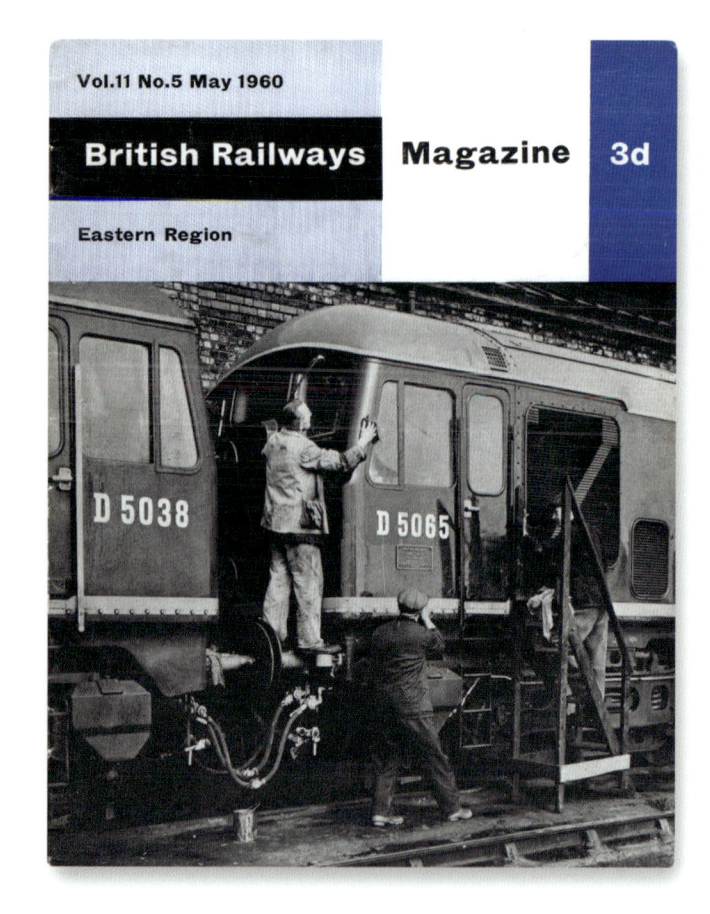

British Railways celebrates its D5000 series locomotive, 1960.

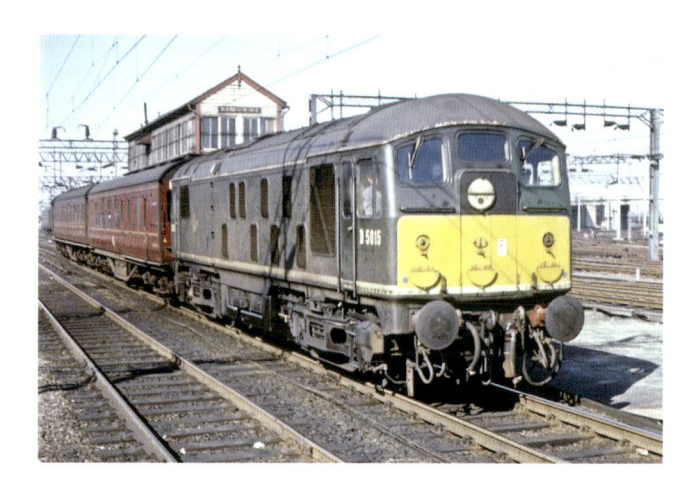

D5000 (class 24) locomotive D5015 at Bletchley, March 1965. The colour scheme is dark green with a single blue-grey or white stripe at skirt level. A yellow panel has been added to the lower cab front to improve sighting of the locomotive by track workers.

126

D5151 series (class 25)

The first two lots of the D5151 series, going into service from April 1961, continued the D5000 superstructure style, with the exception of a box mounted on the cab dome containing roller blinds to give headcode information.[37] Air horns were contained in cylindrical projections on either side of this unit. A third run of the type, in the series D5233–D5299 (class 25/2), was amended after input by Wilkes & Ashmore. With no need for gangway doors, the fronts could be simplified, and all cab windows aligned along the lower edges. After study of the performance given by W&A's D5300 series (class 26) superstructure, ventilation louvres were repositioned in the roof area of the D5151. W&A created a dark and mid-green livery for the revised body design.

First form of D5151 (class 25/1) superstructure, a development of the D5000 series. The orange panel was another experiment in making the locomotives more visible to prevent accidents involving line-side staff.

Right: Wilkes & Ashmore were invited to amend the D5151 cab front design for the third production batch. All front cab windows were aligned horizontally and vehicles were painted in a colour scheme of two greens recommended by Wilkes & Ashmore. This is D7534 at Nottingham, March 1965.

D5300 (class 26), D6500 (class 33) and D5347 (class 27)

Birmingham Railway Carriage & Wagon Company (BRCW) also built a Type 2 locomotive for British Railways' *Pilot Scheme*, and this manufacturer accommodated some of the design guidance from Wilkes & Ashmore. D5300 was a more elegant essay on the basic requirements of the body superstructure for this type. Cab fronts were rounded, the windows deeper either side of the gangway doors, and the cab side windows aligned with those in the fronts. W&A applied the same livery as their class 30: dark green with a light grey waist band and window surrounds.[38] As we can see in the full-size cab model, the numerals were to be of the Gill Sans letter form. The first of the series went into service from July 1958, a few weeks before British Railways' in-house D5000 locomotives. After the positive results of the D5500 and D5300 series, Wilkes & Ashmore asked that the Design Panel allow them to work on locomotives *with* the engineers, not after the mechanical aspects had been decided. This request was facilitated wherever possible. Brought into service from June 1961, this series by the Birmingham Railway Carriage & Wagon Company used the D5300 (class 26) superstructure, with the addition of headcode display boxes on the cab roof domes, in place of ventilator cowlings. Livery style was continued from the D5300 series.

Development of the D5300 (class 26) body style shown through scale model of July 1956 (above), and full size cab mock-up of October 1956 (left). The colours are not documented.

Above: D6500 series design represented a variation of the D5300.

Above: D6556 (class 33) operating at Salisbury in August 1964.

Top and above: D5347 (class 27) locomotives shared many similarities with the D5300 superstructure. These locomotives are seen in their later livery of British Rail's Rail Blue with yellow cab fronts.

Multiple-unit trains

After some intervention by the British Transport Commission Design Panel and its consultants Wilkes & Ashmore, a small number of diesel and electric multiple-units were produced with more attractive body styling and wrap-around windows, informed by study of European rail vehicles and contemporary trends in motor car design based on north American examples. Technical innovation aided the appearance work: in 1957 British Railways had been working with motor car and white goods body makers Pressed Steel, to make lightweight steel passenger carriages. The Bristol Aeroplane Company was investigating glass reinforced plastic (GRP) for the same purpose: it could be moulded into any form around a steel crash-resistant structure, facilitating the design of more sophisticated unit ends than could be achieved by welding metal plates together. In tandem with Design Research Unit and others, Wilkes & Ashmore also improved the interiors of multiple-units, selecting woods, plastic laminates and textiles for surfaces.

'Trans-Pennine' (class 124) diesel multiple-unit, and AM3 (class 303), AM9 (class 309) and a family of electric multiple-units for the Southern Region all benefitted from the attention of Wilkes & Ashmore. At the request of James Ness, general manager of British Railways' Scottish Region, the AM3 'Blue Trains' built 1959–61 for the Glasgow suburban electrification scheme had full width cab fronts with generously rounded convex forms and wraparound windscreens to give passengers the best view of the landscape. Adopted also for the class 124 (built 1960), this feature is similar to North American automobile styling seen in vehicles styled by Harley Earl at General Motors from about 1954, and first seen in Britain with the Vauxhall Victor *F series* of 1957; it evidences the designers' roots in the motor industry. The three cab windows with slender pillars made visibility exceptional. Curve profiles were emphasised by the panel above the cab windows and two levels of rain gutter strips. Misha Black, and John Diamond of Diamond, Hodgkinson & Partners, styled the passenger interiors for the AM3.

Design drawing for the AM3 (class 303) multiple-unit train by Peter Ashmore, to a design by Don Tustin of Wilkes & Ashmore.

To give passengers a panoramic view of the Scottish landscape, AM3 trains had glass screens behind the driving compartments.

Passenger saloon in an AM3 train. The interiors were styled by Design Research Unit, who chose several different colour schemes, all to be used across the vehicle fleet.

To evaluate the AM3 design a complete train was made in mock-up form.

Exterior of an AM3 train when new. The bright blue livery with black and yellow waist lining followed F H K Henrion's branding for the Glasgow suburban rail system, and made reference to traditional Scottish railway colours.

Class 124 diesel multiple-unit designed by Wilkes & Ashmore for Trans-Pennine services.

AM3 train at Balloch Central in July 1966, with the later addition of a yellow panel to the cab fronts.

A Trans-Pennine train at Marsden, Lancashire, in British Rail Corporate Image livery, 1978.

131

Commissioned in February 1959, Wilkes & Ashmore were briefed to envisage a two-car unit for holiday season tourists to view the Scottish landscape. Its design was modelled on North American two-level road coaches.[39] The end styling has a likeness to the D7000 locomotive, and the raised section windows are directly comparable to the D9000 series locomotive. Had it been built, this was to be painted in light yellow and ochre, or Scottish Region blue.

Perspective drawing of the proposed observation train for the Scottish Highlands, 1959.

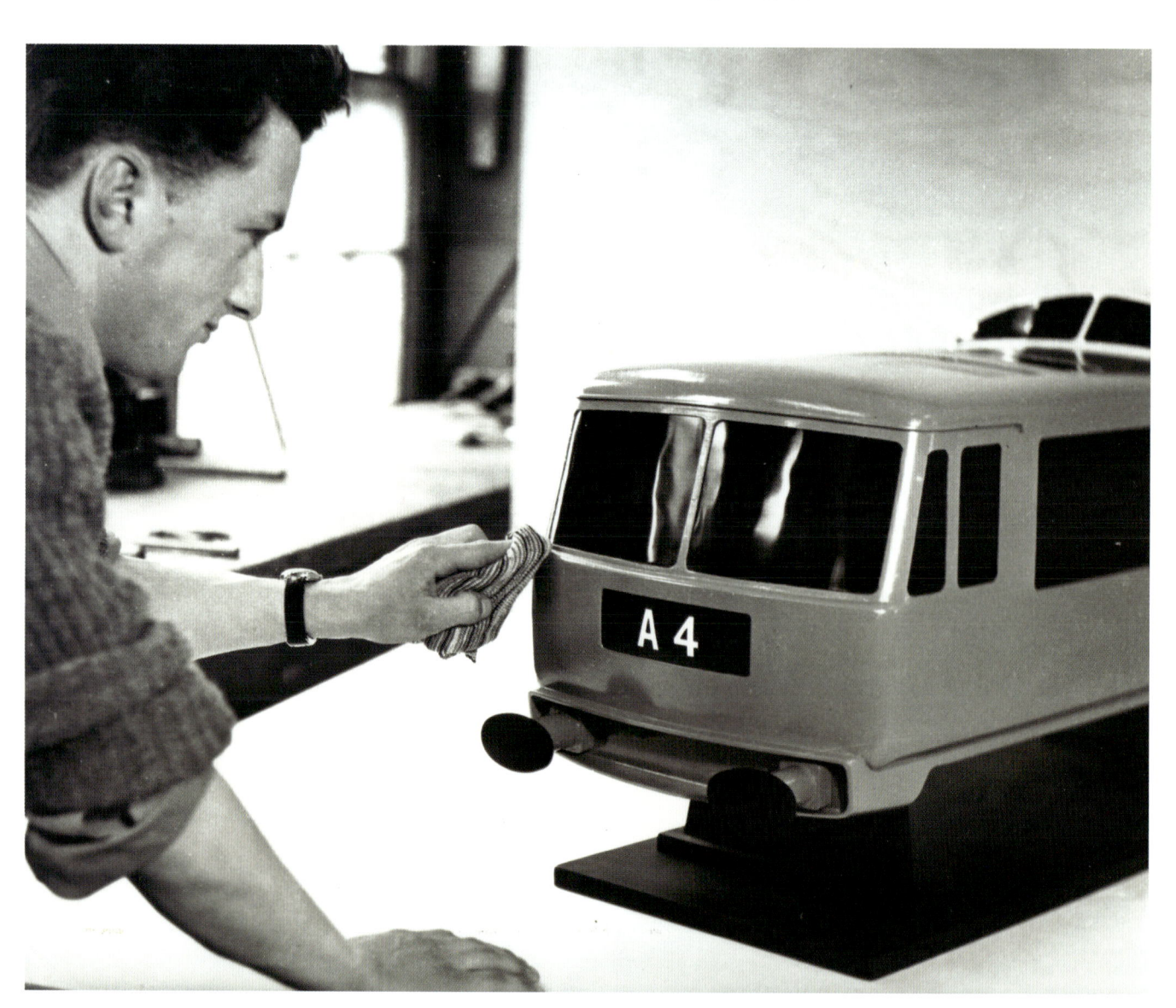

At Wilkes & Ashmore's Horsham, Sussex, studios a technician prepares a display model of the observation train in 1959.

AM5 (class 305)

Wilkes & Ashmore drafted designs in 1957 for the trains which would transport passengers over electrified lines in east and north east London, known as the 'Chenford' routes. Ted Wilkes softened the abrupt angles of the Wolverton style unit fronts by giving them concave forms. The pattern of five marker lights had been used by London Transport on its 1938 tube stock, and by British Railways on early units for the Eastern Region. A monochrome drawing suggests one overall superstructure colour, with contrasting window surrounds like the D5300/D5500/D6500/D7000 locomotives.

After AM3 and AM5 electric multiple-units, Wilkes & Ashmore took on the styling of express trains on the Eastern Region's London and Clacton-on-Sea/Walton on the Naze line, and for the Southern Region's London-Brighton route. Drawings by the consultants define alternative approaches to the matter of improving unit end design. Unlike the AM3 and class 124, York–built AM9 (class 309) units of 1962–63 featured a gangway connection to the convex cab fronts. Their interiors resulted from considerable design work: seats featured built-in ashtrays; passengers had reading lamps; the buffet cars had decorations incorporated into the veneered screens. In later years the wraparound cab windscreens were replaced by two flat sections either side of a corner pillar, an ugly but serviceable solution attributed to a tendency for the curved glasses to come out of their mounts, maintenance costs, and the need to improve vandal-resistance.

Right: Side view of AM9 train cab, showing the wrap-around windows. These trains were painted all-over passenger coach maroon, with gold/yellow and black waist lining.

Drawing by Peter Ashmore of the proposed design for the AM5 multiple-unit, 1957. It was not brought to production.

Front view of AM9 (class 309) multiple-unit designed by Wilkes & Ashmore for express services between London and Essex seaside resorts.

133

Second class passenger saloon in a 4CIG unit.

First class compartments in a 4VEP unit.

Driving cab front of a 4REP multiple-unit train, with improved design by Kenneth Sadler of Wilkes & Ashmore.

The 4CIG and 4BIG units were built at York from 1964 for Southern Region express services. 4VEP stock was built for electrification of the Waterloo-Bournemouth service in 1967. Painted all-over Rail Blue, with polished aluminium double arrow symbols on the cab sides at unit ends. Basic in provision, the interiors followed a colour scheme of blue, grey and white *Formica* and *Warerite* plastic laminates, brightened a little by orange curtains from Edinburgh Weavers fitted in the first class compartments, blue/green upholstery fabric by Marianne Straub, and orange curtains also by Straub, in a pattern called 'Aries' made by Tamesa Fabrics.[40]

134

Diesel electric trains (class 3D/207) for the Oxted, Surrey area lines were some of the last passenger units to be built at Eastleigh. They featured a variation of the AM9 appearance with the additional influence of existing Southern Region stock. In place of the three panels of sheet metal, the fronts were gently curved in the horizontal plane and rounded into the carriage sides and roof. Partial streamlining included recesses for pipe and cable 'jumper' connections, and tidied grab rails. Units operated from 1962. The 4CIG trains produced at York to replace old units on the Brighton line from 1964, had the same improved ends, with added corridor connections.[41]

British Railways' Swindon works built the class 123 as a diesel-engined version of the AM9 (309) sets. Introduced in April 1963, these ten three- or four-car trains were for 'Inter-City' routes: Cardiff Birmingham-Derby, Cardiff-Bristol, and a projected Brighton-Cardiff service. Class 123 had gangway connections in the unit ends between the wrap-round windows. The connections made driving cabs draughty; a panel of yellow was needed as a visual warning for track workers. This gave rise to an ingenious design solution: Wilkes & Ashmore had used moulded glass reinforced plastic for the unit outer ends of the class 124 DMU; they applied the same technology to develop a cover for the gangway, coloured yellow.

Class 123 train at Doncaster, 1979, without the gangway cover.

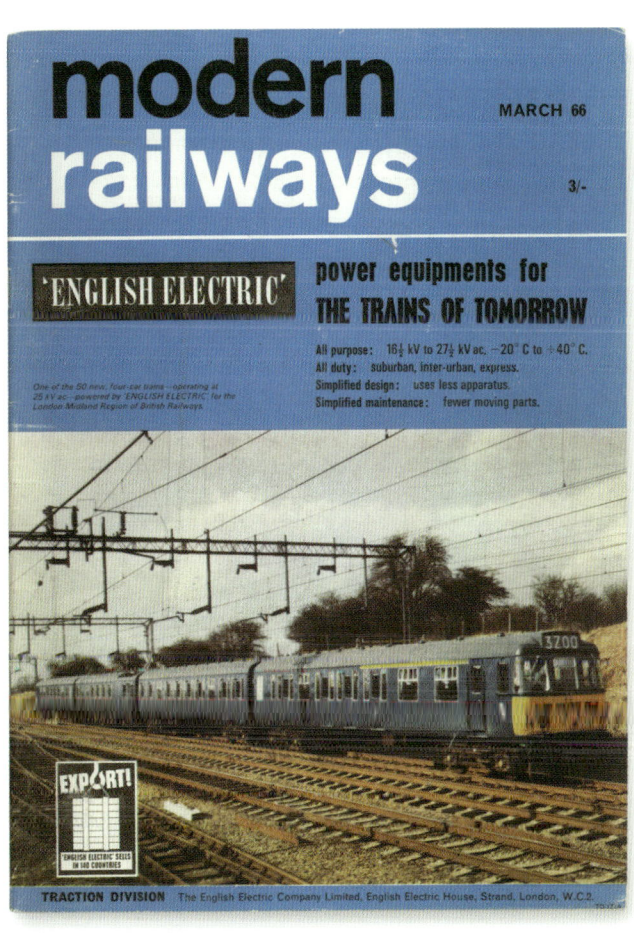

Top and above: AM10 (class 310) electric multiple-units continued the general appearances of the AM3, here re-interpreted by British Rail workshops. Recesses added below the windows for cable and pipe connections on these trains disrupted the clean design of the Wilkes & Ashmore original.

135

D9000 series (class 55)

During the Second World War, the English Electric Group of companies acquired the engine builder D Napier & Son, and with it a diesel power unit developed by Napier's from an original designed for German Junkers aircraft. Known as the 'Deltic' because its triangular cylinder configuration, pairs of these motors also found a use in fast patrol boats for the British Royal Navy.[42] English Electric adapted the power unit for a prototype diesel-electric locomotive, announced in 1955 as the most powerful anywhere in the world. By the late 1950s British Railways Eastern Region, which operated the East Coast Main Line between London and Scotland, knew it needed faster modern trains to remain competitive. British Railways, who were then commissioning various models from different manufacturers under the *Modernisation Plan Pilot Scheme* saw the potential of the prototype.

Promoted by the Eastern Region's Line Traffic Manager G F Fiennes as a means of competing with domestic airline services and a nascent motorway network, twenty two of the type was ordered in 1958. Its appearance immediately came under the scrutiny of Design Panel consultants Wilkes & Ashmore. The prototype was considered overly styled: a ponderous and brash interpretation of North American locomotive design rendered in light blue with ungainly grey stripes. Ted Wilkes and Jack Ward worked with the engineers to reduce the vehicle weight, lengthen the body, and specify a colour scheme which would further reduce the apparent bulk: dark green with a yellow-green panel at skirt level. To hide the particles of dust created when the train braked, brown paint was specified for the underframe area. Motivated by automotive design, most evident in the styling of Vauxhall family saloons such as the 'Victor' and 'Cresta' in England, W&A suggested a three-part cab window, wrapped around at each side. They also proposed a radical redesign of the bonnets, raking them forwards to sharpen the side profile, adding an air intake and clustering the lamps either side of a headboard unit.[43] Bodysides were to be tapered inwards at the tumblehome. A large-scale model was made and discussed at length with the Design Panel, but the modifications were rejected by British Railways and English Electric as too costly and time-consuming to implement.[44] Production examples of the D9000 series began operation on the East Coast Main Line in February 1961; a full service operated from June 1962.

Prototype English Electric-built 'Deltic' locomotive, when being withdrawn from British Railways.

Wilkes & Ashmore proposal for the restyling of the 'Deltic' superstructure.

Wilkes & Ashmore model for their version of the 'Deltic' locomotive.

Production D9000 (class 55) series D9018 *Ballymoss* at Darlington in July 1964.

D9016 *Gordon Highlander* at Gateshead, July 1965. The livery of green and yellow-green developed by Wilkes & Ashmore is evident here.

D9016 *Gordon Highlander* in British Rail Rail Blue. The mass of the locomotive is revealed by this colour scheme.

137

D7000 series (class 35) Hymek

British Railways' Western Region had a particular interest in diesel-hydraulic locomotives, and a tradition of distinctive modern design exemplified by the diesel railcars built for the Great Western Railway. Independently of the *Modernisation Plan Pilot Scheme*, the Region commissioned the D7000 series (later class 35), colloquially referred to as the 'Hymek' because of its mechanical units. Built by Beyer Peacock, and operating in service from May 1961, the superstructure was designed by Don Tustin at Wilkes & Ashmore during 1959. This was the first new British Railways locomotive with two windscreens instead of three. Between the windows a pronounced crease reprised a distinctive feature seen in Great Western railcars and the class 120/126 diesel multiple-units (see page 52). The cab fronts included a prominent recess around the windows, a feature developed from the D5500. Intended to imply a wraparound appearance to the window area, the recess had a practical use in enabling the necessary cab door height to be obtained.[45] Tustin's particular taste influenced the marked raking forward of the side window recesses. It had looked good on the Glasgow suburban (303) and Swindon Inter-City multiple-units; here it was further stressed to increase the locomotive's apparent length and 'give an effect of power and speed'.[46] Considered by Ted Wilkes to have been unsuccessful, however, the feature was not repeated for other vehicles. Cab roofs were made lower than the engine compartment as a further horizontal accent. The buffer beam enclosed in a cowling was a feature continued from D5500, to show it as a distinct and deliberate part of the design. Like the D9000, the D7000 painting scheme was dark green with a yellow-green band at skirt level.

Cab front detail of the D7000 series (class 35) locomotive, designed by Don Tustin at Wilkes & Ashmore.

The influence of contemporary car styling - designer Don Tustin had worked for the Ford Motor Company - is clear in this side view of the D7000 series.

D7000 locomotives shared with the D9000 series the livery of dark green with a yellow-green skirting.

New forms for new power: the Type 4 prototypes

If it was to remain competitive in passenger and freight operations, British Railways had to procure more powerful locomotives than those built to existing specifications. An invitation was extended to locomotive manufacturers for the design of vehicles based on updated, and uprated, requirements. Four prototypes emerged from this process, one going into full production and another forming the test-bed for a future model. To promote a consistent appearance, three projects were supervised by Wilkes & Ashmore: D0280 *Falcon* (completed October 1961), D0260 *Lion* (in service April 1962), and D1500 (in service September 1962). Both D0280 and D0260 had been drawn in outline form by the end of 1960. The English Electric DP2 (operated for tests from May 1962) utilised an adapted English Electric superstructure and is discussed in a subsequent section below.

D0280 *Falcon* (class 53) was built by Brush Traction at Loughborough, and released to British Railways for trials in October 1961. In common with the work by Design Research Unit on the D800 design (see page 150), *Falcon* was the first British Railways' project in which the consultants worked with the engineers from the locomotive's conception.[47] Records confirm that *Falcon* was designed during the same period as D1500 and D0260 *Lion*, with full reporting of the design process being made to the Design Panel on a regular basis.[48] D0280 *Falcon* featured the twin cab windscreens which characterised several Brush products. Unlike other Wilkes & Ashmore designs, the cab fronts were brought cleanly down to the buffers, creating the impression of deeper panels below the windows than either the D7000, D1500 or D0260 *Lion* locomotives. The windows appeared somewhat high in the fronts, because the floor of the driving compartments was itself set high. This caused the side windows to be recessed so they did not cut into the roof edges, a condition only partly relieved by the continuous slope of the body sides. Structural techniques used for aircraft construction were borrowed to make the vehicle superstructure lighter. Ventilation grilles and engine room windows were arranged symmetrically in the body sides, the higher level apertures placed in a single strip above four larger openings. To enhance the visual appearance all window frames were flush with the body skin.

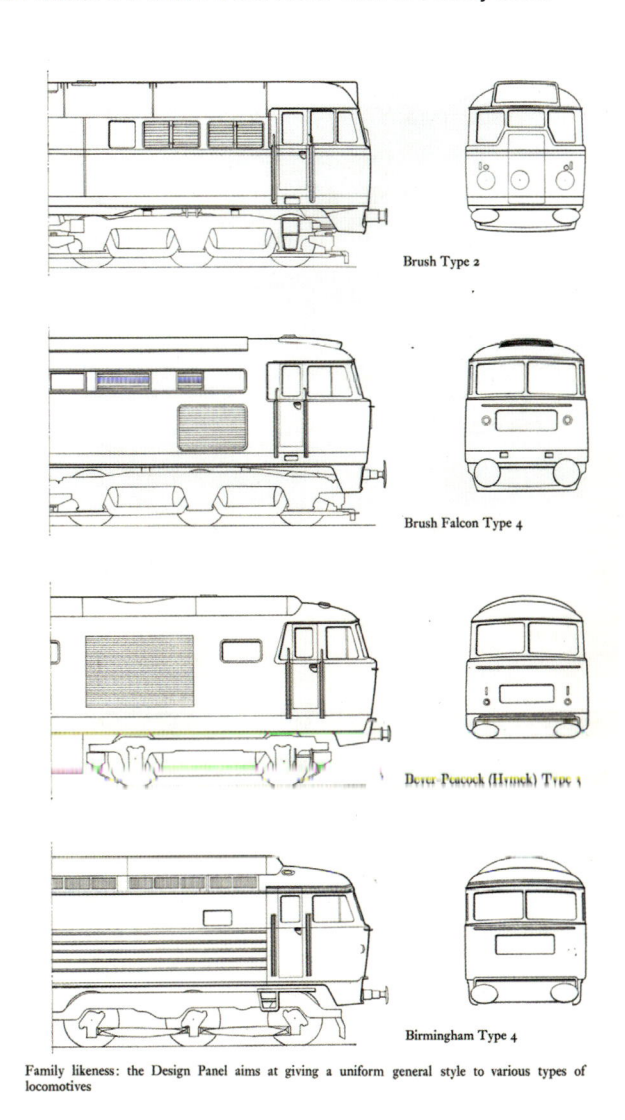

Family likeness: the Design Panel aims at giving a uniform general style to various types of locomotives

Drawing by Wilkes & Ashmore comparing the cab front designs of D5500, D0280, D7000, and D0260 superstructures, 1962.

Formulated by Wilkes & Ashmore in the same spirit of speculation as the locomotive, *Falcon* appeared in light olive green with darker bronze green around the body side windows, louvres and lower body edge. To complement the greens, the buffer beam was orange rather than the usual red.[49] After inspecting *Falcon* in these colours, W&A asked that cab window surrounds be painted in the darker bronze green. Around the time *Falcon* first operated on the British Railways network, the bronze green was replaced by light brown.[50] The *Falcon* name was first applied as a light blue transfer depicting the eponymous bird, which represented the name of Brush's Loughborough works. In March 1962, against the consultants' wishes, cast aluminium nameplates and letters were made to replace the transfers. *Falcon* was subsequently hired by British Rail, and in January 1965 repainted in an adapted Wilkes & Ashmore livery of dark and light green, with an additional light green panel around the body side windows and grilles. From February 1971 *Falcon* wore the standard Rail Blue paint, with cab ends painted entirely in yellow.[51]

Brush Traction intended to sell the *Falcon* locomotive in international markets.

D0280 *Falcon* in the Brush Traction workshops when new.

D0280 *Falcon* in service at Kings Cross, London, September 1962.

D0260 *Lion*, originally to be called *Trigon* or *Trident*,[52] was built by the Birmingham Railway Carriage and Wagon Company (BRCW) as an attempt to secure new orders and so help to save their manufacturing operation. Wilkes & Ashmore had worked successfully with BRCW on the D5300 series; with *Lion* their relationship was severely strained because the builders would not cooperate with design recommendations. Work on *Lion* started in 1959, but because of delays the locomotive was still being developed at the end of 1961, for completion in

A manufacturer's image of D0280 published in 1962 showing the original livery of light and mid-green.

early 1962. The manufacturers were asked to follow the British Railways specification of placing two windscreens in cab fronts of two flat planes set at an obtuse angle to each other. In the near vertical body sides the consultants incorporated horizontal flutes for additional strength, as an alternative to giving rigidity by curving them. BRCW ignored guidance on the roof design, producing a form with a bulging dome over the engine room. There were changes to detail too: instead of being a horizontal feature, the front grab-rail was turned down at each side of the cab front, upsetting the longitudinal profile. BRCW painted the locomotive body and all underframe parts a very impractical white. Gold strips highlighted the body side flutes, suggesting that the builders had borrowed from contemporary north American motor car design. Unattractive cast name plates were fitted on the body sides.

Wilkes & Ashmore had wanted to use *Lion* to test a potential standard British Railways colour scheme. Surviving text descriptions and artist's impressions indicate a livery of two different greys, the darker shade aligned with the height of the yellow patch then being introduced as a warning to trackside workers of an approaching locomotive.[53] Grey imparted solidity with speed, brightness with resilience. Choosing grey was anti-tradition, matching British Railways vehicles with the colours of contemporary machinery and aircraft. The consultants considered

Lion to be their best design, commenting that if their recommendations for colour had been followed, then:

'...everything [would fall] correctly into place. The cab is one with the body; the ribs become a structural feature and not applied decoration; the raised roof hatches become a separate feature from the main roof instead of an ugly blister; the cowling around the buffer beam makes sense; the bogies and undergear become less disturbing; and the whole locomotive looks longer, lower and more mobile... it is small wonder that the [press] article criticising the "Lion" failed to see any unifying features. They have all been obliterated by the manufacturers.'[54]

Lion ran in regular British Railways service for several months. Following technical faults it was withdrawn towards the end of 1963.[55]

Wilkes & Ashmore artwork for D0260 *Lion*, here with the fictional number D8500. This shows the positive effect of painting the locomotive in two shades of grey as the designers intended, rather than all-over white

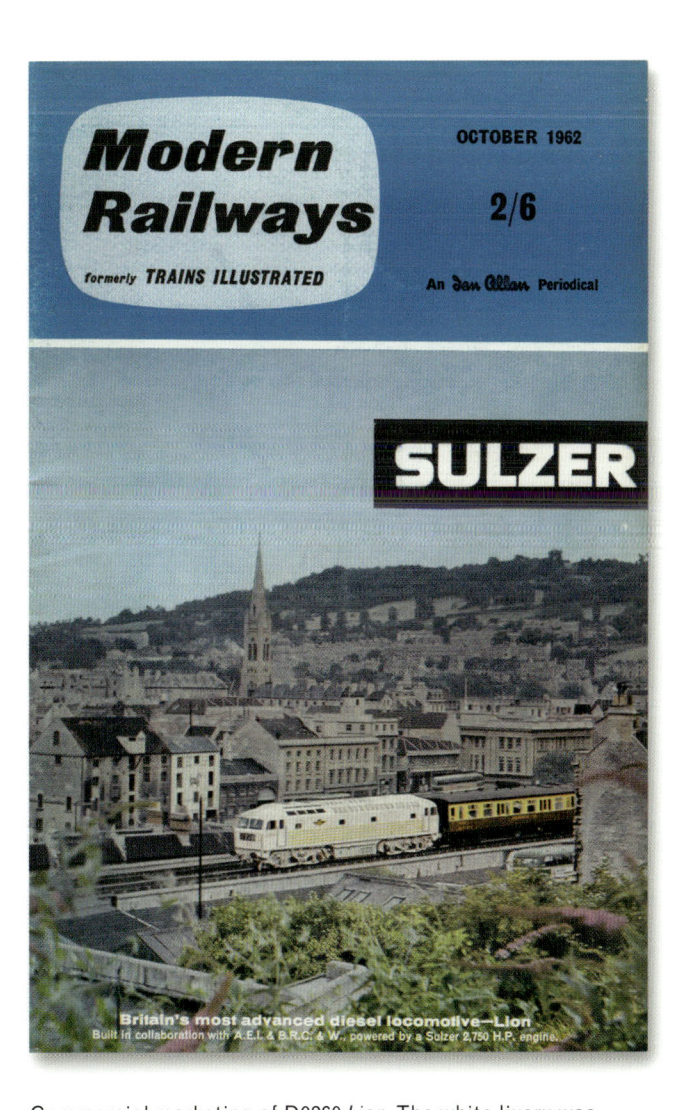

Commercial marketing of D0260 *Lion*. The white livery was unique in British Railways, and somewhat impractical.

141

D1500 series (class 47)

Brush Traction developed a second Wilkes & Ashmore design alongside, and shortly after, D0280 *Falcon*. This was the first unit of what became the D1500 series. Industrial designer Peter Cambridge worked with Ted Wilkes to shape the vertical bodysides of the monocoque superstructure, tapering them inwards at each end.[56] The body was smaller than that of *Falcon*, and cleaner in appearance as all grilles were let into the roof, leaving just two windows and a door on each side. Cab fronts formed from aluminium alloy complied with the pattern of two raked planes meeting at a narrow ledge with a gently curved profile. To create a small vertical return, or step, between cab door and body side, the side windows were raked inwards towards the roof. Fibreglass cab and engine room roof sections further reduced the weight of the locomotive. Domed cab roofs curved upwards to align with the engine room roof, with a central cowling similar to that used for D5300, D6500, and D0280. D1500 brought the first opportunity for Wilkes & Ashmore to integrate the yellow warning panel with the livery and provide visual interest for the otherwise plain bulk of the locomotive.[57] Two colour schemes were drafted, the second of mid-green sandwiched between dark green being selected. The mid-green band lined up with the yellow warning panels on cab fronts. This was a good compromise, because it allowed locomotive painters to use up stocks of standard British Railways locomotive green and simultaneously adopt a new livery.

Ergonomics were beginning to be understood as an important factor in driver comfort, and therefore safety. Wilkes & Ashmore commissioned a full-size mock-up of the D1500 control desk to gather operator's comments and advice. Locomotives of this series commenced operation in September 1962; in time 512 examples would work across the British railway system.

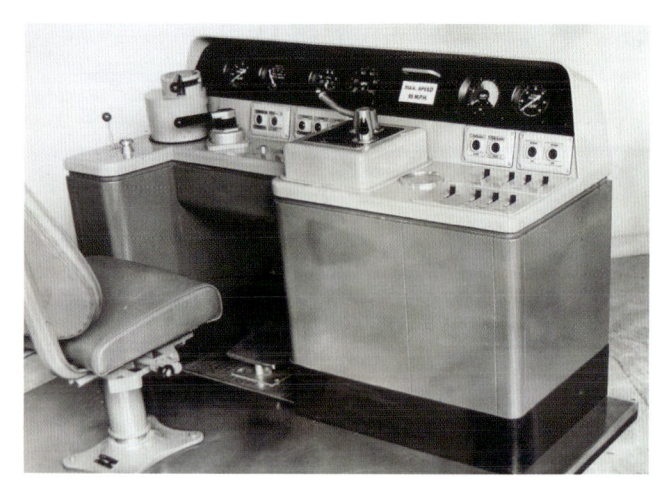

Mock-up of the driver's control desk for the D1500 series locomotive.

D1500 (class 47) locomotive D1826 at Westhouses, Derbyshire, March 1965.

Cab profile of the D1500 type. Kirkby in Ashfield, Nottinghamshire, March 1965.

BRUSH

2750 h.p.

Co-Co DIESEL ELECTRIC LOCOMOTIVES

Above: Sales brochure for the D1500 type. Illustration by Michael Davighi.

Opposite: The success of the D1500 body style and livery resulted in it being licensed, with minor variations in body detail, for operation in other countries. The Clayton Equipment Company took an order from Cuban National Railways for ten locomotives in 1963.[58] They went into service from summer 1965. The version illustrated was operated by Rhodesian Railways.[59]

New livery styles

By March 1962 Wilkes & Ashmore were sufficiently pleased with the *Falcon* and D1500 painting schemes, to produce a paper communicating their thoughts on colours suitable for modern locomotives on a modern railway. Commenting that 'slightly drab colours look more at home in this country', the consultants discussed the criteria for an effective locomotive colour scheme, with the relevant practical and aesthetic aspects.[60] Dark colours worked better in the polluted environment of the railway. Colours must complement the passenger vehicles, which were then mostly green, maroon or chocolate brown and cream. Livery schemes needed to convey to the public what we would now call brand values. Evaluating the options, Wilkes & Ashmore said that some hues could be rejected immediately: most blues; middle to dark greens (too similar to historical examples); bright red or yellow, silver, and other light or pastel colours (too bright, too exuberant, and hard to keep clean); middle to dark brown (incompatible with maroon coaches). The remaining palette comprised dull yellow, sand yellow, plain grey, green-grey, blue-grey, and light to mid-brown, a range known by some designers as 'Thames mud'. Outstanding in the list, and important because it has fascinated historians and railway modellers, is the inclusion of 'Stroudley Yellow' or 'Improved Engine Green', a colour introduced to the London, Brighton and South Coast Railway by its Locomotive Superintendent William Stroudley after 1870.[61] Stroudley Yellow joined the colour range because it was proposed by British Transport Commission Design Panel adviser, artist and railway writer Brian Haresnape. He particularly favoured 'Golden Ochre' - a modern copy of 'Improved Engine Green' - and suggested it to the Design Panel: it was adopted for tests in late 1962.[62] With *Falcon* the designers had tried two shades of grey-green with some success: definitely modern yet in keeping with the railway environment. Taking the most direct route through the remaining colour possibilities, W&A concluded their report with the recommendation that the future standard locomotive livery comprise two shades of grey having a very slight green cast: contemporary, durable, and complementary to most other rolling stock colours.[63]

In January 1963 the consultants reflected on progress in their approach to locomotive design - particularly the cab front formed by two angled planes with a horizontal ledge - as improving through the successive designs for D5500, D7000, D0260 *Lion*, and D0280 *Falcon*. D1500 was felt to be a compromised project, because 'engineering and dimensional requirements proved unusually awkward.'[64] To explain this last statement, in the D1500 there was sufficient body height to accommodate the driving cab spaces without the substantial recess to the window area needed for the D7000 series and D0260 *Lion*. The consequence of being able to set the windows lower for D1500 was a shorter, deeper cab roof, which then appeared too bulky for the body. Such factors as these are the critical everyday business of the locomotive designer.

Above: D6700 (class 37) series locomotives in operation, another example of the refusal by manufacturer English Electric to abandon North American styling.

D6700 (class 37)

After experience of transforming the 'Deltic' prototype into a fleet of locomotives, the Design Panel tried again to address the reluctance of builder English Electric to abandon its preference for the North American 'nose' styling of locomotives. In original form the bonnet fronts reduced opportunities for any streamlining, and the cab doors cut into the roof line because of the relationship between straight sides and roof. Wilkes & Ashmore was invited in February 1963 to comment on how it could apply the flat cab front to the D6700 superstructure, prior to the last batches of the vehicle being ordered in January and February 1964. Ted Wilkes suggested setting aside the bonnet type body altogether, offering instead a semi-streamlined adaptation of the D7000, D0280 and D1500 superstructures, with an added horizontal crease in the bodysides.[65] Had the design advice been heeded, later examples of the locomotive would have looked very different, but English Electric did not accept the proposals.

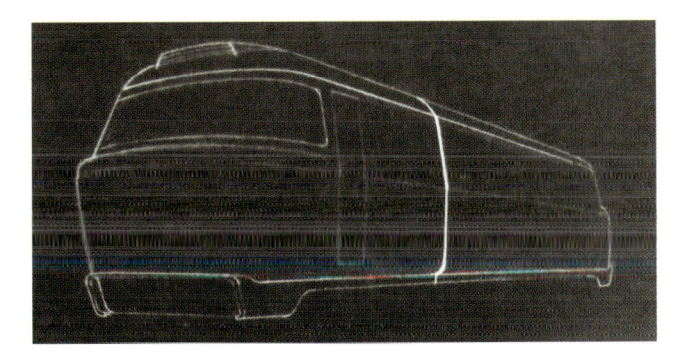

Sketch drawing by Wilkes & Ashmore proposing a semi-streamlined superstructure for the D6700 series.

Production appearance of the D400 (class 50) type.

D400 (class 50)

When English Electric needed a vehicle to develop new technology for British Railways in the early 1960s in competition with Brush Traction, they once again selected a body with bonnets, not dissimilar to that used for the 'Deltic'. An obvious marketing ploy was to reference this engineering success, so the trial locomotive was named D(eltic) P(rototype) 2. British Rail ordered this design for a new fleet which would become the class 50 (D400) series, put into English Electric's own version of the flat front superstructure developed by Wilkes & Ashmore. Asked to advise on *DP2* in January–March 1966, Wilkes & Ashmore identified several areas for improvement, most based on the odd combination of a vertical crease between the windscreens and a horizontal crease between the upper and lower cab fronts. Taken together, these features gave an awkwardly drooping appearance which looked neither powerful nor fast. The thick pillar between the cab windows was disruptive - it should be made as thin as possible. Most obviously out of place was the ungainly headcode box carried on the cab roof dome, because of both its bulk and the awkward junction it made with the angled cab windows. W&A noted that the body would look better if the deep chamfer along the skirting was replaced by a tumblehome on all four sides. The historical resistance shown by English Electric to any outside guidance, as we saw with handling of advice given on the D6700 body, would problematise the class 50 too; barring adjustments to the positioning of doors and windows, the manufacturers did not accept the suggested amendments to their plans.[66]

The D400 cab front (left) was a less successful version of the D1500 (right).

145

Semi-streamlining for higher speeds: Kestrel

One last locomotive project came to the Wilkes & Ashmore office before the practice ceased its consultancy work. This was the *Kestrel*, sponsored by manufacturers Hawker Siddeley, who owned Brush Traction. In light of 'Deltic' performance, and at the same time as the Type 4 prototype trials discussed above, British Railways decided to procure locomotives with higher power (3500–5000hp) capability. The Design Panel's George Williams asked W&A to consider the form of such a locomotive in October 1962. With the prospect of increased speeds, semi-streamlining would be a necessary shift from the consultants' own flat-front designs. First conceived as a single-ended, single driving position, powered vehicle hauling a set of coaches, this was in effect a precursor of the *Advanced Passenger* and *High Speed Trains*. Given this potential step towards superstructure forms new to Britain, Williams approached another automotive industry expert in high-performance vehicles: designer of the *E-type* Jaguar car, Malcolm Sayer. In a wind tunnel at Loughborough College of Technology, Sayer tested a form adapted from the dimensions of the D1500 locomotive. He then amended the shape to achieve maximum airflow efficiency.

Williams asked W&A to comment on the semi-streamlining in December 1963. The consultants felt the proposal heavy and not visually effective; Sayer's modifications had reduced the attractiveness of the form, without giving substantial advantage. Suggesting its own adjustments to the Sayers outline, W&A drew the front plane forward below the windscreens to produce a more pronounced horizontal ridge. This also made the cab roof appear flatter, and therefore faster. The horizontal window margins were made parallel. Beyond the semi-streamlined cab ends, which were comparable to the German Federal Railways' *E03* electric locomotive developed from 1961, the body shared a common appearance with other Wilkes & Ashmore projects. In side profile we can see how the two raked planes of previous W&A cab fronts have been adjusted, the connecting ledge removed and both planes curved away from the horizontal centreline to give the impression of more solidity and speed. The consultants suggested that this should be the standard form of cab for future British Railways locomotives, adjusted in scale according to the application.

Preliminary sketch by Wilkes & Ashmore for a semi-streamlined multiple-unit, 1964.

Model of the cab front of the multiple-unit, after wind tunnel testing.

D1500 and semi-streamlined unit models compared, 1964.

146

Colour scheme for the *Kestrel* locomotive which was developed from the original multiple-unit concept.

Full size mock-up of the *Kestrel* cab in the Brush Traction works at Loughborough, November 1967.

Designer Anthony Hill working on a locomotive superstructure design, with model of *Kestrel* control panel in foreground.

Left above and below, right above: Model *Kestrel* control panel and handbrake wheel, used for evaluation by operating staff.

A final W&A model of July 1964 presented the engine in a livery of blue, with yellow warning panel; Ted Wilkes described the project to the Institute of Locomotive Engineers in August 1964.[67, 68] Brush Traction was aware of possible new business building high-speed trains. British Railways was not interested in developing the idea, so the consultants applied their research to the Brush opportunity, producing drawings and supervising building of a full-size mock-up to show how the front body section of *Kestrel* might look.[69] Brush Traction took the *Kestrel* design in-house in July 1965, giving it to their Industrial Design Manager and former automotive designer Anthony Hill.[70] Hill knew Wilkes & Ashmore's David Higgins, Perry King and Kenneth Sadler from his time as a student at the Royal College of Art in London. He had previously styled vehicles for the Ford Motor Company; he brought his ergonomic and aesthetic knowledge of car dashboards to the design of the control console for *Kestrel*. Hill worked within the available, cramped spaces to improve the driving position by moving from the engineer's array of flat panels, as was the practice in the power generation and manufacturing industries, to an inclined layout which reflected the need for the driver to sit for long periods giving full attention to controls and indicators.

It is evident that the colours of the *Kestrel* superstructure were determined by Wilkes & Ashmore. They had devised a colour scheme of yellow, beige and brown for a version of the D1500 locomotive which Brush Traction built for the colonial Rhodesian Railways (now the National Railways of Zimbabwe) in 1962. Matched to the horizontal positioning of Rail Blue and Pearl Grey which British Rail had adopted for its passenger coach livery in 1964, and the intended appearance of the D1500 and D0260 *Lion* locomotives, *Kestrel* was painted in bands of yellow and brown. Unusual as it may seem in the context of green or blue trains, this was an entirely logical idea. Observing that the semi-streamlined *Kestrel* did not have conventional cab fronts framed by angled junctions with the body sides, it was natural to extend the clean, easily visible yellow visual warning panel around the entire locomotive as a deliberate design feature. The lower area of brown complemented the yellow section, and worked well with the the blue of the coaches, whilst also hiding the inevitable accumulation of brake dust. A thin white waistline separated the two body colours to give each a defined edge.[71]

There were difficulties for *Kestrel* in service. British Rail did not have track of appropriate type to support high speed locomotives of its weight, operating at sustained high speeds. If British Rail were to order a series of these machines, it would need to reconsider the approved sponsoring of its *APT* project, and the policy of electrification schemes. Ultimately, the decision was made to progress with diesel-electric multiple-unit development, resulting in the *High Speed Train*. In 1971 *Kestrel* was sold to the Soviet Union, coinciding with its being shown at the USSR International Exhibition of Railway Rolling Stock in Moscow, 1–20 July 1971.[72]

HS4000 *Kestrel* operating at Cricklewood, London, in July 1969. Continuing the standard yellow warning panel around the entire superstructure mitigated the usual visual interruption caused by a panel which is conventionally confined to the vehicle ends.

Design Research Unit

This second consultancy advising the Design Panel would become so closely linked with innovation for Britain's railways, that it has eclipsed recognition of Wilkes & Ashmore's accomplishments. Their work on locomotive design is discussed below; their project for a far-reaching corporate identity programme to transform British Railways into British Rail is detailed in Chapter Five. Milner Gray, Misha (later Sir Misha) Black[73] and Marcus Brumwell founded Design Research Unit (DRU) and worked to bring together art and design in what was then a novel form of multi-disciplinary design agency, able to handle any scale or type of design challenge in two or three dimensions. DRU were involved in the seminal 'Britain Can Make It' exhibition at London's Victoria and Albert Museum in 1946, and produced exhibitions, interiors and signage for the 1951 *Festival of Britain*. Design Research Unit led on interior design projects for buildings and ships, created the City of Westminster street name signs which have become a London icon, made brand marks for breweries, cigarette companies and made a substantial contribution to the appearance of modern commerce during in the second half of the twentieth century.

The BTC Design Panel's George Williams knew Milner Gray. In 1956, while president of the Society of Industrial Artists, the Unit's Misha Black was appointed by the British Transport Commission as a consultant for diesel and electric locomotives. Black asked J P 'Joe' McCrum to design the superstructures for the D6100 (class 21)/D6300 (class 22), and D600 (class 41) locomotives. John Beresford-Evans, who joined DRU in 1958, worked with Black and is associated with the main design work for the superstructures of the D800 (class 42), D1000 (class 52), E5000 (class HA/class 71, built 1959) and E3001 (1959) types. With this last locomotive Beresford-Evans established a standard appearance for five versions (AL1–AL5, classes 81–85) of the same specification locomotive built to operate the first section of the electrified West Coast Main Line.

D600 (class 41) 'Warship'

Made by the North British Locomotive Company, the small batch of D600 series locomotives - D600–D604 - did not form part of the *Modernisation Plan Pilot Scheme*, but was an attempt by the British Transport Commission to pursue locomotive development independently of the Western Region's strategy. Introduced in January 1958, D600 was also the first locomotive to have a superstructure attributed to Design Research Unit. We know this to be incorrect: D600 was designed by Joe McCrum, a northern Irish furniture designer working from his home in Glasgow.

In contrast to Wilkes & Ashmore, who aimed to give horizontal emphasis to their vehicles by promoting rectangular cab fronts, the superstructure of the D600 series and locomotives styled by Design Research Unit used the locomotive's cross-section to produce cab fronts which followed the roof contour. McCrum crafted a contracted, more angular form of the 'nose'-type cab front, imparting to D600 a definitively 'western' character. The bonnet form gave sufficient clearance over the gangway doors to allow an arrangement of just two windscreens, which in turn made possible the inclusion of the vertical crease which was a feature of several Great Western Railway/British Railways Western Region vehicles. McCrum employed sharp edges at changes of panel direction, and a shallow fold along the body sides for rigidity.

Drawing by J P McCrum, circa 1959, of the front end for the D600 locomotive body. The short nose is a compromise between North American and European styles.

149

D6100 (class 21) and D6300 (class 22)

Part of the official *Pilot Scheme* locomotive trials, the D6100 diesel-electric locomotive by Joe McCrum represented a further revision of the bonnet form of superstructure, with the element reduced - at the request of the Design Panel - to a near-flat panel with single vertical crease. This amendment was consistent for this smaller scale relative to the D600 superstructure. At the same time, an externally similar locomotive employing hydraulic transmission was assembled in a small batch of six for comparison (D6300–D6305), these becoming class 22. D6100 operated in service from December 1958, D6300 from January 1959. Twenty D6100 series locomotives were later rebuilt as class 29.

D6100 series (class 21) locomotive D6123 in July 1966 after rebuilding, and redesignation into class 29. The engine is decorated with a version of the dark and light green livery.

Locomotive D6123, at Perth, Scotland, showing the window arrangement preferred by Joe McCrum and Design Research Unit.

D800/D833 (class 42/class 43) 'Warship'

K W C Grand, the Western Region's Chief Regional Officer in 1958, and also formerly Assistant General Manager of the Great Western Railway, had considerable influence over the Western Region maintaining independence from the British Transport Commission in publicity, design and rolling stock. He was quoted as remarking in 1953, when the break-up of the nationalised transport system was being debated in Parliament: 'standardisation is now a fetish in British Railways. I believe it may mean standardisation of brains. When you get this, it is the end of progress.'[74] Sir John Elliot, Chairman of the Railway Executive 1951–53, said in Grand's obituary that 'for Keith, state ownership was anathema... he never made any secret of his loathing of the tight control by the British Transport Commission and its agent, the Railway Executive; or of his determination to do all he could behind the scenes to destroy it.'[75] This attitude would see the Western Region choose to work beyond the specifications of the *Modernisation Plan Pilot Scheme*. While the Commission had the D600 type made, the Western Region made its own choice of a new locomotive. This was the D800 series in use from 1958, and the visually similar D833 operational from 1960. D800/D833 were to have looked similar to the D1000 (class 52) 'Western' type, but the building programme gave insufficient time to refine the form. Instead, the Western Region asked DRU to re-proportion the superstructure of the German Federal Railways' *V200* locomotive of 1954. Why copy the *V200*? It was a proven, relatively new machine, and choosing it was a deliberate strategy by the Western Region to underwrite their faith in diesel-hydraulic power units. The designers made few revisions to the shape, except to reduce the overall scale and re-proportion the fronts, increasing the area of cab windows and reducing the bulk of the curved nose. The Western Region's signature vertical crease was introduced between the two cab windows. Body sides were finished flat.

Left: Design Research Unit's D800 (class 42) 'Warship' locomotive D826 *Jupiter* at Waterloo, September 1964. The livery scheme is based on the pre-1962 British Railways/Wilkes & Ashmore painting specification for such vehicles: all-over dark green with a horizontal stripe of pale grey-blue or white.

E5000 type HA (class 71) and E6000 type JA (class 73)

A brief regional diversion is necessary here to note the form of superstructure created when John Beresford-Evans assumed the task of drafting locomotive superstructures at Design Research Unit. For the Southern Region's E5000 series of 1958 he developed the idiom of accenting the vehicle cross-section, making it unmistakable by dispensing with any substantial forward projecting detail: the cab front became a plain slab raked back from the buffer beam, and radiused into the roof and body. Curved sides added to the overall effect of mass. Type JA was the Southern Region's own version of the HA machine. It was announced as Britain's first electro-diesel, a hybrid which could operate over electrified or non-electrified lines. The clean, flat-sided superstructure received a cab profile like that of the D1500 locomotive, and a squared-off version of the cab window styling seen on the E5000 type. Bodysides were of steel sheet lined with aluminium; cab roofs, doors and drivers' desks were of glass-reinforced polyester. It operated from 1962.

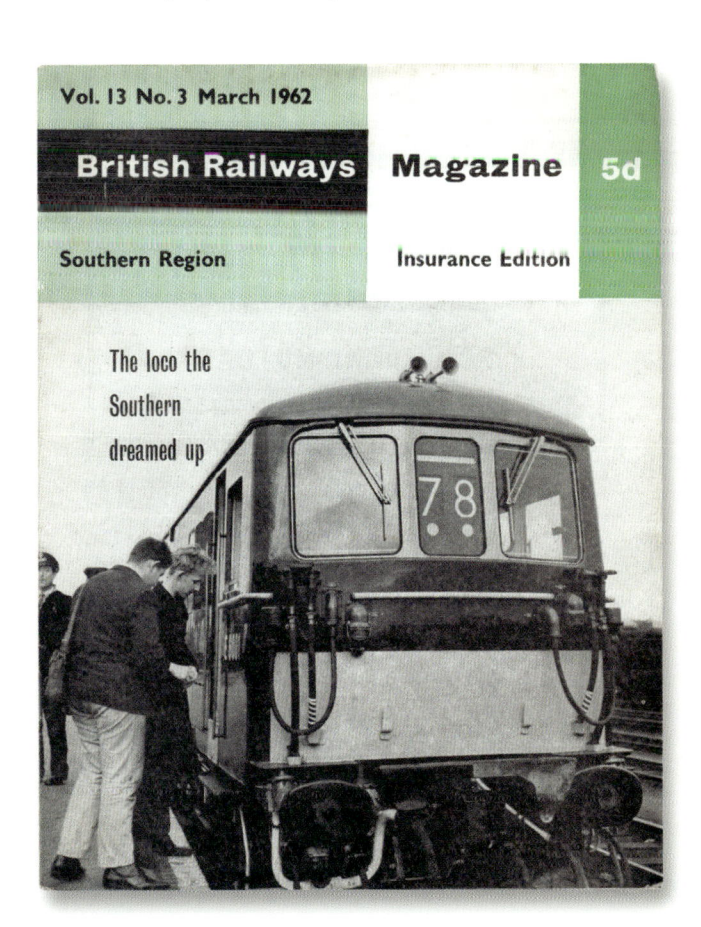

E5000 (class 71) locomotive E5022 exhibited at Battersea, London, in 1960.

Illustration of an E5000 series locomotive used to advertise the British Railways' Southern Region 'Golden Arrow' train.

Above: The 'Golden Arrow' service was a boat train, linking London with ferry services to continental Europe.

Left: E6000/JA type (class 73) locomotive when new.

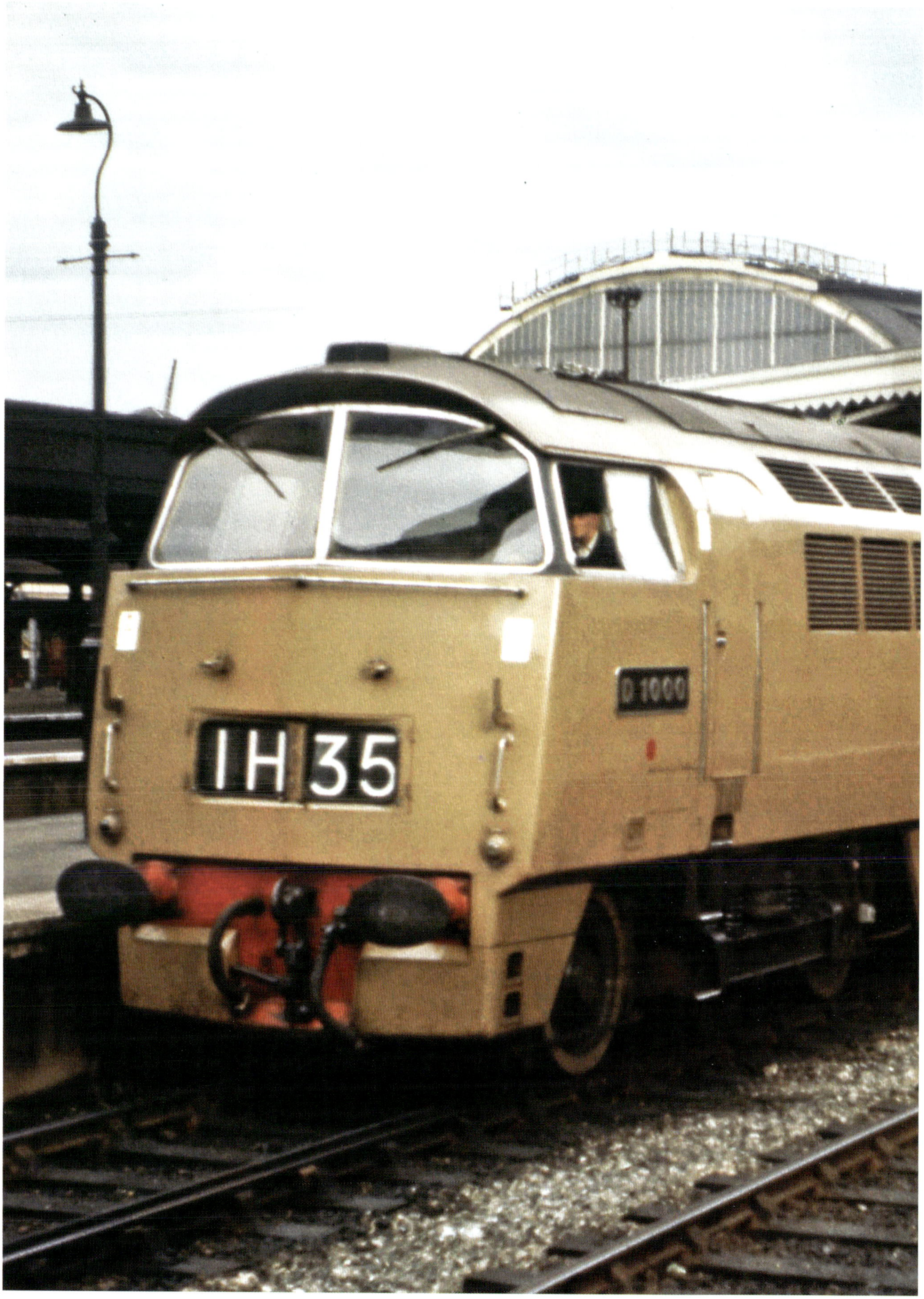
IH35
D 1000

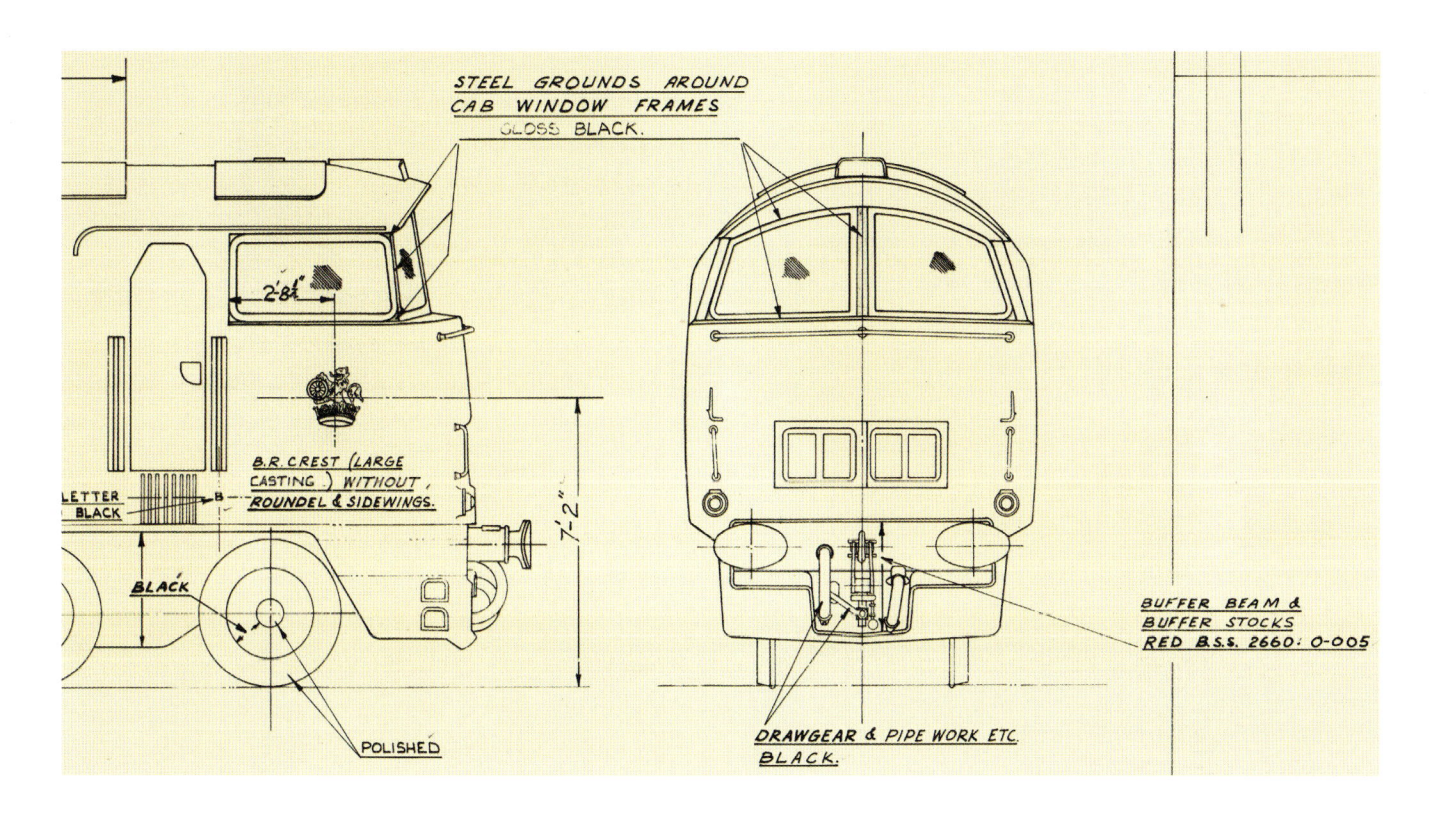

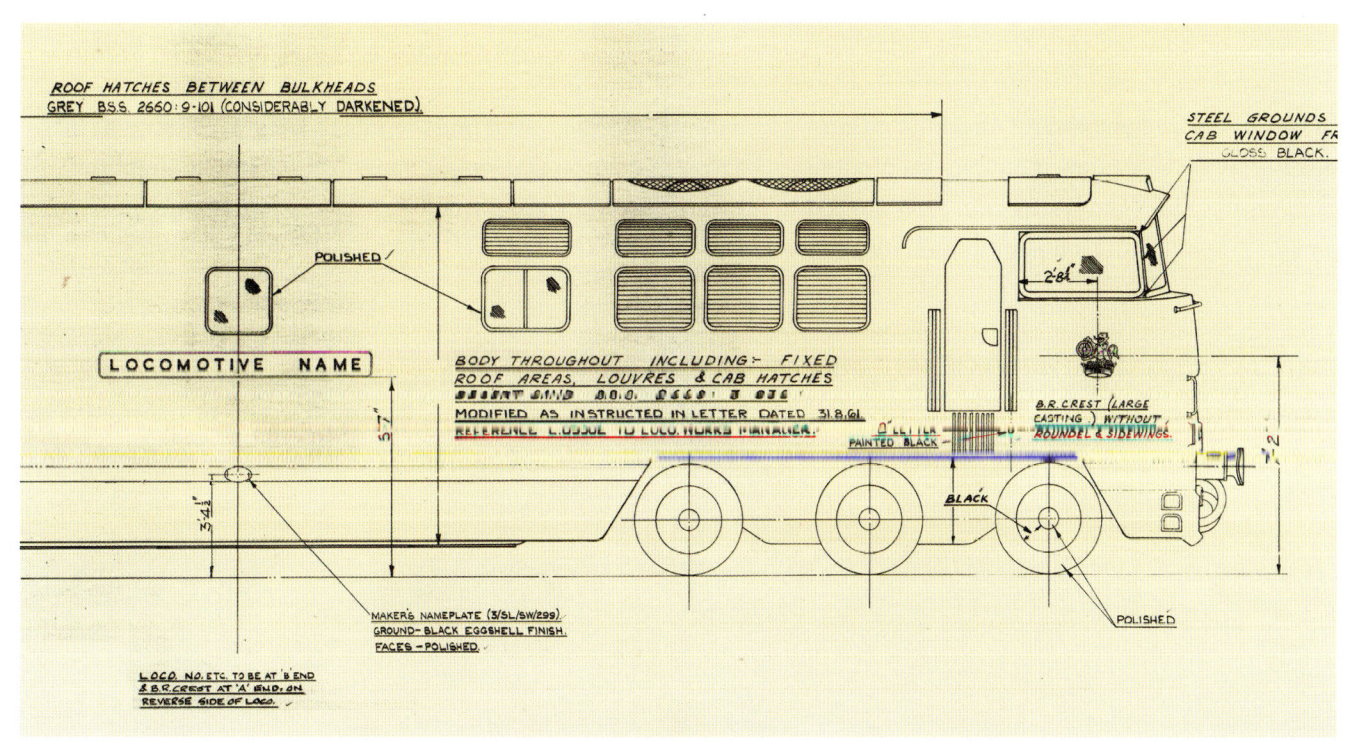

Above and top: British Railways' painting scheme drawing for D1000 *Western Enterprise*.

Left: D1000 series locomotive D1000 *Western Enterprise* at Paddington, London, in September 1962. The livery of pale beige (Desert Sand) was applied as an experiment in updating Great Western Railway colour schemes.

D1000 (later class 52)

The largest diesel-hydraulic locomotive made for the Western Region has become a classic of industrial design. Christian Barman, BTC Chief Publicity Officer, had worked for the Great Western Railway after the Second World War. He was a colleague of senior Great Western and Western Region official K W C Grand. Barman is noted as suggesting to Grand in 1958 'that the 2700hp locomotive [the D1000 series] should be designed with a distinctive styling which would be recognised as typically W R [Western Region].'[76] Consequently the design of the D1000 was a combination of innovation in engineering, form and colour. It continued the pitched front of the E5000 type, augmenting it considerably by taking the windscreens up below the peaked projection of the roof. Below the windscreens a subtle vertical ridge maintained Western Region tradition. Borrowing from German railway practice, the cab side windows were slanted into the roof as continuations of the windscreens. Milner Gray, Misha Black's partner at DRU, designed cast metal crests for the locomotive. The Western Region also wanted to find a new regional livery, choosing the D1000 series to test colours. D1000 carried a matt paint finish when put into service on 20 December 1961, in a shade referred to as 'Desert Sand'. Yellow-grey hues were known to Misha Black through his overseas research travels, a point which has led to the choice of livery for D1000 being attributed to Black. It is now evident however, that the true colour of D1000 was 'Cobweb', a warm light beige.[77] It was hoped that a complete train would eventually be produced in 'Cobweb' and off-white - Wilkes & Ashmore were directed by Christian Barman to apply it to their 'Coach of the Future' discussed in Chapter Five - so we can conclude that it was an attempt to find a version of Great Western Railway chocolate brown and cream more suited to the 1960s. D1001 was painted maroon to match the passenger coach livery, and D1002–1005 of February–June 1962 painted green to show the effect of this traditional railway colour on the novel form of the locomotive. On Brian Haresnape's prompting the Design Panel had D1015 *Western Champion* painted in Golden Ochre when new in January 1963, matching the revised coach livery exhibited at the London *Design Centre*.[78] To test colour visibility in track conditions, D5500 series locomotive D5579 also briefly featured an ochre paint.

154

AL1 to AL5 (classes 81 to 85)

When Design Research Unit's Herbert Read revised his seminal text on three-dimensional design *Art & Industry* in 1966, the book cover featured locomotive E3001 (AL1/class 81) as an exemplar of good form and function.[79] John Beresford-Evans, Read's colleague at DRU, had developed a standard superstructure for the locomotives which would haul trains on the electrified West Coast Main Line when it opened in September 1960.[80] A resemblance to other Design Research Unit locomotives is evident in the austere appearance: raked back single plane fronts, now combined with the Wilkes & Ashmore form of domed roof. A single recess held the windscreens together visually, and the lower edges of the superstructure were turned inwards.

Beresford-Evans' specification was variously interpreted by the five manufacturers, with E3001 series of 1959 and E3056 series (AL5/class 85) of 1961 closest to his intentions. For British Railways blue was the colour of modernity, although it was used tentatively at first. The 'Blue Pullman' diesel multiple-units by architect Jack Howe, and the Glasgow suburban electric trains by industrial designers Wilkes & Ashmore, had introduced two bright blues to the post-war railway in 1960, these vibrant shades proclaiming a distinct identity which was clean and progressive. Design Research Unit specified a shade called 'Electric Blue' for the AL1–AL5 locomotives; another blue advanced by DRU would be the universal colour for locomotives across Britain after 1965. White surrounds to the cab windows copied Wilkes & Ashmore painting schemes. Milner Gray commissioned cast metal lion & crown crests for the body sides. A conscious effort was made to bring the superstructure of electric locomotives closer in appearance to the contemporary D1500 series engine, when AL6 (E3101 series/class 86) was designed for production during 1965–66. The class began operation in the then new colour of Rail Blue.

In the next chapter, we will see how Design Research Unit extended their consultancy remit to encompass the complete visual image of Britain's railways.

Left: D1000 type D1037 *Western Empress* in all-over green livery at London Paddington, September 1962.

Right: AL6 (class 86) E3163 at Longsight, Manchester, August 1965.

Evidence that John Beresford Evans and Misha Black styled both the E5000 and E3000 series locomotives.

AL1 (class 81) locomotive E3018 in electric blue livery at Stafford, June 1964.

Left to right: Two AL6 and one AL5 locomotive showing the detail differences in cab front treatments.

155

Chapter 5 →
Design researched
1960–81

'BR's present visual image in terms of symbols, lettering and colour is negative and Victorian and certainly out of step with technical advance. Far too much of the front BR shows to the public - train liveries, uniforms, signposting, etc - remains an ill-thought perpetuation of steam-age railway fashion. The railways have lost their persona as an undertaking in this medley of confusing visual associations and become out of focus to the public eye.'[1]

In explaining British Railways' need for a modern appearance, George Williams advanced an unequivocal manifesto for change, change driven by politics, economics, and the sustained desire to make Britain, through the asset of the railway, entirely modern. The context in which George Williams promoted a transformation of the railways is essential to any understanding of why it was needed. Like his colleagues in the wider British design culture, Williams understood design as a means of providing continuous improvements to the quality of life. He saw trains operating alongside new, fast motorways and under skies increasingly dotted with jet passenger aircraft: both modes in which comfort exceeded that of ordinary railway travel. Passenger journeys were increasingly between expanding population centres, urban developments whose citizens were migrating with varying degrees of enthusiasm from low-rise houses to tall blocks, a hangover of pre-Second World War European practice. In city and town centres, shopping precincts replaced traditional outdoor streets. An ostensible convenience pervaded society, as the corporate acted to organise the individual.

Chapter Three made evident the important advances in British Railways vehicles which flowed from the Design Panel's meticulous selecting and briefing of consultants. Momentum for modernity grew quickly after the 'Blue Pullman' made its high-speed debut in 1960. This new industrial glamour was not lost on the Conservative government, ever keen for signs of commercial advantage in nationally-owned businesses. Railway managers were very happy too: their working lives were once more populated with objects of which they could be proud, after years under a pall of deterioration. The Panel gained confidence, championed by its Chairman and senior railway manager T H Summerson. British Railways had become increasingly aware of business opportunities, many benefitting from design input. On Christian Barman's retirement in September 1962, George Williams was promoted to Director of Industrial Design, a new post on the Design Panel which recognised his work and brought him greater influence. By the first few years of the 1960s the success of the Panel's work on locomotives and vehicle design would bring it more support and influence, sufficient for it to be tasked with changing the entire visual appearance of the railway. When Labour returned to government during 1964–70, a new image for the railways suited its programme of transforming Britain into a new technologically advanced nation. Williams had been incrementally updating locomotives and rolling stock for almost a decade. Mindful of the need to give new life to British Railways after the shock of the *Reshaping Plan* published in 1963, Williams, with his friend and senior partner at Design Research Unit Milner Gray, concurred that British Railways needed an entirely new corporate image to brand and style it as a single entity at the heart of British life from city centre to Highland village.

Working with Ellis Miles (Design Officer - Industrial and Graphic) and Jack Bloomfield (Design Officer - Research), Williams could now address a multitude of projects of all scales, from a paper retirement certificate to 'the design problems of locomotives, carriages, special multiple-unit trains, ships' interiors, tableware, emblems, typography, litter bins, station furniture, lighting, seating, trolleys, ships' flags, signal gantries and equipment, overhead electrical gear, liveries, road and rail freight transport vehicles and items needed to run a transport service.'[2] The huge accomplishment of this change to Britain's railways, which was necessary to rehabilitate an ageing and broken infrastructure in the face of competition from the new motorway system and inland air travel, was achieved through a process of total design. From this expanded, comprehensive approach came the British Rail *Corporate Identity Manual*, a pioneering document with international influence. We consider the programme below. Williams died suddenly in November 1965, too soon to witness the considerable effects which proceeded from implementation of the corporate image strategy, but the legacy of Design Panel work under his supervision was momentous. Architect James Cousins, who like George Williams had worked for the Council of Industrial Design, joined British Rail as Director of Industrial Design from autumn 1966. He saw the Department through the launch of British Rail's new image, taking on increasingly substantial speculative design projects including 'the aesthetic and amenity design, both internal and external of such fixed and moveable equipment as is widely used by the Board's passengers, customers and staff or is prominently visible to them or the general public.' Mary Adams, deputy chair of the Consumers' Association, was the first woman to join the Design Panel.[3] In later years Cousins would experience a reversal of corporate policy which challenged much that he, and Williams before him, had achieved. This chapter's second section takes the story on from 1966, considering innovation in graphic and industrial design for trains, before moving into the designed surroundings of architecture and clothing, from the 1970s up to partial separation of the system in 1982.

Design by the River Clyde

A vision of how a fully thought-through corporate image might rejuvenate the railways, was first given with the Design Panel and graphic designer F H K Henrion project for the Glasgow suburban electrification system. Henrion created a special logo which abandoned any reference to the British Transport Commission or Railway Executive. For signs and publicity, he arranged two interlocked chevrons coloured blue and yellow, arranged across each other horizontally on a black ground. The yellow chevron was said to represent the pantograph by which the train collected power from the overhead line; the blue chevron represented the River Clyde. At the suggestion of the Ministry of Transport, Jock Kinneir's *Transport* lettering featured at Glasgow suburban stations. A likely link here is that Sir Walter Worboys of Imperial Chemical Industries, who sat on the Design Panel, chaired the government committee tasked with making recommendations for road signs.

Lettering designed for British motorways featured in the Glasgow suburban system identity.

Exterior of a Glasgow suburban station, about 1962. The branding showed British Railways the importance of a new corporate image.

Glasgow suburban electrification scheme symbol designed by F H K Henrion.

Redefining passenger comfort

Wilkes & Ashmore (W&A) undertook consultancy work on the future form of British Railways/British Rail standard passenger vehicles. They worked with architects John and Sylvia Reid, and silversmith-industrial designer Robert Welch. From a first prototype shown in 1963 as the 'Coach of the Future', the project progressed through an eight carriage operational train called the 'xp64', and on to the Mark II carriage, of which nearly two thousand were built. The duration of this project and its several outcomes is linked with evolution of the British Rail corporate image programme; it is therefore discussed in stages through this chapter.

Jack Howe's high speed diesel-electric 'Blue Pullman' train provided an example of good practice in design for passenger comfort. Having made numerous research journeys around Britain, Howe reported to the Design Panel in 1959. He cited advantageous improvements to all aspects of the passenger areas from floor to ceiling.[4] T H Summerson, Chairman of the Design Panel, added his authority to the need for new carriages in 1962.[5] Known as the Mk II Carriage Project from 1961, a lengthy development process would see many aspects of industrial design challenged. Aluminium alloy, glass reinforced plastics, plastic laminates and fluorescent lighting all prompted a fresh approach to vehicle interiors. After sketching ideas for George Williams of the Design Panel, the design team built three full-size sections of vehicle during July–October 1961: a First class compartment, a Second class open saloon, and an access vestibule with toilet cubicle.[6] W&A crafted all the fittings including seats, coat hooks, litter bins, lavatory door locks, and ashtrays. Metalwork designer David Mellor, who would later make a range of cutlery for British Rail, created the luggage racks. John and Sylvia Reid chose wood veneers for wall surfaces and commissioned special carpeting; Gaby Schreiber advised on textiles. W&A designed the then revolutionary glass fibre

159

'shell' type seat after using an adjustable seating rig to evaluate seating positions and comfort. They introduced magazine racks and tray tables in the backs of seats. Before he moved to Italy to work with Ettore Sottsass, Perry King designed the lock and vacant/engaged indicator for the lavatory door. The wc pan and wash basin were the work of Robert Welch.[7]

Looking ahead to a full train hauled by locomotive D1000 - discussed on page 154 - Christian Barman specified an external colour scheme of pale beige - the same colour as the locomotive - and off-white. Before exhibition, and at Brian Haresnape's suggestion, the painting scheme was revised to ochre and light grey. The disposition of these colours followed almost exactly that of Jack Howe's high-speed diesel-electric 'Blue Pullman' trains. This pattern, and the feature of light grey as a panel around the windows, would be continued in the corporate livery adopted as the national colour scheme for passenger vehicles in 1965.

Litter bin and ashtrays in aluminium for the 'Coach of the Future', 1962.

Above: Another compartment in the mock-up, with painted artwork by Richard Butler. Seats incorporate ashtrays in the arm rests, with airline type reading lights in the luggage racks overhead.

Left: First class compartment in the 'Coach of the Future' mock-up, when exhibited at London's *Design Centre* in 1963.

160

At their Horsham studios the Wilkes & Ashmore team worked continuously for 72 hours to complete the sample 'Coach of the Future' carriage sections. Perry King (left) works on a window detail, in discussion with Jack Ward.

In the Wilkes & Ashmore workshop craftsmen shape the coach mock-up from full-size drawings.

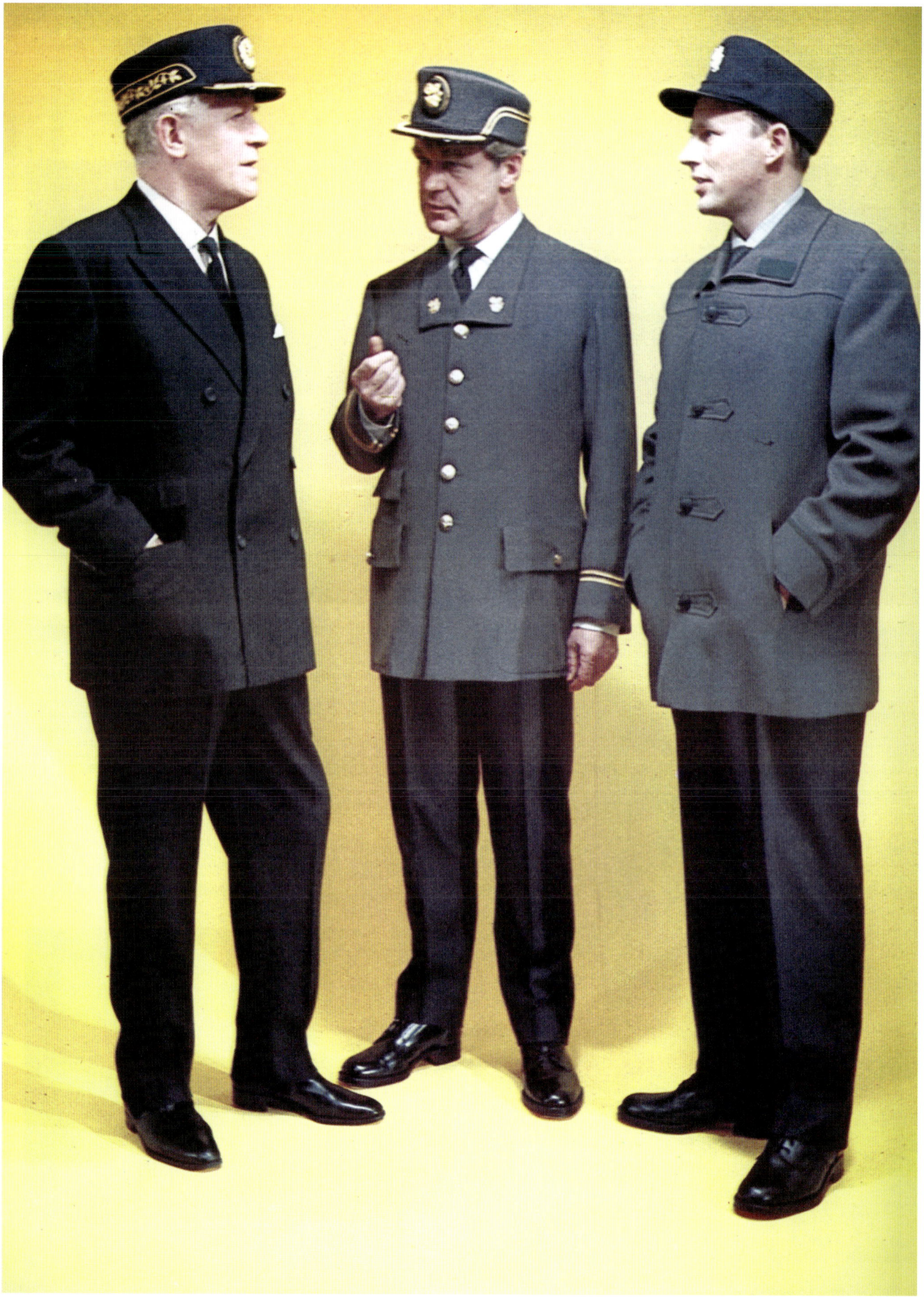

Dressing the organisation

If the trains were to wear new uniforms, so too should the staff. A working group of Jack Bloomfield (BTC Design Officer) and Milner Gray and Kenneth Lamble (DRU), agreed to focus on clothing the porter, ticket collector, station inspector and station master. The brief was further rationalised to devise three basic sets of workwear for porter, middle grades of collector/inspector, and station master; attire for women workers was not considered at this point. The aim was to arrive at a uniform which staff would be proud to wear, which did not show the dirt, and which could fit most body types. In outline, tailoring was based on non-battle military dress. All garments would be in shades of charcoal grey, the jackets lighter than the trousers. Collars were turned down, with wide spread corners lying flat on the shoulders - a casual-formal shape popular in the early 1960s. The high set lapels with horizontal lower margins could have colour flashes to define rank. To remove any fastening that might snag when working, the porter would wear a denim slip-over smock in dark grey with sleeves of a cloth striped with the regional colour. This was before a single national British Rail brand had been agreed, so staff ties too could denote the individual region.[8] Initial ideas were evaluated by Bloomfield, Gray and Lamble when they made a trip to inspect railway uniforms in Switzerland, Italy, Austria, West Germany, Norway, Sweden and Finland.[9] A common feature of most uniforms, and one which confirm the first recommendations, was the widespread fashion for single-breasted jackets. The touring group found a 'kepi' ski cap worn by Swedish Railway workers particularly attractive, and would eventually adopt it for all British Rail uniformed staff.[10] Samples of uniform materials and badges were given by the railway companies to aid development.

Back in London, DRU sent Gerry Barney and David Dathan to research workwear in use at Liverpool Street station; Dathan then developed the detailing with Kenneth Lamble, and samples were made by Lamble's tailor in London's Savile Row for presentation to the Design Panel.[11] By July 1962 a range of outfits had been made, expanded to include porter, ticket collector, inspector, station master, and senior station master. Jackets were of straight side or 'box' cut to give ease of movement when working, single-breasted with four buttons for the ticket collector and five for the inspector and station master. Tailoring included separate shoulder yokes for the collector. There was as yet no approved new insignia: the 1956 lion & crown crest still identified the organisation. The ticket collector, inspector and station master wore small lion & crown collar emblems; on the collector's jacket these were backed by rectangular coloured fabric patches and supplemented by the word 'collector' as an embroidered patch on the right breast. Following navy and airline practice, cuff rings of metallic Russia braid were provided to indicate grades on the jacket sleeves.[12] Ordinarily based in an office environment, the senior station master wore a conventional double-breasted suit without additional markings.

A straight sided pill-box hat, a form of which had been worn by Great Western Railway staff, was re-introduced. Its shape, with additional side panels based on a fold-down neck flap, was modelled on the Swedish Railways' ski-cap. Along the margins of the side panels, which curved down either side at the front in line with the peak, braid matching the jacket cuff bands was added to denote grades from ticket collector to station master. Porters wore no braid; senior station masters' caps were decorated with a band of 'Traveller's Joy' embroidered in gold with gold braid on the peak. For the first three uniform grades, the proposed cap badge was the 1956-issue lion & crown crest: porters would wear a white metal symbol on a red background with a vertical black line below the symbol. A chrome lion & crown identified the collector, and a gold lion & crown the inspector, both on a coloured felt pad. Station masters and senior station masters would retain the post-1956 wreathed insignia, on a padded mid-blue backing. The range of uniforms was first shown to the public in March 1963.[13]

New Design for British Railways

George Williams advocated to industry the commercial and aesthetic benefits of improving the appearance of products. The Council of Industrial Design realised that showing 'improved' objects to the public was another form of communicating its message: it launched a *Design Centre* in London in April 1956.[14] A *Scottish Design Centre* opened in Glasgow in 1957. In our present time the notion of officially-approved, centrally co-ordinated visual surroundings seems at odds with free-market consumer choice, but in 1957 it was seen as a remedy for the burgeoning clamour of unregulated commercial design. The CoID - renamed the Design Council in 1972 - granted a label of endorsement to goods which it considered to have good characteristics of appearance and function, selling many of them in a shop at its *Centre*. An exhibition space hosted extended displays of design culture: it would make the look of the railways a mainstream public concern by staging several presentations concentrating on British Railways and British Rail.[15]

Before British Railways was reinvented as British Rail, Williams promoted the work of his department at the *Design Centre*. 'New Design for British Railways' enjoyed 80,000 visitors between 27 February and 23 March 1963 before touring to the *Scottish Design Centre*, to Moscow in the Soviet Union the following year, and as an exhibition train called 'The New Railways' which toured to 38 locations in May–October 1964. As a snapshot of Design Panel activity, this made a timely point to look back on its first seven years, during which the railway work by consultants Wilkes & Ashmore (vehicle superstructure design) and Design Research Unit (vehicles, uniforms, graphics) gained ground and intensity. 'New Design for British Railways' celebrated the diversity of projects and indicated the potential for an extension of design management across all activities throughout the network. Experiments in livery, staff dress, vehicle and graphic design formed the core of the display. The range of transformed work-wear imparted a contemporary

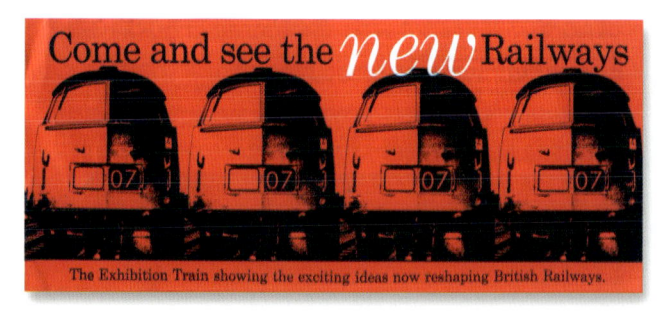

Promotional leaflet for the exhibition train taking British Rail design around Britain in 1964.

'Coach of the Future' Second class saloon in the colour scheme of beige and off-white to match locomotive D1000.

Part of the architecture display in 'New Design for British Railways' at the London Design Centre, 1963.

yet familiar human countenance to the state system. Wilkes & Ashmore contributed three full-size carriage mock-ups so that visitors could actually sit in the 'Coach of the Future'. Small models of vehicles pointed towards new forms and possible colours: D1015 (class 52) *Western Champion* carried the 'Golden Ochre' livery suggested by Brian Haresnape; a D7000 series 'Hymek' locomotive and six coaches were shown in light grey and ochre,[16] afterwards described by the consultants as 'a rather dirty yellow'.[17] With positive public approval, in a matter of months the idea of a single corporate image became a practical reality.

Before a completely new painting scheme came forward as part of the corporate image, some road and rail freight vehicles were given new colours by the Design Panel. Road delivery lorries, tractors and containers became yellow with a red and black 'freight arrow' symbol; general purpose freight wagons took bauxite red to hide the dirt; insulated containers were fittingly made ice blue.

Towards a Corporate Image

'The designer's part is to analyse, create, visualise and co-ordinate the design as a whole.'[18]

Reviewing the success of the 'New Design for British Railways' exhibition, Milner Gray suggested to George Williams that the British Railways Board must have a complete change of visual appearance. A cue was taken from the Glasgow area electrification project of 1960, to determine how a modern image might be applied nationally. Gray directed the Design Research Unit team of Kenneth Lamble, Rupert Armstrong, Collis Clements and Ron Braddick. For the Board's Department of Industrial Design, Jack Bloomfield dealt with three-dimensional subjects, and Ellis Miles took charge of the branding. The corporate image would comprise a symbol or mark, a logotype which combined the mark with a special alphabet encompassing all necessary characters for conceivable uses, standard colours for publicity and signs, vehicle liveries, and staff uniforms. It would be applied nationally as a monolithic identity. When the endeavour commenced in August 1963, Design Research Unit members and other consultants were assigned to each aspect of the project. Gray, Lamble and Clements would deal with the mark, graphics and uniforms. Independent consultant Jock Kinneir - formerly of DRU - collaborated on design of the lettering with his colleague Margaret Calvert. Misha Black and John Beresford-Evans developed the livery.

'xp64: the Train of Tomorrow'

British Railways officers had visited the USA in 1957 to look at railway operation and design. Whilst noting that most passenger services were in decline due to competition from the automobile and domestic air travel, some innovative practice was observed. American coaching stock featured extensive use of plastics, as melamine laminate sheets for the lining of vehicle interiors, and as moulded glass-reinforced plastic for seat units. The visitors also saw better sound insulation, and air suspension. These all found a place in specifications for new British passenger carriages. After the 1963 'Coach of the Future', Wilkes & Ashmore worked with other consultants and British Railways' Derby workshops to design a complete train known as 'xp64' - the 'xp' meaning express passenger, a new designation for premium services. It consisted of D1500 series (class 47) locomotive D1733, eight new coaches (three corridor firsts, two corridor seconds, three open seconds) and four refurbished Mark I vehicles.[19] Doors wider than usual and designed to fold on the jack-knife principle to save space, would give better passenger access. Once on board, travellers could experience improvements through developments in use of space, bigger windows, lighting, and better toilet compartments assembled from four prefabricated plastic parts. The consultants arranged colour schemes too: the second class saloon for smokers was upholstered in yellow, grey and blue wool textiles, and that for non-smoking areas in blue and green. English cherry or Rio rosewood veneer lined some wall surfaces. Aluminium fittings were anodised satin gold or silver. To gather public comments and operating experience, 'xp64' ran between London and Edinburgh as 'The Talisman' from June 1964, in a livery of blue and pale ivory with dark brown underframes.

Mark II passenger coach of 1967 developed from the xp64 prototypes.

Second class saloon in a Mark II coach, with seats upholstered in moquette designed by Marianne Straub, 1970.

First class compartment in a Mark II coach, 1970.

Detail of the innovation in wider doors introduced with the Mark IIB coach. The orange interior is to highlight the vestibule area.

From 'xp64', a standard form of passenger vehicle designated the Mark II coach featured first class accommodation in compartments, and second class seating in open saloons, copying 'xp64' practice. The Mark IIa included a whole range of ergonomic developments, more sound insulation, new vestibules and gangways, new lighter bogies of the B4 type, and metal alloys and plastics replacing wood and steel for coach bodies and seating. For end walls in these coaches teak veneer was used. Design Research Unit evolved a sleeping car compartment for overnight travel.[20] Air-conditioned versions were later developed: by creating entirely enclosed carriages, external sound was substantially reduced.

Development of passenger coaches continued through 1964 in preparation for London Midland Region electric services to Manchester and Liverpool which would begin in 1966. A number were of *Pullman* standard - the highest quality on British Rail - designed by Jack Howe as a continuation of his ideas from the 'Blue Pullman' trains.[21] For these vehicles British Rail introduced the *Pullman* version of its new corporate livery: Rail Blue as a band enclosing the windows on a Rail Grey coach body, with Rail Blue 'Pullman' lettering. Howe selected pale grey padded plastic for the carriage interior walls, with blue/black or orange/black carpets. Rosewood veneer lined the saloon ends. Wilkes & Ashmore developed a reclining seat for the train interiors, upholstered in black plastic and blue or rust coloured wool fabric.[22] Luggage racks with integral lamp units repeated the 'Blue Pullman' design. Details including the ashtrays were designed by Graham Knox at Wilkes & Ashmore.

The range of uniforms developed for station staff during 1962–63 required little revision. It was augmented in April 1964 to include the train-borne guard, driver and secondman (the driver's assistant - a legacy from steam locomotive crews). Facing the public, it made sense for the guard to wear another variation of the station staffs' apparel: a firm cap with lion & crown crest badge on a blue felt oval, with one line of silver Russia braid around the edge of the hat flap. The guard's jacket featured smaller lion & crown crests on light brown flashes, and 'Guard' embroidered on the right jacket breast. Driver and secondman wore lighter navy blue suits, and soft ski caps of a grease and waterproof material. Three gold stars on the jacket lapels denoted a driver, and one white metal star the secondman. Jacket buttons featured a monogram formed from seriffed capital letters 'B' and 'R' overlapping vertically.

Jack Howe sitting in a mock-up of the *Pullman* coach he developed with Wilkes & Ashmore.

The adjustable seating devised for *Pullman* vehicles is advertised by British Rail.

Rail Alphabet

Jock Kinneir's *Transport* lettering had found an application on the Glasgow suburban electrified network, and limited used elsewhere on totem nameplates in regional colours, and for other station signs in black on white (for example at Coventry). When Design Research Unit decided an alphabet was required for the British Rail corporate image, *Transport* seemed an obvious choice. Margaret Calvert argued that the *Transport* letter was made for signs to be read when travelling at speed, whereas railway passengers were pedestrians with more time to apprehend visual information.[23] Swiss designers had considerable influence in communication graphics from mid-1950s. For the Haas'sche Schriftgiesserei (Haas'sche Type foundry), Max Miedinger and Eduard Hoffmann designed *Neue Haas Grotesk* in 1957–58. Soon redrawn and published as *Helvetica*, the font became popular internationally in the 1960s. *Helvetica* seemed universal; it looked utilitarian and attractive too. It was not readily available in England when new. Gerry Barney at DRU and Margaret Calvert at Kinneir Associates both essayed a version of it. Soon Calvert's form of *Rail Alphabet* joined the new visual identity, made to a sophisticated system of rules controlling how the letters would be used in relation to each other and their context. *Rail Alphabet* was available in a range of sizes for signing purposes, to give calm and coherent directions and instructions to passengers across the system. Noticing its suitability for railway transport, the lettering was adopted by DSB *Danske Statsbaner* (Danish State Railways) and NSB *Norges Statsbaner* (Norwegian State Railways).

Livery and colour

'The fundamental changes in the concepts of rail transport that are taking place should be seen to be new and stimulating changes.'[24]

Conceiving of a corporate image in its entirety ensures that all components of the brand image are related. Bringing new colour to the railway was a cheap and effective means of communicating new ideas. Colour schemes for locomotives, multiple-units and passenger vehicles were devised by the Design Research Unit team who had styled the superstructures for the 'Warship' and 'Western' locomotives: Misha Black and John Beresford-Evans. They posited that a single unified livery scheme was needed for all trains, to be notable to passengers and generate pride among staff. At the same time as Wilkes & Ashmore were reporting on colours for future locomotives (see page 144), Black and Beresford-Evans reviewed historic railway liveries in Britain, mindful not to negate tradition. They found that the bright hues promoted by Victorian railway companies were often practical and eye-catching, but too fussy for modern practice. Those painting schemes assembled piecemeal by British Railways from its predecessors, were reminiscent of private companies and not coherent. Individual colours were assessed for contemporary relevance: black was too dark, green too dull, red too much associated with the London Midland Region to be universal. Yellow might be upbeat, but it was hard to select a shade which would not show the dirt or look insipid. Travel in Europe - where Black and Beresford-Evans saw Swiss railcars painted deep blue with light ivory added as a panel at window level - offered confirmation that the blue trains in British Railways' service were the examples from which to build a fresh identity. Choosing a combination of two colours had to be informed by the need for the contrast between them to be perceived in any lighting conditions, and for the colours to be so distinct as to complement each other.

A 'strong rich blue, inclining to peacock blue, with the least darkening by black or thinning by white' would be the primary hue.[25] Debates abound on the precise blues tested in use; certainly the blue applied to the 'xp64' locomotive and coaches was lighter than the final shade. Named BR Rail Blue, the approved colour belonged to a hue group called Monastral Blue, or Phthalocyanine Blue BN, a durable, fade resistant blue-green which looked powerful without being bright, and carried dirt well.[26] (Misha Black liked this colour so much he used it to brand London Transport's new Victoria line in 1968.) Local trains were to be blue all over. Long-distance coach liveries were largely revisions of painting formats originated by Jack Howe in 1959, and Wilkes & Ashmore in 1963, with blue as the main body colour and a panel of 'pale grey, inclining to the blue, that makes so sharp a contrast as to seem white' around the windows - this became BR Rail Grey.[27] We have talked about the idea of total design - a process encompassing thorough investigation of a design problem to produce a comprehensive design solution. Black and Beresford-Evans acquired samples of dirt from coaches and locomotives at Paddington, Birmingham and Swindon, so that a paint colour could be selected for those parts of vehicles below the body.[28]

Locomotives, which by the early 1960s had many different sizes and superstructure styles, would be entirely blue except for the cab fronts - to be painted golden yellow as a visual warning device. There were now two house colours present in the corporate identity: BR Rail Blue and BR Rail Grey. A bright accent was needed to provide contrast. Design Research Unit commissioned several red paint samples without success before arriving at the third house colour: BR Flame Red. Rail Blue and Rail Red were so new that they had to be approved by the British Standards Institution before being accepted as official colours.[29]

British Railways had an uneasy history of commissioning brand marks: the Railway Executive totem of 1948 was widely criticised as a poor imitation of the London Transport bar and circle, suffering from the lacklustre nicknames 'hotdog' and 'double-sausage'. The indeterminate totem had become ubiquitous in the rail environment on publicity and signs, competing with the British Transport Commission's lion & wheel mark for vehicles, which had its own colloquial title: 'a lion riding a bicycle'. When the Commission obtained its grant of heraldic arms in 1956, it made the crest of lion & crown its new operating symbol; unfortunately this had even less emphasis than the previous two. Finding a new mark would exercise DRU for a considerable time, without producing a result. Ultimately, cutting across the conventions of profession and hierarchy, every member of DRU was invited to draft a symbol. Some fifty to sixty of these were gathered together in a display for George Williams and Ellis Miles to make their selection.

Two sketches gained approval. They were chosen because they could be reproduced equally well in monochrome and colour, in print or on vehicles and uniforms. Collis Clements of the DRU corporate image team had proposed two interlinked circles with an arrow implying direction and movement. Gerry Barney was not a trained designer, but a craftsman working with the design team to produce lettering for DRU projects.[30] With nothing to lose he responded to the open call for ideas. Barney's sketch, which he recalls being made on a scrap of paper during the morning commute, had no explicit meaning but neatly inferred 'two-way traffic arrows on parallel lines representing tracks.'[31] It used typographical principles succinctly and without flamboyance, to appear distinctive *and* universal.

A story has circulated that Clement's symbol was abandoned after it was released to the media: Barney disputes this. Gerry Barney's mark was approved for the rebrand of British Rail. Finally the organisation had a device with which to announce its transformation. It would quickly be applied to many uses, as DRU demonstrated its versatility. There were samples of carpet and curtains designed by June Fraser of DRU, in which the symbol became the repeating motif in different colour stripes; it adorned matchbook covers, cutlery, glassware and ashtrays; workers identified by double arrow insignia operated vehicles displaying the mark, through stations signed with two and three-dimensional versions.

The task of creating a comprehensive visual identity had been accomplished. In April 1964 Dr Richard Beeching was able to report in the

Financial Times that British Railways would adopt a symbol, name-style and logotype, and house colours, as a unilateral change across the system.

Top: Visitors to the exhibition launching British Rail corporate identity in 1965 received a wall sheet communicating every aspect of the new image.

Above: Gerry Barney's sketch of Collis Clements' symbol, the alternative to the double arrow.

Top: Four of many possible symbols for BR: a lion, arrows crossing parallel lines, a Union Jack arrow, and railway sidings converging on a Union Jack. The theme of railway tracks is evident in all these; a desire to appear European rather than British ruled out the heraldic motifs.

Above: Gerry Barney's double arrow symbol in its sign and publicity form on a slab of British Rail Publicity Red.

173

'The New Face of British Railways'

Two years after George Williams had tantalised the public with speculative plans for rail transport, he was able to return to the London *Design Centre* in 1965 with a fully-defined exhibition. This was a summary of projects for vehicles and architecture which had been in progress for some time, with a striking difference. Open during 5–23 January 1965, the display toured afterwards to Liverpool and Dublin. The leaflet given to visitors - which the producers intended be displayed as a wall sheet - carried on its cover the double arrow in its purest form on a background of BR Publicity Red. On opening the first fold, the same bright colour proclaimed the new operating title: British Rail. With the double arrow and this name 'one national undertaking... Everything seen and used frequently by the public, every station, every sign, every piece of printed matter, will be given an instantly recognisable family likeness.'[32] Modernity was communicated in every section of the leaflet: electrification of passenger trains; high-speed container-based *Freightliner* services; electronic signalling; functional new stations. A second unfolding revealed the prototype uniform, new publicity, new signs, and 'Elements of the Corporate Identity' including an early version of the book which would gather all these elements together: the *Corporate Identity Manual*.

Distant as it may seem from the business of running a railway, a ring binder of style sheets would become the single point of reference for the entire appearance of British Rail. It was also the culmination of the intense efforts of the Design Panel over a decade, and George William's last project. Ellis Miles chaired the working party which created and assembled the *Corporate Identity Manual*, and he wrote the text. Kenneth Lamble, Rupert Armstrong, Gerald Barney and Collis Clements represented Design Research Unit. Typographer and communication designer Herbert Spencer advised on the use of the symbol and logotype in print.[33] Angela Reeves designed the *Manual*, working closely with Ron Braddick who was the DRU studio manager in charge of production at that time.[34] Clements commissioned the illustrations. Chairman Richard Beeching signed the Foreword which commended the *Manual* to British Rail staff, but it was actually authored by Design Research Unit's Milner Gray with George Williams. Following the strict system of graphics identified with post-war Swiss design, there were precise rules governing application of the new brand to vehicles, buildings, signs, uniforms and publicity. To this end, the *Manual* was expected to provide design specifications for every two- and three-dimensional aspect of the British Rail environment. At its fullest, the *Manual* comprised four binders; the content for the first two came together in just under a year. All the original artworks were painted onto glass plates as definitive records, and the specification documents filled a room at the British Rail offices.[35] The *Manual* went into circulation in July 1965 with an initial edition of 750 copies, ensuring its guidelines were rapidly extended and promulgated throughout all British Rail activities. Receipt of each copy had to be personally acknowledged. Once the *Manual* had press coverage, examples were requested by companies far beyond British Rail, as an exemplar of how to brand an organisation. Many parts of the business adhered closely to the corporate identity for twenty years; some, such as the catering division called 'Traveller's Fare', drifted into their own styling as they perceived changes in the market.

To look at the *Manual* in more detail, we will follow its structure to consider selected sections: 1 Basic Elements: symbol, logotype, lettering, colour; 2 Printed Publicity; 3 Architecture and Signposting; 4 Rolling Stock; (5 Lineside Equipment - not discussed here); 6 Road Vehicles; 7 Ships; 8 Liner Trains; (9 Uniforms - not discussed); (10 Stationery - not discussed); (11 Miscellaneous - not discussed).

Corporate Identity Manual

British Railways Board, 222 Marylebone Road, London N.W.1.

Sheet 2/06 — Printed Publicity: Symbol and logotype in colour for rail publicity (Apr 1965)

a. Symbol and logotype reversed out of panels of BR Publicity Red

b. Symbol reversed out of panel of BR Publicity Red, logotype reversed out of solid or tone panel of black

c. Symbol and logotype in BR Publicity Red reversed panels

d. Symbol in BR Publicity Red, logotype in black within reversed panels

Sheet 2/08 — Printed Publicity: Symbol and logotype with regional identification (Apr 1965)

a. Form and proportions to be followed for London Midland Region. To appear in BR Publicity Red or black

b. Alternative arrangement for a.

c. Form and proportions to be followed for North Eastern Region. To appear in BR Publicity Red or black

d. Alternative arrangement for c.

Sheet 2/02 — Printed Publicity: House colours for printed applications (Apr 1965)

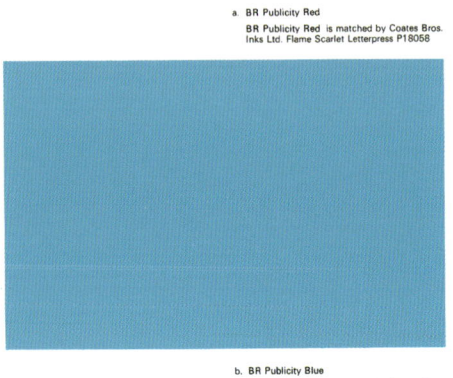

a. BR Publicity Red
BR Publicity Red is matched by Coates Bros. Inks Ltd. Flame Scarlet Letterpress P18058

b. BR Publicity Blue
BR Publicity Blue is matched by Coates Bros. Inks Ltd. Permanent Brilliant Blue. Letterpress P22018

Sheet 2/21 — Printed Publicity: Use of Symbol with other identifications (Apr 1966)

Use: By agreement with British Rail Hovercraft Ltd and the Director of Industrial Design
Colour: Publicity Blue for printed application
B.R. Rail Blue for liveries
B.S. 0-012 for signs

Basic Elements
Rail alphabet black letters

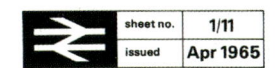

sheet no. 1/11
issued Apr 1965

abcdefghijklmnopqrs
tuvwxyz&-.,'()
ABCDEFGHIJKLMNOP
QRSTUVWXYZ
1234567890

For notes on the use of this alphabet refer to Sheet 1/10.

Gerry Barney's double arrow could be used in solid form, in outline, or reversed out (in negative) on a rectangular 'slab', in black, white or colour without changing its characteristics. For a government agency, the British Railways Board was surprisingly efficient in seeking legal protection for its mark. In June 1965, before the *Corporate Identity Manual* was published, the Board ensured that Design Research Unit assigned to it the copyright in the double arrow: Milner Gray and Gerry Barney both signed the letter of transfer.[36] Barney's symbol was married with Margaret Calvert's lettering to make a logotype. Enclosed in a separate frame, the wording was infinitely yet consistently variable to suit regions, functions or trading activities. When British Rail began operating hovercraft to France, the logotype crossed the English Channel. It advertised ferry routes to the Republic of Ireland and the Netherlands too. Catering outlets at stations and on trains had their own versions of the logotype. In enlarged and modified form, the logotype made a template for exterior signs at stations. Application of the symbol and logotype to new uses was supervised by British Rail's Corporate Identity Steering Committee, a function of the Industrial Design Department.

Bulky compendiums of all the public train services throughout a region were redesigned. In some instances the cover colour was matched to the region, a curious perpetuation of the Railway Executive coding that the corporate image was intended to eradicate. On other books the colours seemed to be chosen for their brightness: the Western Region used a similar crimson to the London Midland Region, and the Eastern Region

Opposite page and above: The British Rail *Corporate Identity Manual* contained loose-leaf pages describing in detail the form and use of the brand. It provided permutations for different contexts, evolving as British Rail changed the way it marketed its services, and found new needs for the branding.

took a soft blue-green. Between 1965 and 1969 the book covers showed only words, except for the Southern Region whose three divisional timetables included diagrams of principal routes. From 1970, some featured an outline map of the regional coverage: this was universal by 1973. More convenient for passengers on the move, cards and booklets dispensed from racks in ticket halls began to be produced from 1964, to a layout by Herbert Spencer. He employed coloured inks printed on white for some booklets, and conceived of the distinguishing panel of colour intended to identify one booklet from another by route, not region. Spencer used visual proportions to balance the colour panel with its white neighbour; pocket timetables continued the Spencer design of 1964; until 1968 they were of horizontal and vertical formats; after this the vertical type persisted. The essence of Spencer's layout would prevail until 1981.

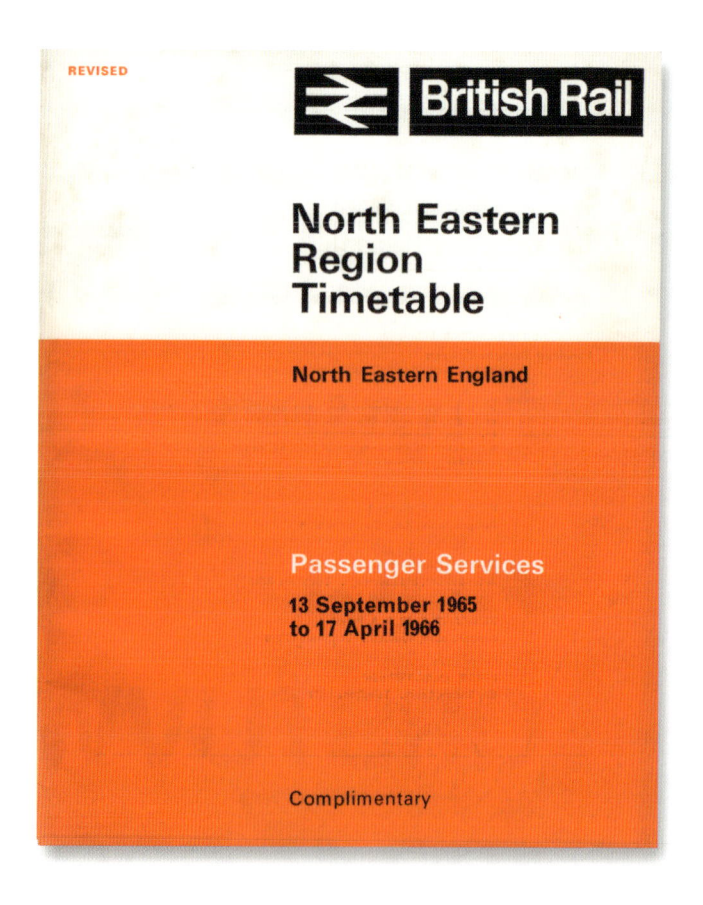

Book and pocket card or folder timetables featured a cover designed to recommendations by typographer Herbert Spencer.

178

The railway estate would need a great deal of work to modernise or restore it. As staffing levels reduced, maintenance also decreased. New name signs on station exteriors, and directional signs around the buildings on platforms, would at least give a superficial sense of renewal. British Rail's Industrial Design Department established a Signing Secretariat staffed by Alan Applegate and Bill Barby to rationalise the profusion of visual information in the railway environment. Design Research Unit working with Kinneir Associates, contrived a 'plank' system of rectangular units which could be fixed singly or in multiple according to the information displayed. Many stations advertised their name reversed out of Rail Blue or black, with the double arrow on a Flame Red slab or plain ground. The separation of Design Panel and architectural teams meant that the re-signing of buildings took a considerable time. As an example, by 1970 many Southern Region stations still displayed the post-1948 green and white enamel signs, some even retaining items from circa 1923.[37] When implemented, fitting of new nameboards and other signs on platforms initiated the wholesale removal of the 'totem' nameplates, which soon became desirable items for collectors.[38]

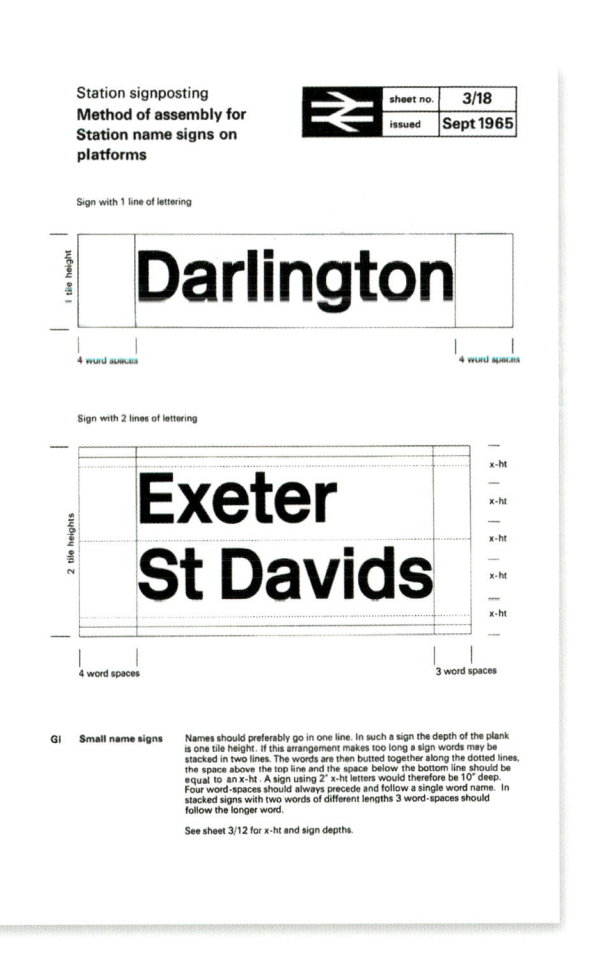

A directive of 9 June 1966 confirmed Monastral/ Rail Blue, with Warning Yellow ends for locomotives and multiple-units, as the 'National train livery', although some new locomotives had been painted in this colour since early 1965. By January 1967 *Modern Railways* was reporting on the effects of the livery applied to locomotives and multiple-units.[39] Vehicles would now be marked by the double-arrow symbol, and white numerals/letters. Main-line passenger vehicles displayed Rail Grey bands outlined in white as window surrounds along their length; for *Pullman* coaches this pattern was reversed to produce a Rail Blue strip on a Rail Grey body. Multiple-unit trains were plain Rail Blue with yellow ends. 'Liner trains' of freight containers would replace assorted wagons: these vehicles show a Flame Red stripe livery which would work equally well on rail or on road. Ship hulls were naturally suited to Rail Blue above the waterline, whatever the weather. Their superstructures were white, with Flame Red funnels. Novel as the creators of the corporate image knew it to be, they respected marine tradition by showing the symbol reversed, or backwards, on the port side of the funnel and fleet flag.

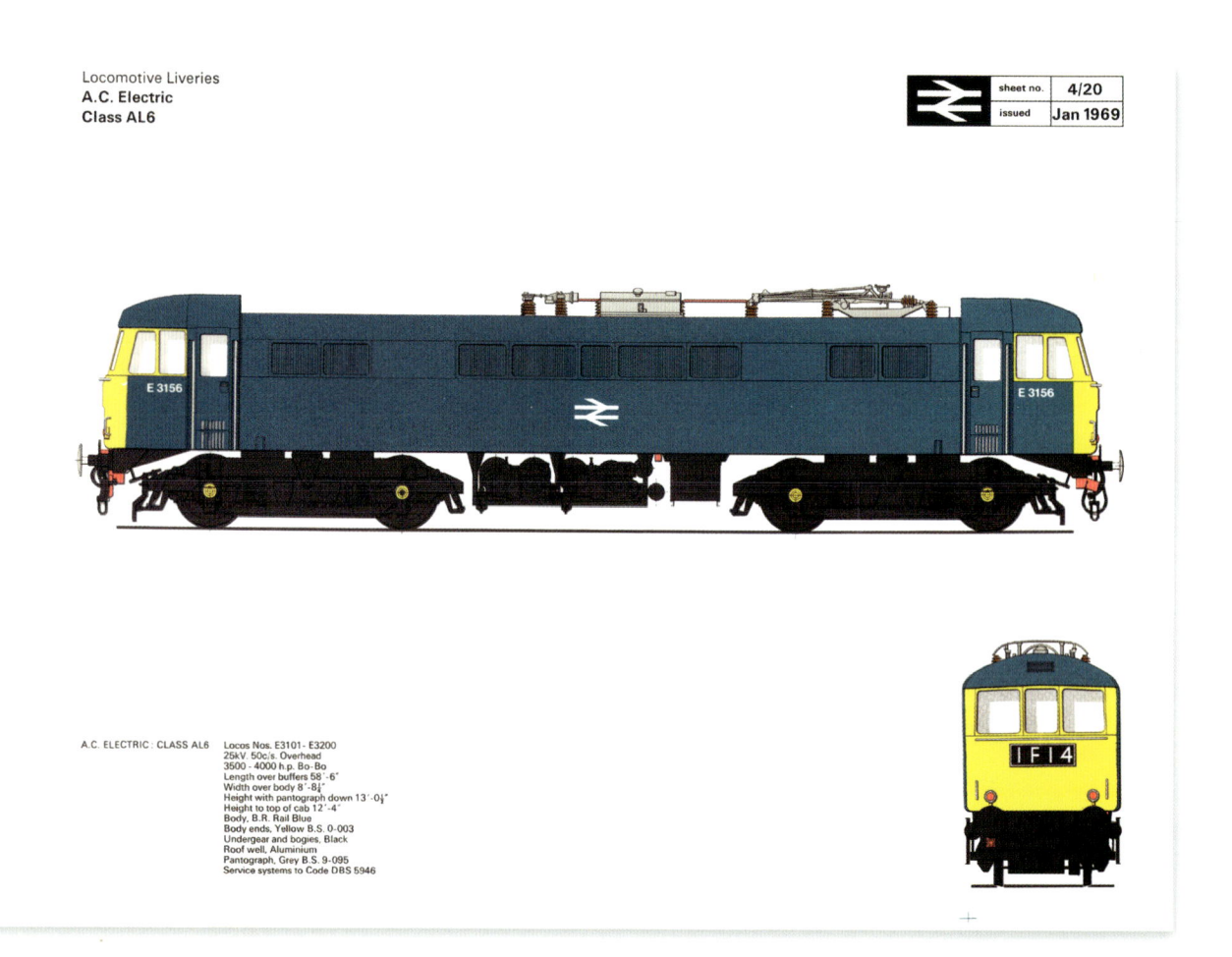

Locomotive Liveries
A.C. Electric
Class AL6

sheet no. 4/20
issued Jan 1969

A.C. ELECTRIC : CLASS AL6
Locos Nos. E3101- E3200
25kV. 50c/s. Overhead
3500 - 4000 h.p. Bo-Bo
Length over buffers 58'-6"
Width over body 8'-8¼"
Height with pantograph down 13'-0½"
Height to top of cab 12'-4"
Body, B.R. Rail Blue
Body ends, Yellow B.S. 0-003
Undergear and bogies, Black
Roof well, Aluminium
Pantograph, Grey B.S. 9-095
Service systems to Code DBS 5946

Rolling Stock Liveries
Mark 1 Carriage
First class Corridor

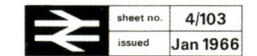

sheet no. 4/103
issued Jan 1966

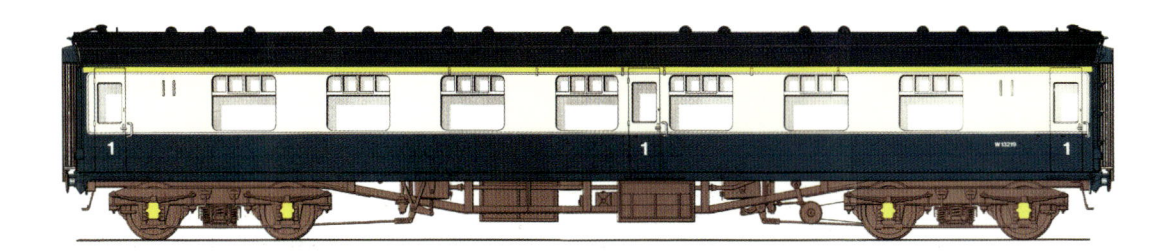

MARK 1 CARRIAGE First class, Corridor
Length over body 64'-6"
Width over body 9'-0"
Height rail to roof 12'-9½"
Main body, B.R. Rail Blue
Window band, Grey B.S. 9-095
Roof, Dark Grey B.S. 9-098
Underparts, Dark Brown B.S. 3-039

Ships Liveries
T.S.S. Dover

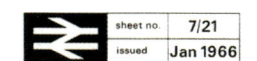

sheet no. 7/21
issued Jan 1966

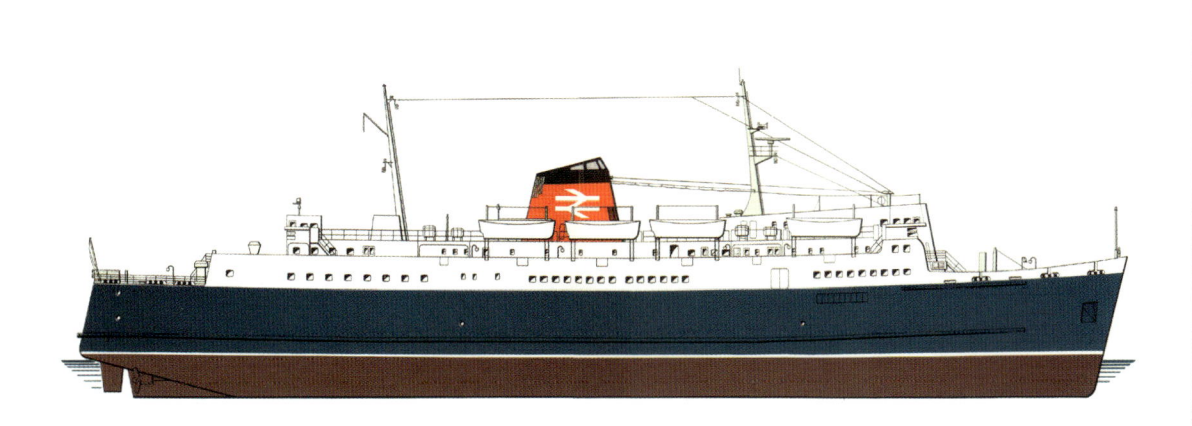

T.S.S. DOVER Car Ferry between Dover-Boulogne
Gross tonnage 3601.7, Length 369'-0", Breadth 57'-2", Draught 12'-9"
Built 1965 by Swan Hunter and Wigham Richardson Ltd.
Colours, B.R. Rail Blue, B.R. Flame Red, B.R. Marine Grey, Dark Brown, White, Black

181

Section 9 of the *Corporate Identity Manual* defined uniforms for men. For full issue throughout British Rail, a double arrow replaced the lion & crown crests on caps and jacket lapels for all staff except station master/senior station master. Jacket collar lapels were reduced in size, and porters issued with traditional waistcoats rather than smocks. Cuff and cap braid was adjusted too: porters would now be identified with a single line of red piping. The booklet *Your New Uniform* guided staff in correct attire.[40]

An increasing number of female employees joined British Rail in roles modelled on airline stewardesses and the crews of prestige services in other countries, such as the Canadian National Railways' *Turbo Train*. Dress for female staff working as couriers on rail-air link services began to appear around 1969. *Seaspeed* hovercraft purserettes wore 'Hoversuits' made from a synthetic jersey textile called *Koratron*, which was knitted in a tube before being treated with heat and pressure to retain a permanent, seamless, easy-care form.[41] More accommodating knitted and woven garments for *Rail-Air Link* 'hostesses' featured the British Rail symbol and colours in assorted trend-conscious permutations. When the *Advanced Passenger Train* was promoted at 'Transpo 72' in Washington DC, USA, female members of the exhibition team wore metallic *Koratron* dresses and headgear.

Left: Moulded synthetic uniforms made to promote British Rail internationally as a future-thinking, fashionable organisation.

Top left: British Rail male station staff uniform, 1968.

Top right: *Rail-Air Link* hostesses, 1969.

Left and above: Moulded knitted tube uniforms for Seaspeed hovercraft purserettes, 1970.

The next train: Into the 1970s with British Rail

Barbara Castle (later Baroness Castle of Blackburn) became Minister of Transport in December 1965, by which time Sir Stanley Raymond had replaced Dr Richard Beeching as chairman of the British Railways Board. Raymond resigned in 1967, and was succeeded by Henry (later Sir Henry) Johnson; Richard (later Sir Richard) Marsh served as chairman 1971–76 and Peter (later Sir Peter) Parker 1976–83. Castle wanted to create a commercial railway, supported by understanding the real cost of the social railway in order to maintain it most economically. This approach, which culminated in the *Transport Act 1968*, would affect the maintenance, or otherwise, of the railway built environment and the design of rolling stock. In the same year, the *National Traction Plan* surveyed motive power requirements. From 1970, as a consequence of the 1968 act, sections of the network had to be shared with Passenger Transport Executives created in the West Midlands, Merseyside, Tyneside and Greater Manchester. TOPS, a computer system imported from North America, came into use in 1972: at this point many locomotives were renumbered into classes.

British Rail's operating deficit grew rapidly in the early 1970s; reduction of the rail network ensuing from the *Reshaping of British Railways* report had not brought the predicted profitability. Growth in projections of private car use forced a further look at the usefulness of rail to relieve congestion and reduce pollution. The railway became a place for positive development once more. Urban railways could relieve pressures on urban roads; rural routes might help protect the environment and perform a community purpose. To serve this strategy, cleaner and more economic types of train were needed. For a range of tasks, both lightweight railbuses and more powerful electric or diesel-electric locomotives and multiple-units would be introduced. Planned growth of the Inter-City network - through electrification of suburban areas and main lines - would be accelerated by new rolling stock, including the *High Speed Train (HST)* as an interim measure before full electrification of the main lines, and the *Advanced Passenger Train*. From 1976 Peter Parker pushed design strongly, trying to get much wider engagement across British Rail. He worked with pioneer of design management Peter Gorb, who had founded the Design Management Unit at the London Business School. As a result the Design Panel, now chaired by former London Transport officer David McKenna, strived to integrate design with business. British Rail could permit talented individuals to move around through promotion or transfer, spreading good practice in a way that was less possible in private industry. Effects of this process might be slow, but when seen across the distinct approaches taken by the business sectors from 1982, did produce a renaissance in the appearance of the British Rail network by the late 1980s.

'The Next Train...', a 1969 exhibition at London's *Design Centre*, presented speculative ideas of how rail travel in the 1970s might be improved by design.[42] It featured models of the *Advanced Passenger Train* and *High Speed Train*, a hovercraft (for British Rail's sea routes), mock-ups of the Mark III passenger rail carriage and ship's cabins, and a potential 6000hp locomotive with superstructure by industrial designer and silversmith Atholl Hill, who would later craft the superstructure for the *Advanced Passenger Train* in its *APT-E* and *APT-P* forms.[43] To specifications provided by British Rail, William Mitchell, who had made the decorative vestibule panels for the Midland and Western Pullman and class 309 multiple-units, fabricated a mock-up one bay long of a proposed coach interior.[44] A prototype passenger seat was also shown: its designer Kenneth Grange soon became an important player in the development of the *High Speed Train*. After London, elements of the display toured Europe in 1971, starting at the Louvre in Paris. An exhibition train visited twenty two cities on the railway network to further promote British Rail design successes and aspirations.[45]

Promotional graphic for the 1969 British Rail exhibition, featuring a version of the *Advanced Passenger Train*, 1969.

Simulated interior of the Mark III coach shown at 'The Next Train...' exhibition, London, 1969.

Model of a heavy freight locomotive styled by Atholl Hill, 1969.

A heavy freight locomotive

As economic prospects fluctuated, so British Rail traction policy shifted from electrification to diesel prime-mover and back again. The scale of new infrastructure provision necessary for electric trains made internal combustion seem an expedient remedy to traction needs. British Rail's most powerful locomotive was the 3300hp D9000 series (class 55), but only 22 existed. As a reaction to the numerous motive power types left over from the *Modernisation Plan Pilot Scheme*, with their different mechanical and maintenance requirements, a limited series of locomotives built to standard specifications made good sense. An ever-present demand for faster passenger trains and capacity to haul heavier or express freight, with plans for a future Channel Tunnel rail service, would need locomotives of up to 8000hp. T C B 'Terry' Miller, who succeeded J F Harrison as Chief Engineer (Traction & Rolling Stock), issued *Locomotives for the 1970s* in 1969.[46] At this time British Rail had an incomplete schedule of electrification schemes, meaning both diesel and electric locomotives would be wanted; they could, according to this proposal, use common mechanical parts. The report outlined a limited selection of engines with an equally restrained family of locomotive bodies sharing cab design and chassis, with permutations to suit the power source and wheel arrangement. Atholl Hill, part of the Industrial Design Department, was seconded to the research team 1½ days a week for three years, in order to close the gap between vehicle innovation and appearance. Hill shaped the cab fronts as sharp, angular forms, combining features of the D1000 (later class 52) 'Western' and D1500 (later class 47) series, altered into a tougher, more decisively aggressive shape. Between acutely raked windscreens, a projecting unit taken up into the cab roof dome contained the headcode panel. Ventilation louvres extending down into the body sides gave the appearance of a high roof over the engine room. Locomotives with this form were expected to be in service from 1972. The plan was not implemented, but aspects of the technology found their way into the class 87 and class 56 locomotives.

Convention and conflict: the 'Advanced Passenger Train' and 'High Speed Train'

Athol Hill was also lead designer on the *Advanced Passenger Train APT-E* prototype (gas turbine-powered) and *APT-P* (electrically-powered) superstructures. British Railways' Advanced Projects Group first imagined an express passenger train in 1962, when the main lines were still operated with steam engines pulling lines of individual, and frequently antique, coaches. The Railway Technical Centre at Derby was established in 1964 to concentrate engineering expertise. It did more than this, however, because British Railways looked to the rapidly developing jet aeroplane travel industry - a significant competitor - for inspiration. Senior staff at the centre, including Director of Research Dr Sydney Jones, were recruited to support an official plan to radically alter rail transport. Leading the *Advanced Passenger Train* project, Jones predicted future passenger train speeds of 200–300mph. Dr Alan Wickens of Sydney Jones' team studied the dynamics of wheel on rail, and train movement at high speed. From about 1966 Wickens worked on systems for tilting vehicles so that they could take curves faster. With central government funds flowing into this exciting vision, the project began to materialise new kinds of train based on multiple-units, with integrated driving cabs and power equipment. As we shall see, two somewhat different approaches and outcomes would follow, with the engineers and the Research Department engaged on conflicting ventures: 'one group working on the next generation of diesel-electric locomotives while another parallel group works on the much more speculative *Advanced Passenger Train*.'[47]

Plaster model for what would become the *APT* by Wilkes & Ashmore, 1964.

Early British Rail model for the *APT*, with a curved and faceted nose to the front, 1970.

186

Consultants Wilkes & Ashmore took several rolling stock schemes through to completion; they were also on-hand to make models with which British Railways/British Rail could catch the eye of government officials in the unending quest for finance. When Minister of Transport Barbara Castle made a visit to the Railway Technical Centre at Derby in April 1967, she entered past a highly speculative small-scale multiple-unit which had been commissioned from Wilkes & Ashmore by George Williams before he died. It was a model for a turbo-jet train based on a sketch made by E G M Wilkes in 1963 for a fully streamlined locomotive front, intended to be a detachable pod which would allow different lengths of train to be formed.[48] Evidently based on a light aircraft fuselage, it predated the streamlined form of the Japanese *Shinkansen* train. It also shared similarities with the W&A artwork for the two-car magnetic levitation *Limpet* hovertrain, which British Railways hoped to create through collaboration with Manchester University.[49] The pointed nose below an array of cab windows can be compared with the contemporary Aérospatiale and British Aircraft Corporation *Concorde* supersonic passenger jet airliner. This was never intended to be a serious pattern for a real unit, and it gave no impression of the power or strength which British Rail desired to show in underlining the innovation of the *Advanced Passenger Train*. It did, however, become the first of several aircraft-inspired models made for various purposes between 1967 and 1969, when British Rail, aware of similar European developments, announced that the *APT-E* would be funded to proceed.

British Rail display for 'European Conservation Year', November 1969.

Another early model of *APT*, with roof cowlings for the gas turbine power units. This was used as the basis for the logo on page 185.

Chairman of the Design Council and the Royal Society of Arts Lord Hayter, is shown models of the *APT* and *HSDT* at the launch of the British Rail 'European Conservation Year' exhibition train, 1969.

At this point Atholl Hill of the Industrial Design Department was handed the task of giving credible form to the *APT-E*, which had so far operated as a collection of test rigs. To tilt and still fit within the constraints of bridges and tunnels, the train was designed with an egg-shaped cross-section formed by two flat surfaces on each side, joined by a segmental curve below the windows. Hill drew the sides together in streamlined form at the unit ends, the four planes producing a faceted wedge profile. Moulded glass reinforced plastic made it possible to create the complex angles. To ensure the driver's window would be impact resistant - even at 150 mph - only a small area of glass was used, set high in a rectangular recess between tapering flanks. Three pairs of fairings on the power unit roofs enclosed ventilation and exhaust ports for the gas turbines. Metro-Cammell built the driving car bodies from sheet aluminium, over which a band of Rail Blue at window level wrapped up and across the cab roofs as a continuous strip. Ends were painted Warning Yellow. Ergonomist Paul Branton advised on the layout of the driving cab and passenger seating. Architectural practice Sir Basil Spence, Bonnington and Collins detailed the train interior, sourcing components which could be rearranged according to the class of travel and function of the vehicle. A four-car evaluation train was ready for running in July 1972; when testing ceased in April 1976 it was donated to the National Railway Museum at York.

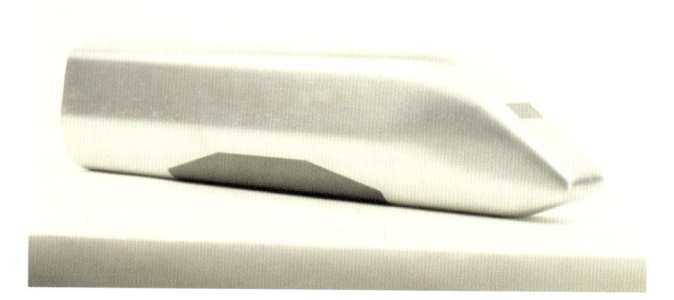

Above: Concept model for the *APT-E* by Atholl Hill, circa 1970.

Right top: *APT* designer Atholl Hill in prototype seat, circa 1969.

Right middle: Developed model for *APT-E*, with colour scheme proposal, about 1971.

Right bottom: Full size mock-up of *APT-E* interior, by architects Sir Basil Spence, Bonnington and Collins, September 1973.

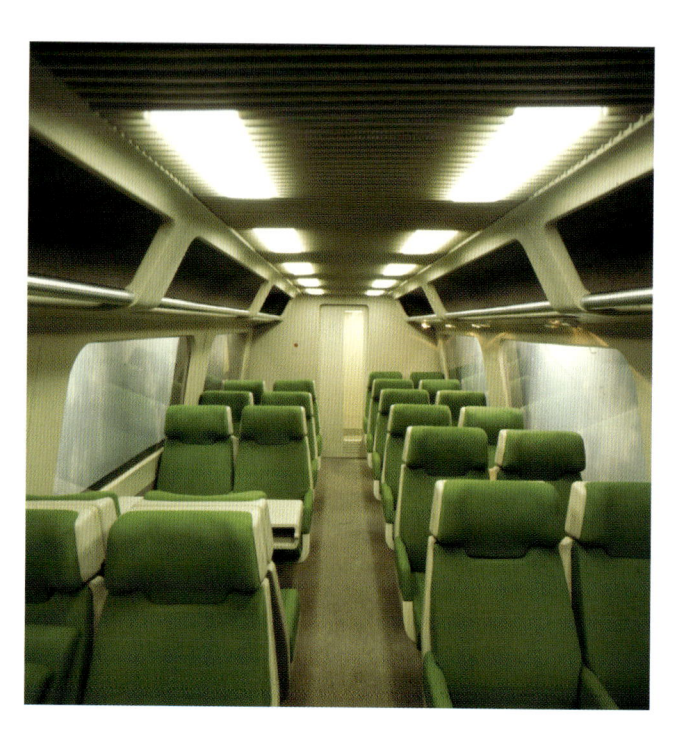

Full size mock-up of *APT-E* interior, 1972-73. The folding tables and prepared meal trays were innovations to accompany the new services.

Prototype *APT-E* toilet compartment, 1973. Moulded plastics would be used extensively to aid installation and maintenance.

Cover of the promotional booklet for *APT-E*, 1972.

Above: Investigating the additional demands which would be placed on seating as trains began to tilt and move at higher speeds, British Rail designer Jack Bloomfield and ergonomist Paul Branton experimented with a 'sling' seat in 1969. Borrowing from innovation in space craft design, the *Terylene* polyester fabric support was suspended from a metal frame like a hammock to give it tension and optimal body support.[50] Prototypes were made by specialist company Portsmouth Aviation, and the design was then refined by Kenneth Grange of Pentagram. One version was granted a patent in the USA

Above: A portion of *APT* in its prototype revised form featured at the 'International Transport Exhibition', Hamburg, 1979.

189

Advanced Passenger Train revived

APT-P, also called *APT-250*, became the class 370 electrically-powered prototype version of the *Advanced Passenger Train*, for future use on the West Coast Main Line London–Glasgow services. The fourteen vehicles in a complete train were configured as two- and six-car non-powered sections with a single driving cab at one end, formed either side of two 4000hp motor vehicles containing the power collecting and transforming equipment, the motors and the driven wheels. Front and rear bogies supported the ends of the six-car units; intermediate bogies bore an articulated connection between coaches. Each half was provided with a restaurant/buffet car. Atholl Hill again provided the design, modifying the profile from *APT-E* to make a wider, shorter wedge nose, using the reduced distance between front bogie and body end. More adjustments - a cab window flush with the external skin, cab side windows, a waistline curved down either side of cab and light clusters below the horizontal crease across the nose - brought the appearance closer to that of the *HST*. Passengers enjoyed an interior resembling an airliner. Much use was made of beige moulded glass reinforced plastic for wall linings, bulkheads and interior fittings. All passenger coaches were of the open-plan or saloon type: first class passengers sat in blue tartan seats, second class in red tartan. Ribbed ceiling panels were made from vacuum-formed plastic with rectangular plastic shades to the fluorescent lights. Below the windows, carpet and moquette fabric lined the walls and floor; in the catering vehicles carpeting covered bar front, floor, wall and ceiling. Colour schemes varied between the six catering vehicles.

An *APT-P* model of 1974 was presented in aluminium with longitudinal bands in two shades of blue, swept over the cab roofs like the *APT-E*. As built, this was revised to what would later be the InterCity 'Executive' colour scheme: a dark grey window level band on a white upper body, with white and red waist bands above a beige lower body. The legend 'InterCity APT' in large white letters identified some motor cars; others displayed an equally substantial white double arrow symbol. Cab ends carried Warning Yellow above the horizontal crease in the nose. Latterly, in line with British Rail livery changes, a black panel was painted around the cab windows. Nose fronts had various versions of the logotype, comprising a double arrow (outline to early 1984, then solid), 'InterCity' (solid) and 'APT' (in outline form to early 1984, and then in solid form).

Three complete *APT-P* sets were available from mid-1978. They were tested until 1980, beginning regular passenger runs between Glasgow and London on 7 December 1981. Technical faults led to more testing in 1982, and passenger runs in 1983–84. A fleet or squadron of sets coded *APT-S* was expected to follow in the early 1980s. *HST*, however, was so effective that the *Advanced Passenger Train* project was abandoned in 1986, regarded by government as an inconclusive, complex and expensive development project. The experience of *APT* would lead to the *InterCity 225* concept, using a conventional locomotive in push-pull format with conventional coaches.

Second class saloon in *APT-P*, identified by its custom-designed tartan seat upholstery.

Bar counter in the *APT-P*. Moulded fibreglass and carpeting created a sense of luxurious contemporary travel.

Top: Poster and postcard advertising *APT-P* train services.

Above: The nose of *APT-P* appeared as a shortened, simplified version of its predecessor *APT-E*.

Left: Mock-up second class saloon in *APT-P,* January 1977. The headrests have covers featuring the train, adapted from the design of an earlier motif seen on page 185.

191

HST - the High Speed Train

British Rail envisaged tilting train technology being most suited for the curved alignment of the West Coast Main Line. Not wishing to limit the availability of rolling stock for other trunk services, and reluctant to ignore the calls of some British Rail officers to rely upon more proven solutions, permission was given to the Derby mechanical and electrical engineering team to develop a new version of the conventional diesel-electric multiple-unit, concurrently with *APT*. A *High Speed Diesel Train (HSDT)* could be an interim solution to the accelerating of service times, while tracks were improved and routes adapted for faster speeds. Once again, Wilkes & Ashmore made the initial model to illustrate ideas; this was shown at 'The next train...' exhibition in London in 1969, and toured Europe. In autumn 1970 the *High Speed Diesel Train* was publicised as a project: it would have an operating speed of 125mph, and go into service from 1975.

Kenneth (later Sir Kenneth) Grange, industrial designer and founding-partner in the group Pentagram, became engaged with work for British Rail when he was asked to refined the form and function of Jack Bloomfield's netting passenger seat.[51] Grange was then asked to draft a livery for the *High Speed Diesel Train*. He was able to extend this commission to restyling the train's power car fronts.[52] He had worked in the office of Jack Howe & Partners when it was designing the 'Blue Pullman' diesel-electric multiple-units, so he knew this type of vehicle. British Rail provided Grange with a model of a cab end which had been made for wind tunnel testing.[53] After discussion with a British Rail engineer and the aerodynamicist working on the *Advanced Passenger Train*, a revised front was made.[54] This had a bulbous form resembling the streamlined version of William Stanier's 'Coronation' Class 4-6-2 locomotive built for the London, Midland and Scottish Railway from 1937. In autumn 1970 a class 86 locomotive fitted with a streamlined plastic nose cone was used to test the design's aerodynamics.[55]

Wilkes & Ashmore model for the *HSDT*, 1967.

Fibreglass streamlined front fitted to a class 86 locomotive for tests in autumn 1970.

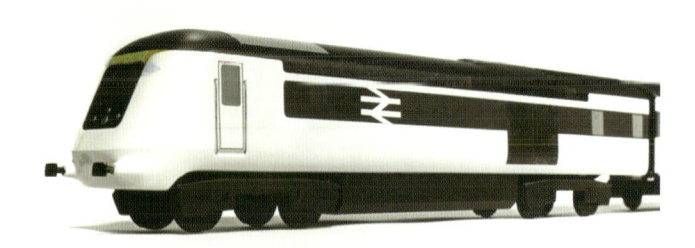

Model of locomotive 41.001, one end of the *HSDT* unit.

Brochure for the *High Speed (Diesel) Train*, after the front had been restyled without buffer units.

When Grange took on the appearance design for the *High Speed Diesel Train*, he employed glass reinforced plastic technology to give each power car a self-assured wedge-shaped front, formed by raking the single plane of the cab front forwards down almost to the line of the buffers, and then drawing it in again at a pronounced horizontal crease. Grange continued the crease around the body sides, blending it with the curved tumblehome above the bogies. A single window area in the sloping cab front was divided horizontally into two sections to take advantage of the largest size of the specified armoured glass then made, with the lower section containing the head and tail lamps. Smoothed fairings enclosed the buffer stocks. Cab access doors contained small windows, with others provided along the power car sides. The form's aerodynamic properties were tested in a wind tunnel by Grange's assistant Roger Jones.

Two power cars were completed in 1970–71. At first they were understood to be locomotives, and numbered accordingly, as .001 and .002 of class 41, now with the contracted title *High Speed Train*. British Rail's new lightweight steel Mark 3 passenger coaches made up the full train unit. Prototyped in 1970, at 23 metres the Mark 3 was longer than the Mark II, with full air-conditioning, chemical toilets and a higher operating speed. A single body structure would be used for all versions of this vehicle, from open saloons to kitchens, buffets and sleeping cars. Doors were wider than on previous coaches, and continued the feature from the Mark II of being hinged into the carriage ends. Coach interiors - panelling, furnishings and seats - were designed for variable seating positions; greater accessibility for all passengers was considered by the ergonomist Paul Branton.

Right: First class passenger coach in production version of the *HST*, 1977.

Nose profile of operational prototype *HST* 252.001 at Swindon, June 1976.

Proposed second class saloon in *HST*, circa 1973.

The complete seven-coach, two-power-car high-speed train, re-designated as a DEMU, was renumbered as class 252.001 in 1974. In summer 1972, in common with the *APT*, the first *HST* train was available for test runs. Like the *APT*, it was affected by a trade union dispute with British Rail which stalled evaluation until spring 1973. *HST* established a new world speed record for diesel traction of 141mph on 11 June 1973, pushed up to 143mph the next day.[56] Unit 252.001 was withdrawn February 1977, by which time a fleet of *HST* trains was in production. The first was given a public display in September 1975; the last was completed in 1982. They differed from the prototype in appearance, after additional work by Kenneth Grange. Most obvious of the changes was the removal of the buffers - because *HST* units would not normally couple to other vehicles - allowing the fronts to be clean wedges with cowlings in front of the wheels. Grange made the angle at which the two cab planes met more acute, increasing the projection of the front to maintain its aerodynamic performance. A shallower cab window - using the larger size of armoured glass which could now be manufactured - was complemented by a transparent strip containing the lamp units either side of a grille for the air horns. Side windows were fitted into the rounded cab corners, and the arrangement of windows and grilles in the body sides made much neater. After experimenting with colour schemes, the unit livery was altered too: a Rail Blue band formed the middle section of the sides and cab front, with warning panel yellow above and below. The point where large openings were let into the bodysides was used to reverse the position of the Rail Blue so that it conformed to the passenger carriage livery. This meeting of colours followed the slope of the cab fronts. *High Speed Trains* operating London–Bristol/South Wales/Cornwall services from October 1976 formed class 253; the majority of trains for the Eastern Region London–Newcastle/Edinburgh route had eight passenger coaches and formed class 254. Trains and marketing materials featured the branding *Inter-City 125*. The *HST* won a Design Council award in 1978. It remains in service in 2016.

Three *HST* class 253 trains in the blue and yellow livery devised for them by Kenneth Grange, August 1976.

Timetable book cover, with image by Danish artist Per Arnoldi.

Brush Traction manufactured equipment for a version of the *HST*-type power cars built in Australia. This operated as the *XPT* between the states of Victoria, New South Wales and Queensland from 1982.

Class 87 electric locomotive, a 5000hp, 100mph machine, built by British Rail Engineering at Crewe, and introduced from 1973 for the extension of electric services on the West Coast Main Line to Carlisle and Glasgow. The in-house team combined Wilkes & Ashmore and Design Research Unit appearance features to make a slab-sided superstructure with flat lower ends, two raked back windscreens and shallow cab roofs. Ventilation grilles and windows in the bodysides were arranged in a single strip. The locomotives continued in *InterCity* use, changing liveries as the sector branding changed.

The Brush-designed Class 56 was made for hauling heavy coal trains. Its superstructure was a simplified version of the D1500/class 47 series; omission of roof ventilator cowlings made the cab dome more pronounced on this locomotive. Electroputere of Romania built the first batch, which began operating in 1976. Production was afterwards continued by British Rail Engineering Limited at Doncaster. This engine is seen in a later livery, discussed in Chapter Six.

Away from the main lines

By the mid-1970s Passenger Transport Executives, those sections of local authorities providing travel services across urban areas and conurbations, needed new rolling stock, without wanting to pay the cost of traditional rail vehicles. As the main builder, and certainly the main customer of railway vehicles in Britain, British Rail began to address these needs by taking a bespoke design of diesel multiple-unit and exploring cheaper options. We will consider the bespoke multiple-unit first.

Class 210 diesel train when new.

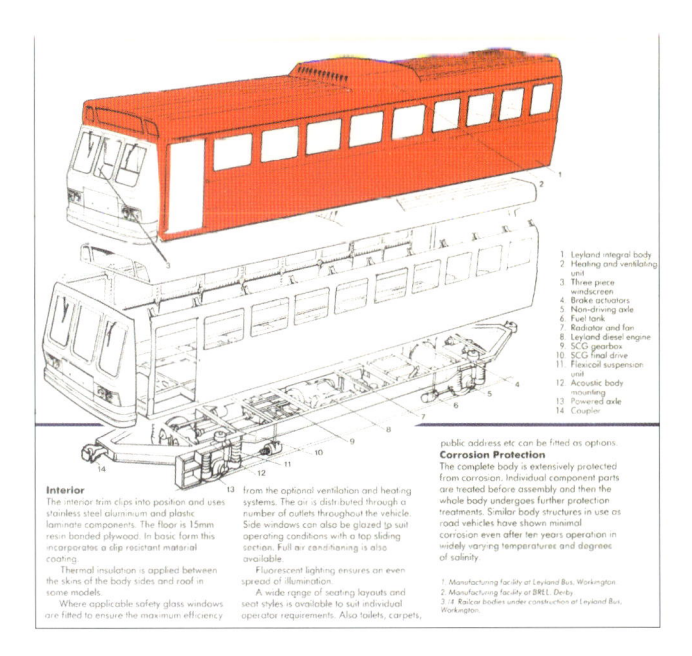

The British Rail-Leyland railbus combined road vehicle body and rail chassis.

Class 210 diesel multiple-unit

Tested in 1981, the class 210 was to be a universal replacement for the original DMUs on commuter services and in busy urban areas. It would also allow older fleets to be moved to other routes. With a body based on the Mark 3 carriage, unit end styling was of the same square, unresolved appearance as that used by the class 317/1 and 455/8 EMUs discussed below. Following Southern Region DEMU practice, the 210 had an engine compartment behind one driving cab. Sliding doors were passenger operated. Operating in service from 1982 until the mid-1980s, the three-car (210.002) and four-car (210.001) trains were found to be over complex, and therefore uneconomical to build and maintain in the numbers required by British Rail and the Passenger Transport Executives.

Road to rail

Fortunately innovation at British Rail took different forms: a radical alternative to the class 210 was the bus on wheels, or railbus, project which commenced in 1976. Buses adapted for railway use had proved a cheap alternative to railway vehicles throughout the twentieth century; the General Motors *Aerotrain* of the mid–1950s had utilised bus bodies in an attempt to create an upmarket passenger service. The British Rail railbus project beginning in the 1970s is a story which inverts the account of the *Advanced Passenger* and *High Speed Trains*, because here the conventional solution - class 210 - was rejected in favour of a novel concept derived from *Advanced Passenger Train* research. Evolving through five types - classes 140 to 144 - the railbus was effective for lines where economy was a major factor in maintaining a social railway service. A second more conventional diesel multiple-unit - class 150 - was developed for better resourced routes. Leyland Bus and Truck, part of the state-owned British Leyland group, had created a special factory at Workington, Cumbria, in 1971 to mass produce a single-deck bus called the *National*, which it supplied to many regional bus operators within the similarly state-owned National Bus Company. Planned for high volume output across a limited range of vehicle types, Workington offered semi-automated equipment and streamlined processes for body assembly, painting and fitting-out. During 1976 British Rail Engineering asked Leyland to identify a lightweight passenger vehicle body for mounting on a chassis originally developed for four-wheel high speed freight vehicles.[57] Making railbuses would be efficient, and hopefully bring new business to British Leyland as other work declined. Leyland's development team included Basil Hancock and Mike Cornish.[58]

R1

Initially the Leyland *National* bus was adopted in near-original form. In 1977 the Workington plant made up a twelve-metre-long steel body from two identical modular bus front ends, each of four short *National* bay modules riveted together including the single driving position, windscreens, bus-type air operated folding doors, and seats for forty people - all under a ribbed aluminium alloy roof. Arriving at British Rail Engineering, Derby in January 1978, the body was placed onto the high speed freight vehicle chassis. This unpowered hybrid was tested on rails for performance and stability at speeds up to 100mph. Identified as the 'alternative technology experiment', it was made public in June of the same year.

LEV 1

Deemed a success, R1 was fitted with a British Leyland diesel power unit and second driving position; the ten-metre long body was strengthened to meet the government's Railway Inspectorate safety standards. By late 1979 it was referred to as LEV 1, or *Leyland Experimental Vehicle*.[59] LEV 1 travelled to the United States early in 1980 for demonstration tests, and operated in Britain as a research vehicle. A specially formed BRE-Leyland joint venture called Associated Rail Technologies marketed the unit internationally. Glossy brochures noted the technical achievements and stated that the railbuses could be produced for various track gauges, with optional extras including a bar module with cooking facilities. After LEV 1 all units were built to a length of 15 metres. LEV 1 resulted in an order for another experimental single-car unit to be sent to the United States, coded R3.01, or LEV 2. Constructed by Wickhams of Ware in 1980, the 15.3 metre-long body featured cab fronts of the Leyland *National* bus Mk 2 design. It operated on the Boston & Maine Railroad.

Railbus LEV1 on a test run in England, 1979.

Interior of the LEV1 vehicle.

R3.02, R3.03

Further testing of the single-car idea generated R3.02 and R3.03 in 1980, both derived from R3.01. R3.03 was shown at the UITP conference in Dublin in 1981, and operated as a demonstration vehicle.[80] After service with British Rail it was sold to Northern Ireland Railways in 1982. From the interest generated by R3.01, an order was placed in 1984 for another single-car demonstration vehicle, identified as 'USA'. It shared the appearance of the Class 141, but had doors fitted to each corner.

R3.03 railbus as demonstration vehicle, Derby, 1981.

R3.03 in Northern Ireland Railways livery, circa 1982.

'USA' railbus in north America, 1984.

Class 140 (R2)

This unique two-car train was built in 1980 to develop the railbus concept as a multiple-unit. It included a passenger toilet and gangway connection. Replacing the *National* bus cabs, unit fronts for the 140 were built to offer the levels of impact protection required for railway operation. Their flat, functional appearance did nothing to complement the body sides, or to suggest they had been considered by a designer. Nevertheless the high, square form with two-part windows was reprised in the more sophisticated designs of multiple-unit classes 313, 315 and 508. Class 140 proved too sophisticated for cheap mass production; it remained a one-off.

Class 140 two-car railbus.

Interior of the class 140, August 1981.

199

Class 141 (R4)

Made for operation by British Rail with the West Yorkshire Passenger Transport Executive, class 141 was the first production run of the British Rail Engineering-Leyland Railbus project. It followed the class 140 gangwayed two-car-with-toilet arrangement and aspects of model R3. Reordering of the bus assembly system at Workington enabled railway vehicles to be welded and riveted together on automotive production line principles using semi-skilled workers. Bodies painted in spray booths before fitting out and trimming as complete cars gave consistently high standards of finish. Glass reinforced plastic fronts used the same windows as class 140 and other British Rail vehicles of the period, placed into a compressed wedge form between *National* bus destination indicator and lamp clusters. During 1983–84 twenty sets were assembled. From Workington, bodies moved by road transport to Derby for attaching to the chassis.

A class 141 railbus unit in service at Huddersfield, about 1985.

Interior of the class 141, February 1983. The bus heritage is very evident.

In an attempt to secure more business for the Workington factory during a period of austerity, three demonstration vehicles were produced for export. All were based on class 141. One two-car set with high-density seating was built in 1983 for use in Thailand, Malaysia and Singapore (top and middle); it was of sufficient interest for Malayan Railways (KTM) to order a set of railbuses from the Hungarian railway vehicle builder Ganz-MÁVAG, using superstructures made by the Ikarus bus factory. A single unit demonstration went to Denmark in 1984 (above left and right), before moving to Sweden, Norway, West Germany, Holland and Canada. Another is reported to have operated in Greece. Some class 141 units were later sold to Iran for further use.

Class 142 (R5) Pacer

A drawback of the R series prototypes and class 141 units was the narrow (2.5-metre) width of the body modules. By adjusting the framing system of the *National* bus body, engineers increased the transverse dimension to meet the usual British Rail passenger coach standard of 2.81 metres. Now the seating arrangement could be adjusted from double seats either side of the aisle to triple seats and double seats. British Leyland adapted a production line it had used for *Titan* buses to make fifty class 142 sets for use around Greater Manchester, Devon and Cornwall and north-west England. First examples were delivered to British Rail in March 1985, with test runs in June of the same year. Besides the widened body, windows and seats remained of the bus type. Glass reinforced cab fronts fitted over a steel crash structure. The fronts indicated more careful design input than for previous railbuses: mouldings in the side panels were continued around below the windscreens, and lamp clusters were aligned with a grille for the air horns. Driving positions were improved too, with cab side doors omitted. In 1986, 46 additional two-car units were manufactured as class 142/1.

Interior of the prototype class 142 railbus, 1984.

Unit 142001 in Greater Manchester Passenger Transport Executive livery.

202

British Rail sketch for the class 142, undated.

Top: Promotional brochure for class 142 trains.

Above: There were two further Leyland Railbus projects, neither of which went into production. A double-deck version was proposed, presumably using a Leyland bus body. More radical was the 'night coach', where extended bus superstructures would be assembled onto redundant Mk I coach underframes, to provide high-density, low-cost student travel in competition with road coaches. One prototype was built.[61]

Left: Class 142 units working at York, August 1988.

203

Transport for the suburbs

Electrification offered clean and efficient transport. British Rail wished to press ahead with the extensive programme it had planned in 1948, but implemented only in fragments after that time. Suburban systems around London and other big cities were obvious subjects for conversion to either third rail or overhead power supply. Where this conversion was not regarded as economically viable, old diesel multiple-units had to be superseded. These schemes, and aged rolling stock, brought a demand for new rolling stock.

Second iteration of the suburban multiple-unit, 1970.

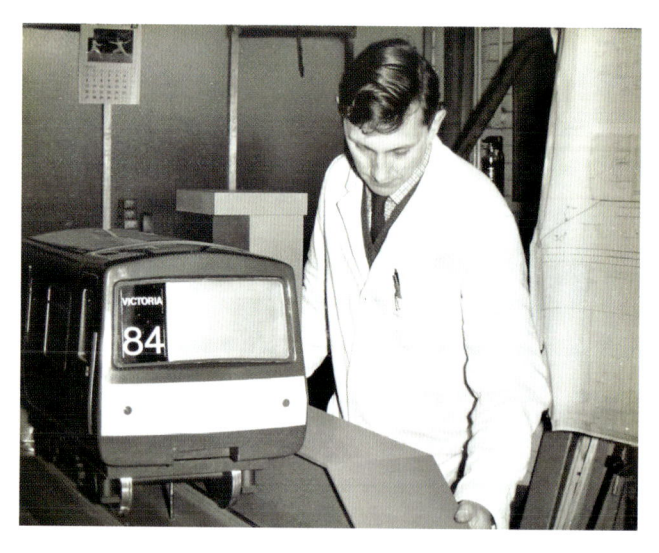

Early model by Wilkes & Ashmore of a suburban train for the Southern Region, about 1966.

Interior mock-up for the high-density suburban train, November 1969.

Above: Southern Region high-density train, with the addition of a corridor connection to the cab front, March 1970

Right: Full-size prototype Southern Region '4 PEP' multiple-unit, May 1980.

204

British Railways' Eastleigh Works had ceased production of passenger vehicles in 1963. When the Southern Region inaugurated plans for a high-density electric multiple-unit with sliding doors in the late 1960s, Wilkes & Ashmore produced a model, and a mock-up was built at Doncaster. It had to appear as modern as its technology was innovative. The unit fronts grew out of a trend for wedge forms, with a deep upper portion projecting forwards at the lower margin, from which the front made a short return. In early 1968, York rail engineers constructed a working prototype to explore the concept. A single wedge on the mock-up became an arrangement of two prisms when a cab centre door was added. The styling detail of enlarging the apparent window size by painting black panels around the glass, which was to be applied to much of British Rail's rolling stock a decade later, was introduced with the train. Vertical chamfers - a means of matching the curved carriage side profile to the square ends - were new too, and copied for several subsequent classes built before and since privatisation. Complete 2- and 4-car units were delivered to the Southern Region during July 1971–June 1972. Produced in unpainted aluminium with red double arrow symbols, 2-car PEP (class 446, unit 2001) ran in passenger service until August 1974, and formed a test unit for development of the class 313. Stored afterwards at the Derby works, one of the last uses for 2001 was testing a planned Network SouthEast livery. The 4-car prototypes (class 445 PEP, units 4001 and 4002) operated in Rail Blue until withdrawal in May 1977.[62]

It was envisaged that PEP type trains would be used on all electrified lines across Britain. This did not happen, but derivatives of the PEP did go into service. Electric multiple-units of classes 313 (1976, for electrification of the Great Northern line in London), 507 (1978, for the London Midland Region), 314 (1979, for Glasgow suburban routes), 508 (1979, for Merseyside but first operated on the Southern Region) and 315 (1980, for Eastern Region London suburban services), were all developed from the PEP.

These units abandoned the flat roof profile of the prototypes, using instead the roof curve to soften the cab front design. In further contrast to the class 445/446, where the wedge form was made using flat sheets of metal, the production cab ends were flat, enclosed by peripheral mouldings angled forward in the horizontal plane to create a recess for the central door; this version shares its appearance with multiple-units prototyped for the Washington Metropolitan Area Transit Authority in early 1970. All window corners were radiused. The centre cab door was painted black, producing two apparently separate yellow panels. Head and tail lights were arranged horizontally. Chamfering of carriage corners, first seen on the PEP units, was continued for these units.

British Rail Engineering developed a common appearance for electric multiple-units of classes 317/1 (built from 1981 for the St Pancras–Bedford route) and 455/8 (for the Southern Region), and class 210 DMU. Carriage bodies were based on the Mk 3 coach design, with four pairs of passenger-operated sliding doors per coach. In the first batches (317/1, 455/8) the cab fronts were flat, with flattened roof domes creating awkward angular corners at cantrail level. A box moulded into the roof dome was intended to contain a roller blind showing the destination, but it was not used. Windows either side of the corridor gangway connections resembled those fitted to the class 141 DMU, having square upper corners and rounded lower corners. Window surrounds were framed in black against the all-yellow fronts.

For Southern Region classes 455/7 (built 1984), 317/2 (built 1985–86), 455/9 (1985) and class 318 (1986, for Scottish Region Ayrshire suburban services), the cab front design was improved by curving the roof-cab margin, and adding a projecting perimeter to the top and side of the cab.

Detail of the fibreglass cab front on a class 313 train, developed from the PEP design.

Class 313 unit 002 in original livery scheme.

Features of a class 313 interior, 2016.

Comparison of class 455/7 rounded front and class 455/8 squared-off front, London Waterloo, May 1985.

Above: Proposal for the revised appearance of class 455 units.

Right: Launch leaflet for the class 455 trains, January 1985.

Introduction of Class 455 sliding door trains in the South London Suburban area

Squared-off cab front of the first class 317 units, July 1983.

207

Unobserved detail

We conclude this chapter by reviewing some of the smaller, but no less important aspects of railway renewal. Catering on trains and at stations had relied on ceramic and glass vessels since the railways began. By the early 1960s plastics came to dominate food service in the airline industry, answering a need for regulation of meal sizes - 'portion control' - and easy transhipment of provisions. Terrestrial cafes and restaurants were impressed by the reliability and convenience of plastic products. Washing-up of articles, and the drudgery of such employment, could largely be eliminated because used plastic and paper packaging, utensils and food waste were placed in crushing machines for onward disposal. British Rail appreciated the opportunity plastic presented, to place its modernised image into the hands of every passenger. Martyn Rowlands, a pioneer of plastics in industrial design, created prototypes for a beaker, tray and cutlery using clear, smoked and opaque plastic. *Advanced Passenger Train* customers enjoyed meals served in an entire set of bespoke plastic vessels shaped by British Rail's Department of Industrial Design. Like the objects themselves, the high quality of design was transient; private companies such as *Maxpax* developed branded cups pre-filled with a teabag or coffee grounds, as stock for drinks dispensers in many different industries. Today this remains the general practice.

Staff dress remained relatively unchanged through the 1970s, with some interesting exceptions. In 1973 the uniform insignia was changed to a larger, three-dimensional double arrow cap badge fixed without any coloured backing.[63] Collar flashes, which had been found to snag on clothing, were replaced by cast plastic rectangles containing the symbol, presented in silver or gold. Trials of new attire made in 1978 resulted in new outfits issued from 1981. Changes to the design reflected fashion more generally, with jackets being cut to a casual shape, and the quasi-military metal badges and braid replaced by bands of red, blue, metallic silver or gold coloured cloth.[64]

Cup and tray for British Rail by expert designer in plastics Martyn Rowlands, August 1969.

Prototype disposable plastic British Rail cutlery by Martyn Rowlands, August 1969.

Pre-filled instant coffee drink product served on British Rail trains during the 1970s and 1980s.

Blouson Jacket
Blue Collar Blue Bands
Senior Railmen and Chargemen

Blouson Jacket
Red Collar Red Bands
Railmen and Leading Railmen

Leaflet of 1978 announcing the programme for testing a revised uniform. The essential features of the 1966 Design Research Unit clothing remain, softened into more relaxed form. Metal insignia is replaced by cloth, and metallic colours by blue and red.

Publicity, tickets and timetables

Because most printed materials directed at the public were commissioned from local design agencies working with their own preferred printing companies, very few items were wholly revised to meet Corporate Identity guidelines beyond featuring the British Rail logotype in various forms. Printing technology advances made it possible for photography to replace typography as the main medium for creating images. British Rail realised publicity must be changed to increase its customer base, and to promote cheap fares, holidays and all of the innovations which would otherwise be unnoticed by the public. In 1965 it could be observed that 'a cardinal rule for all BR publicity offices these days is that graphic publicity must always feature the young, upcoming executive, thoroughly "with it" in dress, or the young family. The railway must always be projected as the discerning travel choice of the modern generation.'[65] An icon of the 1967–69 Inter-City campaign to attract youth was the character 'Monica'. Represented in her most well-known, blonde-haired, form by actress Phoebe Shaw, 'Monica' attracted a fan club of teenagers wanting to imitate her style of dress.

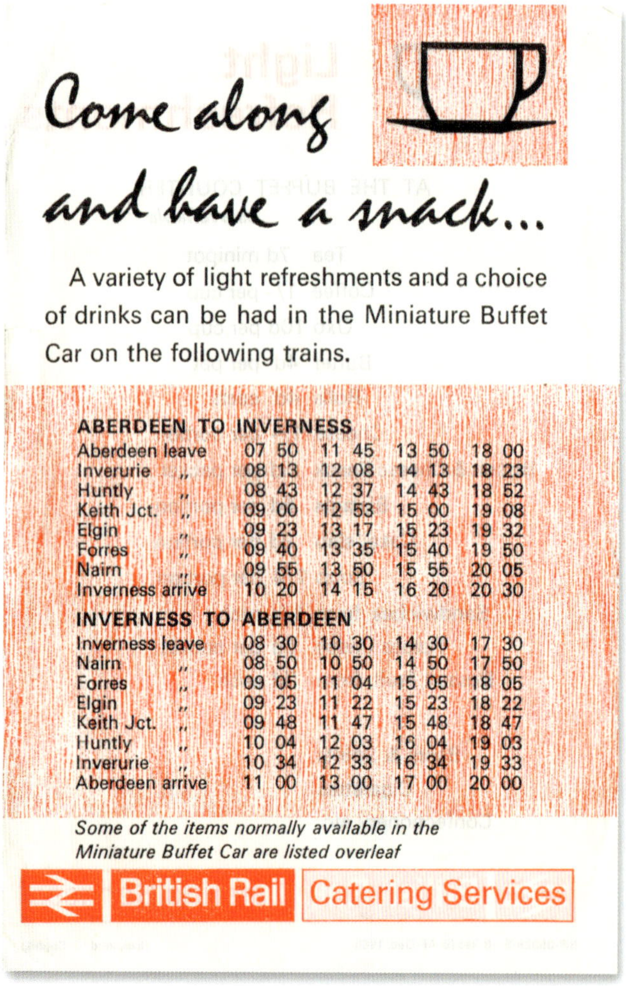

MODERN RAILWAYS

MARCH 70

4/-

See a friend this weekend

Inter-City makes the going easy
(and the coming back)

212

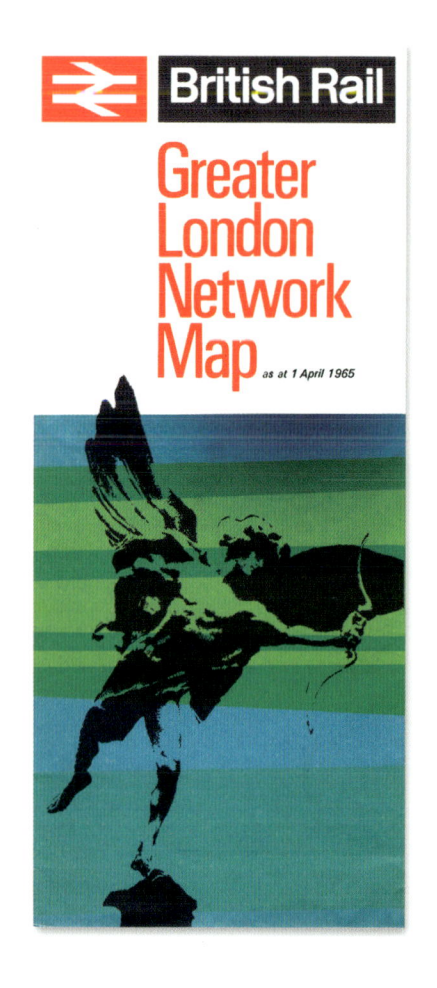

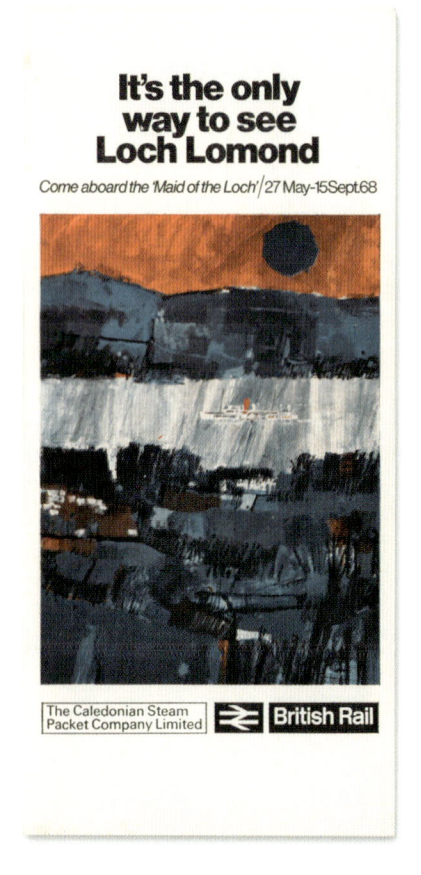

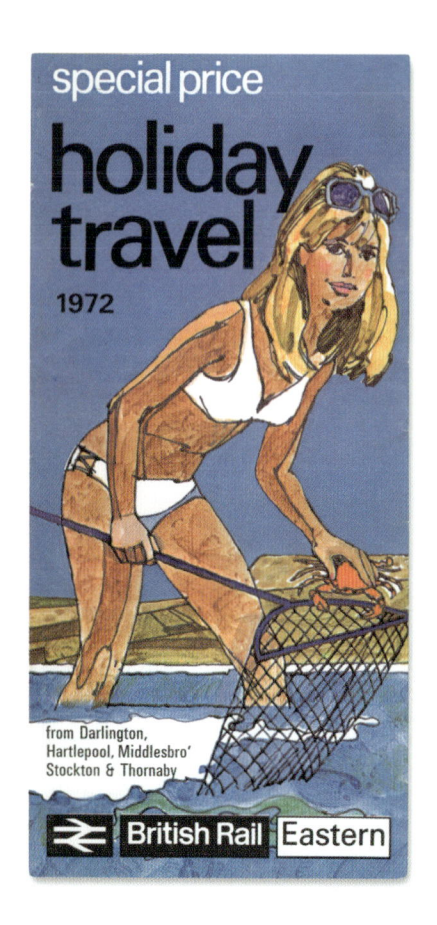

Summer days..

Sea-river-country
So easy by train

British Rail Western Region

Get this ticket*

and the freedom of Scotland

British Rail

take a bargain break

Travel bargains from London
King's Cross, Liverpool Street, and Fenchurch Street
from 5 October 1970

British Rail Eastern

Golden Rail
Personal Choice Holidays 1974

The easy way to take a holiday at any time of the year!

Summer Railaway '75

An invitation to view Lake Windermere in watercolours

SUMMER SCHEDULE 1980

Sealink WINDERMERE

213

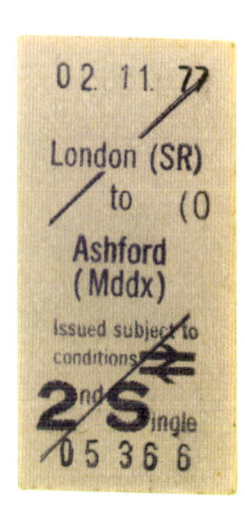

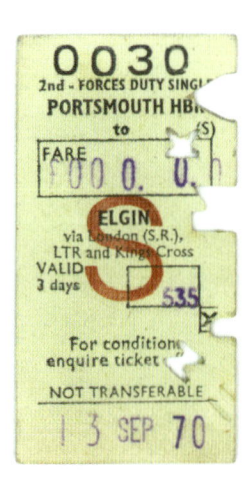

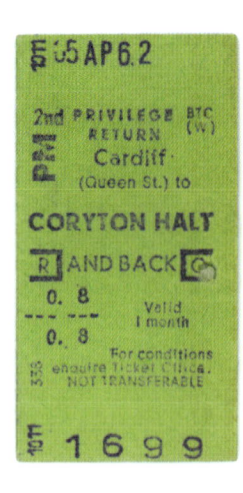

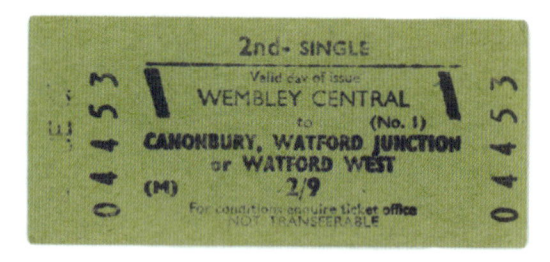

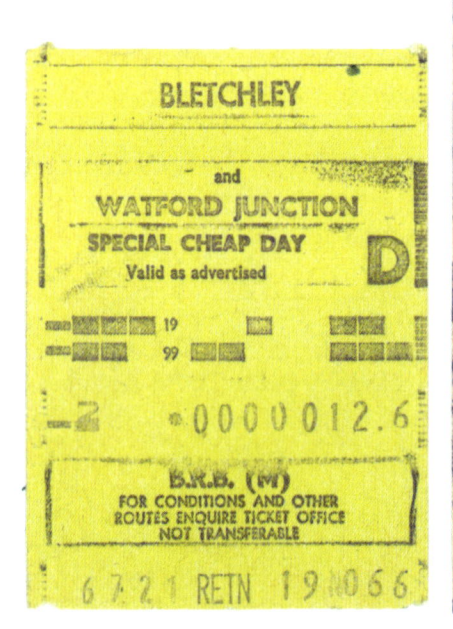

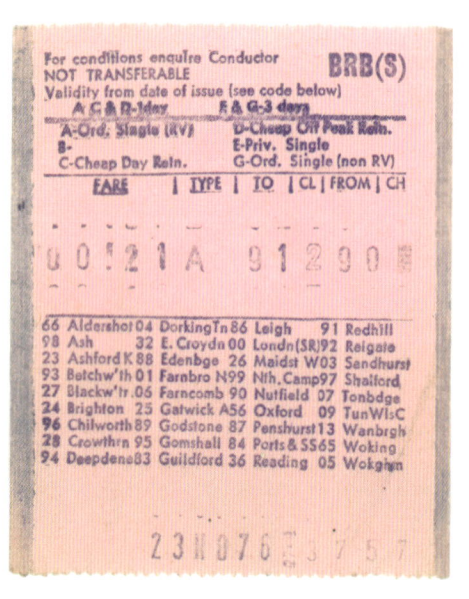

Easily overlooked paper and card tokens for travel, tickets are tiny pieces of machine-made graphic design. Printed in their millions by letterpress techniques, there was a ticket for most journeys, and several levels of fare. Variety did not offer flexibility however, because large stocks of printed objects required space, security, and meticulous accounting. Gradually British Railways acquired semi-automated, but not yet computerised machinery to save on production and staff costs. Beyond the Southern Region, station based equipment changed the appearance of the card ticket to show different elements of information. On trains, portable issuing devices dispensed paper tickets, again using codes to communicate their validity. Uniquely, the Southern Region introduced a one piece ticket in October 1969.[66] Pre-printed with origin and destination, these were of traditional size, but with the information arranged vertically in a rational, modern format. These tickets were validated by insertion into a specially adapted cash register which impressed the issuing point as a three digit code, priced and dated them.[67] Accounting and selling were simplified; litter was reduced, because return tickets did not need to be torn in half. A larger one-piece ticket appeared on other regions in 1973.[68] Mechanically-printed tickets remained the main form of travel authority until computerisation began to have an impact in the mid-1980s.

214

215

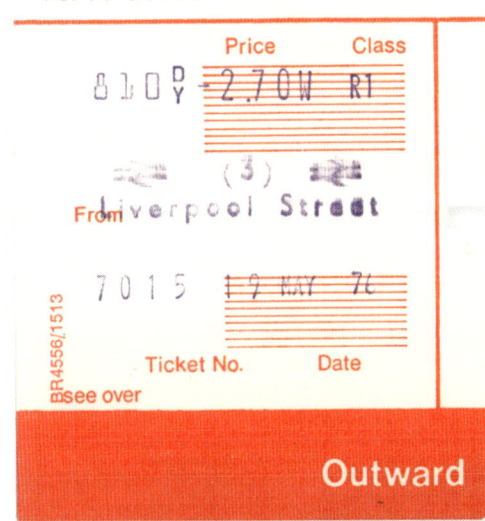

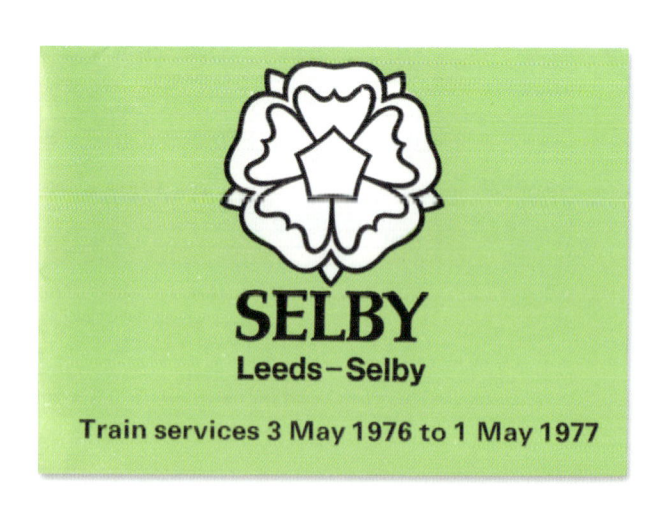

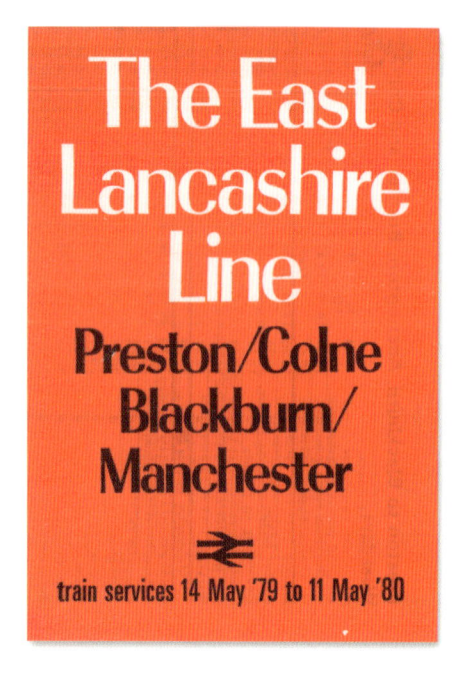

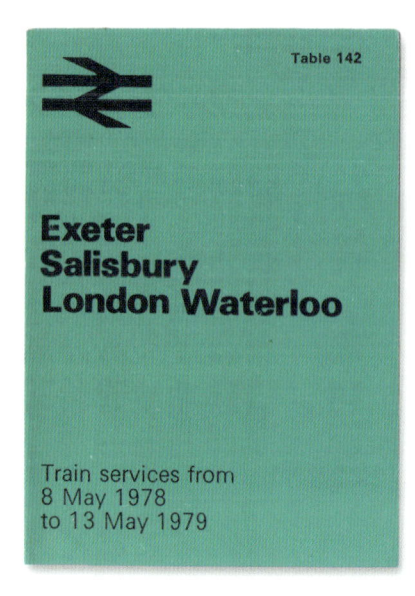

From 1978 the format of pocket timetables was changed. At first, it was a matter of the covers becoming a single colour. Then, to promote particular routes for community and tourist programmes, pictorial details were added as references to the local identity: the first small signs of a drift away from the unified corporate image.

Corporate identity: the legacy

Nostalgia for the 'Rail Blue era' has grown among enthusiasts and modellers in recent years, following a period during the 1980s when the visual impact of modernisation was regarded by many as a nadir in transport design. Neither position reminds us that when new, the achievements of British Rail gained considerable influence - giving a particularly British form of European design back to Europe. The state railway systems in West Germany, the Netherlands, Austria, Norway, Denmark, France and Switzerland all adopted aspects of this comprehensive transport design strategy. The sharing of good practice was reciprocal: Denmark and Norway adopted the lettering designed by Jock Kinneir and Margaret Calvert for British Rail; in time the red of Danish Railways would form a major part of railway corporate identity across Scotland, and the south, west and midlands of England. In the next chapter, we will see how increasingly concerted efforts to move away from a single corporate image once more changed the public face of British Rail.

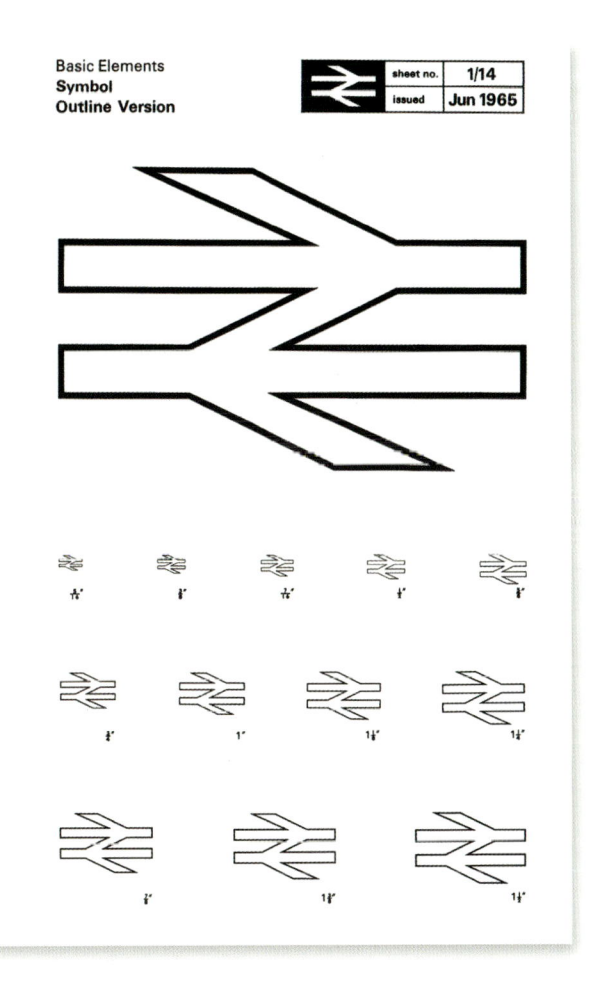

217

Chapter 6 →
The new look: Design diversity and privatisation 1982–97

Britain had returned the Conservative Party to government in 1979. An agenda for this, and indeed subsequent administrations, was the transfer of state controlled monopolies to private ownership. In the early 1980s, British Rail was a monolith looking for ways to move beyond the institutional appearance of its 1965 corporate identity, which by this time had become staid and shabby. It was recognised that the railways could no longer operate to their own standards of appearance and service, but must be updated again to match the rapid improvements in other industries such as retail, private car and air travel. To enhance performance and revenue, the division of British Rail services commenced in 1982, and was largely complete by 1988. Separating the railway into sectors would, it was understood, make management and design more responsive to the needs of different customer groups. For the government, a single corporate image was too reminiscent of centralised control in a period when the state divesting itself of direct responsibility for industry. The new commercial entities - InterCity, London & South East, Provincial, Parcels, and Railfreight - would each require new design work for buildings, uniforms and trains; the single Design Research Unit livery and corporate identity, comprehensive and consistent since 1965, would come to an end.[1]

Under British Rail Chairman Sir Robert Reid, joint managing director of British Rail and Design Panel chairman Jim O'Brien advocated design as an essential tool for bringing state-owned activities to a point where they would be as viable as the private sector.[2] Director of Industrial Design James Cousins spent the last part of his railway career promoting management of design for the sectors. He tried to establish shared principles through the Panel, but it was evident that the sectors would gradually go in their own separate directions. In mitigation of these negative influences, Jim O'Brien linked the sector directors with the Design Panel; he renewed design policy by increasing the collaboration which Cousins had begun with Danish State Railways (DSB). DSB's Jens Nielsen

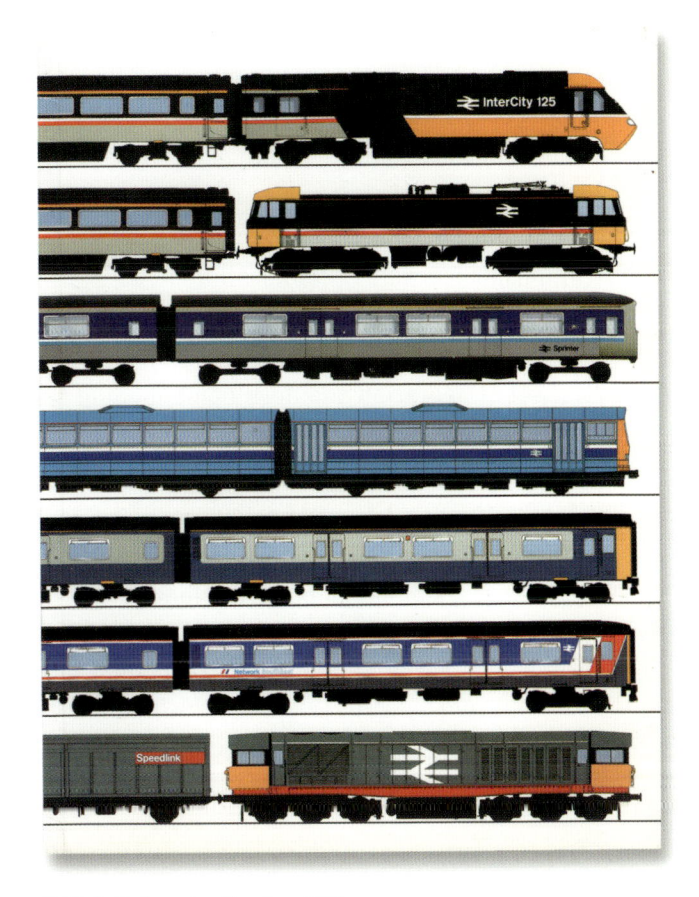

British Rail sector liveries, 1986.

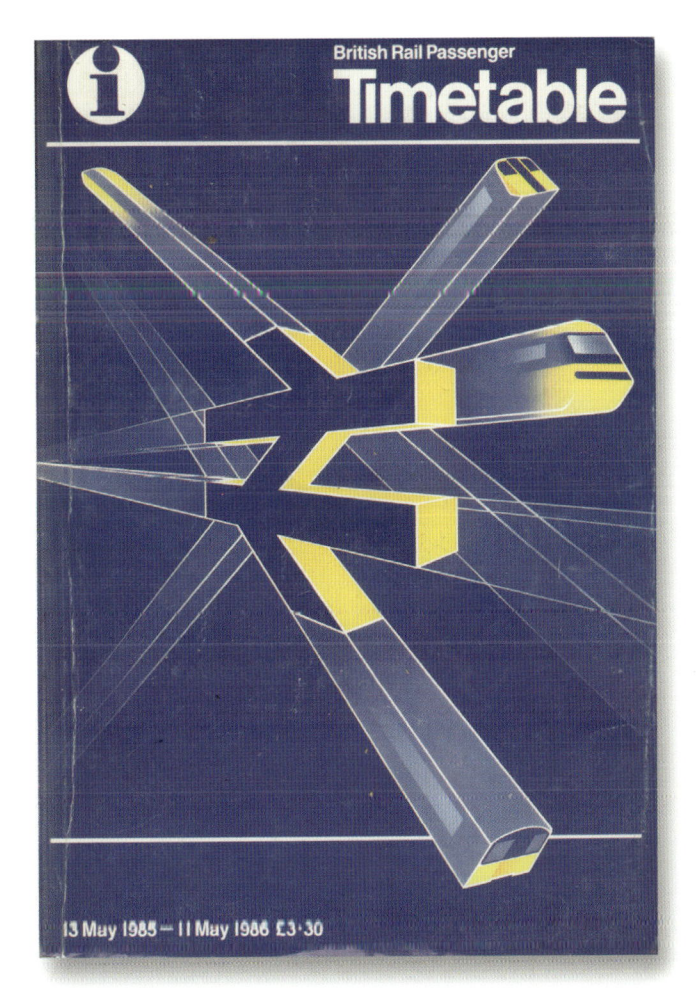

controlled all matters of design, enabling him to bring much greater consistency to a much smaller railway network. The bright red book of Danish railway design published in association with James Cousins and Jens Nielsen, would become an important point of reference for British Rail, and particularly the ScotRail and Network SouthEast brands, as it reinvented its image once more.[3] O'Brien ran a design conference in January 1986 to consider how every aspect of operation and development could be improved by design following DSB examples. Dr John Prideaux spoke for InterCity, and Chris Green for the London & South East sector.

In 1991, three years ahead of privatisation, Chairman Bob (later Sir Bob) Reid issued an optimistic report outlining potential developments for 'a vibrant modern railway entering the next decade.'[4] Three sectors encompassed the entire passenger system: InterCity, Network SouthEast, and Regional Railways. A fourth sector called European Passenger Services, looked ahead to high speed services between London and the continent. Reid's upbeat forecast echoed the sentiments of previous chairmen, noting past successes and galvanising the workforce to further challenges. There was a clear hint to a radically different prospect too, as he noted 'this document does not deal with ownership...consultation will make clear the impact of any change on the future activity and development plans of what must be a high quality rail network and service by the turn of the century.'[5]

Guide to the corporate identity of Danish State Railways, produced in partnership with British Rail's own Industrial Design directorate, 1986.

A new voice

Government reduced the subsidy to British Rail in the mid-1980s. The organisation was forced to look to other travel industries across Europe for ideas. It realised design was an essential priority, if it were to persuade public and politicians that it could compete and be good value. Because the task of transforming the railway system was so big and complex, in November 1986 Dr Jane Priestman was recruited from the British Airports Authority, where she had achieved an extraordinary transformation in the passenger experience.[6] Her work of the previous eleven years at British Airports Authority and in extensive independent practice, meant Priestman was aware of how design mattered at every scale and in every detail, from interiors to landscaping, waiting rooms to driving cabs. Personally, she wanted to make using British Rail a nicer encounter, and wanted to show that railways could again be successful through good design. Desirable sentiments indeed, but after the Kings Cross fire of 1987 and Clapham rail crash of 1988, intentions became imperatives as British Rail was forced to increase its attention to making passenger environments safer and easier to use. To give Priestman effective power, she was made Director of a merged Department of Architecture, Design and Environment. The complexity of Priestman's task emerged in the extensive press coverage around her appointment. Five business sectors, each establishing their own identities, needed to be related to the idea of a single organisation, but would also need to be perceived as attractive stand-alone units as privatisation approached. Priestman had to salvage the essence of the 1965 British Rail Corporate Identity, and supersede it with something new. In advancing the strategy of serving the public's needs in precedence over those of the railway, she would face the industry establishment and its time-honoured ways of working.

By 1988 British Rail's Industrial Design Department was occupied on hundreds of projects. In the new business environment it could neither cope with this many tasks, nor was it felt desirable for an in-house group to author so much work. The department

Jane Priestman, circa 1986.

was reduced in size and refocused on the sectors, adopting the then vogue for becoming design managers working with external consultants. This was expected to be more economical and secure the best outcomes across the sectors' brand, graphics and industrial design needs. Eventually all design was to be handled externally, directed by Priestman or chief architect Rodney Taylor, with Tony Howard for industrial design, trains and environments, Nick Derbyshire for architecture, and Tony Skeggs for graphics. Jane Priestman substantially altered the way design was managed: 'we shall restructure the department so that an increasing amount of work is undertaken by outside design consultants, managed by a core of design professionals within BR.'[7] Services offered by the department included a database of design projects, design awareness training, project management and control of design standards to ensure unity of appearance for each sector. Relationships were developed with consultants: DCA Design, Jones Garrard, Roundel Design and Newell & Sorrell contributed important work which revived the image of the railways. In five years, incrementally, Jane Priestman worked to move British Rail from the homogenous image it had acquired in the 1970s, to a consistently-designed system as smart as any in Europe. Changes were made where they would be most evident: in the transformation of major termini, and the creation of graphics to quickly rebrand fleets including InterCity and Railfreight. Design management policy for a railway heading into privatisation would eventually be diminished: the everyday work of a design department was lost, and consideration for the details of small schemes fell away.

This chapter is structured in sequence by sector: InterCity, London & South East/Network SouthEast, Provincial/Regional Railways, Railfreight, and Parcels/Rail express systems. Each section follows the pattern of considering corporate design, livery, locomotives and rolling stock, architectural and product design, and uniform where this was included in the changes to sector identities.

Inter-City becomes InterCity

British Rail's high-speed rail services had taken on competition from air travel in the 1960s. The Inter-City brand inspired other rail operators around the world to adopt the same name for their own trains. Continuing to develop during the 1970s with the advent of the *High Speed Train*, which was itself promoted as InterCity 125, by the 1980s the brand's success indicated further business growth: it just needed to step out from the image of British Rail. Led by Cyril Bleasdale from 1982, Inter-City operated the routes which made the most profit for British Rail: the East Coast and West Coast Main Lines between London and Scotland, the trunk routes between London, South Wales and the West Country, London and Sheffield, Cross Country between the Midlands and west, routes into East Anglia and the *Gatwick Express* between London Victoria and the airport. Railway managers thought about ways to raise the profile and image of this, the prestige passenger sector. Targeting business travellers and those making leisure journeys too, Inter-City employed every marketing ploy from glamorous posters to television commercials featuring television personalities, and discounted fares publicised with glossy leaflets.

By 1985 the sector name Inter-City had been modernised by the simple but inspired removal of a hyphen: InterCity. This was synchronised with a typographic trend of the time to put brand names together with intermediate capital letters: Network SouthEast would be another example. *Pullman* prestige services were recommenced too. To replace the generic Rail Blue and Rail Grey livery of passenger trains, a new colour scheme of red, white, beige and grey had been adapted from the *APT-P* (class 370) in summer 1983.

Dr John Prideaux directed the InterCity sector 1986–92. Government instituted a policy of giving InterCity no subsidy at all. Every effort would be needed to obtain profitability. Research showed that

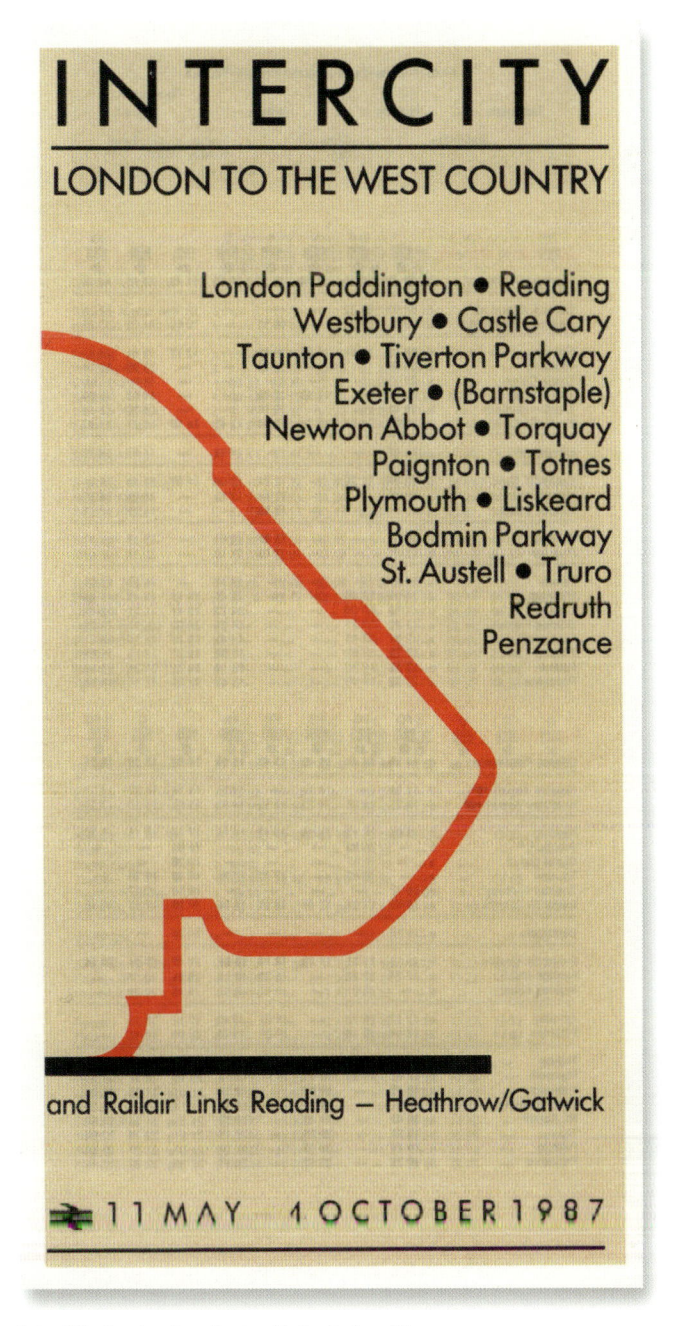

InterCity begins to adopt a distinct visual image.

InterCity had a better public reputation than British Rail, making it sensible to foreground the sector name as the brand. Prideaux wanted good design to state a single message, that his sector was the 'best, fastest, most civilised way to travel centre to centre.'[8] James Cousins gave him a presentation of the many different ways that the sector was being marketed, saying 'you need a brand which speaks of quality, you need to lose all this inconsistency.'[9] Aesthetic, kinaesthetic, and sensory design would be applied to the whole InterCity travel environment. The train livery was adjusted - the grey darkened to match John Prideaux's request for a shade like 'the colour of a black cat's fur when wet'.[10] Designers Newell and Sorrell were introduced by Jane Priestman, who had worked with them at BAA. They completed the removal of the InterCity sector from the shadow of British Rail's reputation, when they created a new logotype with swallow bird motif. The swallow represented a softer image, described as 'freedom, speed, excellence and style'.[11] Premium marketing products took a rich maroon colour; timetables included maroon and grey. National television advertising bolstered efforts to reposition InterCity; the 42 second 'Relax' commercial of 1988, directed by Tony Kaye for Saatchi & Saatchi, conjured an entirely fresh view of railway travel, and secured several prestigious awards.

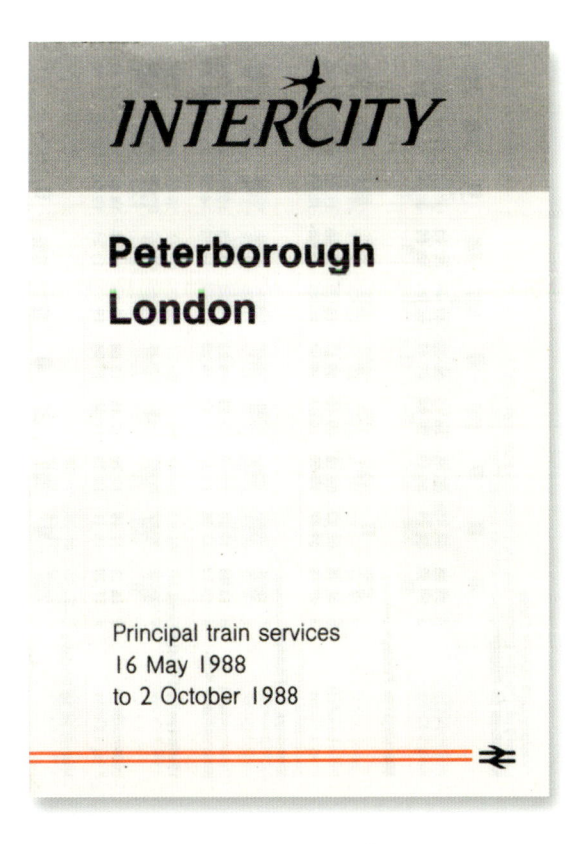

InterCity branding developed by Newell & Sorrell, as a logotype, and on a pocket timetable card.

223

Locomotives and passenger vehicles

Developed from electric locomotive class 87/1, and with a body superstructure by DCA Design (formerly David Carter Associates), the class 90 was also made by British Rail Engineering at Crewe. Introduced in 1988, these locomotives were paired with Mark II and Mark 3 passenger coaches, and a Mark 3 Driving Van Trailer (DVT) a non-motored vehicle with operating cab and luggage/parcel storage space.

Electrification of the East Coast Main Line would need new rolling stock. The InterCity 125 *High Speed Train* (*HST*), itself an evolution of the 'Blue Pullman' multiple-units, offered a successful model for future train formations, combining power, speed and efficiency. To give more flexibility, a 'push-pull' practice found favour, where an independent locomotive was attached to coaches, with a Driving Van Trailer at the other end of the formation. GEC/BREL-built *Electra* 225 class 91 Bo-Bo locomotives operated from 1989, working with up to eleven Mark 4 coaches and a Metro-Cammell Mark 4 Driving Van Trailer.[12] It would haul trains on the East and West Coast Main Lines, with the potential for speeds up to 140mph/225kph, and daily operation at 125mph. DCA Design worked on both *Electra* and the Brush class 9/class 9000 Bo-Bo-Bo locomotives operating *Le Shuttle* vehicle-carrying trains through the Channel Tunnel from 1992.[13] To meet the requirement of operation as a conventional locomotive, *Electra* was styled with

Class 89 locomotive 89001 *Avocet*. Designed by Kenneth Grange, the superstructure of this 125mph, electrically-powered prototype resembled two *High Speed Train* cabs placed back to back, with the somewhat ungainly addition of buffers. Built by British Rail Engineering at Crewe works, it had potential for use on Intercity 225 services, but was not put into production.[14]

224

one wedge-shaped cab front, which would normally face outwards from the unit when operating at high speed. The other cab front was flat, allowing it to match more closely the profile of the passenger coaches, and to provide a second driving position at lower speeds of travel. Power would be taken by pantograph from overhead wires. A similar wedge-form front was adopted for the DVT. Livery for the locomotive and DVT matched the InterCity 'Executive' scheme, with panels of dark grey and red painted over a white ground, in a pattern to emphasise the profile of the cab fronts.

British Rail's own model for the *Electra* locomotive, 1986.

Class 91 91012 at York, undated.

Class 90 locomotive 90024 in InterCity 'Executive' livery, Carlisle, 1990.

Above: Mark 3 Driving Van Trailer 82101, August 1994.

Right: Brochure for the InterCity 225 trains powered by class 91 locomotives.

InterCity 125 *High Speed Train* Mark 3 standard class saloon interior, October 1991.

InterCity 225 Mark 4 standard class coach, October 1991.

InterCity Mark 4 *Pullman* coach.

Pullman version interior of the Mark 4 coach, for prestige business travel.

InterCity introduced sixty new Mk 3b coaches in 1985, and operated two hundred Mk 3a and HST refurbished coaches. For InterCity 225 trains, Mark 4 coaches - based on *Advanced Passenger Train* innovations - were built. Frances Sorrell specified subdued interior colour schemes - standard class: red and grey; first class: pink and grey - to harmonise with passenger spaces at stations, giving the sense of a seamless, high quality experience.

Stations

Important stations had facilities re-planned by InterCity for customer needs. Architects aimed for light colours and clean surfaces. Good lighting and increased visibility using glass walls, addressed concerns around passenger security. Displays of passenger information were improved. Historic buildings underwent restoration. *Pullman* lounges at Kings Cross and Euston termini - equipped with electronic business technology - represented a hybrid of home and office; more were rapidly added at main stations.

New apparel

Anne Tyrrell Design reviewed the railway uniforms issued to 55,000 employees. Her brief was to create smart, flexible, comfortable and fashionable outfits which would give staff confident authority. A core collection of clothing, augmented by a range of accessories to be chosen by the staff, was published in 1988 for a 1990 launch. Caroline Clayton created bespoke uniforms for InterCity On-Board Services staff.

Female station platform personnel.

Male supervisor not in contact with the public.

Above: Female supervisor not in contact with the public.

Left: InterCity uniforms for on-board crew designed by Caroline Clayton, 1991.

InterCity art

Brendan Neiland approached Jane Priestman in 1990 with the idea of using paintings as the basis for posters depicting major InterCity stations. Neiland used his interest in reflected and refracted images to create 'a feeling of space and light but also business and speed activity and noise'. His subjects included stations on the East Coast Main Line, Glasgow Central and Waterloo International.

InterCity separated into six train operating companies and *Gatwick Express* from 1 April 1994. Seen in retrospect, the project to establish InterCity as distinct from British Rail made it both an exemplary travel operator and, importantly, a widely recognised and respected consumer brand.

Painting by Brendan Neiland for the InterCity poster promoting Leeds, Yorkshire, as a travel destination.

London & South East/Network SouthEast

London & South East was a management unit with limited public visibility. Its main design statement was the publication in April 1985 of a brown and orange colour scheme which had been trialled from 1979, attributed to the typographic designer Herbert Spencer. Some multiple-unit passenger trains - classes 309, 411 and 421 - carried this livery.

Chris Green became Managing Director of London & South East in January 1986, having previously transformed the Scottish Region into ScotRail. Priorities for his new role would be the generation of leisure travel to take up spare off-peak capacity on this mainly commuter system, and an increase in revenue to counteract the ongoing reduction in state subsidy. Green's brief to his team was: 'tell London everything is going to change, fast, better.'[15] To provide coordinated promotion of London rail services, and so offer greater convenience to passengers, the sector required a comprehensive marketing review. The result would be Network SouthEast, a radical rebrand to unite railway services as far east as Kings Lynn and Harwich, in an arc around the south coast from Margate to Weymouth, and west towards Exeter. What is now the Paddington to Heathrow rail link was in course of development, with *CrossRail* and *Thameslink 2000* to enhance transport through London on east-west and north-south alignments. The planned Channel Tunnel route would institute high speed commuter services between London and southern England. Publicity - maps and posters - and new ticketing options would stimulate increased passenger volumes, whilst retail units took advantage of the increased use of stations to provide rental income. Launched on 10 June 1986, Network SouthEast was to be bright, efficient and as appealing to travellers as any high street, 'like making people see colour after black and white.'[16]

Ronnie McIntyre, the architect who worked with Chris Green to reinvent ScotRail, used Danish State Railway (DSB) design styling as an important reference.[17] Key to the DSB image was a bright, clean red hue, not dissimilar to British Rail's own Flame Red. Chris Green observed the positive feeling red imparted to ScotRail stations and at certain do-it-yourself warehouses. Red, white and blue seemed appropriately bright colours for Network SouthEast. On buildings and rolling stock, they responded well to the dusty environment of the railway, appearing clean even with less than ideal maintenance.

At Ashford, Kent, in March 1988, two 4CEP multiple-units carry the first Network SouthEast livery, and the London & South East sector colour scheme it replaced. The beige, orange and brown colours had been recommended by Herbert Spencer. John Robertshaw of Jordan Williams devised Network SouthEast's red, white and blue scheme.

Publicity and Livery

The corporate restyling was handled by advertising agency J Walter Thompson with brand designers Jordan Williams. Research showed the double arrow mark brought a negative perception of services. John Robertshaw created a red, blue and grey logo for the sector, based on three lozenges, two of identical size and one marginally narrower. This brand mark, colloquially called the 'rhombus', appeared on trains, and as part of a band along signs on station exteriors and platforms. Robertshaw also prepared a white livery for inner suburban trains, and blue for those on outer suburban routes. This was rejected in favour of one colour scheme for all trains, combining red, white and bright blue: appropriately British, and not directly associated with the colours of any previous British Rail region. On locomotives and multiple-units the first version of the livery was swept up at each end at a sharp angle, and embellished with the double arrow. After intervention by Jane Priestman, the upsweep changed to a curve, and the rhombus replaced the British Rail symbol. The shade of blue was darkened 'to be kinder to the countryside'.[18] All aspects of the brand were detailed in the *Network Design Guide* produced by assistant architect Michael Papps.[19]

Top: One of various trial Network SouthEast liveries, tested on a PEP vehicle in 1985.

Above: Class 50 50035 *Ark Royal* in the first approved locomotive paint scheme.

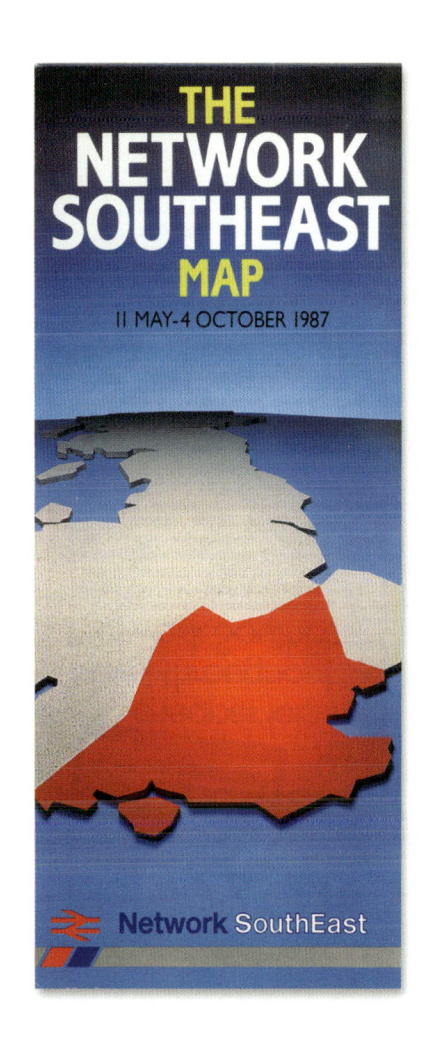

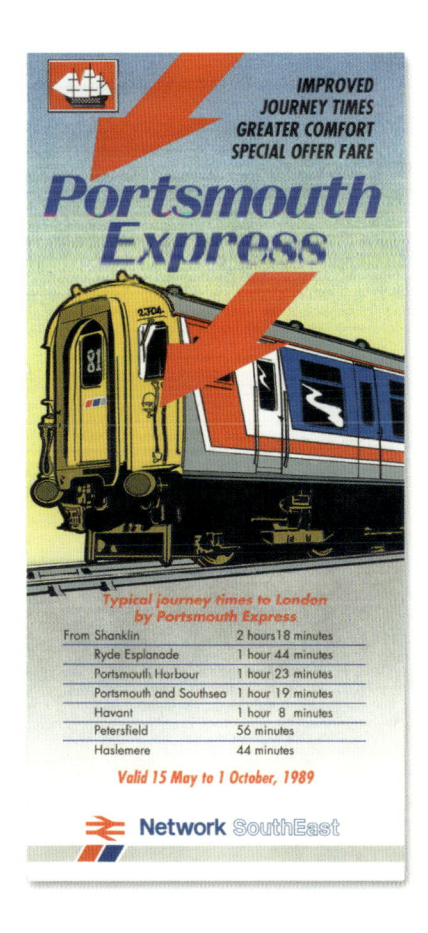

Like the London Underground diagram of lines, the Network SouthEast map drawn by Bernard Slatter promoted greater travel through showing good potential for interchange, and implied direct, convenient services. Folder leaflets were issued to advertise new all-London tickets like the One-Day Capitalcard, and cheap travel deals offered on 'Network Days' covered an area from the south west to eastern England.[20]

Network SouthEast achieved a notable success in their publicity activities, led by the red, white and blue colours of the brand. The sector's design environment was enhanced subtly, but comprehensively, by the artist Edward 'Eddie' Pond.[21] Pond had worked for Jane Priestman at the British Airports Authority. When Priestman became involved in the interiors of the class 442 *Wessex Electrics* multiple-units, Pond seemed a good choice for providing artworks in the passenger spaces. Pond and his design studio made murals fixed as *Perstorp Warerite* laminate panels on the coach bulkheads. Subjects for the illustrations were chosen to reflect the landscape and buildings along routes normally operated by the trains, from the Sussex and Hampshire coasts to the London suburbs, Home Counties and East Anglian countryside. Images followed for the 319 and 321 trains. Murals were also made for hanging in station waiting rooms, and for the rebuilt Poole, Dorset, station. When Network SouthEast refurbished vehicles to the standard of their new trains, Edward Pond Associates provided decorations for Mk I and Mk II coaches, class 421 (4CIG) and class 313 electric multiple-units. Pond images were planned to feature in the class 165, 465 and 471 (not built) trains.

Poster promoting the Dreamland theme park at Margate, Kent by Edward Pond, 1989.

Network SouthEast gave away boxed sets of postcards to advertise the artworks commissioned for its trains.

Above: For vehicle liveries and publicity, each line was given its own brand mark in 1989, from a series devised by Edward Pond Associates. The brands made use of stylised pictures referencing the area served by each line, focussing on red and blue as the predominant colours.[22] These marks appeared on trains, timetables, posters and route maps.

Opposite: Murals in a class 319 multiple-unit coach by Edward Pond Associates, representing St Paul's Cathedral and the Old Royal Naval College, Greenwich.

New and existing rolling stock

Network SouthEast operated over a largely electrified system, using multiple-unit trains which were twenty to thirty years old, built to pre-war and immediately post-war standards of comfort and appearance. Most of the units had doors of the 'slam' type - hung on hinges with manual latches - those for passengers opening outwards. These caused accidents and delays in operation. Compartments and saloons in the vehicles were not suited to high-density loading on busy commuter lines experiencing rapid increases in demand for capacity. To move passengers in greater comfort over an extended system of electrified lines, a series of new trains built by British Rail Engineering were introduced on Network SouthEast. Some were designed exclusively for and by the Network, others were distributed to various parts of the British Rail system. Both diesel and electric multiple-units were commissioned to replace older rolling stock. These units are discussed here, arranged by design type and their original area of operation. British Rail now routinely evaluated future train designs by making full-size mock ups to determine the form and layout of interiors, and to ensure correct ergonomics and comfort for passengers and train crews. Besides the positioning of furniture, hand grabs, luggage racks, litter bins and safety equipment, lighting could be planned at this stage. Special fabrics would be commissioned for the seat covering, and samples made of all the fittings before full production. In this context, Design Panel member Lady Virginia Ogilvy, Countess of Airlie DCVO, advised on upholstery fabrics.

Inauguration of the route linking Network SouthEast areas north and south of the River Thames, 1988.

Class 319 electric multiple-unit, built for *Thameslink* services between Bedford and Brighton.

Early proposal for the class 319 cab front.

Dual voltage trains of class 319 were required for the cross-London *Thameslink* services which commenced on 16 May 1988. The route linked former London Midland and Southern regions in the capital; trains could now be operated between Bedford and Brighton. An artist's impression of the proposed class 319 unit fronts resembled a developed version of the class 142 and 143/144 diesel multiple-units drafted in the same period: a moulded surround to the recessed window area, in this case taken down below the head and tail light clusters. The vertical grille of the air horns was copied from the class 142. It seems that the potential for creating forms in glass reinforced plastic prompted the designers to include some idiosyncratic features, particularly the recesses below the light units, and the yellow panel on the cab centre door. British Rail's Design Panel rejected the concept, and asked Michael Rodber of Jones Garrard to redesign it. Production examples delivered from September 1987 saw the styling tidied and rounded, although some of the original detail had to be retained to save production time and expenditure. To match the Network SouthEast livery, the yellow cab front surround was now coloured grey and the formerly black portion coloured yellow.

Initial concept for new Bournemouth line trains, when part of British Rail's London & South East sector.

Two preliminary - and rejected - British Rail sketch models for the class 442 trains.

Model for the class 442 by Jones Garrard, specifying red for the unit fronts. Another version used blue.

Class 442 *Wessex Electric* trains began public service in May 1988, used for the extension of electric services from Bournemouth to Weymouth. Consultants Jones Garrard produced an aerodynamic cab front design, featuring wrap-around windows and a raked back profile apparently referencing the work of British Railways/British Rail's design consultants Wilkes & Ashmore, who had made the class 124 and 309 multiple-units so distinctive. The angle of rake neatly coincided with the manner in which the Network SouthEast livery was swept upwards at the train ends. Moulded fronts were elaborated as a sculpted fairing around vehicle coupling equipment ahead of the leading bogies at each end. Unit to unit connections were concealed behind panels below the windows. Coaches for the five-car units were based on the British Rail Mark 3 design. Train interiors used a colour scheme of blue in standard class, and dark grey, crimson and red in first class, with mural decorations by Edward Pond Associates. In 2016 class 442 trains form part of the *Gatwick Express* fleet linking London and Gatwick Airport.

Introduced in September 1988, class 321 units were built for routes between London and Essex. Their cab ends had a single raked-back plane, divided horizontally with black window surround above a yellow panel. Like other multiple-units of the time, the cab fronts were enclosed in a moulded surround, in this case extended down as a spoiler in front of the leading bogie. The visually similar class 320 went to the Strathclyde area, and class 322 formed the *Stansted Express* fleet.

British Rail engineers at Derby developed the 465 *Networker* as the 'Advanced Suburban Train'. Early proposals for this type show a composition of rounded rectangular shapes within a concave yellow coloured frame, an appearance which can be compared with the class 143/144 DMUs and class 323 EMU. The windscreen was represented as a continuous dark element across the unit ends, with an asymmetrical extension to incorporate the dot-matrix destination indicator. Interior design reflected new thinking too. Moulded

Class 442 multiple-unit at Bournemouth, 1988.

Class 321 (321/3) unit 321301 when new, 1988.

British Rail Engineering model for the class 465 train, in London & South East sector colours, circa 1985.

individual seats with a new pattern of moquette upholstery featured grab handles for passengers using the gangways; dot matrix displays in the carriages provided journey information to supplement the route maps; passengers had access to lavatory facilities. Units had Network SouthEast livery from new, in an augmented style with red bands wrapping around the blue window-level panels. Two versions of the *Networker* were produced, one for Kent inner suburban lines and one for Liverpool Street/Fenchurch Street–Essex lines; they began service in December 1991. *Networker Turbo* DMU classes 165 and 166 of 1991-92 for *Chiltern* and *Thames* routes used the 465 bodyshell.

Several other trains were specified by Network SouthEast, and exhibited as full-size models. All were superseded by privatisation and not built.[23] The appearance of class 471 (for *Networker* and *Thameslink Express* services) was demonstrated to the public at Margate, and class 341 at Paddington, both in 1991. Intended to be the train for *Crossrail* services, class 341 was designed by a team comprising Network SouthEast, London Underground Limited, and consultants DCA Design of Warwick.[24]

Full size mock-up at Margate of the intended class 471 cab front, March 1991.

Development model for the class 465 *Networker* train, 1988.

First production *Networker*, unit 465001, December 1991.

237

Station improvements for suburbia and beyond

Network SouthEast worked to improve all its stations, starting with the most heavily used sites in the south western sector of London, and selected termini. Architect Ronnie McIntyre guided a comprehensive revision of how the network was presented to the public from street to train, transforming the clinical black and white of the British Rail corporate identity, and traces of green and cream from much older decorations, into a bright, immediately recognisable, red, white and blue with grey colour scheme. Outside stations signs displayed the double arrow, with the station name and/or network logotype. Passenger entrances were also identified with the name in blue lettering, accompanied by the full sector logotype, or the 'rhombus' only if space was restricted. All lampposts, railings, seats, doors, ticket collector booths, ticket barriers, display screen enclosures, digital clock cases, light fittings and litter bins took the signature bright red. Many ticket halls were refurbished with cream marble, or marble-effect, tiles; ticket windows were modernised with wide plate glass panels in red frames.[25]

Liverpool Street

A legacy of nineteenth century railway competition, the terminal stations on adjacent Liverpool Street and Broad Street sites represented a duplication of facilities where land was in short supply, in this north east corner of the City of London. British Rail was not in a position to improve either station without considerable external investment, so it chose to focus on Liverpool Street and release Broad Street for redevelopment. The ten-acre Broad Street site was cleared during July-September 1985, giving way to the *Broadgate* development.[26] *Broadgate* would provide the kind of comprehensive office district which had been envisioned for, but never completed, at Euston. It would incorporate the north east corner of a pedestrian walkway network intended to span the City of London.[27]

Network SouthEast-branded station name frieze in north London, 2016.

Red lamposts, digital clocks, seats and litter bins were signature features of Network SouthEast stations. Passenger concourse of Clacton-on-Sea, Essex, 1992.

Richmond, Surrey, lower level concourse, 1986. This is the exemplar Network SouthEast interior: bright red paint and plastic is combined with cream terrazzo tiling.

Liverpool Street was also subject to redevelopment, the east side being submerged below the gargantuan 135 Bishopsgate. In the face of plans to clear the site entirely - much of the perimeter of the station was demolished - British Rail architect Nick Derbyshire led an extensive restoration programme. Part of the trainshed received a new roof based on the appearance of the original. Buildings designed to be in keeping with the Victorian structure, and each distinguished by pair of towers, provided new entrances on Liverpool Street and Bishopsgate. A mezzanine walkway, inspired in part by the Manchester Royal Exchange Theatre and the café in Copenhagen Central railway station, provided connections across the station without adding to the volume of travellers on the concourse, and added a row of shop units. On Bishopsgate a steel and glass structure, resembling an updated and enlarged version of a Paris *Metro* canopy, stood forward of the new brick screen wall. Just outside the passenger station, a new signal box gave the architects an opportunity to explore undiluted post-modern aesthetics.[28] The renewed Liverpool Street opened officially in December 1991.

Free-standing sign on Bishopsgate advertising the station, 2016.

East entrance on Bishopsgate, 2016.

West entrance on Liverpool Street, 2016.

Liverpool Street concourse, 2016.

East Croydon

To solve the problem of limited ground support, and still produce a station of greater capacity, architects Alan Brookes Associates used the concept of a suspension bridge to make a lightweight, open-plan building at East Croydon, south of London. From two pairs of 30 metre-high masts, space frame girders supported the station roof over a glass box containing passenger spaces, railway offices and a small shopping mall. The masts also served as a convenient and effective landmark for the station. Long glass-walled ramps linked street and platforms, where the platform structures were also replaced. The rebuilt East Croydon opened in August 1992; parts of it have since been renewed or extended once more. Brondesbury Park on the North London Line (now part of London Overground) was selected for an experimental station design. Consultants David Hodge Associates designed a platform shelter with an elliptical roof on metal columns having a post-modern styling of exaggerated diameters. Structures of varying sizes could be built from a kit of parts. Platform surfaces were laid out as semicircles of brick paving, edged by metal bollards. Although this arrangement was not developed across the network, the Hodge Associates shelter saw deployment in many locations. In the face of lobbying from conservation groups striving to preserve railway heritage, several stations were provided with a new building called the 'RA Traditional', or 'RAT', developed by Network SouthEast architect John Fellows with Michael Papps. In common with design trends for roadside restaurants of the period, 'RAT' had a conservative appearance which would satisfy local authority planners and meet passenger needs. It was adaptable to give any scale of facility from a passenger waiting shelter to a combined ticket office, lavatories and waiting room.

Chris Green left Network SouthEast in December 1991, moving to InterCity. He was succeeded by John Nelson, who continued development of the network until privatisation.

East Croydon by Alan Brookes Associates

Platform shelter at Brondesbury Park, by Hodge Associates. The detailing and colours make reference to post-modern architectural trends.

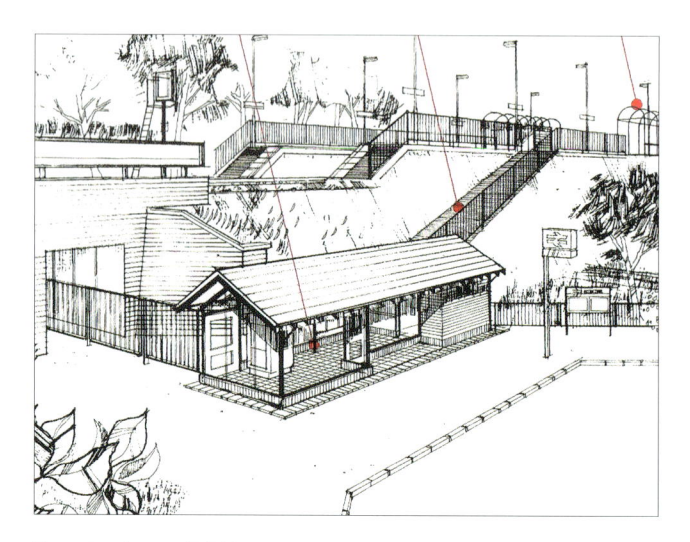

Drawing for an 'RA Traditional' station building at Winnersh, Berkshire, circa 1981.

Provincial sector/ Regional Railways

Away from the main-line InterCity routes, and beyond the Network SouthEast area, trains were operated by the Provincial sector. Vehicles were painted a bright turquoise, with a narrow white band below the windows, and a deep dark blue panel below the white. When Provincial was rebranded as ScotRail in Scotland and Regional Railways in England and Wales, the painting scheme for locomotives and the passenger coaches they hauled was based on the revised InterCity livery, with colours selected to sit comfortably in both town and countryside: light blue, dark blue and grey.

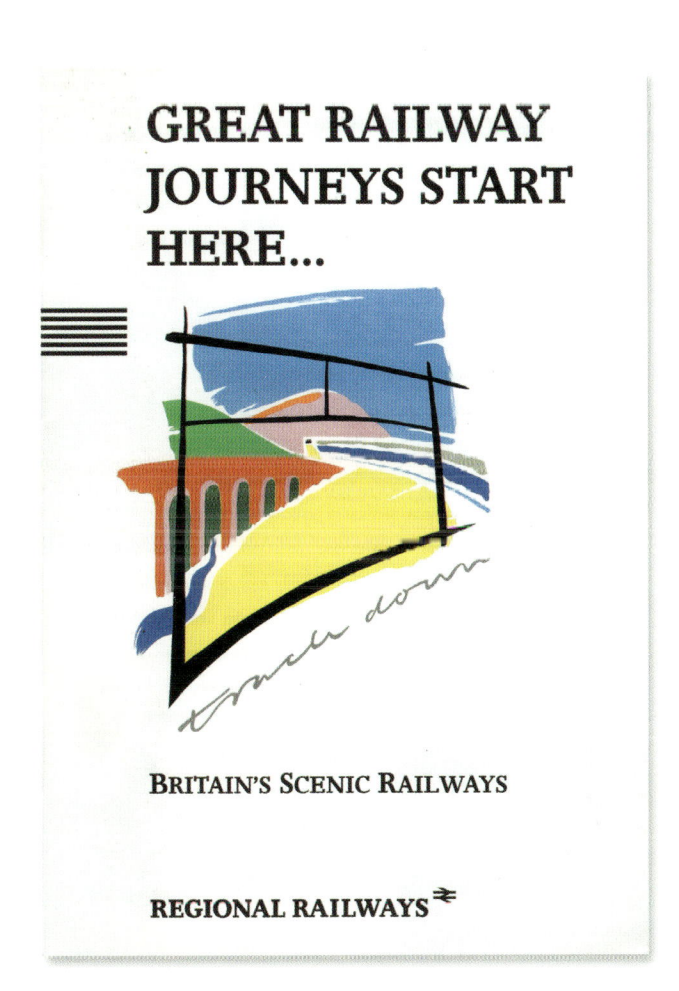

Chris Green made good use of public funds to improve the railway in Scotland. Working with regional architect Ronnie McIntyre, Green made ScotRail the first sector to break away from the standard corporate image. To give better definition to ScotRail and Regional Railways, a new logotype was introduced in Summer 1991. Interestingly the font chosen for this was *Joanna*, designed by the same typographer as the standard British Railways pre-1965 lettering - Eric Gill.[29] A device called the 'fleximark' brought distinctiveness on trains and at stations. This flag-like arrangement of coloured horizontal bands on a white ground was placed at each end of the light blue stripe on train sides, and as a logotype on the edge of printed materials. The number of bands varied according to the application.

Above: Contemporary trends in illustration helped to make the fragmented Regional Railways network appear modern and efficient.

Above right: *Express* was a Regional Railways brand for certain operations.

Regional Railways and ScotRail branding guidelines, including colours and the horizontal stripes of the the 'fleximark'.

Class 143 railbus body at the William Alexander factory, Falkirk, before uniting with its chassis.

Rolling stock

Development of new diesel multiple-units was most evident in the Provincial/Regional Railways sector, and the associated Passenger Transport Executives. We now consider the main classes developed before privatisation. These vehicles should be understood as compromises between the relatively limited resources available to the sector, and the choice of vehicles commissioned in response to the pressing need for withdrawal of older trains. Post-privatisation train operating companies continue to work with this challenging legacy.

Classes 143 and 144

A disappointment for British Leyland bus manufacturing was that no more orders were received from British Rail after class 142/1. Instead, the two-car class 143 and 144 units were built by another coach body maker, William Alexander of Falkirk, using mechanical parts from Andrew Barclay & Sons (class 143) and British Rail Engineering (class 144). Again made with modules devised for bus assembly, these trains had cab fronts incorporating curves and chamfers to create the most resolved and smart of all the railbus types. In common with other railbus and multiple-units of the period, the three cab windows were styled as a single unit by being set in a black surround. Class 143 began service in 1985, working for Tyne & Wear PTE and Provincial sector; class 144 followed in 1986, going to West Yorkshire PTE.

In contrast to the railbuses, the class 150 *Sprinter* introduced in January 1986 had conventional bogie-mounted coaches based on the Mark 3 design. Built by British Rail Engineering at York during 1984-87, the first units featured three windows recessed in a black surround forming part of the moulded fibreglass cab fronts. Class 150/2 of 1986 had gangway connections added, changing the appearance to that of the contemporary class 455/7 EMU. *Sprinters* have operated in many parts of Britain.

Class 144 diesel railbus 144017, 1987.

Class 150 *Sprinter* brochure, 1986.

Metropolitan-Cammell/West Midlands Passenger Transport Executive class 151 railbus, 1985.

Diesel multiple-unit 155333 at Cardiff, July 1988.

Moquette seat fabrics used by Provincial Sector/Regional Railways.

Metropolitan-Cammell worked with West Midlands Passenger Transport Executive to make the class 151 lightweight railbus project. Tested from early 1985, it was a contemporary, and potential competitor, of British Rail's own class 150 *Sprinter*. Designed by Noël Haring & Associates, a dominant styling characteristic for the two three-car prototypes was the body profile formed by a pronounced longitudinal ridge, low in the body sides. Parallel to this a shallow projection was formed above door level. Moulded fibreglass unit ends followed the angle of the profile to form a low-set horizontal wedge, from which the front-side corners tapered inwards to roof and chassis. Within this angular composition a black trapezoid with curved sides and rounded lower corners contained the three windows. Large pods on the carriage roofs contained air heating/cooling equipment. Class 151 trains had an unpainted aluminium body with the Provincial Services sector livery of light and dark blue stripes swept up behind the unit fronts, much like the Southern Region PEP trains. Gangway connections made the units fully walk-through; positioning of seats ensured they were aligned with windows, an improvement on British Rail's contemporary passenger coaches. The cost of manufacture and delays in delivery resulted in the 151 being set aside in favour of the class 150.

The modular nature of Leyland's railed vehicles made it possible to, quite literally, extend its class 142 DMU product to create the 23 metre long coaches of the class 155 *Super Sprinter* for cross country services. Built from 1986, these two-coach trains commenced service during 1987–88. Unit outer ends incorporated a gangway connection, producing the appearance of a class 150/2 DMU or class 455/7 EMU but with a squarer frame to the front moulding. From 1991 the majority of class 155 trains were split into two, creating the single-car class 153 fleet. Metro-Cammell's class 156 first operated in November 1987 looked similar to the class 155, but without a moulded perimeter to the cab fronts.

Designers' sketch for class 158 unit, May 1988.

Rebuilt from the class 158, this is a class 159 in South West Trains livery at London Waterloo, 2016.

158 *Express Sprinter* units were built by British Rail Engineering in 1989-92, to replace locomotive-hauled trains for express services on non-electrified lines. These two- and three-car units were some of the last vehicles made by the state-owned railway. They are a revised and improved version of previous *Sprinter* designs, having a marked narrowing of the body towards the roof exaggerating the height. A lavatory cubicle in every carriage and full air conditioning increased passenger comfort. Interior design used a colour scheme of grey and white for plastic lined walls and ceiling, with dark grey upholstery for the individual moulded light grey plastic seats. British Rail Engineering Limited built a version of the class 158 for the State Railway of Thailand.

Regional Railways also required new electric multiple-units for services around Manchester and the West Midlands. Supplied from 1992 to meet this need, Hunslet Transportation Projects' class 323 used some of the styling of the contemporary *Networker* trains.

Electric multiple-unit 323213 on left, next to 304033, Birmingham, March 1990

245

Railfreight

As soon as it became a sector in 1982, Railfreight published a new livery to break away from corporate Rail Blue. Brian Haresnape, and Ellis Miles of the British Rail Department of Industrial Design, studied agricultural equipment, noting that bright colours were effective in difficult operating conditions. First applied to freight wagons, the mid-grey bodysides and Flame Red details worked well together, and with the Warning Yellow colour of cab sides and fronts. A white double arrow symbol filled the full-height of the locomotive body. This scheme came from the creation of the so-called 'large logo' identity for Rail Blue locomotives, trialled in 1978 and applied to classes 37, 47 and 50 from 1980.

Class 58

Made for freight work, British Rail Engineering's class 58 of 1983 had a superstructure of plain, straightforward design. A revision of the D8000 (class 20) body style, the superstructure had a cab at each end to resolve the visibility issues of driving hood type locomotives. It was painted in the Railfreight grey and red livery from new, with the feature of cabside decals printed to simulate cast metal nameplates, bearing the legend 'Railfreight'.

Class 60

Roger Jones and Michael Rodber of Jones Garrard designed the superstructure for the Railfreight Class 60 locomotive, built by Brush Traction at Loughborough.[30] To avoid repeating historic British locomotive forms, two front end treatments were proposed. Full size models of both assembled in summer 1987 made possible a thorough assessment of the ideas. One idea used a raked forward cab similar to several locomotives of SNCF French Railways, including classes BB15000, BB22000 and CC72000. The class 60 design selected for production was an updated and simplified version of the class 47 outline, with angled joints replacing the curves of the earlier type to obtain the best defined form most economically. Vertical body sides met the roof and cab fronts at chamfered corners, emphasising the apparent strength of the vehicle; this was a feature of some French and Italian locomotives designed in the same period. The fronts themselves combined the upper sloped backwards windscreen area, with a concave lower section having a square central recess above a more deeply set-back strip containing the lamp clusters. To match the British Rail locomotive and multiple-unit livery, the windows were set into a black surround. From new, locomotives were painted in the Railfreight sub-sector colour schemes.

Former D5500 series engine 31102 in original Railfreight sector livery, Manchester Victoria, June 1986.

Class 47 47007 *Stratford*, 1986.

The simplicity and power of the first Railfreight painting scheme is shown well on locomotive 20023, April 1985.

Class 58 58002, April 1984.

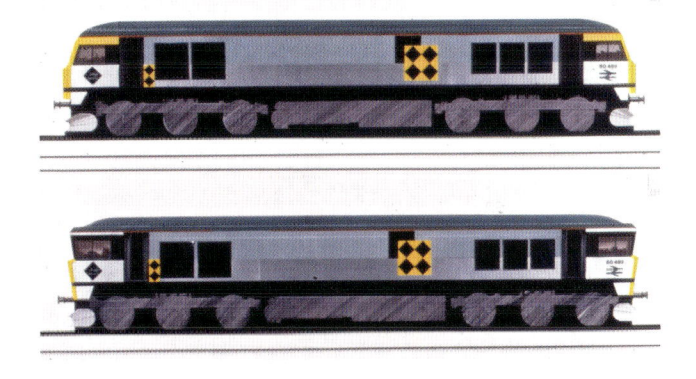

Side elevations of the two superstructure concepts for class 60.

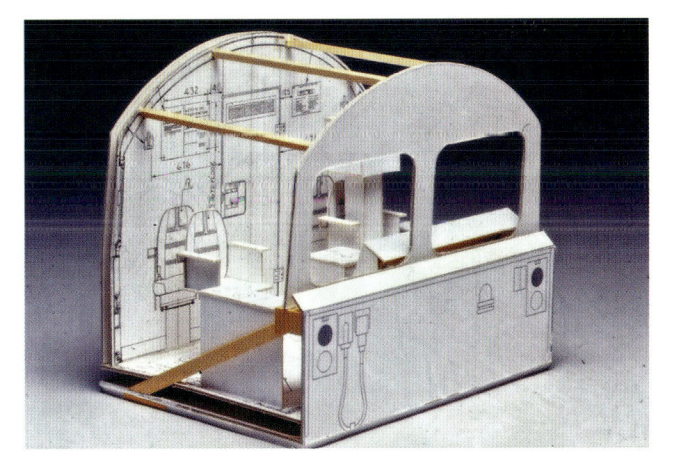

Card model for the 'French' form of the class 60 driving cab.

Model of the second design for class 60.

Built by Brush Traction (Loughborough) and ABB Transportation Systems (Zurich) for British Rail and SNCF Fret, the class 92 locomotive would haul cross-Channel freight trains and night passenger services over tracks with different electric power supplies. Designed by Jones Garrard, it shared the basic body style of the class 60. Important detail differences in the cab fronts included the rounding of the lower panels either side of the central recess, lamp clusters relocated behind clear sections in the lower panels, and a similarly treated headlamp in the cab roof dome. Delivered to Railfreight from 1994, further locomotives were built for Channel Tunnel related activities and identified by metal plates in the form of concentric circles representing the tunnel.

247

Railfreight sub-sector liveries

Railfreight's grey-red-yellow livery proved useful but unglamorous. The sector wanted a competitive image to move its business from a substantial loss into operating profit. Roger Jones of Jones Garrard, designers of the class 60 locomotive superstructure discussed above, introduced Roundel Design to British Rail, because it was felt that the new vehicle would look best in an equally new paint scheme.[31] Extending this idea throughout Railfreight, a fresh identity would help the business focus and restructure its activities into sub-sectors.

A regime of regular vehicle washing in the cleaner environment of electrification suggested lighter colours could work well. Roundel chose a painting scheme of horizontal mid- and light grey bands, with dark charcoal grey for vehicle roofs. The greys were revised to darker versions when the effect of light bleaching them was seen at full-size on a locomotive. Roundel specified six related Railfreight sector symbols: the 'parent' Railfreight, and Railfreight Distribution, Railfreight Petroleum, Railfreight Metals, Railfreight Coal, and Railfreight Construction. The identifying device of the Polish Air Force provided a basis for the symbol. It was developed by the designers with primary colours for motifs referencing heraldic designs, and the nature of the materials being transported. The motifs would work equally well on locomotives, signs, or business cards; they would be easily recognised in most environmental conditions. Marker strips at cab door edges repeated the theme of the sub-sector symbol. To embellish the locomotives further, giving prestige and a sense of ownership which would inspire staff and customers, metal double arrows were fixed to one side of each cab. The tradition of locomotive decoration and local loyalty generated specially-made diamond plates, cast in aluminium with images based on suggestions by staff, referring to the depot at which each locomotive was to be based.[32] Roundel's Railfreight livery launched in October 1987; it would be applied to locomotives of classes 08, 37, 47, 50, 56, 58, 60 and 86. Non-sector locomotives were painted plain dark grey, later altered by adding yellow panels to the upper bodysides, similar to a Dutch Railways (NS - Nederlandse Spoorwegen) livery.

First idea for a Railfreight livery by Roundel Design, applied to an 00 gauge model class 37 locomotive.

Class 37 locomotive 37504 with Railfreight Metals subsector symbol, June 1990.

Class 58 58039 in Railfreight Coal subsector livery, June 1990.

Locomotive 60006 *Great Gable* marked with Railfreight Construction subsector decals, October 1990.

Privatisation of British Rail freight services saw the sub-sector liveries superseded in October 1994 by those of three businesses. Where two colours of grey had given consistency to what remained a state-owned fleet, the multicoloured locomotives of Load Haul, Transrail Freight and Mainline Freight pointed towards sale and the plethora of painting schemes which have ensued. Venture Design Consultants devised the Load Haul livery of black with orange, grey and white, featuring a chevron form block with orange shadow, on a base of black and orange. The Transrail Freight mark by Peartree Design Associates comprised a wheel on rail: a white 'T' on a blue disc in a red ring, above two red bars, applied over two greys of Railfreight livery.[33] Halpen, Grey, Vermeer created a pattern of wheels on a rail in silver on blue, or blue and yellow on white for Mainline Freight. When the freight businesses were acquired by North American operator Wisconsin Central in 1996, the three liveries were superseded by a maroon and gold livery, which has itself now largely been replaced by other operators' colours.

Class 37 37694 in full Railfreight Coal sub-sector colours, showing the main symbol, door-side flash panel, and cast metal depot plaque for Glasgow's Eastfield Traction Maintenance Depot, June 1990.

Symbol for Transrail Freight, 1994.

The family of Railfreight sub-sector devices: clockwise from top left: General, Petroleum, Coal, Construction, Distribution, Metals.

249

Parcels/Rail express systems

British Rail operations to move parcels and mail around the country passed to a sector called Rail express systems, or R.e.s. Roundel Design made a livery using Post Office Red, dark grey and light blue rectangular flashes; this was applied to vehicles from October 1991. Roundel's Mike Denny states that there was no direct meaning behind this scheme, but it does suggest positivity and movement. Like the Railfreight sub-sector format, locomotives carried cast metal double arrow symbols on cab sides, and some received cast metal nameplates.

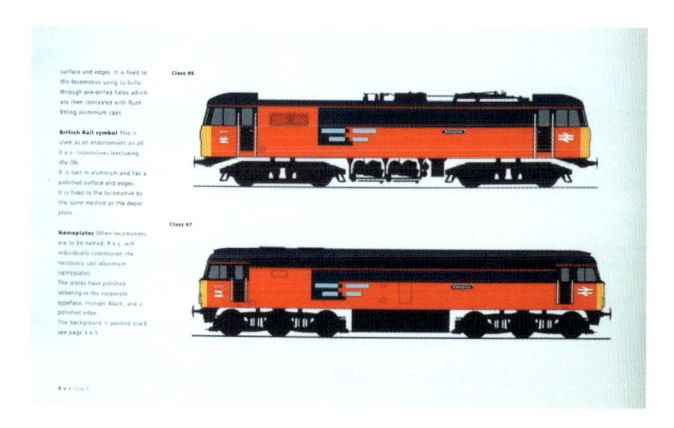

From the branding manual, drawings for the R.e.s. liveries to be shown on class 86 and 47 locomotives, 1991.

Under the Channel

European Passenger Services was formed as a subsidiary of British Rail, to work with French Railways (SNCF) and Belgian Railways (SNCB). A new main line in Kent would route trains between London and the Channel Tunnel, enabling the extension of InterCity services from Scottish and English cities to Europe. In an international competition, Jones Garrard, as part of Transport Design Consortium, produced the winning scheme for Eurostar passenger trains (British Rail class 373). These eighteen vehicle trains have an integral locomotive at each end, and are therefore electric multiple-units. To share the design work equitably, the competition managers allocated the train exteriors to Mike Rodber at Jones Garrard, the driving cab and buffet interiors to Tilney Lumsden Shane, and the remaining passenger interiors to French and Belgian design practices. Operating at very high-speed for much of the route, true streamlining was a key factor in the design process. The 38 trains have a cross-section as close to a rectangle as possible within the dimensional limits of the loading gauge. Nose fronts are of wedge form, made visually powerful by their side profile and broad taper. A single

R.e.s. livery adapted for locomotives 47798 *Prince William* and 47799 *Prince Henry* allocated to the Royal Train.

central cab window is fitted above an integrated lamp unit, beneath which a large moulded spoiler increases the aerodynamic properties and sculptural mass of the units. Continuous vertical louvres in the locomotive sides provide ventilation for the traction equipment. Minale Tattersfield created the Eurostar branding and train livery, using colours which were popular at this time: silver, dark blue and yellow. In 2016 Eurostar also operates class 374 *e320* units.

To haul trains of passenger vehicles through the Tunnel, the *Le Shuttle* Bo-Bo-Bo (class ESL 9000) locomotive was produced. DCA Design developed the superstructure appearance. The leading front of the locomotives has a wedge form designed to operate well in the air pressure of the

Channel Tunnel, minimise visual distractions for the driver, and be collision-resistant: the moulded fibreglass nose contains a special structure to absorb impact forces. Chamfers between cab front and body sides are continued up and along the roof margins, housing ventilation grilles. Looking perfectly suited to these vehicles, they also subtly reflect French railway styling practices. Locomotives were named after contemporary opera singers. Regular *Le Shuttle* freight services began on 19 May 1994; passenger and vehicle transporting service started 3 October 1994. Fashion designer Pierre Balmain was responsible for *Le Shuttle* staff uniforms.

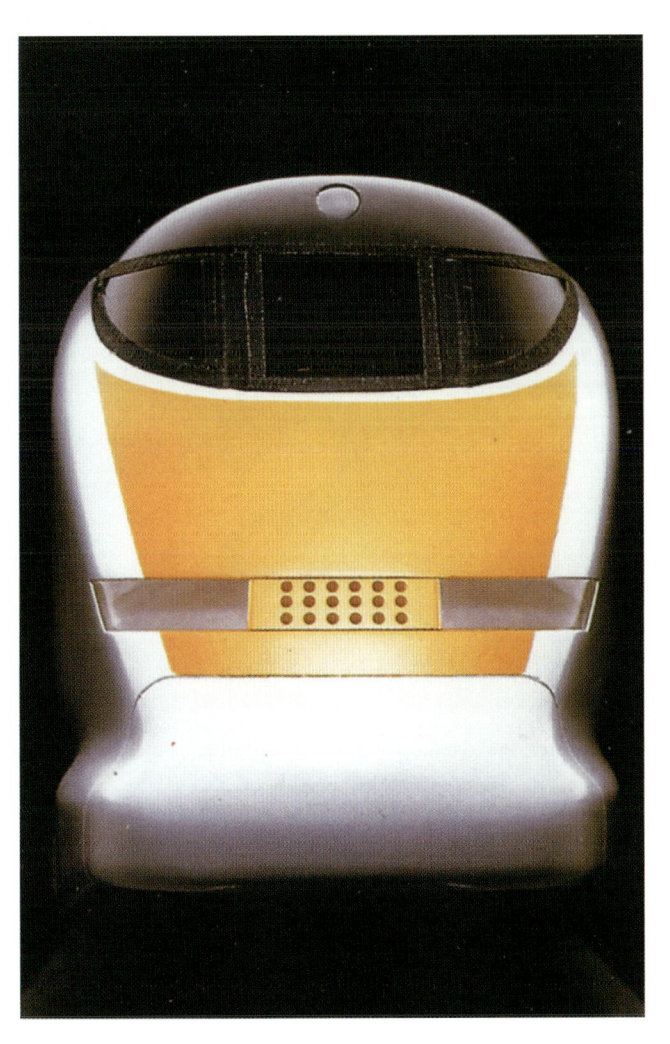

Model for the class 373 Eurostar electric multiple-unit front end, 1988.

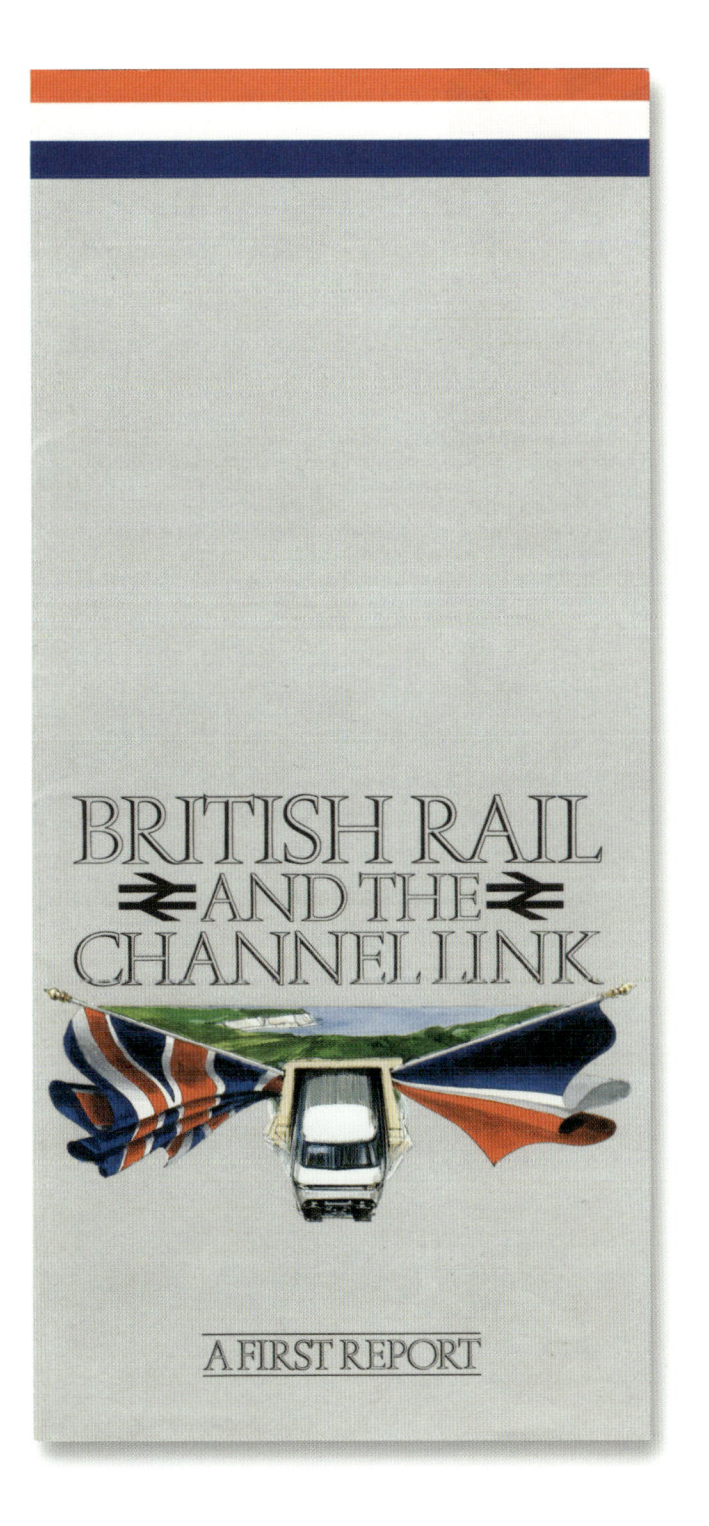

Waterloo International

It was decided that the first London International Terminal of the Eurostar service would be built at Waterloo station. Jane Priestman selected architects Nicholas Grimshaw & Partners with engineers YRM Anthony Hunt Associates for the new trainshed and associated spaces. The project occupied a restricted site known as the 'Windsor side' platforms and had the exceptional - for British Rail - requirement of having to accommodate some border control facilities in addition to the usual passenger and staff spaces. A plan was contrived whereby the different passenger check-in, border control, waiting, catering, departure and arrival areas were placed on different levels, stacked below the five new platforms. Deliberately made to look different from the adjoining domestic railway station, a modern form of trainshed followed the alignment of Eurostar tracks: two longitudinal runs of bow string arches, meeting at a pivot point to adjust to the changing width of the space being covered. The Eurostar concourse was set below that of the main station, to give direct access from the Underground railway. Colours were limited to the Eurostar branding of blue, grey and yellow. Rodney Kinsman provided seating for passenger areas. Along the ceiling of the departure lounge, robotic sculptures of a fish common to the English Channel moved with increasing agitation prior to the departure of a train. The terminal won several prestigious architecture awards. Eurostar operations transferred to London St Pancras in 2007.

Model by Nicholas Grimshaw & Partners architects for Waterloo International Eurostar terminal, 1992.

Top: Detail of the trainshed structure at Waterloo International, 2016.

Above: Main line station seating by Rodney Kinsman RDI of OMK Design, circa 1991. This developed into the *Trax* range used in transportation spaces worldwide.

252

An ending

The *Railways Act* 1993 and consequent privatisation, saw British Rail dispersed into several parts. Infrastructure passed to *Railtrack* (formed 1994, privatised 1996). British Rail-owned Train Operating Companies, all acting as franchisees, replaced the sectors on 1 April 1994. Franchises were awarded to private undertakings during 1994–97. Rail express systems was sold in 1995, the former Railfreight businesses in 1996, and full privatisation was deemed to have occurred on 1 April 1997. Assets were divided. The trains themselves were moved to Rolling Stock Companies (ROSCOs), who lease them to train operators on a wholly commercial basis. Several operators have emerged from road transport companies; their focus on design cannot be the same as that given by a single, network-wide organisation. The British Rail Residuary Body held responsibility for various remnants of British Rail; it was itself abolished in September 2013. Today, National Rail continues to use the double arrow symbol, which is a registered trademark of the Secretary of State for the Department of Transport. There is one last point of interest: technically the British Railways Board still exists, because its legal obligations in relation to the Channel Tunnel are embodied in a joint long-term usage contract with the French national railway (SNCF).

What is the inheritance of so much intensive effort by so many talented men and women, underwritten by many millions of pounds of public money? What of the work now residing mostly in archives, at heritage railway sites and in catalogues of model railway trains, but not as it should be fully accepted in the mainstream of design culture? Just this: British railway graphics, corporate identity, architecture, fashion, vehicle and industrial design, formed one of the greatest modernising projects of post-war Britain, and changed the way the world designed transport.

Top and above: Pocket timetables produced as British Rail prepared Network SouthEast for sale to the private sector.

Notes to the text

Chapter 1

1. See https://www.gov.uk/government/uploads/system/uploads/attachment_data/file/427339/the-northern-powerhouse-tagged.pdf [accessed 31 December 2015].

2. After study as an artist and illustrator, Brian Haresnape (1937–1992) combined his training and interest in railways to work as a journalist, commercial artist and teacher for clients including Shell, British Railways, and Kingston School of Art. Remembered as a quiet and reserved man, he was adviser to the British Transport Commission Design Panel, and capitalised on this close relationship to become the leading writer on railway design for more than two decades from the early 1960s. For twelve years he combined part time teaching at various schools with freelance commercial art, his clients including British Rail, Shell, and the BBC. Haresnape was elected Fellow of the Royal Society of Arts in 1969. Haresnape moved to southern France in the early 1980s to open a café bar and pursue his interest in jazz music; he was reportedly murdered while travelling in Barcelona. Brian Haresnape's legacy is several books and many articles on the development of design for the British railway system, and it forms the genesis for this present work.

Chapter 2

1. See for example: Anon., *Forward: The LNER development programme*, (n p: London & North Eastern Railway, 1946), and Christian Barman, *Next Station: A Railway Plans for the Future*, (London: George Allen & Unwin, 1947).

2. Anon., *Modernisation and Re-equipment of British Railways*, (London: British Transport Commission, December 1954). http://www.railwaysarchive.co.uk/documents/BTC_Mod001.pdf [accessed 2 February 2016].

3. Michael Bonavia: 1945–47 Assistant (Public Liaison) to Chief General Manager, LNER; 1948–50 Assistant Secretary (Works and Development) British Transport Commission; 1950–53 Principal Works and Development Officer, BTC; Chief Officer (New Works), Railway Executive 1953–56 Chief Officer (New Works), BTC; 1956–59 Principal Officer (Modernisation) Eastern Region, BR.

4. Dr Michael Bonavia, to David Lawrence, 3 June 1995.

5. Cecil Walter Thomas OBE, FRBS (1885–1976).

6. 'The BTC Seal', *The Railway Magazine*, vol. 94, no. 574, (March and April 1948), p 127.

7. Dr Michael Bonavia, to David Lawrence, 3 June 1995.

8. Harold F Hutchison, London Transport Publicity Officer, writing to A B B Valentine, board member, London Transport Executive, commented that 'it would be wrong for us to even suggest to the Railway Executive what kind of symbol they should use, and that we should not raise the thorny question of the inclusion of a mention of the British Transport Commission'. Memorandum of 23 January 1948.

9. A J White (?–?) joined the Great Northern Railway in 1913. After war service 1914–18, he became a Traffic Apprentice to the LNER. White was: Assistant to the Industrial Agent, LNER 1929; Commercial Advertising Agent 1933; Advertising Manager 1945; Advertising Officer, Railway Executive January 1948; Assistant Chief Regional Officer, Eastern Region October 1948; Assistant General Manager, Eastern Region at retirement in November 1959. White had an important role in the modernisation of the Eastern Region, including stations, route widening, and electrification.

10. Michael Bonavia was Assistant Secretary (Development and Works), British Transport Commission 1948–50; Principal Works and Development Officer 1950–56, Principal Officer (Modernisation) 1956–59.

11. Dr Michael Bonavia, to David Lawrence, 3 June 1995.

12. 'Memorandum of meeting held at the offices of the Railway Executive, 3rd Feb. 1948.' Initially the London Midland version of the totem symbol was to be coloured white, with crimson lake lettering and outlines. At least one example of this scheme found its way into use at London's Kensington Olympia station.

13. Dr Michael Bonavia to David Lawrence, 3 June 1995.

14. Anon., 'Transport symbol disappointment', *Design*, no. 93, September 1956, p 49.

15. A number of books and World Wide Web resources offer detailed studies of British Railways' output. See the websites www.originalrailwayposters.co.uk, and Greg Norden's www.travellingartgallery.com [both accessed 13 February 2016]. The *Poster to Poster* book series by Richard Furness is very good.

16. www.timetableworld.com is a useful resource: [accessed 13 February 2016].

17. The main manufacturer was J R Gaunt with, in decreasing order of production, John Pinches, L Simpson, and Toye.

18. A comprehensive survey of badge manufacturers indicates the following: **'British Railways'** (white metal): Eastern Region (ER): J R Gaunt, J Pinches, L Simpson; London Midland Region (LMR), Southern Region (SR), Western Region (WR): J R Gaunt, J Pinches, L Simpson, Toye; North Eastern Region (NER): J R Gaunt, J Pinches, Toye; Scottish Region (ScR): J R Gaunt, J Pinches. **'British Railways'** (yellow metal): ER: J R Gaunt, J Pinches; LMR: J Pinches; NER: J R Gaunt; ScR: J R Gaunt, J Pinches; SR: J R Gaunt J Pinches; WR: J R Gaunt, J Pinches. **'Excess Luggage'**: all regions: J R Gaunt. **'Foreman'** (white metal): ER: not known; LMR, NER, ScR, SR, WR: J R Gaunt, J Pinches. **'Guard'** (white metal): ER: not known; LMR, ScR, SR: J R Gaunt; NER, WR: not known. **'Guard'** (yellow metal): ER, LMR, NER: J R Gaunt; ScR not known; SR, WR: J R Gaunt, J Pinches. **'Porter'**: LMR, NER, ScR, SR, WR: J R Gaunt; ER: not known. **'Ticket Collector'** (white metal): ER: not known; LMR, NER, ScR, WR: J R Gaunt.

19. Examples of the lion & wheel badge recorded to date are: White metal with enamel in regional colour: **'British Railways'**: ER, LMR, ScR, SR, WR; **'Guard'**: all regions*; **'Porter'**: ER*, LMR, NER*, SR*, WR*; **'Station Master'**: ER, SR; **'Ticket Collector'**: LMR*, ScR*, SR, WR. Yellow metal with enamel in regional colour: **'British Railways'**: all regions*; **'Foreman'**: ER*, LMR, NER*, ScR*, SR, WR*; 'Inspector': all regions*; **'Station Master'**: ER*, LMR, NER*, ScR*, SR*, WR*; **'Yard Master'**: ER*, LMR*, NER, ScR*, SR*, WR*. These badges do not carry a manufacturer's identifying mark. It is likely that some of these badges now in circulation were drawn from unissued stocks, and never worn in service. Badges marked with an asterisk (*) were exhibited at the National Railway Museum in 2015.

20. Manufacturers for the ribbon type cap badges: **'British Railways'** (white metal): ER, ScR: J R Gaunt; LMR, NER, WR: no example seen; SR: not known; **'Excess Luggage'** (yellow metal): ER, ScR, LMR, NER, WR: J R Gaunt; SR: not known. The **'Excess Luggage'** badge was subsequently shortened, with a lighter weight, condensed text: all regions: J R Gaunt. **'Foreman'** (yellow metal): ER not known; LMR: Dowler, J R Gaunt, unmarked; NER, ScR, SR, WR: J R Gaunt, unmarked; **'Guard'** (white metal): ER, LMR: not known; NER: J R Gaunt, unmarked; ScR, SR: J R Gaunt; **'Guard'** (yellow metal): ER: not known; LMR, ScR, WR: J R Gaunt; NER, SR: J R Gaunt, unmarked; **'Porter'** (white metal): ER: not known; LMR: J R Gaunt; NER, SR: Fattorini & Sons, J R Gaunt, unmarked; ScR: Fattorini & Sons, J R Gaunt; WR: not known. The **'Ticket Collector'** badge was produced in yellow metal with a 4.5 inches length and a block letter for the text: ER: not known; LMR, NER: (unmarked); ScR: J R Gaunt, unmarked; SR: J R Gaunt, unmarked; WR: not known, one example seen in white metal. The **'Ticket Collector'** badge was subsequently shortened, with a lighter weight, condensed text: all regions: J R Gaunt.

21. Authoritative accounts of the colour schemes vary in their detail.

22. The blue livery was associated with regional locomotive classes thus: LMR: 7P; ER and NER: A1, A3, A4, W1; WR: *King*; SR: *Merchant Navy*; ScR: 7P, A3, A4, A10.

23. From 1949, express passenger locomotive classes in green livery included: LMR: 6P *Royal Scot*, 5X, 5XP *Jubilee* and *Patriot*; ER and NER: A2, B2, B3, B17; WR: *Castle, Star*; SR: *West Country, Battle of Britain, Lord Nelson, King Arthur*; ScR: *Royal Scot*, 5XP *Jubilee*, A2.

24. Proceedings of the British Railways (Western Region) London Lecture and Debating Society: Session 1960-61: No. 467: Design and Transport by Mr. T. H. Summerson, D.L., J.P. (Chairman, Design Panel, B.T.C.): Read at the meeting on 5th January 1961, p 12.

25. See: http://www.bulleidlocos.org.uk/_oth/coCoElectric.aspx [accessed 13 November 2015].

26. Between 1956 and 1958, in advance of the AM5 trains being built, Michael Bonavia, a senior officer of the British Railways Eastern Region management in the late 1950s, worked to improve the quality of rolling stock which would be needed for electrification of suburban lines in north east London. From consultation with his colleagues on the Southern Region Bonavia knew that passenger-operated 'slam' doors caused accidents and delays. He lobbied Assistant General Manager A J White - designer of the 'totem' symbol - arguing that the new stock should have power-operated sliding doors, as it was effectively a London Underground type service. White did not accept the rationale, and the trains were built to pre-war design standards.

27. Cravens' two diesel multiple-unit builds were classes 105/106 (built 1956–59), and 112/113 (built 1960). They shared the same body style, made distinctive by the choice of two near-square cab windows set in a raked back plane. The rain gutters curved upwards on either side of the destination indicator window offered a further distinguishing feature.

28. Pressed Steel, manufacturers of the class 303 EMU, contributed two DMU classes: the three-car unit 117 (built 1959–61) and single-car 121 (built 1960). The cab front design followed Derby practice seen in classes 107 and 115 of 1960.

29. D Wickham made just five of its two-car class 109 units. These were the most elaborately styled of any early British Railways DMU, taking inspiration from streamlining effects used on pre-war road motor coaches. Driving windows were compressed between side corner pillars, the central window narrower than the outer two. Above the windows the roof gutter swept down at either end of the destination indicator in a way which was more aesthetically appropriate to transport vehicles of the 1930s.

30. Class 131 DMU was a conversion of class 122.

31. See: http://www.railwaysarchive.co.uk/documents/BTC_Mod001.pdf.

Chapter 3

1. Dr Frederick Francis Charles Curtis DrIng FRIBA (1903–1975) became Assistant Architect to the Southern Railway in 1934, and worked for Adams, Holden and Pearson 1935–36. He was appointed Architect to the Great Western Railway in 1946, when he succeeded Brian Lewis (1906–1991). Effectively staying in post through nationalisation, Curtis was the first Chief Architect to British Railways Western Region, and subsequently Chief Architect to the British Transport Commission, retiring in 1968.

2. Bernard Kaukas (1922–2014).

3. Howard Ernest Bernard Cavanagh ARIBA AADip (1909–1960) joined the Great Western Railway Architect's office in 1945. In 1946 he became assistant to the then Chief Architect Brian Lewis, and was then Assistant Architect to Dr Frederick Curtis from 1947. Cavanagh was made Architect, British Railways Western Region in 1949, and supervised the joint British Railways-London Transport stations from Hanger Lane to West Ruislip. He died in a sailing accident in 1960.

4. See David Lawrence, *Underground Architecture*, (Harrow Weald: Capital Transport, 1994), and *Bright Underground Spaces: The Railway Stations of Charles Holden*, (Harrow Weald: Capital Transport, 2008).

5. See for example Becontree, Upney, Heathway and Southend East (all 1932), Chalkwell (1933), Leigh on Sea and Upminster Bridge (both 1934), and Elm Park (1935).

6. Leasowe, Moreton and Meols stations were of similar styling.

7. Anon., *Passenger Stations: Standards for Planning and Equipment*, (Euston: The Railway Executive, London Midland Region, August 1948).

8. Ibid., p 5.

9. Ibid., p 70. The London Midland regional colour was given as BS540 Crimson.

10. F F C Curtis, 'British Railways Architecture', *The Architect and Building News*, vol. 216, no. 13, 4 November 1959, pp 394–410.

11. For a full description of this colour scheme, and many other related to Britain's railway companies, see the *HMRS Livery Register* series. The Southern Region is discussed in L Tavender, *HMRS Livery Register no.3: LSWR and Southern*, (Bromley: The Historical Model Railway Society, 1970).

12. Source: www.metadyne.co.uk/D_ml_stations.html [accessed 4 April 2015].

13. The Railway Executive, *Sign Standards: Letters; Figures; Totem; Arrow*, (np: The Railway Executive, April 1948), and the Railway Executive, *Code of Instructions for Station Name and Direction Signs*, (np: the Railway Executive, 27th September 1948).

14. Sir John Elliot; Michael Esau, *On and Off the Rails*, (London: George Allen & Unwin, 1982).

15. Examples of the Transport alphabet on name signs include Balcombe, Barnehurst, Esher, Fratton, Hampton, London Road (Guildford), Maze Hill, Oxshott, Shoreham and Woldingham, and a directional sign with the legend 'WAY OUT'; all were Southern Region, and all were made in a lighter shade of green than the original Southern Region station nameplates.

16. Western Region stations involved in this project included Bourne End, Devonport, Hayes & Harlington, and Langley (Buckinghamshire). Torquay used Gill Sans rather than a grotesque font. Other variations arose when the original form of these name signs began to look outdated. Wraysbury (Southern Region) gained at least one example with the white outlining omitted. For Girvan (Scottish Region), cut-out pieces of blue and white plastic made for a somewhat crude totem.

17. This is the Rome Second Statzione Termini by Eugenio Montuori, Hannibal Vitellozzi, Massimo Castellazzi, Vasco Fadigati and Achilles Pintonello with engineer Leo Calini, completing the abandoned design by Angiolo Mazzoni.

18. 'New E.R. and S.R. station colours', *Modern Railways*, vol. XVIII, no. 179, August 1963, p 81.

19. Ibid.

20. Anon., 'Project for Harlow Town', *The Architect and Building News*, vol. 216, no. 13, 4 November 1959, p 409.

21. Anon., 'Conoid shell roofed station at Manchester', *The Architect and Building News*, vol. 216, no. 13, 4 November 1959, pp 404–8.

22. Max Clendinning to David Lawrence, 14 April 2015.

23. Ibid.

24. British Railways London Midland Region, 'Announcing Manchester's New Super Station', *News Special (Manchester Edition)*, no. 2, August 1959.

25. The architectural team for Manchester Piccadilly was led by N C Millin.

26. 'New Station at St Helens', *Modern Railways*, vol. XV, no. 160, January 1962, p 22.

27. Stations rebuilt in this period but not discussed here include: Oldham Mumps, Radcliffe Central, Willesden Junction High Level and Cheddington (all 1956); Chelford (no date available).

28. Anon., 'The prefabricated station: East Didsbury', *The Architect and Building News*, vol. 216, no. 13, 4 November 1959, pp 396–400.

29. 'The prefabricated station: Heald Green', *The Architect and Building News*, vol. 216, no. 13, 4 November 1959, pp 401–2.

30. Donald Insall, 'All Change: the future of British railway stations: 2 The Present Dilemma', *Architectural Review*, February (1966), pp 115–16.

31. See Alison and Peter Smithson, *The Euston Arch and the Growth of the London, Midland & Scottish Railway*, (London: Thames and Hudson, 1968).

32. *Interior Design*, February 1972, p 102.

33. CLASP is the acronym for Consortium Local Authority Special Programme. It received the Bronze Medal of the Royal Institution of British Archiects, and an award at the Milan Triennale.

34. Nigel Wikeley, 'New stations for the Southern', *Modern Railways*, vol. XXIII, no. 231, December 1967, p 643.

35. Ibid., p 644.

36. The CLASP stations were Sunbury (1965); Fleet (1966); Crawley (1967); Ashtead, Aylesham, Belmont, Belvedere, Charlton, Crayford, New Eltham, Slade Green (all 1968); Berrylands and Hampton Wick (both 1969); Catford and Poole (both 1970); Brockley, East Grinstead, Kidbrooke, Longfield, Lower Sydenham, Rainham, Sunningdale, (all 1972); Wool (by December 1972); Forest Hill, Hassocks, Meopham, Strood, Virginia Water, West Byfleet, Wokingham (all 1973).

37. Western Region stations at Oxford (1971), Bristol Parkway (1972), Gloucester (1977). For Alfreton & Mansfield Parkway see: *Modern Railways*, vol. XXX, no. 298, July 1973, pp 270–71.

38. Nigel Wikeley, 'New stations for the Southern', *Modern Railways*, vol. XXIII, no. 231, December 1967, p 646.

39. British Rail Southern Region, *Southern Report Number 6*, (n. p.: British Rail Southern, 12 December 1972), p 2. See also: Anon., 'Maze Hill SR prototype station', *Modern Railways*, vol. XXIX, no. 289, October 1972, p 369.

40. Sam Lambert, 'New gateway to the north: King's Cross extension', *Architects' Journal*, vol. 159, no. 5, 30 November 1974, p 204; Anon., 'Kings Cross station improvements', *Modern Railways*, vol. XXIX, no. 282, March 1972, p 117; Anon., 'Transformation at Kings Cross', *Modern Railways*, vol. XXX, no. 300, September 1973, pp 364–65.

41. Anon., 'Telephone Exchange and Signal Box, New Street Station, Birmingham', *Building*, vol. CCXIII, no. 6483, 18 August 1967, pp 73–8.

42. Paul Hamilton, 'The power signal box: a railway building of a new type', *Architectural Review*, vol. 138, no. 825, November 1965, pp 333–5. Hamilton led the teams which designed Bletchley, Coventry, Harlow Mill, Nuneaton, Rugby, Tilbury Riverside, Watford, Willesden and Wolverhampton boxes.

Chapter 4

1. British Transport Commission, *Various internal reports concerning industrial design, 1956-1964*, The National Archives (TNA): AN 163/5.

2. Richard Drew Russell (1903-1981), brother of designer Sir Gordon Russell, trained as an architect. He was also much involved in product and industrial design. From 1951 he was head of the School of Wood, Metals and Plastics at the Royal College of Art, and continued his architectural work as a partner in the practice of Russell, Hodgson and Leigh.

3. John Barnes (1913–89), ultimately Chairman of Allen Bowden industrial designers in Leamington Spa, was a prolific product designer who worked on many objects from domestic goods such as room heaters and wash basins to textile manufacturing machines, cameras, cars, exhibition stands, telephones, and liveries for bicycles. Barnes designed car bodies for Donald Healey, three locomotives for the British Transport Commission, and a driver's master control for a British electric multiple-unit train.

4. In 1957 Jack Howe was appointed design consultant to the British Transport Commission, to work on the new diesel Pullman trains being developed for the Western and London Midland Regions as part of the modernisation programme for British Railways. He was appointed Royal Designer for Industry in 1961 and served as President of the Society of Industrial Artists and Designers in 1963-64; he was awarded the Duke of Edinburgh's Design Prize in 1969.

5. British Transport Commission, *Various internal reports concerning industrial design, 1956-1964*, TNA: AN 163/5.

6. Christian Barman OBE RDI (1898–1980). In 1935 Christian Barman was invited by Frank Pick to take up the post of Publicity Officer at London Transport. He played a key role in presenting its design policy until 1941. After a period as assistant director of Post-War Building at the Ministry of Works he was Public Relations Adviser, Great Western Railway, 1945–47 and was head of publicity for the British Transport Commission 1947-62.

7. Christian Barman, *The Things We See: Public Transport*, (Harmondsworth: Penguin Books, 1949), pp 3–4.

8. Ibid., p 15.

9. Anon., 'Men in the News', *The Commercial Motor*, vol. CV, no. 2697, 8 March 1957, p 34.

10. A full list of projects in which the Design Panel had input during the period June 1956–January 1964 is given here. Locomotive series: D1/200/600/800/1000/1500/5000/5300/5500/5700/5900/6100/6300/7000/8000/8200/8400/8500/9000; E3001/5000. Multiple-units: the interior and exterior of high-speed diesel-electric trains, class 303 and class 309 electric multiple-units, class 124 Trans–Pennine diesel multiple-unit; new interior finishes for several existing and new trains on routes across England and Scotland: East Kent phases I and II, London–Brighton, Hertford–Bishops Stortford, Enfield–Chingford, Manchester–Crewe, Ayr–Girvan, London–Oxted, St Pancras–Bedford, Liverpool–Manchester, Euston–Manchester, Marylebone–Aylesbury, Scottish diesel multiple-units, Southern Region electric multiple-units. Passenger coaches: replacement Pullman cars, standard carriage interior schemes, interiors for four types of catering carriage, observation car for the Scottish Region (to sketch and model stage only). Architecture: *The Code of Practice for Minor Station Improvements*. Road and rail freight vehicles and emblem. Glasgow suburban electrification livery, symbol and station colour schemes. British Road Services badge. Station staff uniforms. Work in progress at 16 January 1964: a new 25Kv ac electric locomotive (Class 86), a high-speed diesel locomotive (*Kestrel*), the 'xp64' train, fronts for Southern Region electric multiple-units.

11. Wilkes & Ashmore. *Notes on the cab design of the English Electric Locomotive as shown on E.E. drawing V.3200/152*, March 1966. National Railway Museum library and archive centre (NRM): 2002-8349/12.

12. E G M Wilkes, The Appearance and Amenity Design of Rolling Stock: Paper to be read at the Institution of Locomotive Engineers, August 1964. NRM: 2002-8349/9.

13. Anon., 'Report on Railway Progress', *Design*, no. 106, October 1957, pp 25-29.

14. Contractors included Cravens, and the Birmingham Railway Carriage and Wagon Company. See Anon., 'Report on Railway Progress', *Design*, no. 106, October 1957, pp 25-29.

15. 'New Ideas in Rail Transport: Demonstrated at Battersea Exhibition', *British Railways Magazine: Southern Region*, vol. 8, no. 8, August 1957, pp 202-3.

16. Anon., 'Report on Railway Progress', *Design*, no. 106, October 1957, pp 25-29. Vilhem Koren was a Norwegian freelance motor car stylist, whose clients included Alfa Romeo and Rolls-Royce. Frank E Dudas (1928–2011) was a Canadian industrial designer who trained at the Royal College of Art in London.

17. Fairbanks-Morse employed the influential industrial designer Raymond Loewy to style their H-10-44 1000hp 'yard switcher' shunting locomotive.

18. John Barnes designed various industrial products for British Thomson-Houston (BT H). In May 1955 he gave the company two alternative designs for the D8500 superstructure (neither was illustrated in his papers. BT-H reference B14/125, John Barnes design number 1851. See John Barnes, *Product Design Register*, 1 Jan 1946–1 Jan 1959, V&A Archive of Art and Design (V&A): GB 73 AAD/2013/3/1/1.

19. First proposals for D8500 are dated 18 July 1961, when Barnes provided a perspective drawing, coloured elevation and some full-size detail drawings. John Barnes, Design Register as from 1-1-59 i.e. 2278, 1 Jan 1959–11 Mar 1963, V&A: GB 73 AAD/2013/3/1/2. British Transport Commission reference number B21/38; John Barnes design number JB 2855. A colour scheme was proposed by Barnes on 25 August 1961: cab roof Sherwood Green 177.25321, cab sides and engine compartments BS2660 5-061 Pine green, sides below superstructure bright red. British Transport Commission reference number B21/38; John Barnes design number JB 2863. By November 1961 the colours were adjusted to: cab roof BS2660 9-101 Charcoal grey, cab sides BS2660 5-065 Clover leaf and engine compartments BS2660 5-061 Pine green. British Transport Commission reference number B21/38; John Barnes design number JB 2934/A. On 6 April 1962 the colours were changed once more to: cab sides Sherwood green 177.25321 and engine compartments British Railways locomotive green. British Transport Commission reference number B21/38; John Barnes design number JB 2992.

20. John Barnes, *Product Design Register*, 1 Jan 1959–11 Mar 1963, V&A: GB 73 AAD/2013/3/1/2 and GB 73 AAD/2013/3/1/3. British Transport Commission reference number B21/39; John Barnes design numbers JB 3207 (scale colour elevations, 10 July 1963), JB 3243 (visual of locomotive, 23 September 1963), JB 3308 (painting scheme, 2 March 1964). Proposed disposition of colours was: body BS2660 4-056 Mustard; cab BS2660 5-058 Gossamer; roof BS2660 3-038 Congo brown.

21. Pale Nanking (or Nankin) Blue was originally identified in glazes for Chinese porcelain items produced during the Kangxi period of the early 18th century.

22. See the British Pathe film 'Cement Murals' of 1960: http://www.britishpathe.com/video/cement-murals [accessed 28 March 2016].

23. Mary Schoeser, *Marianne Straub*, (London: Design Council, 1984), p 92.

24. The full coach interior decoration schedule is as follows: First cass scheme one: Passenger saloon walls: French Grey *Lanide*; partitions/doors: Rio Rosewood; 'Cortina Kingfisher' irregular blue trace on black ground; seats: red/navy blue stripe upholstery with grey hide and grey *Lanide* details, black *Lanide* arm sides and pedestal; table tops: French Grey *Lanide*; metal fittings: aluminium anodised satin pale gold; Lavatories: wall behind wash basin: Clover Pink 'Hopscotch' laminate, other three walls: Pale Pink 'Filigree' laminate, outside walls: Red Tapestry pattern laminate, wall opposite window: Flame 'Carousel' red/grey pattern laminate, other three walls: Grey 'Filigree' laminate, outside walls Pale Blue 'Tapestry' laminate. First cass scheme two: Passenger saloon walls: French Grey *Lanide*; partitions/doors: Macassar Ebony; carpet: 'Cortina Cardinal' irregular red trace on black ground; seats: blue/navy blue stripe upholstery with grey hide and grey *Lanide* details, black *Lanide* arm sides and pedestal; table tops: French Grey *Lanide*; aluminium anodised satin pale gold; Lavatories: wall behind wash basin: Clover Pink 'Hopscotch' laminate, other three walls: Pale Pink 'Filigree' laminate, outside walls: Red Tapestry pattern laminate, wall opposite window: Flame 'Carousel' red/grey pattern laminate, other three walls: Grey 'Filigree' laminate, outside walls Pale Blue 'Tapestry' laminate. Second clss: Passenger saloon walls: Grey *Vynide*; partitions/doors: blue/white linen pattern laminate; seats: blue/navy blue stripe upholstery with grey hide and grey *Lanide* details, black *Lanide* arm sides and pedestal; table tops: French Grey *Lanide*; aluminium anodised satin silver; Lavatories: wall opposite window: Chinese Blue 'Hopscotch' blue/green pattern laminate, other three walls: Payne's Grey 'Filigree' laminate, outside walls: Blue-grey linen pattern laminate.

25. London Midland Region Pullman route: London-Manchester; Western Region Pullman routes: London (Paddington)-Leamington Spa (General)-Solihull-Birmingham (Snow Hill)-Wolverhampton (Low Level), and Bristol (Temple Meads)-Bath Spa-London (Paddington).

26. Ted Wilkes (1914–c1993) attended Berkhamsted School and Watford Art School. First worked as an artist on the staff of a motoring magazine. With an interest in motor racing, Wilkes built his own vehicles to compete in hill climbing events. During World War Two he worked at Commer Cars in Luton. This

company was a member of the Rootes Group, as was Humber-Hillman who made cars and commercial vehicles in Coventry. Wilkes was moved from Commer Cars to Humber-Hillman circa 1944 and was given the position of ' Chief Stylist' for the group. He left the firm in 1952 and set up a design practice in Horsham, West Sussex. Wilkes retired in 1976.

27. Peter Ashmore (1923–????) was born at Coventry. He started work as a junior draughtsman in the car body design department of Humber-Hillman's Coventry works, where he met Jack Ward about 1943. Both were engaged on designing armoured cars for the war effort. With preference for art over engineering, Ashmore was allowed to attend Coventry Art School on a day-release basis. At the end of the war he transferred to the Humber-Hillman Vehicle Styling department where he worked for Ted Wilkes for some time, before moving to Allen-Bowden in Leamington Spa. He was an active partner in Wilkes & Ashmore 1953–1959 when he left to work alone as a commercial artist. He had a contact in London known as ' Astral Arts ' for whom he produced large airbrushed drawings of cars which were used as originals for advertising brochures. Ashmore's talent for illustration brought him commissions for the children's magazines *Look & Learn* and *The Eagle* during the 1960s–1970s, to which he contributed artworks ranging from motor cars and marine vessels to cut-away views of buildings.

28. Jack Ward was born at Coventry in 1922. Educated at Coventry Technical College, in he 1938 went to work at the Humber-Hillman car works where he was encouraged to take up an apprenticeship with the car body design staff. After about three years working in various departments in the factory Ward moved circa 1942/43 to the design department where he met Peter Ashmore. At the end of the Second World War, Ward left Humber-Hillman to work for Brush Traction in Loughborough. From there he moved to other motor manufacturers, including Standard Triumph. During this period Ward spent two years with Allen-Bowden industrial designers in Leamington Spa, where he met up with Peter Ashmore again. In 1954 Ward left Standard Triumph to join Ted Wilkes and Peter Ashmore as the third partner of Wilkes & Ashmore in Horsham. The practice, eventually renamed Wilkes & Ward, continued to operate from Jack Ward's home in West Sussex into the 1990s.

29. At 3, Blatchford Road, Horsham, West Sussex. Other clients for whom Wilkes & Ashmore designed significant projects included the Central Electricity Generating Board (power supply control desks), the Monotype Corporation (mock-ups of a range of machinery for the printing industry), and the Pressed Steel Company (designing and made mock ups of a range of refrigerators and dishwashers); Ferranti Limited (several designs for 'main frame' computers including engineering and all working drawings and supervision of manufacture), the Ever Ready Company (re-designing and making models of their complete range of hand torches, lamps and portable radios), ICI (designing and engineering the enclosing bodywork for a salt transporting vehicle).

30. Perry King trained in industrial design at Birmingham College of Arts and Crafts, tutors including jeweller and industrial designer Naum Slutszky (1894–1965), who had come from the Bauhaus, Weimar, Germany. He joined Wilkes & Ashmore in 1959, leaving in 1963 to work for Ettore Sottsass in Milan, Italy. The design of the innovative *Valentine* typewriter for Olivetti in 1969 is credited to Sottsass and King. In 2016 Perry King continues to co-direct the Milan-based consultancy King & Miranda Design.

31. David Higgins, industrial designer at Wilkes & Ashmore 1958–62, to David Lawrence, 5 July 2015.

32. Brian Haresnape, 'Design in 1961 - a Retrospect', *Modern Railways*, vol. XV, no. 162, March 1962, p 191.

33. Wilkes & Ashmore. *Design work for British Railways: Progress Report 8*, 30 January 1957. NRM: 2002-8349/1/8.

34. Wilkes & Ashmore. *English Electric Type 3 Locomotive: Notes on the design recommendations*, February 1963. NRM: 2002-8349/6.

35. Early examples were allocated to class 30, but after a change of engine units all were placed in class 31.

36. Wilkes & Ashmore. *Notes on the relationship between the appearance and the engineering and operational requirements of the Hymek, Falcon, Lion, and Hawker-Siddeley (Brush Type 4) locomotives*, January 1963. NRM: 2002-8349/5.

37. D5151–D5175 (class 25/0) were produced in the Darlington workshops, and D5176-D5232 (class 25/1) at Darlington and Derby.

38. Wilkes & Ashmore. *Locomotive Appearance Design Progress Report 6*, 18th October 1956. NRM: 2002-8349/1/6.

39. Wilkes & Ashmore, British Railways Observation Train: Report on Design Progress up to 29th October 1960, TNA: AN 163/15.

40. Laminates used in 1966–67 electric multiple-unit trains have been identified as 'Snow White', 'Persian Blue Linen', 'Grey Moresco' and 'Grey Linen' *Warerite* (second class areas), with 'Dove Grey Softglow' and 'Polar White' *Formica* in first class areas.

41. The 4 CIG (class 421) 1964, 4BIG (class 420, renumbered 422) 1965, 4 REP (class 441, renumbered 430 then renumbered 432) of 1966, 3- and 4-TC (class 442, renumbered 491, then renumbered 438) of 1966 and 4VEP (class 423) 1967 all featured the same rounded form of front ends developed by Wilkes & Ashmore. See also: Anon. 'The SR's new Brighton express units', *Modern Railways*, vol. XXI, no. 196, January 1965, pp 20–22, and Anon. 'Rolling stock for the SR's Bournemouth electrification', *Modern Railways*, vol. XXIII, no. 225, June 1967, pp 301–4.

42. See http://www.ptfnasty.com/ptfDeltic.html [accessed 30 May 2015].

43. See Cecil J Allen, G F Fiennes, Roger Ford, B A Haresnape, Brian Perren, *The Deltics: A Symposium* [second revised edition] (Shepperton: Ian Allan, 1977), illustrations between pp 16–17.

44. Ibid., B A Haresnape, 'The Deltic Styling controversy' pp 36–37.

45. Wilkes & Ashmore. *Beyer Peacock Type 3 1700 H. P. Diesel Hydraulic Locomotive for The British Transport Commission: Design Notes*, September 1959. NRM: 2002-8349/2.

46. Wilkes & Ashmore. *Beyer Peacock Type 3 1700 H. P. Diesel Hydraulic Locomotive for The British Transport Commission: Design Notes*, September 1959. NRM: 2002-8349/2.

47. Wilkes & Ashmore. *Notes on the cab design of the English Electric Locomotive as shown on I.E. drawing V.3200/152*, March 1966. NRM: 2002-8349/12.

48. Wilkes & Ashmore. *Design work for British Railways: Progress Report, July-September 1961*, October 1961. NRM: 2002-8349/1/11.

49. Wilkes & Ashmore. *Design work for British Railways: Progress Report, July-September 1961*, October 1961. NRM: 2002-8349/1/11.

50. This colour may be BS381C 3-044 Golden Brown, which was the Museum of British Transport's interpretation of William Stroudley's Improved Engine Green.

51. At this point the locomotive was renumbered 1200. It was reportedly scrapped in Spring 1976.

52. The origin of *Trigon* is unclear; *Trident* was rejected because it was expected to be given to a 'Warship' class locomotive.

53. Wilkes & Ashmore. *Recommendations for a new locomotive livery*, March 1962. NRM: 2002-8349/3.

54. Wilkes & Ashmore. *Notes on the relationship between the appearance and the engineering and operational requirements of the Hymek, Falcon, Lion, and Hawker Siddeley (Brush Type 4) locomotives*, January 1963. NRM: 2002-8349/5.

55. *Lion* was reportedly scrapped in 1965.

56. Peter Cambridge (1929–2010) trained as an industrial designer at the Central School of Arts and Crafts in London. He worked for the Ford Motor Company styling studio, on models including the *Anglia, Consul* and *Cortina*. From Ford, Cambridge was seconded to work on the Lotus *Elite Type 14* during 1956–57, creating its interior. He also worked on Lotus's *Elan Plus2* and *Europa*. After working in the USA on the Bell Jet Ranger helicopter, he led the Design Council in Wales 1974–89.

57. Wilkes & Ashmore. *Locomotive Appearance Design: Progress Report 3*, 14 April 1956. NRM: 2002-8349/1/3. The darker colour is given as 'Olive Green' in 'The Hawker-Siddeley 2,750 h.p. Type 4 diesel-electric for B.R.', *Modern Railways*, vol. XVII, no. 173, February 1963, p 96. Kenneth G Sadler, industrial designer at Wilkes & Ashmore, to David Lawrence, 15 July 2015.

58. 'Main line diesel-electric locomotives for Cuba', *The Railway Gazette*, 7 January 1966.

59. See TNA: ZPER 9/135.

60. Wilkes & Ashmore, notes on *Recommended Colour Scheme for Rhodesian Railways Locomotive*, May 1962, NRM: 2002-8349/4.

61. There is no single definition for this colour. Sources suggest the best example of the original hue can be seen on the model of London, Brighton and South Coast Railway class D2 steam locomotive 'Como', number 308, made by Dr J Bradbury Winter between 1884 and 1915, and displayed in Brighton Museum & Art Gallery. Design Research Unit obtained a reference from the former Museum of British Transport at Clapham, London, of BS2660 3-044 Golden Brown, noting also that Stroudley's 'Improved Engine Green' for the LB&SCR could be compared to British Colour Council (BCC) reference 227.8, whilst the shade he had used for the Highland Railway before 1870 gave a match with BCC reference 227.7.

62. Chris Leigh railway writer and former colleague of Brian Haresnape to David Lawrence, 22 April 2015. Mike Papps, British Rail architect and colleague of

Brian Haresnape in the late 1960s, corroborated this statement to David Lawrence, 12 October 2015. Brian Haresnape used his own artwork of a locomotive painted in this livery for one of his first books on railway design, published in 1968: Brian Haresnape, *Railway Design since 1830: Volume 1 1830–1914*, (Shepperton: Ian Allan, 1968), p 108.

63. Wilkes & Ashmore. *Locomotive Appearance Design: Progress Report 3*, 14 April 1956. NRM: 2002-8349/1/3.

64. Wilkes & Ashmore. *Notes on the relationship between the appearance and the engineering and operational requirements of the Hymek, Falcon, Lion, and Hawker-Siddeley (Brush Type 4) locomotives*, January 1963. NRM: 2002-8349/5.

65. It is assumed that what became the final ninety locomotives of the D6700 series would have been subject to the revisions discussed here.

66. Wilkes & Ashmore. *Notes on the cab design of the English Electric Locomotive as shown on I.E. drawing V.3200/152*, March 1966. NRM: 2002-8349/12.

67. Wilkes & Ashmore. *Design recommendations for the streamlining of a high speed locomotive*, July 1964. NRM: 2002-8349/8.

68. E G M Wilkes. *The Appearance & Amenity Design of Rolling Stock: Paper to read at the Institution of Locomotive Engineers*, August 1964. NRM: 2002-8349/9.

69. E G M Wilkes, *Designing for the Railways* [private paper], circa 1990.

70. Anthony Hill designed objects across the Brush businesses, reporting directly to Brush Director of Engineering Dr L R Blake, who had previously managed the fast breeder nuclear reactor at Dounreay, Scotland. Hill had worked for the Ford Motor Company on projects including the Mark IV Zephyr and Zodiac. Hill designed and produced his own prototype city car call the *TiCi* in 1974.

71. Wilkes & Ashmore. *Notes on Recommended Colour Scheme for Rhodesian Railways Locomotive*, May 1962. NRM: 2002-8349/4.

72. Anon., 'Kestrel locomotive bought by USSR', *Modern Railways*, vol. XXVII, no. 273, June 1971, p 290. *Kestrel* designer E G M Wilkes stated that *Kestrel* was 'dismantled at a workshop 50 miles east of Leningrad in mid 1988' (see E G M Wilkes, *Designing for the Railways* [private paper], circa 1990); other sources suggest it was scrapped in 1993.

73. Misha Black was born in Baku, Azerbaijan. On moving to England he began designing posters, exhibition stands and interiors. He met Milner Gray in 1933, founding Design Research Unit with him and Marcus Brumwell a decade later. Black was a consultant to British Railways/British Rail 1956–66, and to London Transport for the Victoria and Jubilee lines, 1963-75. He was professor of Industrial Design at the Royal College of Art, London 1959–75, and a great promoter of design education and culture.

74. The Rt Hon Herbert Morrison MP, quoting K W C Grand in: British Transport Commission, *Hansard*, HC Deb 21 October 1953 [accessed 5 June 2015].

75. Sir John Elliot, 'Mr K. W. C. Grand.' , *The Times* [London, England], 21 November 1983, p 12. *The Times Digital Archive*. [accessed 10 January 2016].

76. From the notes of a meeting at the Loco Drawing Office, Swindon, 26 November 1958, quoted in *Western Enterprise: A celebration in pictures and words of the Western class 2,700hp diesel hydraulic locomotives. Designed and developed at Swindon. Built at Swindon and Crewe*, 1961–1964. (Reading: British Rail Western, London Division, April 1975), p 2.

77. BS2660: 1955 *Colours for Building and Decorative Paints*, shade 3-036 Cobweb.

78. Whilst it may seem a leap too far from the railway environment, it is worth noting that many designers would have been familiar with the near-ubiquitous Penguin paperback books. Produced in their millions, the books were colour coded: Orange for fiction, green for crime, dark blue for biography, cerise for travel and adventure, red for plays. The related imprint of Pelican Books used a turquoise ink derived from the same dye as the blue introduced by British Rail from 1965. Might it be possible that this set of colours guided thoughts about locomotive liveries?

79. Herbert Read, *Art & Industry: the principles of industrial design* [first published 1934], (London: Faber and Faber, 1966).

80. To promote the new trains, a mock-up of a 3300hp locomotive cab was exhibited at Manchester department store *Lewis's* in September 1960.

Chapter 5

1. George Williams, 'British Railways and Industrial Design- 4: Why BR needs a new design idiom', *Modern Railways*, vol. XXI, no. 201, June 1965, p 329.

2. George Williams, 'Working on the Railroad', *SIA Journal*, no. 115, September 1962, p 1.

3. James S Cousins, 'Role of the BRB Design Panel', *Modern Railways*, vol. XXV, no. 251, August 1969, p 398. Design Panel membership in 1969 included chairman John Ratter, James Cousins, British Rail Chief Architect Bernard Kaukas, Mary Adams, shipping line owner and art and design patron Sir Colin Anderson, and Sir Paul Reilly, director of the Design Council.

4. Jack Howe, *The Design of Railway Passenger Rolling Stock: Report by Jack Howe FRIBA FSIA*, 17 July 1959, TNA: AN 163/12.

5. T H Summerson, *Design of Main Line Carriages*, January 1962, TNA: AN 163/21.

6. Wilkes & Ashmore. *Design work for British Railways: Progress Report, July–September 1961*, October 1961. NRM: 2002-8349/1/11.

7. Wilkes & Ashmore. *Comparison between the new Mark 3 Coach and XP64*, November 1966. National Railway Museum library and archive centre reference 2002-8349/13, and Wilkes & Ashmore. *Prototype Train xp 64 Exhibition Carriages* (1960–1965). NRM: 2002-8349/14.

8. Design Research Unit, B.T.C. *Uniforms: Formulation of Basic Design Proposals as a Guide for Compiling General Report DRU 1/485, 28/5/62*, TNA: AN163/24.

9. The stations visited during the May 1962 tour were: Luzern, Switzerland; Milan Central, Italy; Innsbruck, Austria; Hamburg, Germany; Oslo, Norway; Stockholm, Sweden; Helsinki, Finland. Design Research Unit, *Appendix A: Report by Investigating Team on Visit to Continent - May 1962*, TNA AN 163/25.

10. Design Research Unit, BR Staff Uniforms: Appendix A, - May 1962, TNA AN 163/25.

11. David Dathan via Gerald Barney to David Lawrence, 11 February 2016.

12. Uniform colours were as follows:

	Cap	Jacket	Trousers
Porter	Dark grey	Dark grey	Dark grey
Ticket collector (one silver band)	Med grey	Med grey	Dark grey
Station inspector (two gold bands)	Med grey	Med grey	Dark grey
Station master (small/medium stations, three gold bands)	Dark grey	Dark grey	Dark grey

13. Robert Spark, 'Design policy into practice: Uniforms', *Design*, 171, March 1963, pp 64–65.

14. The London *Design Centre* occupied premises at 28 Haymarket, near Piccadilly Circus, from 1956 to 1994 when Design Council activities were substantially curtailed.

15. An incomplete list of railway-oriented exhibitions at the London *Design Centre* includes: 'New Design for British Railways' (27 February–23 March 1963); 'The New Face of British Railways' *Design Centre* London (5–23 January 1965); 'The next train...' (16 July–16 August 1969); 'The train now arriving...' (September–October 1975); 'On the move' (3 April 1985–12 May 1985).

16. Brian Haresnape, 'Towards a B. R. "house style"', *Modern Railways*, vol. XVII, no. 175, April 1963, p 238.

17. Wilkes & Ashmore, *notes on Recommended Colour Scheme for Rhodesian Railways Locomotive*, May 1962, NRM reference 2002-8349/4.

18. E G M Wilkes, 'British Railways and Industrial Design - 1: A designer's look at BR rolling stock today', *Modern Railways*, vol. XXI, no. 201, June 1965, p 325.

19. Anon., *British Railways project xp64* [public information brochure], n p: British Railways Board, 1964.

20. Robert Spark, 'London Manchester Liverpool: BR's new line in passenger appeal', *Design*, 211, July 1966, p 57.

21. Ibid., pp 53–57.

22. Ibid., p 54.

23. Margaret Calvert to David Lawrence, 18 January 2016.

24. Design Research Unit (Misha Black and John Beresford-Evans), *A report on a livery for British Railways: Part 1*, 27/5/63, TNA: AN 163/27.

25. Design Research Unit (Misha Black and John Beresford-Evans), *A report on a livery for British Railways: Part 1*, 27/5/63, TNA: AN 163/27.

26. Monastral or Phthalocyanine/'Phtalo' Blue was first synthesised in the 1920s, and manufactured commercially by Imperial Chemical Industries during the 1930s. The distinctive blue covers of *Pelican* paperback books were printed using this pigment. It is numbered BS114, and the nearest Pantone® match is 316C. Phthalo Blue can also be obtained as an artists' colour.

27. Design Research Unit (Misha Black and John Beresford-Evans), *A report on a livery for British Railways: Part 1*, 27/5/63, TNA: AN 163/27.

28. The colour chosen was BS2660 3-045 Middle Brown.

29. Rail Blue (ICI colour ST12404) and Rail Red were given unique numbers in the BS381C:1964 colour range - BS114 and BS593 respectively. Rail

258

Grey (ICI colour SL6929) is BS2660 9-095 Minerva grey.

30. Gerry Barney in an interview with David Lawrence, 28 January 2016. Born in 1939, he attended Ealing Art School. He joined DRU in 1961 as a lettering artist, and left in 1965 to work at Wolff, Olins. Barney subsequently did the lettering and portrait of H M the Queen for the first British decimal coins. He was a founding partner of design practice Sedley Place.

31. Design Research Unit, *British Rail Corporate Identity Manual*, (London: Design Research Unit/British Railways Board, July 1965), p 1/01.

32. Anon., *The new face of British Railways* [folder leaflet], (London: British Railways Board, 1965).

33. British Transport Commission, Corporate Identity Programme: Design Manual: 1st meeting of the Working Party for Corporate Identity Manual, September 1964, TNA: AN 160/217.

34. Gerald Barney to David Lawrence, 11 February 2016.

35. There is an unattributed anecdote that the contents of this room were scheduled for preservation, but lost in the scramble to clear space as privatisation approached during the early 1990s.

36. British Transport Commission, *Corporate Identity Programme: Protection for BR Symbol*, The National Archives: AN 160/791. The British Railways Board paid a fee of 350 guineas (about £5100 at 2016 values) for a finished artwork of the mark, this being the authoritative version of the symbol.

37. Nigel Wikeley & John Middleton, *Railway Stations: Southern Region*, (Seaton: Peco Publications & Publicity, 1971).

38. See for example Dave Brennand & Richard Furness, *The book of British Railways Station Totems*, (Stroud: Sutton Publishing/Wickford: Gloucester & Essex Railway Publishing, 2002).

39. See *Modern Railways*, vol. XXIII, no. 220, January 1967, pp 2–3.

40. The list of staff grade insignia on head-wear as at April 1966 is: **Porter**: red double arrow cap badge, one line of red Russia braid around cap; **Foreman** and **Ticket Collector**: silver double arrow cap badge, one line of silver braid around cap, silver braid on peak; **Travelling Ticket Inspector**: gold double arrow badge, two lines of gold braid around cap; **Station Inspector** and **Junior Station Master**: lion & wheel with laurel wreath on blue felt pad, two lines of gold braid around cap, gold braid on peak; **Senior Station Master**: lion & wheel with laurel wreath on blue felt pad, three lines of gold braid around cap; gold braid on peak; **Guard**: silver double arrow on blue oval pad, one or two lines of silver or white braid around cap, silver braid on peak; **Secondman**: silver double arrow on black plastic pad; **Driver**: gold double arrow on blue oval plastic pad (subsequently changed to felt) arranged horizontally.

41. *Koratron* comprised a knitted mix of *Dacron* and *Farelle* fibres, and was invented by Koret of California, Inc., in 1961. The 'Hoversuits' were made by L C Clothes of Folkestone, Kent, England.

42. Anon., '"The Next Train..." BR's exhibition at the Design Centre - July 16 to August 16', *Modern Railways*, vol. XXV, no. 252, September 1969, pp 452–3. The exhibition was designed by Hamper & Purcell, and toured to the Scottish Design Centre, Glasgow in autumn 1969.

43. Richard Carr, 'British Rail: The Way Ahead', *Design*, 248, August 1969, pp 18–20.

44. In his book *Self Portrait: The Eyes Within*, and in an interview with David Lawrence, William Mitchell claims to have produced complete prototype coach bodies and interior fittings for the *Advanced Passenger* and *High Speed* trains. Mitchell suggests that the commission came from George Williams in 1969, when in fact Williams had died in late 1965. Mitchell's former assistant John Warne suggests that instead a single seating bay was produced: this is likely to have been featured in 'The Next Train...' exhibition of 1969.

45. Anon., 'BR exhibition train for Europe', *Modern Railways*, vol. XXVII, no. 272, May 1971, p 234.

46. British Rail Chief Engineer (Traction & Rolling Stock), *Locomotives for the 1970s*, March 1969. See also Anon., 'Design for higher speeds', *Railway Magazine*, vol. 116, no. 835, November 1970, p 599.

47. Richard Carr, 'British Rail: The Way Ahead', *Design*, 248, August 1969, p 18.

48. E L Cornwell, 'BR's advanced turbo-train project', *Modern Railways*, vol. XXIII, no. 224, May 1967, p 234.

49. The linear induction motor propelled electric train was published in 1963: Robert Spark, 'Looking ahead', *Design*, 171, March 1963, p 79. For further background see Charles F. Klapper, 'Tracked hovercraft-a threat to orthodox railways?', *Modern Railways*, vol. XXI, no. 196, January 1965, pp 14–15.

50. Anon., 'BR's experimental "sling" seat, *Modern Railways*, vol. XXV, no. 249, June 1969, p 294; Anon., 'Net suspension seat', *Modern Railways*, vol. XXV, no. 251, August 1969, p 403.

51. In a long career, Sir Kenneth Grange has designed many familiar objects of the British environment, including bus passenger waiting shelters (whilst in the office of fellow industrial designer Jack Howe), parking meters, food processors, cameras, *Anglepoise* lamps, computer housings, razors and architectural ironmongery. See: Fiona MacCarthy, Deyan Sudjic, Gemma Curtin, Penny Sparke, Jonathan Glancey and Barbara Chandler, *Kenneth Grange: Making Britain Modern*, (London: Design Museum/Black Dog Publishing, 2011).

52. For a description of the restyling project, see 'How to draw a train' and 'Inter-City 125' by Kenneth Grange in *Living by design*, (London: Lund Humphries, 1978), pp 276–77 and pp 278–283.

53. Sir Kenneth Grange to David Lawrence, 9 August 2015.

54. Roger Jones of Jones Garrard - designers of the class 60 and class 92 locomotives, class 319, 373 and 442 electric multiple-units - was an assistant to Kenneth Grange at this time, and ran the *High Speed Train* model wind tunnel tests at what was then the Borough Polytechnic in London. Roger Jones to David Lawrence, 10 May 2016.

55. See *Modern Railways*, vol. XXVI, no. 267, December 1970, p 530. The locomotive was class 86 E3173, and ran in this form in October 1970 and May 1971.

56. *Speed for the Seventies: HST* [publicity brochure], (London: British Railways Board, 1973).

57. This chassis incorporated the 'Flexicoil' suspension system made for the *Advanced Passenger Train* project. One of the first vehicles built for the project was High Speed Freight Vehicle 1 (HSFV1), British Rail vehicle number RDB511023.

58. The chronology of this section is based on: B S Hancock, *The Leyland Railbus Body* [a paper given for the Willis Faber Manufacturing Effectiveness Award/Institute of Mechanical Engineers 1986], (Leyland: Leyland Bus, 1986).

59. British Rail vehicle number RDB975874. Also sometimes referred to as the *Lightweight Experimental Vehicle*.

60. British Rail vehicle number RDB977020.

61. David Burnicle, former Technical Director (Rail) at Leyland Bus Ltd, to David Lawrence, 17 November 2015. British Rail vehicle number RDB977091, using underframe from Mark I coach E21234.

62. The PEP units were also identified as the 2- and 4-PER trains. See Anon., 'Replacements for the "4-SUBS"', *Railway Magazine*, vol. 117, no. 846, October 1971, pp 524–6.

63. 1973 cap badge issue: **Porter**: red double arrow; **Guard**: chrome double arrow; **Driver** and **Secondman**: gilt double arrow; **Rail Express parcels drivers**: blue double arrow; **Inspector**: larger gilt double arrow.

64. Staff grades were renamed prior to the 1981 uniform general issue. Insignia was as follows: **Railman** (one red bar on sleeve) red cap band, red cloth double arrow cap badge; **Leading Railman** (two red bars) red cap band, red cloth double arrow; **Senior Railman** (two blue bars) light blue cap band, red cloth double arrow; **Chargeman** (three blue bars) light blue cap band, red cloth double arrow. From 1983: **Guard** (two silver bars, 'Guard' name on left jacket breast, silver double arrow on cap, two rows of silver braid) and **Station Supervisors** ('Supervisor' name on left jacket breast, gold double arrow on cap). From 1984: **Senior Guard** and **Inspector**: 'Travellers Joy' embroidery on cap band, gold embroidered arrow with wreath on red felt patch.

65. G Freeman Allen, 'Blueprint for BR passenger travel', *Modern Railways*, vol. XXI, no. 204, September 1965, p 499.

66. 'New one piece ticket', *Southern Report*, no. 1, (British Rail Southern Region, 19 March 1970), p 1; 'End of two-part return ticket', *Modern Railways*, vol. XXV, no. 255, December 1969, p 635.

67. This was the NCR21 type machine.

68. Referred to as the NCR51 ticket.

Chapter 6

1. Anecdotally this period marked the literal dismantling of the Design Research Unit corporate identity. British Rail had maintained a room at its Paddington offices, of files documenting every aspect of its design standards as developed from 1965. The room contents were moved to British Rail's *Southern House* in Croydon, and then on to an attic store at Kings Cross. Ultimately the records were discarded. Tony Hayward, former industrial design manager, British Rail, to David Lawrence, June 2015.

2. Design Panel membership in 1984 included Director of Industrial Design James Cousins, Director of InterCity sector Cyril Bleasdale, Director of London & South East sector Chris Green, British Rail Chief Architect Roy Moorcroft, Danish State Railways' Director of Design Jens Nielsen, Director of the British Design Council Lord Paul Reilly, structural and civil engineer for Ove Arup & Partners Povl Ahm, David Maroni - a director at Olivetti, Alan Williams, railway writer, Grant Woodruff - British Rail Director of Public Affairs, and Virginia Ogilvy, The Countess of Airlie DCVO.

3. Jens Nielsen, *DSB design: Danish Railway Design*, (Copenhagen: Danish Design Council, May 1984).

4. Anon., *Future Rail: The Next Decade*, np: British Railways Board, July 1991, p 1.

5. Ibid.

6. Jane Priestman trained as a textile designer at Liverpool College of Art. She was subsequently a designer for Heals and Marks & Spencer, working in independent practice (mid-1950s–1975) designing interiors, exhibitions and displays. Priestman implemented the Wolf Olins corporate identity for BAA and developed a comprehensive design policy for the business. She recruited Sir Norman foster to design the Stansted Airport buildings, and supervised design for Heathrow Terminal 4 and the North Terminal at Gatwick. Priestman sat on the London Regional Transport Design Panel 1985-88. She was appointed OBE in 1991.

7. Jane Priestman, Foreword, in: British Railways Board, *Architecture and Design for British Railways*, (London: British Railways Board, circa 1990).

8. Dr John Prideaux to David Lawrence, 24 September 2015.

9. Ibid.

10. Ibid.

11. 'The Emblem', *Intercity Design Guidelines*, August 1988.

12. See: Tolu Solanke, *Avocet: In Pursuit of Style*, (London: IOD, 2013).

13. *Class 91 25kV BoBo locomotives for British Rail*, (Manchester: GEC Transportation Projects, nd).

14. David Carter Associates was formed in 1960. The practice designed domestic objects like electric heaters, telephone and kitchen equipment, hand tools and items for the gas supply industry.

15. Chris Green to David Lawrence, 25 September 2015.

16. Former Network SouthEast architect Michael Papps to David Lawrence, 25 September 2015.

17. Ronnie McIntyre had been deputy chief Architect with the London, Midland and Scottish Railways prior to his British Railways/British Rail career.

18. See *'Marketing the Network'*, Modern Railways, vol. 44, no. 470 (November 1987), p 575.

19. Ken Cordner, 'Design led by Commerce', *Modern Railways*, vol. 45, no. 479, August 1988, p 415.

20. See Network SouthEast *Network Design Guide*.

21. Trained as a textile designer, Edward Pond (1929–2012) established Edward Pond Associates in 1976. Pond also created *Polypops Products* to design and sell cardboard children's toys, and the *Paperchase* chain of stores.

22. It has been difficult to locate a single source documenting all Network SouthEast line identities. The following references have been useful: http://www.networksoutheast.net/route-brands.html [accessed 2 January 2016]; http://www.srpublicity.co.uk/nse/nse01.htm#t1 [accessed 2 January 2016]; Mark Lawrence, *Network SouthEast: From Sectorisation to Privatisation*, (Sparkford: Oxford Publishing Company, 1994); Chris Green & Mike Vincent, *The Network SouthEast Story 1982-2014*, (Hersham: Oxford Publishing Company, 2014). Documented line marks are: Anglia Electrics (badge of the Anglia Regiment, 1989, renamed Great Eastern and West Anglia by 1993); Chiltern (Chiltern hills, 1989, renamed Chiltern Line by 1993); Chiltern Turbo; Essex Electrics; Great Northern (King's Cross station, 1989) or Great Northern Line; Island Line (outline of Isle of Wight, 1989); Kent Coast (badge of the Cinque Ports, 1989); Kent Link (1989); London Tilbury & Southend (Thames Barge, 1989); Marsh Link; Northampton Line (barge art rendering of Grand Union canal, 1989); North Downs (badge of Tonbridge, 1989); North London Lines (colours of former 'Harlequin line' symbol, 1989); Oxted Line; Portsmouth Line (HMS Victory, 1989, renamed Solent and Wessex by 1993); South London Lines (Crystal Palace, 1989); South Western Lines (Victory Arch, Waterloo station, 1989) (two versions); Sussex Coast (Brighton Pavilion, 1989); Thames (arms of Oxford colleges, 1989, renamed Thames Line by 1993); Thameslink (city skyline, 1989); Thames Turbo; Uckfield Line (Hever Castle); Wessex Electrics (heraldic helmet, 1989, renamed Solent and Wessex by 1993); West of England (heraldic arms of Exeter, 1989).

23. Class 331 would be the *Networker* for the London, Tilbury & Southend line; class 332 a *Networker* to Heathrow Airport. For the LT&S and Crossrail lines, class 341 was exhibited as a single coach full-size mock-up at Paddington station in 1991. Developed from the *Networker*, the 341 cab fronts were to include a single windscreen set in a smaller area of yellow, surrounded by a contoured frame painted light grey. The 341 was to be operated from 1995. Express classes 371 (operating over *Thameslink 2000* routes) and 471 (for Kent Coast services) would be faster versions of the *Networker*. Class 381 would carry commuters over the Channel Tunnel Rail Link. The 171 *Turbo Express* intended for Waterloo-Exeter and Paddington-Oxford services was supplanted by the class 159 DMU.

24. Alan Williams, 'Crossrail train unveiled', *Modern Railways*, vol. 49, no. 520, January 1992, p 7.

25. Stations built, rebuilt or refurbished by Network SouthEast include: 1986: Richmond - the pilot redecorated station, used for Network launch day, Southampton Airport Parkway, Welham Green, Weymouth, Winnersh Triangle; 1987: Bicester Town, Corby, Haddenham and Thame Parkway, Lake; 1988: Arlesey, How Wood, Islip, Littlehampton, Martin's Heron, Newbury Racecourse; 1990: City Thameslink (renamed St Paul's Thameslink 1991), Hedge End, Stansted Airport; 1991: Smallbrook Interchange.

26. See: *The New Liverpool Street Story: Part One: 'Say goodbye to Broad Street'*, (London: British Rail Property Board, 1986). Architects Arup Associates produced the design for Broadgate.

27. This walkway system is commonly referred to as the 'Pedway'. Fragments of it survive around the Barbican arts and residential complex, near Bishopsgate and along the north bank of the river Thames, but in 2015 most of had been abandoned or removed.

28. A detailed account of the work is given in: Nick Derbyshire, with an Introduction by Colin Amery, *Liverpool Street: a station for the twenty-first century*, (Cambridge: Granta Editions, 1991).

29. The full name for the font is Joanna® MT Extra Bold.

30. See www.jonesgarrardmove.com [accessed 4 June 2015].

31. Roundel Design Group began as the in-house design department of Imperial Chemical Industries (ICI). The practice completed corporate identities for many international transport systems, including *Railfreight, Rail express systems, Great Western, Heathrow Connect* and *Southern* in the UK. Mike Denny, partner, Roundel design, to David Lawrence, 13 January 2016. Roundel merged with Chaos Design in 2012; the combined organisation was rebranded as Chaos in September 2013. See: http://www.chaosdesign.com [accessed 29 December 2015].

32. Eleven of these depot plates could be seen displayed at the National Railway Museum, York, in 2015: West Highland Terrier (Glasgow Eastfield); Cockney Sparrow (Stratford - this replaced an earlier plaque showing a perching sparrow, Cooling Towers (Toton), Leopard (Crewe); Charging goat (Cardiff Canton); Rolling wheel (Buxton); Colliery wheel (Knottingly); Battersea Power Station (Stewarts Lane); Oast houses (Hither Green); Star and banner (Immingham); Viking ship (Grangemouth). Other plates known to have been made were: Kingfisher (Thornaby); Lizard (St Blazey); Rose (Tinsley); Greyhound (Willesden); Rampant horse (Westbury); Flaming torch (Ripple Lane); Fox (Carlisle Currock); Hammer and anvil (Motherwell); Saddle (Bescot); Eagle (Crewe International); Spitfire aircraft (Eastleigh); Panther (Leicester); Kite bird (Margam); Hare (March); Bison (Engineering Development Unit, Derby); Unicorn (Bristol Barton Hill); Galleon (Barry, Wales, Wagon Depot); Horse-Invicta (Dollands Moor); Seagull (Saltley); Horse-Suffolk Punch (Ipswich Wagon Repair Depot); Ocean liner (Southampton Wagon Repair Depot) Golden Hind sailing ship (Plymouth, locomotive 50149 *Defiance* only; nameplates on this locomotive had yellow backgrounds).

33. Colin J Marsden, 'Bright new identities for TLF businesses', *Railway Magazine*, vol. 140, no. 1121, September 1994, p 12.

Glossary of design terms and abbreviations

AL	Alternating current locomotive
AM	Alternating current multiple-unit
Cant rail	Horizontal line between roof and body side
Chamfer	Narrow angled plane at the joint of two planes
Cowling	Shaped enclosure placed around equipment to give it a simpler, ordered, smoothed or streamlined appearance
DEMU	Diesel electric multiple-unit
DMMU	Diesel mechanical multiple-unit
DMU	Diesel multiple-unit
Dome	Cab or engine room roof curved on two axes
Fairing	Moulded form around the buffer beam or some other projecting element
Flare	Increase/decrease in the width of a three-dimensional form
Frontal skirt	Portion of body panel below and/or behind the buffer beam area
GRP	Glass reinforced plastic
Ledge	A narrow horizontal panel
Livery	The arrangement or scheme of colours used to decorate a locomotive, multiple-unit or coach
Logotype	A combination of symbol and words to create a distinctive brand mark: the double arrow with wording 'British Rail' is a logotype
Monocoque	Method of construction in which the vehicle body is self-supporting, bearing the weight of equipment, and all the loads expected in normal operation
Mounting step	A form of short ladder giving access to an operating cab door
Operating cab	Portion of the locomotive containing the equipment used by personnel to control the vehicle
Pillar	Vertical support between windscreens
Pitch	Angle of inclination from the vertical of a windscreen
Plane	Surface with a uniform flatness
Radius	A curve in a plane or at a meeting of two planes
Rake	See pitch
Recess	A portion of vehicle body side which is set-in from the main surface
Skirt	Portion of body panel below the body sides
Splay	A surface making an oblique angle with another or others
Superstructure	The vehicle body, including fronts, sides, roof, ventilation units and windscreens, made to house the power and control equipment, and the operating personnel
Swept back	The effect of a pitch or rake in a plane on contingent parts of the locomotive body
Tumblehome	The turning inwards of body front or sides towards or at the lower margin
Underframe or undergear	structure, attached equipment, bogies (if any), suspension, wheels and other related components below the body of a vehicle
Waist line	A horizontal feature or zone around a vehicle, at a level typically just below the cab driving windows

Glossary of colours

It may never be possible to provide a complete guide to the colours used for British Railways/British Rail vehicle liveries and architectural painting schemes. Records are fragmented, and much has been expended by railway historians on conjecture which cannot always be substantiated. Here is presented a guide to those colours which are documented, in order that the reader may gain an insight into particular hues, and trends in the role of colour in design for Britain's railways. For this glossary original references have been drawn from the papers of Wilkes & Ashmore at the National Railway Museum Search Engine library and archive centre, John Barnes' and Misha Black's papers at the Victoria & Albert Museum Archive of Art and Design, Design Research Unit reports and Design Panel papers (especially British Railways Board: Design Panel, Standardisation of paint colours, reference AN 160/677) held at the National Archives, British Rail design manuals, and interviews with designers. These colours have been checked by cross-referencing them to contemporary BS381C: 1955 Colours for ready mixed paints and BS2660: 1955 Colours for building and decorative paints, and the excellent paint colour database www.e-paint.co.uk. CMYK references based on, but not necessarily identical to the British Standard colours are taken from the *e-paint* database have been included to aid modelmakers. Where given for print colours, the CMYK specifications are for coated paper. N/A = further detail not available.

Proposed station colours, London Midland Region, 1948

[Numbers are from the BS381C: 1955 range]

Country stations

	Red brick	Buff brick	Stone	Timber
Doors	413	445	445	445
Frames	365	White	White	White
Steelwork	692	Black	694	635
Awning soffits	365	White	397	365
Awning fascias	365	365	397	365
Poster boards (railway)	Black	Black	Black	Black
Poster boards (commercial)	223	223	223	223
Ticket machines	166	166	166	166
Station name signs	540	540	540	540
Directional signs	Way Out	Way Out	Way Out	Way Out

Town stations

	Red brick	Buff brick	Stone	Timber
Doors	278	278	278	278
Frames	628	635	635	365
Steelwork	635	Black	Black	413
Awning soffits	365	365	365	365
Awning fascias	628	365	365	365
Poster boards (railway)	Black	Black	Black	Black
Poster boards (commercial)	223	223	223	223
Ticket machines	166	166	166	166
Station name signs	540	540	540	540
Directional signs	Way Out	Way Out	Way Out	Way Out

British Railways 'locomotive green'

BS381 224 (CMYK 5; 0; 15; 71)

Wilkes and Ashmore locomotive and passenger coach colours

Diesel locomotive superstructure scheme, 1957:

All-over colour: BS2660 6-074 (CMYK 67; 0; 42; 72)

Window surrounds: (class 26) BS2660 9-095 (CMYK 0; 2; 7; 30)

Window surrounds: (class 30) BS2660 7-078 (CMYK 9; 0; 4; 40)

Colour bands: (class 24, 26, 30) BS2660 7-078 (CMYK 9; 0; 4; 40)

D5300 prototype March 1957:

All-over colour: BS2660 9-095 (CMYK 0; 2; 7; 30)

Window surrounds: BS2660 5-060 (CMYK 1; 0; 23; 40)

Waistband: white

Roof: BS2660 9-101 (CMYK 0; 1; 7; 60)

Buffer beams: BS2660 0-005 (CMYK 0; 73; 85; 22)

D7000 and D9000, 1960:

All-over colour: BS2660 6-074, (CMYK 67; 0; 42; 72)

Skirting band: BS 2660 5-062 (CMYK 0; 0; 45; 18)

[this shade varies on different manufacturers colour cards]

High-speed diesel multiple-units (Blue Pullmans)

All-over colour: probably BS 381 174 (CMYK 60; 2; 0; 41)

Proposed new standard British Railways locomotive livery, March 1962 [to be tested on D0260 Lion]:

All-over colour to be a shade between:

BS634 (CMYK 1; 0; 16; 61)

and BS635 (CMYK 9; 0; 12; 69)

Secondary colour (to be used with the main colour above) to be a shade between:

BS2660 4-049 (CMYK 0; 7; 26; 39)

and BS634 (CMYK 1; 0; 16; 61)

Glasgow Suburban system, 1960

All-over colour: BS381 109 (CMYK 63; 23; 0; 51)

Original D0280 Falcon colour scheme:

All-over colour:

BS278 (CMYK 4; 0; 38; 49)

or BS 2660 5-063 (CMYK 0; 11; 67; 44)

Ventilation louvre panel and skirting:

BS222 (CMYK 0; 0; 67; 64)

or BS2660 4-050 (CMYK 0; 15; 58; 57)

Buffer beam: BS 591 (CMYK 0; 63; 96; 18)

Revised D0280 Falcon colour scheme:

All-over colour:

BS278 (CMYK 4; 0; 38; 49)

or BS 2660 5-063 (CMYK 0; 11; 67; 44)

Window surrounds, ventilation louvre panel, and skirting:

BS381 320 (CMYK 0; 28; 54; 42)

or BS2660 3-044 (CMYK 0; 43; 77; 42)

[this is the former Museum of British Transport version of the debated colour 'Improved Engine Green']

Buffer beam: BS 591 (CMYK 0; 63; 96; 18)

D1500 first scheme, circa 1961:

All-over colour: BS 2660 6-074 (CMYK 67; 0; 42; 72)

Skirting:

BS 2660 5-063 (CMYK 0; 11; 67; 44)

or BS 2660 5-060 (CMYK 1; 0; 23; 40)

Buffer beam: BS2660 0-005, (CMYK 0; 73; 85; 22)

D1500 approved scheme, 1962:

All-over colour:

BS2660 6-074 (CMYK 67; 0; 42; 72)

or BS381C 282 (CMYK 36; 0; 30; 66)

Middle band:

5-060 (CMYK 1; 0; 23; 40)

or BS381C 275 (CMYK 20; 0; 22; 33)

Buffer beam: BS2660 0-005 (CMYK 0; 73; 85; 22)

Warning panel: BS2660 0-003 (CMYK 0; 32; 100; 5)

High-speed multiple-unit power car model, July 1964

All-over colour: BS2660 7-085 (CMYK 62; 14; 0; 55)

Warning panel: BS2660 0-003 (CMYK 0; 32; 100; 5)

Rhodesian Railways scheme, May 1962

These colours informed the final livery for *Kestrel*.

All-over colour: BS368

Band around body: BS364

Lettering: 'R R': BS 415

'Coach of the Future', 1963

Scheme proposed by Christian Barman based on updated Western Region traditions:

All-over colour: BS2660 3-036 (CMYK 0; 12; 27; 38)

Window panels: BS2660 9-095 (CMYK 0; 2; 7; 30)

Revised colours attributed to Brian Haresnape:

All-over colour:

BS2660 4-056 (CMYK 0; 16; 56; 25)

or BS2660 4-057 (CMYK 0; 26; 93; 15)

Window panels: BS2660 5-058 (CMYK 0; 1; 19; 20)

Kestrel colour scheme, 1966

Upper body: BS2660 0-003, (CMYK 0, 32, 100, 5)

Lower body:

BS2660 3-038 (CMYK 0; 20; 39; 66)

or BS2660 3-039 (CMYK 0; 29; 35; 80)

John Barnes' schemes for D8500 (class 17)

August 1961:

Cab roof: Sherwood Green 177.25321 N/A

Cab sides and engine compartments: BS2660 5-061 (CMYK 19; 0; 22; 66)

November 1961:

Cab sides: BS2660 5-065 (CMYK 15; 0; 40; 60)

Engine compartments: BS2660 5-061 (CMYK 19; 0; 22; 66)

Cab roof: BS2660 9-101 (CMYK 0; 1; 7; 60)

John Barnes' scheme for D9500, July 1963:

Body: BS2660 4-056 (CMYK 0; 16; 56; 25)

Cab sides: BS2660 5-058 (CMYK 0; 1; 19; 20)

Running gear and cab roof: BS2660 3-038 (CMYK 0; 20; 39; 66)

British Railways freight colours, May 1963

Undergear: BS2660 3-045 (CMYK 0; 32; 56; 55)

Insulated wagons: BS381 112 (CMYK 42; 8; 0; 30)

Southern Region (dc) locomotives and multiple-units

A green close to: BS2660 6-073 (CMYK 64; 0; 21; 66)

London Midland (ac) locomotives

BS381 107 (CMYK 66; 24; 0; 39)

or BS381 175 (CMYK: 57; 28; 0; 29)

D1000 'Desert Sand' livery, 1961

All-over colour: BS2660 3-036 (CMYK 0; 12; 27; 38)

Cab window surround: Black

Experimental blues 1963-65

The Design Panel completed work on a new livery 11 July 1963, for application to the 'xp64' eight-car prototype train. Further work was undertaken with ICI Paints in July 1964 to create a richer, deeper blue, of mid-gloss finish. By September 1964 several colour samples had been prepared by British Railways' Protective Coatings Laboratory at Derby, for evaluation by the Design Panel working with Design Research Unit.

BS381C 103 (CMYK 49; 7; 0; 55)

Replaced by: BS381 113 (CMYK: 48; 11; 0; 55)

Rail Blue was subsequently created as: BS381 114 (CMYK 100; 12; 0; 70)

Test warning patch colour: BS381C 557 (CMYK 0; 47; 77; 16)

xp64 passenger coach window panels: BS381C 697 (CMYK: 11; 0; 2; 26)

Travellers-Fare branding

Rail Red: BS381C 593 (CMYK 0; 65; 74; 20)

Yellow: BS381C 309 (CMYK 0; 16; 96; 8)

British Rail house colours 1965

Rail Red: BS381C 593 (CMYK 0; 65; 74; 20)

Rail Blue: BS381C 114 (CMYK 100; 12; 0; 70)

Rail Grey: BS381C 627 (CMYK 1; 0; 4; 31)

British Rail 'national livery', from 1965

Locomotives and multiple-units:

All-over colour: BS114 (CMYK 100; 12; 0; 70)

Warning panel: BS2660 0-003 (CMYK 0; 32; 100; 5)

Roofs: diesel locomotives: BS2660 9-101 (CMYK 0; 1; 7; 60)

Main line passenger coaches:

All-over colour: BS114 (CMYK 100; 12; 0; 70)

Window band: BS2660 9-095 (CMYK 0; 2; 7; 30) outlined in white

Roof: BS2660 9-098 (CMYK 26; 10; 0; 73)

Under gear and bogies: BS2660 3-039 (CMYK 0; 29; 35; 80)

Cantrail band to indicate First class: BS2660 0-003. (CMYK 0; 32; 100; 5)

Cantrail band to indicate Buffet car: BS381C 593 (CMYK 0; 65; 74; 20)

Other rolling stock, 1965

Freight Brown: BS381C 446 (CMYK 0; 52; 09; 50)

Dark or 'Brake duet' brown: BS2660 3-039 (CMYK 0; 29; 35; 80)

Dark Grey (roofs): BS381C 633 (CMYK 25; 8; 0; 75)

Arctic Blue (insulated wagons): BS381C 112 (CMYK 42; 8; 0; 30)

High Speed Train diesel electric power car class 253

Rail Blue: BS381C 114 (CMYK 100; 12; 0; 70)

Rail Grey: BS381C 627 (CMYK 1; 0; 4; 31)

Yellow: BS381C 356 (CMYK 0; 31; 100; 5)

Roof, undergear and bogies: Black.

London & South East Sector, 1984

Dark Brown: British Rail 81/220 N/A

Light Brown: British Rail 81/221 N/A

Orange: British Rail 81/232 N/A

Railfreight by Roundel Design, 1987:

Railfreight Yellow: BS4880 08 E 51, (CMYK 0, 31, 95, 7)

Railfreight Red: BS4880 04 E 53, (CMYK 0, 64, 69, 25)

Railfreight Blue: BS4880 18 E 53, (CMYK 100, 23, 0, 38)

Light Grey (Rail): BS4800 00 A 05, (CMYK 0, 1, 2, 31)

Mid Grey (Flint): BS4800 00 A 09, (CMYK 2, 2, 0, 48)

Dark Grey (Executive): BS4800 00 A 13, (CMYK 1, 1, 0, 64)

Network SouthEast passenger shelters:

Columns:

BS4800 04 D 45 (CMYK 0; 53; 55; 47)

and BS4800 20 C 40 (CMYK 31; 20; 0; 67)

Canopy:

BS4800 00 E 55 (CMYK 0; 0; 3; 5)

and BS4800 18 B 17 (CMYK 4; 0; 1; 20)

or BS4800 18 B 21 (CMYK 5; 0; 0; 39)

or BS4800 18 B 25 (CMYK 10; 3; 0; 55)

Regional Railways and ScotRail Livery

Dark Blue: Pantone® 281C

Light Blue: Pantone® 306C

Silver Grey: Pantone® 5455C

Silver White: Pantone® White

Executive dark grey: Pantone® 425C

Warning yellow: Pantone® 123C

InterCity, August 1988 livery

There is not an exact match between print and livery colours

Red: British Rail 81/204

Falcon Grey: British Rail specification Dark Grey 81/246

Executive light grey: British Rail specification Light Grey 81/200

Silver white: British Rail specification BR 81/240 N/A

Black

Reference sources and further reading

Books

Anon., *London Architectural monographs: Liverpool Street Station*, (London: Academy Editions, 1978).

Anon., *Modern Railways pictorial profile: 1 high speed trains–IC125*, (Shepperton: Ian Allan, 1983).

Anon., *Modern Railways pictorial profile: 10 The 'Blue Pullmans'*, (Shepperton: Ian Allan, August-October 1985).

Anon., *Quest for Speed: The official story of East Coast enterprise*, (np: British Rail Eastern Region, December 1977).

Anon., *This is British Rail*, (London: British Railways Board, May 1979).

Anon., *Western Enterprise: A celebration in pictures and words of the Western class 2,700hp diesel hydraulic locomotives*, (Reading: British Rail Western Region, April 1975).

Cecil J Allen, G F Fiennes, Roger Ford, B A Haresnape, Brian Perren, *The Deltics: A Symposium* [second revised edition] (Shepperton: Ian Allan, 1977).

V R Anderson and G K Fox, *A Pictorial Record of L.M.S. Architecture* (Oxford: Oxford Publishing Company, 1981).

Christian Barman, *Next Station: A Railway Plans for the Future*, (London: George Allen & Unwin, 1947).

Christian Barman, *The Things We See: Public Transport*, (Harmondsworth: Penguin Books, 1949).

Christian Barman, *An Introduction to Railway Architecture*, (London: Art and Technics, 1950).

Christian Barman, *The Man who built London Transport*, (Newton Abbot: David & Charles, 1979).

Stephen Bayley and John Ward [eds.], *Kenneth Grange at the Boilerhouse: An Exhibition of British Product Design*, (London: The Conran Foundation, 1983).

Ken Baynes, *Industrial Design & the Community*, (London: Lund Humphries, 1967).

J Beresford–Evans, *Form in Engineering Design: the study of appearance during design and development*, (Oxford: Clarendon Press, 1954).

Marcus Binney and David Pearce [eds.], *Railway Architecture*, (London: Bloomsbury Books, 1985).

John and Avril Blake, *The Practical Idealists: Twenty–five years of designing for industry*, (London: Lund Humphries, 1969).

Avril Blake, *Misha Black*, (London: The Design Council, 1984).

Michael Bonavia, *The Organisation of British Railways*, (London: Ian Allan, 1971).

Michael R Bonavia, *The Birth of British Rail*, (London: George Allen & Unwin, 1979).

Michael R Bonavia, *British Rail: the First 25 Years*, (Newton Abbot: David & Charles, 1981).

Dave Brennand & Richard Furness, *The book of British Railways Station Totems*, (Stroud: Sutton Publishing/Wickford: Gloucester & Essex Railway Publishing, 2002).

Noel Carrington, *Industrial Design in Britain*, (London: George Allen & Unwin, 1976).

Linda Clarke, John Ives, Stuart Rankin and Paul Simons, *Aspects of Railway Architecture*, (London: British Railways Board, 1984).

Michelle Cotton, *Design Research Unit 1942–72*, (np: Koenig Books, 2011).

James Cousins, *British Rail Design*, (Copenhagen: Danish Design Council, 1986).

Nick Derbyshire, with an introduction by Colin Amery, *Liverpool Street: a station for the twenty-first century*, (Cambridge: Granta Editions, 1991).

George Dow, *Railway heraldry and other insignia*, (Newton Abbot: David & Charles, 1973).

Sir John Elliot; Michael Esau, *On and Off the Rails*. (London: George Allen & Unwin, 1982).

Chris Green & Mike Vincent, *The Network SouthEast Story 1982–2014*, (Hersham: Oxford Publishing Company, 2014).

T R Gourvish, *British Railways 1948–73: A Business history*, (Cambridge: Cambridge University Press, 1986).

Brian Haresnape, *Railway Design since 1830: Volume 1: 1830–1914* (London: Ian Allan, 1968).

Brian Haresnape, *Railway Design since 1830: Volume 2: 1914–1969,* (London: Ian Allan, 1969).

Brian Haresnape, *British Rail, 1948–78: a journey by design*, (Shepperton : Ian Allan, 1979).

Brian Haresnape, *Design for steam: 1830–1960*, (London: Ian Allan, 1981).

Brian Haresnape, *British Rail 1948–83: a journey by design* [revised edition], (Shepperton: Ian Allan, 1983).

Brian Haresnape, *Railway Liveries 1923–1947*, (Shepperton: Ian Allan, 1989).

Brian Haresnape; revised by Colin Boocock, *Railway Liveries: BR steam 1948–1968*, (Shepperton: Ian Allan, 1989).

Elain Harwood, 'Reappraising British Railways', in Julian Holder and Steven Parissien [eds.], *Studies in British Art: 13: The Architecture of British Transport in the Twentieth Century*, (New Haven & London: Yale University Press, 2004), pp 75–104.

Geoffrey Hughes, *LNER,* (London: Guild Publishing, 1986).

Nick Jardine, *British Railway Stations in Colour: For the Modeller and Historian* (Hinckley: Midland Publishing, 2002).

Stewart Joy, *The Train that Ran Away: a business history of British Railways 1948–68*, (London: Ian Allan, 1973).

G M Kichenside, *Railway Carriage Album* [first published 1966], (London: Ian Allan, 1980).

G H Lake, *British Railways' Standard Liveries*, (London: A W Hambling, 1949).

David Lawrence, *Underground Architecture*, (Harrow Weald: Capital Transport, 1994).

David Lawrence, *Bright Underground Spaces: The Railway Stations of Charles Holden*, (Harrow Weald: Capital Transport, 2008).

Mark Lawrence, *Network SouthEast: From Sectorisation to Privatisation*, (Sparkford: Oxford Publishing Company, 1994).

Raymond Loewy, *Industrial Design* [first published 1988], (New York: Overlook Duckworth, 2007).

Lionel Lynes, *Railway Carriages and Wagons, Theories and Practices*, (London: Locomotive Publishing, 1959).

Fiona MacCarthy, Deyan Sudjic, Gemma Curtin, Penny Sparke, Jonathan Glancey and Barbara Chandler, *Kenneth Grange: Making Britain Modern*, (London: Design Museum/Black Dog Publishing, 2011).

Jens Nielsen, *DSB design: Danish Railway Design*, (Copenhagen: Danish Design Council, May 1984).

Pentagram, *Living by Design*, (London: Lund Humphries, 1978).

Herbert Read, *Art & Industry: the principles of industrial design* [first published 1934], (London: Faber and Faber, 1966).

Andrew Saint, *Not Buildings but a Method of Building...: The achievement of the post–war Hertfordshire School Building Programme*, (Hertford: Hertfordshire Publications, 1990).

Tolu Solanke, *Avocet: In Pursuit of Style*, (London: IOD, 2013).

Mary Schoeser, *Marianne Straub*, (London: Design Council, 1984).

Alison and Peter Smithson, *The Euston Arch and the Growth of the London, Midland & Scottish Railway*, (London: Thames and Hudson, 1968).

S W Stevens-Stratten, with drawings by R S Carter, *British Rail Main-Line Diesels* [first published 1963], (London: Ian Allan, revised and enlarged edition 1975).

Walter Dorwin Teague, *Design This Day: The Technique of Order in the Machine Age*, (New York: Harcourt, Brace and Company, 1940).

Barbara Tilson [ed.], *Made in Birmingham: Design and Industry 1889–1989*, (Studley: Design History Society/K A F Brewin Books, 1989).

Mike Vincent & Chris Green [eds.], *The InterCity Story*, (Sparkford: Oxford Publishing Company, 1994).

Jacquey Visick, *British Rail Architecture, Design and Environment*, (London: British Railways Board, 1989).

Nigel Wikeley & John Middleton, *Railway Stations: Southern Region*, (Seaton: Peco Publications & Publicity, 1971).

Selected journal articles

Anon., 'A.E.I.-Birmingham-Sulzer 2,750 h.p. diesel prototype', Modern Railways, vol. XVI, no. 166, July 1962, pp 18–21.

Anon., 'BR orders Mk III coach prototypes', *Modern Railways*, vol. XXVI, no. 265, October 1970, pp 434–5.

Anon., 'The B. R. standard diesel-electric Type 1 locomotive', *Modern Railways*, vol. XVI, no. 171, December 1962, pp 381–82.

Anon., 'British Consortium in Trains for Europe', *Modern Railways*, vol. 47, no. 497, February 1990, pp 69–70.

Anon., 'British Rail Stations', *Building*, vol. CCXIII, no. 6486, 8 September 1967, pp 97–104.

Anon., 'Class 89 takes shape', *Modern Railways*, vol. 42, no. 439, April 1985, p 167.

Anon., 'The Class 141 railbus: 1: A technical description', *Modern Railways*, vol. 40, no. 412, January 1983, pp 18–19.

Anon., 'The Class 141 railbus: 2: 'the reaction of the Passenger Transport Executives', *Modern Railways*, vol. 40, no. 413, February 1983, pp 69–71.

Anon., 'Class 151: a technical description', *Modern Railways*, vol. 42, no. 440, May 1985, pp 250–1.

Anon., 'The Clayton Type 1', *Modern Railways*, vol. XVI, no. 171, December 1962, p 380.

Selected journal articles (continued)

Anon., 'Design: It's the first outward sign of BR's business efficiency', *Railnews*, August 1987, pp 10–11.

Anon., 'Education is keynote of new BR travel publicity', *Modern Railways*, vol. XXI, no. 197, February 1965, pp 72–3.

Anon., 'Euston Station: London's oldest terminal rebuilt as an envelope for a £15m total travel concept centre', *Building*, vol. CCXV, no. 6545, 25 October 1968, pp 103–10.

Anon., 'InterCity's New Look', *Modern Railways*, vol. 46, no. 488, May 1989, p 240.

Anon., 'Into the interior', *British Railways Eastern Region Magazine*, vol. 14, no. 4, April 1963, pp 102–8.

Anon., 'LMR begins reconstruction of Birmingham New Street', *Modern Railways*, vol. XIX, no. 189, June 1964, pp 404–5 and 409.

Anon., 'Manchester Piccadilly', *Modern Railways*, vol. XXII, no. 216, September 1966, above pp 484–5.

Anon., 'Maze Hill SR prototype station', *Modern Railways*, vol. XXIX, no. 289, October 1972, p 369.

Anon., 'Modernised Kent Coast unit', *Modern Railways*, vol. XXXIII, no. 328, pp 24–7.

Anon., 'New BR high-density stock for the Southern', *Modern Railways*, vol. XXVIII, no. 278, November 1971, pp 185–8.

Anon., 'New Class 56 diesel locomotives for British Rail', *Modern Railways*, vol. XXXIII, no. 333, June 1976, pp 224–5.

Anon., 'New Ideas in Rail Transport', *British Railways Magazine*, vol. 8, no. 8, August 1957, pp 202–3.

Anon., 'New image for BR', *Modern Railways*, vol. XIX, no. 189, June 1964, p 369.

Anon., 'New Inter-City diesel multiple-units for W. R.', *Modern Railways*, vol. XVII, no. 175, April 1963, pp 266–7.

Anon., 'New NER stations', *Modern Railways*, vol. XIX, no. 189, June 1964, p 377.

Anon., '"The Next Train..." BR's exhibition at the Design Centre - July 16 to August 16', *Modern Railways*, vol. XXV, no. 252, September 1969, pp 452–3.

Anon., 'The Oxted line diesel-electric multiple-units', *Modern Railways*, vol. XVI, no. 171, December 1962, pp 383–4.

Anon., 'The progress of British Transport', *London Transport Magazine*, vol. V, nos. 5 & 6, August-September 1950, pp 6–7, 27.

Anon., 'Railfreight's true colours', *Modern Railways*, vol. 44, no. 471, December 1987, pp 628–9.

Anon., 'Replacements for the "4-SUBS"', *Railway Magazine*, vol. 117, no. 846, October 1971, pp 524–6.

Anon.,'Report on Railway Progress', *Design*, no. 106, October 1957, pp 25–9.

Anon. 'Rolling stock for the SR's Bournemouth electrification', *Modern Railways*, vol. XXIII, no. 225, June 1967, pp 301–4.

Anon. 'The SR's new Brighton express units', *Modern Railways*, vol. XXI, no. 196, January 1965, pp 20–22.

James Abbott, 'Designing the Network', *Modern Railways*, vol. 44, no. 460, January 1987, pp 25–9.

G Freeman Allen, '"Blue Trains" treble North Clyde revenue', *Modern Railways,* vol. XXI, no. 196, January 1965, pp 36–40.

Vic Allen, 'New boss of BR design', *Creative Review*, vol. 6, no. 11, November 1986, pp 70–3.

British Railways London Midland Region, 'Ahead of Schedule: London Road ready for August 28', *News Special (Manchester Edition)*, no. 4, August 1960.

Richard Carr, 'Ton-up Locomotive', *Design*, no. 235, July 1968, pp 48–51.

Richard Carr, 'British Rail: The Way Ahead', *Design*, no. 248, August 1969, pp 18–23.

E L Cornwell, 'BR's advanced turbo-train project', *Modern Railways*, vol. XXIII, no. 224, May 1967, pp 234–5.

E L Cornwell, 'BR unveils its 125mph high-speed train', *Modern Railways*, vol. XXIX, no. 285, June 1972, pp 212–15.

E L Cornwell, 'Brush 4,000 H. P. "Kestrel": World's most powerful single-engined diesel locomotive', *Modern Railways*, vol. XXIII, no. 231, December 1967, pp 639–42, 672.

James S Cousins, 'Role of the BRB Design Panel', *Modern Railways*, vol. XXV, no. 251, August 1969, pp 398–401.

James S Cousins, 'British Rail industry in the seventies-6: Industrial design for railways', *Modern Railways*, vol. XXVII, no. 272, May 1971, pp 216–20, 222.

F F C Curtis, 'British Railways Architecture', *The Architect and Building News*, vol. 216, no. 13, 4 November 1959, pp 394–410.

Alec Davis, 'Design policy into practice: Graphics', *Design*, no. 171, March 1963, pp 72–7.

Paul Hamilton, 'The power signal box: a railway building of a new type', *Architectural Review*, vol. 138, no. 825, November 1965, pp 333–5.

Brian Haresnape, 'British Rail: the new image', *Modern Railways*, vol. XXI, no. 196, January 1965, pp 26–34.

Brian Haresnape, 'Design for the total travel environment: A report on papers presented to the recent Rail International Design Environment Conference in London', *Modern Railways*, vol. XXVI, no. 258, March 1970, pp 120–4.

Brian Haresnape, 'The incomplete environment–the railway carriage: Part Two', *Modern Railways*, vol. XXIX, no. 286, March 1962, pp 251–3.

Brian Haresnape, 'The new image emerges on the LMR', *Modern Railways*, vol. XXI, no. 202, July 1965, pp 368–70.

Brian Haresnape, 'Towards a B. R. "house style"', *Modern Railways*, vol. XVII, no. 175, April 1963, pp 234–8.

Brian Haresnape, 'XP64 New standard carriage project', *Modern Railways*, vol. XIX, no. 190, July 1964, pp 2–9.

Michael Harris, 'Closely Observed Images: Design in train by Edward Pond', *Modern Railways*, vol. 47, no. 501, June 1990, pp 308–10.

Corin Hughes-Stanton, 'Pass to greater rail comfort: The New British Railways Passenger Express Train', *SIA Journal*, no. 137, July 1964, pp 8–13, 16.

Sutherland Lyall, 'Priestess of the profitable', *Refurbishment*, 11 November 1988, pp 8–9.

Archie McNab, 'Modernising British Transport no. 5: Stations and station equipment', *Design*, no. 148, April 1961, pp 53–63.

Bryan Morgan, 'Modernisation of British rail architecture', *Modern Railways*, vol. XXIV, no. 235, April 1968, pp 208–11.

Bryan Morgan, 'Modernisation of British rail architecture', *Modern Railways*, vol. XXIV, no. 236, May 1968, pp 256–62.

Marcus Newman and Henry Stanton, 'Birmingham's new station and train service opened', *Modern Railways*, vol. XXIII, no. 224, May 1967, pp 245–7.

John Nunneley [Chief Passenger Manager, British Railways Board], 'BR's 1967 Inter-city campaign: A "first in TV selling of train travel', *Modern Railways*, vol. XXIII, no. 222, March 1967, pp 120–2, 125.

G C Pettitt, '"Crossrail Linkline" stations', *Modern Railways*, vol. 37, no. 384, September 1980, p 419.

J M Richards, 'Domesticating the Iron Horse', *The Architectural Review*, June 1942, pp 129–30, 135–6.

A E Robson, 'Diesel multiple-unit development on British Railways', *Modern Railways*, vol. XV, no. 164, May 1962, pp 308–15.

Hannah Schlee, 'Posters on Line', *Design and Industries Association Yearbook 1990*, pp 17–18.

Robert Spark, 'Design policy: Enter an Androcles', *Design*, no. 171, March 1963, pp 43–4.

Robert Spark, 'Looking ahead', *Design*, no. 171, March 1963, pp 78–9.

Robert Spark, 'XP64 sets new standards in British railway travel', *Design*, no. 189, September 1964, pp 42–5.

Robert Spark, 'London Manchester Liverpool: BR's new line in passenger appeal', *Design*, no. 211, July 1966, pp 53–7.

Nigel Wikeley, 'New stations for the Southern', *Modern Railways*, vol. XXIII, no. 231, December 1967, pp 643–6.

E G M Wilkes, 'Design on the railway', *Modern Railways*, vol. XVI, no. 166, July 1962, p 69.

E G M Wilkes, 'British Railways and Industrial Design - 1: A designer's look at BR rolling stock today', *Modern Railways*, vol. XXI, no. 201, June 1965, pp 324–7.

George Williams, 'What good Design Means', *The Commercial Motor*, vol. XCV, no. 2446, 28 March 1952, p 239.

George Williams, 'Working on the Railroad', *SIA Journal*, no. 115, September 1962, pp 1–2.

George Williams, 'British Railways and Industrial Design - 4: Why BR needs a new design idiom', *Modern Railways*, vol. XXI, no. 201, June 1965, p 329.

Margaret Wilson, 'Three years of the "Blue Pullmans"', *Modern Railways*, vol. XVIII, no. 178, July 1963, pp 22–6.

P F Winding, 'Re-shaping the LMR's north Western Line - 1', *Modern Railways*, vol. XX, no. 193, October 1964, pp 247–9, 253–4.

Brochures and Reports

Anon., *4,000HP Diesel Electric Locomotive* [sales brochure], (Loughborough: Brush Electrical Engineering Co. Ltd., 15 January 1968).

Anon., *The 1250 h.p. A1A-A1A Locomotive*, (Loughborough: Brush Traction Limited, August 1959).

Anon., *Another first for Hawker Siddeley: The 4000 h.p. Kestrel* [a special supplement to the Hawker Siddeley Review, vol. 5, no. 4], (Loughborough: Hawker Siddeley Limited, nd).

Anon., *BR a working clothes guide*, (np: British Rail, June 1990).

Anon., *Britain's New Railways*, (London: Railway

Industry Association/British Railways Board, 1988).

Anon., *British Rail is Travelling....1970*, (London: British Railways Board, 1970).

Anon., *British Railways project xp64* [public information brochure], (np: British Railways Board, 1964).

Anon., *Brush 2750 h.p. Co-Co Diesel Electric Locomotives*, (Loughborough: Brush Electrical Engineering Co. Ltd., nd).

Anon., *Forward: The LNER development programme*, (np: London & North Eastern Railway, 1946).

Anon., *Future Rail: The Next Decade*, (np: British Railways Board, July 1991).

Anon., *Modernisation Eastern Region*, (np: British Railways Board [Eastern Region], 1960).

Anon., *The new face of British Railways* [folder leaflet], (London: British Railways Board, 1965).

Anon., *Passenger Stations: Standards for Planning and Equipment*, (Euston: The Railway Executive, London Midland Region, August 1948).

Anon., *Tomorrow's train today*, (London: British Railways Board, September 1980).

John Barnes, *Press Cuttings, 1956–1989*, V&A: AAD/2013/3/6/1.

John Barnes, *Product Design Registers*, 1946–1980, V&A: AAD/2013/3/1/1– GB 73 AAD/2013/3/1/3.

Misha Black, *industrial design files 1951–59*, V&A: AAD/1980/3/6.

Misha Black, industrial design files 1959–69, V&A: AAD/1980/3/7.

Misha Black, *cuttings and articles 1940–58*, V&A: AAD/1980/3/142.

Misha Black, *cuttings and articles 1957–63*, V&A: AAD/1980/3/143.

Misha Black, *cuttings and articles 1963–77*, V&A: AAD/1980/3/144.

George Blake, *Glasgow Electric: The story of Scotland's New Electric Railway*, (np: British Railways, Scotland, November 1960).

British Rail, *Architecture Design and Environment*, (London: British Railways Board, 1989).

British Rail Chief Engineer (Traction & Rolling Stock), *Locomotives for the 1970s*, March 1969).

British Railways, *Proceedings of the British Railways (Western Region) London Lecture and Debating Society: Session 1960–61: No. 467: Design and Transport by Mr. T. H. Summerson, D.L., J.P. (Chairman, Design Panel, B.T.C.): Read at the meeting on 5th January 1961*.

British Railways, *Report of the Light Weight Trains Committee*, March 1952.

British Railways Board, *Architecture and Design for British Railways*, (London: British Railways Board, 1990).

British Railways Board: Director of Architecture, Design & Environment, *Railfreight Design Guide*, (London: British Railways Board, 1988).

British Transport Commission, *Corporate Identity Programme: Design Manual: 1st meeting of the Working Party for Corporate Identity Manual, September 1964*, TNA: AN 160/217.

British Transport Commission, *Corporate Identity Programme: Protection for BR Symbol*, TNA: AN 160/791.

British Transport Commission, *Design Panel Progress Report No 5: Year ending 31 December 1960*, (London: British Transport Commission, 1961).

British Transport Commission, *Design Panel Progress Report No 6: Year ending 31 December 1961*, (London: British Transport Commission, 1962).

British Transport Commission, *Modernisation of British Railways: Report on diesel and electric traction and the passenger services of the future based on proposals of the area boards*, April 1957.

British Transport Commission: Design Panel: Architects' Study Group, *Recommended Code of Practice for Minor Station Improvements*, 1961.

British Transport Commission, *Various internal reports concerning industrial design, 1956–1964*, TNA: AN 163/5.

Brush Electrical Engineering Company, *Falcon 2800hp Diesel Electric Locomotive* [sales brochure], (Loughborough: Brush Electrical Engineering Company, 1962).

Design Research Unit (Misha Black and John Beresford-Evans), *A report on a livery for British Railways: Part 1*, 27/5/63, TNA: AN 163/27.

Design Research Unit (Misha Black and John Beresford-Evans), *A report on a livery for British Railways: Part 2*, 27/5/63, TNA: AN 163/28.

Design Research Unit, B*R Staff Uniforms: Appendix A: Report by Investigating Team on Visit to Continent - May 1962*, TNA: AN 163/25.

Design Research Unit, *B.T.C. Uniforms: Formulation of Basic Design Proposals as a Guide for Compiling General Report DRU 1/485*, 28/5/62, TNA: AN163/24.

Design Research Unit, *Uniforms for the Railways Staff: Record photographs - as at July 1962*, TNA: AN 163/26.

B S Hancock, *The Leyland Railbus Body [a paper given for the Willis Faber Manufacturing Effectiveness Award 1986]*, (Leyland: Leyland Bus, 1986).

Jack Howe, *The Design of Railway Passenger Rolling Stock: Report by Jack Howe FRIBA FSIA*, 17 July 1959, TNA: AN 163/12.

The Railway Executive, *Sign Standards: Letters; Figures; Totem; Arrow*, (np: the Railway Executive, April 1948).

The Railway Executive, *Code of Instructions for Station Name and Direction Signs*, (np: the Railway Executive, 27th September 1948).

E G M Wilkes. *The Appearance & Amenity Design of Rolling Stock: Paper to read at the Institution of Locomotive Engineers*, August 1964. NRM: 2002-8349/9.

E G M Wilkes, *Designing for the Railways* [private paper], circa 1990.

Wilkes & Ashmore. *Beyer Peacock Type 3 1700 H. P. Diesel Hydraulic Locomotive for The British Transport Commission: Design Notes*, September 1959. NRM: 2002-8349/2.

Wilkes & Ashmore, *British Railways Observation Train: Report on Design Progress up to 29th October 1960*, TNA: AN 163/15.

Wilkes & Ashmore. *English Electric Type 3 Locomotive: Notes on the design recommendations*, February 1963. NRM: 2002-8349/6.

Wilkes & Ashmore. Locomotive Appearance Design: Progress Report 1, 7 March 1956. NRM: 2002-8349/1/1.

Wilkes & Ashmore. *Locomotive Appearance Design: Progress Report 3*, 14 April 1956. NRM: 2002-8349/1/3.

Wilkes & Ashmore. *Locomotive Appearance Design: Progress Report 4*, 14 June 1956. NRM: 2002-8349/1/4.

Wilkes & Ashmore. *Locomotive Appearance Design Progress Report 6*, 18th October 1956. NRM: 2002-8349/1/6.

Wilkes & Ashmore. *Notes on the cab design of the English Electric Locomotive as shown on I.E. drawing V.3200/152*, March 1966. NRM: 2002-8349/12.

Wilkes & Ashmore. *Notes on Recommended Colour Scheme for Rhodesian Railways Locomotive*, May 1962. NRM: 2002-8349/4.

Wilkes & Ashmore. *Notes on the relationship between the appearance and the engineering and operational requirements of the Hymek, Falcon, Lion, and Hawker-Siddeley (Brush Type 4) locomotives*, January 1963. NRM: 2002-8349/5.

Wilkes & Ashmore. *Prototype Train XP 64 Exhibition Carriages (1960–1965)*. NRM: 2002-8349/14.

Wilkes & Ashmore. *Recommendations for a new locomotive livery*, March 1962. NRM: 2002-8349/3.

Journals and magazines consulted

The Architect and Building News; The Architects' Journal; The Architectural Review; BackTrack; British Railways Magazine: Eastern Region; British Railways Magazine: London Midland Region; British Railways Magazine: Southern Region; Building Design; Creative Review; Daily Telegraph; Design; Financial Times; Heritage Outlook; The Locomotive Railway Carriage & Wagon Review; Model Railway Constructor; Modern Railways; Modern Railways Pictorial; Motive Power Monthly; Overseas Railways; Rail; Rail Express; Railnews; The Railway Gazette; The Railway Magazine; Railways Illustrated; Rassengna; Refurbishment; SIA Journal, Southern Report; Third Rail; The Times; Traction; Trains Illustrated; Trains Illustrated Express Trains; Western Division News.

Index

Adams, Mary 158
Advanced Passenger Train
   (*APT*) 146, 182, 184, 185, 186, 187, 192, 194, 197, 208
   (*APT-250*) 190
   (*APT-E*) 187, 188, 189, 190
   (*APT-E*): *interiors* for 188, 189
   (*APT-P*) (*class 370*) 190–1
   (*APT-P*) (*class 370*) interiors for 190–1
   (*APT-P*) (*class 370*) liveries for 190–1
   (*APT-S*) 190
Aérospatiale 187
Applegate, Alan 179
Architects
   Adams, Holden and Pearson 58, 60, 61
   Alan Brookes Associates 240
   Archigram 86
   Arthur, J A 58
   Baden-Powell, Charlotte 74
   Bicknell, John (1929–97) 74, 101
   Birchett, Dennis 81
   Brawne, Michael (1925–2003) 74
   Casson, (Sir) Hugh (1910–99) 113
   Cavanagh, Howard (1909–60) 58, 69
   Clendinning, Max (1924–) 74, 79
   Collins, John 76
   Cunliffe, Roger (1932–) 74
   Curtis, F F C (1903–75) 58, 60, 113
   Dannatt, Trevor (1920–) 113
   de Saulles, Patrick 74, 82
   Derbyshire, Nick 221, 239
   Easton, John Murray (1889–1975) 60
   Edwards, M J C 76
   Farmer and Dark 113
   Fellows, John 240
   Fletcher, E J 98
   Goldhill, David 74, 82
   Green, H E 100
   Hamilton, Paul (1924–2004) 74, 76, 77, 101
   Hamlyn, W H 60, 62
   Hardy, Sydney 58, 100
   Headley, W R 'Bob' 58, 86
   Hoile, John 101
   Holden, Charles (1875–1960) 60, 62, 81, 86, 98
   Jones, R H 69
   Kaukas, Bernard (1922–2014) 58
   Kennett, John 69
   Llewelyn-Davies, (Lord) Richard (1912–81) 62, 63, 64, 95
   MacIver, Peter 60
   Martin, (Sir) Leslie (1908–2000) 62, 63, 64, 95
   McIntyre, Ronnie 229, 238, 241
   Miller, Peter 113
   Moorcroft, R L 'Roy' 58, 86
   Newton, Peter 82
   Nicholas Grimshaw & Partners 252
   Niemeyer, Oscar 79
   Pacitti, Cosimo 82
   Papps, Michael 240
   Pittaway, H H 58
   Powell, H H 58
   Quin, Diana P 101
   Rawson, Keith 76
   Reyniers, Peter 75
   Robertson, Howard (1888–1963) 60
   Shorten, Derrick 70, 74, 76
   Sir Basil Spence, Bonnington and Collins 188
   Snow, T A 82
   Taylor, Paul 74
   Taylor, Rodney 221
   Thorpe, A N 58
   Turner, Roy 69
   van der Rohe, Ludwig Mies 76, 84, 98
   Ward, John 75
   Wheeler, Maurice 74, 82
   Wikeley, N D T 58, 95, 98
   Wyatt, J S 69, 82
Architecture
   colour schemes for stations 64, 74, 76, 95, 238, 252
   influence of European examples 57, 60, 101
   London Underground: influence on British

   railway station design 57, 60, 62, 81, 86, 98
   prefabrication 62, 63, 81, 82, 83
   prefabrication: CLASP 94, 95
   prefabrication: D70 96–99
   prefabrication: 'Mark II' 82, 83
   prefabrication: 'Mod-X' 82, 83
   public sector 57
   RA traditional building type (RAT) 240
   renewal of stations 179
   stations: for InterCity 226
Arkle, E W 108
Art & Industry [periodical] 155
Art Deco 60
Artists
   Arnoldi, Per 195
   Baldwin, Frederick William (1899–1980) 25
   Broadhead, Dobson 25
   Buckle, Claude (1905–73) 80
   Butler, Richard (1921–2005) 160
   Calvert, Margaret 68, 78
   Cowern, Raymond Teague (1913–86) 24
   Dannatt, Trevor (1920–) 45
   Eckersley, Tom (1914–97) 21, 23, 30
   Gill, Eric (1882–1940) 11, 12, 232, 233, 241
   Hodgkinson 24
   Johnston, Edward (1872–1944) 11
   Merriott, Jack (1901–68) 24, 25
   Millett, David 120
   Mitchell, William (1925–) 120, 184
   Neiland, Brendan (1941–) 228
   Pond, Edward (1929–2013) 232, 233
   Roselman 25
   Sorrell, Alan (1904–1974) 61
Arts & Crafts 106
Ashfield, Lord 67
Associated British Railways 9
Associated Rail Technologies 198
Bakelite plastic 73
Barby, Bill 179
Barman, Christian (1898–1980) 108, 109, 122, 154, 157, 160
Barman, Christian: on design for transport 108
Barney, Gerald 171, 172, 173, 174, 177
Beeching, (Lord) Richard (1913–85) 85, 105, 172, 184
Belgian National Railways (SNCB) 250
Bentley S2 Continental Drop Head Coupe motor car 115
Bentley S3 Continental Drop Head Coupe motor car 115
Birmingham Art School 106
Bleasdale, Cyril 222
'Blue Pullman' high-speed diesel train 118–121, 155, 157, 160
Bonavia, Michael (1909–99) 11, 12
Bond, Roland 36
Boston & Maine Railroad 198
Braddick, Ron 174
Branton, Paul (1916–90) 188, 189, 193
Brasilia 79
Bristol Aeroplane Company 130
Bristol Pullman 118–21
British Aircraft Corporation 187
British Airports Authority (BAA) 221, 232
British European Airways 116
British Rail Engineering: works
   Crewe 196, 224
   Doncaster 196
British Rail Residuary Body 253
British Rail
   Corporate Identity 168, 173, 210, 217, 219, 221, 222
   Corporate Identity Steering Committee 177
   Corporate identity: Catering Services 93
   Corporate Identity: influence on European transport systems 217
   Department of Architecture, Design and

   Environment 221
   division into sectors 219
   logotype 210
   privatisation of 253
   regions: colours for 177
   Research Department 186
British Rail: sectors
   European Passenger Services 220, 250
   InterCity 219, 220, 222–3
   InterCity: logotype 223
   InterCity: privatisation of 228
   InterCity: publicity 223, 228
   InterCity: rebranding of 222–3
   London & South East 219, 220, 222, 228
   London & South East: liveries for 228–30
   Network SouthEast 220, 222, 228
   Network SouthEast: liveries for 228–30
   Network SouthEast: privatisation of 253
   Network SouthEast: publicity 230–3
   Parcels 219, 222, 250
   Provincial 219, 241–5
   Rail express systems (R.e.s) 222, 250
   Rail express systems (R.e.s): liveries for 250
   Rail express systems (R.e.s): privatisation of 253
   Railfreight 219, 222, 246
   Railfreight: liveries for 246, 248–9
   Railfreight: privatisation of 249, 253
   Railfreight: sub-sectors 248–9
   Regional Railways 220, 222, 241–5
   Regional Railways: branding 241–2
   Regional Railways: publicity 241
   ScotRail 220, 222, 228, 229, 241
   ScotRail: branding 241–2
British Rail: Signing Secretariat 179
British Railways' Advanced Projects Group 186
British Railways Board: founding of 105
British Railways' regions
   colours for 12, 16, 17, 20, 21, 32, 65, 66, 67
   tradition 10
   Eastern 10, 12, 17, 18, 20, 42, 46, 58, 64, 69, 72, 73, 74, 75, 80, 98, 100, 133, 136
   London Midland 10, 12, 18, 19, 20, 42, 46, 58, 64, 65, 80, 82, 83, 86, 100, 108, 171
   North Eastern 10, 12, 21, 42, 58, 64, 68, 74
   North Western 10
   Scottish 10, 12, 17, 18, 58, 64, 65, 66, 130, 132, 207, 228
   Southern 10, 12, 13, 17, 20 ,21, 39, 40, 41, 42, 48, 49, 58, 64, 66, 68, 69, 74, 75, 95, 98, 100, 135, 151, 197, 204, 205, 214
   Western 10, 12, 19, 20, 39, 42, 52, 57, 58, 60, 64, 68, 69, 95, 138, 149, 150, 154
British Railways' works
   Derby 48, 49, 50, 51, 116, 168, 205
   Doncaster 42, 46, 113, 205
   Eastleigh 42, 48, 135, 205
   Swindon 48, 49, 52, 135
   Wolverton 46, 48, 133
   York 42, 48, 133, 134, 135, 205
British Railways: rebranded as British Rail 168, 173
British Transport Commission
   area boards 10
   demise of 105
   Design Panel 9, 10, 52, 54, 74, 101, 105, 108, 109, 111, 113, 122, 128, 130, 136, 139, 144, 145, 146, 149, 157, 158, 159, 166, 167
   Design Panel: Architects' Study Group 74
British Transport Commission: Executives
   Docks & Inland Waterways 10, 11, 14
   Hotels 10
   London Transport 10, 11
   Railway 10, 11, 12, 14, 40, 54, 150, 150
   Railway: demise of 10
   Road Haulage 10
   Road Passenger 10
   Road Transport 10
British Transport Commission: grant of heraldic arms 15, 172
British Transport Commission: *Modernisation Plan* 40

≋ 268

British Transport Commission: symbols
   lion & crown 15, 163, 165, 170, 172
   lion & wheel 11
British Transport Commission: trading names
   British Railways 11
   British Road Services 11
   British Transport 11
Broadgate development, London 238
Bulleid, O V S (1882–1970) 41
Canadian National Railways' Turbo Train 182
Castle, (Baroness) Barbara 184, 187
Catering products: plastic 208
Channel Tunnel 185, 225, 228, 247, 250
Code of Instructions for Station Name and direction Signs [design manual], 1948 66
Code of Practice for minor station improvements, 1961 [booklet] 74
Colours
   'BR Flame Red' 172, 179, 180, 229, 246
   'BR Publicity Blue' 176
   'BR Publicity Red' 173, 174, 176
   'BR Rail Blue' 155, 172, 179, 180–1, 222, 246
   'BR Rail Grey' 172, 180–1, 222
   'Cobweb' 154
   'Desert Sand' 152–3, 154
   'Electric Blue' 155
   'Golden Ochre' 144, 154, 160, 166
   'Improved Engine Green' 144
   'Monastral Blue' 172, 180–1, 222
   'Nanking Blue' 118, 119, 121
   'Phthalocyanine Blue BN' 172
   'Stroudley Yellow' 144
Concorde supersonic airliner 187
Consumers' Association 158
Copenhagen Central railway station 239
Cornish, Mike 198
Corporate Identity Manual 158, 172, 174–7, 179, 180–1, 182
Council of Industrial Design (CoID) 106, 108, 109, 166
Cousins, James 11, 158, 219, 220, 223
Cox, Ernest Stewart (1900–92) 36
CrossRail 228, 237
Cuban National Railways 143
Dandridge, C G G 12
Danish Railway Design 220
Danish State Railways (*DSB Danske Statsbaner*) 171, 217, 220, 229
de Havilland *Comet* 118
'Deltic' motor 136
Design Centre 166, 174, 184
Design Council 106, 166, 187, 194
Design Management 184, 221
Designers
   Allen-Bowden 115, 122
   Armstrong, Rupert 168, 174
   Ashmore, Peter 106, 109, 118, 119, 122, 130, 133
   Balmain, Pierre 251
   Barnes, John (1913–89) 105, 115, 116, 117, 122
   Beresford-Evans, John 106, 149, 151, 154, 155, 168, 171, 172
   Black, Sir Misha (1910–77) 106, 118, 122, 130, 149, 154, 168, 171, 172
   Bloomfield, Jack 158, 163, 168, 189, 192
   Braddick, Ron 168
   Brumwell, Marcus (1901–83) 149
   Calvert, Margaret 168, 171, 177, 217
   Cambridge, Peter 122, 142
   Carter, David 106
   Clayton, Caroline 227
   Clements, Collis 168, 172, 173, 174
   Coombs, Jill 122
   David Hodge Associates 240
   Day, Robin (1915–2010) 69, 72, 73, 113
   DCA Design 106, 221, 224, 237, 250
   Denny, Mike 250

Design Research Unit 85, 106, 109, 130, 139, 149, 150, 154, 155, 158, 166, 171, 174, 177, 196, 219
Design Research Unit: on locomotive superstructures 149, 150, 151, 154, 155
Diamond, John 130
Dudas, Frank E (1928–2011) 115
Earl, Harley 130
Fraser, June 172
Grange, (Sir) Kenneth (1929–) 184, 189, 192–3, 194
Gray, Milner (1899–1997) 149, 154, 158, 163, 174, 177
Gray, Milner: on British Railways' public image 168
Halpen, Grey, Vermeer 249
Henrion, F H K (1914–90) 131, 158, 159
Higgins, David 122
Hill, Anthony (1939–) 147, 148
Hill, Atholl (1935–) 106, 184, 185, 186, 188
Howe, Jack (1911–2003) 105, 116, 117, 118–9, 155, 159, 160, 170, 172, 192
Hulme Chadwick & Partners 90
Jones Garrard 106, 221, 235, 236, 246, 247, 248, 250
Jordan Williams 230
King, Perry 122, 160, 161
Kinneir, Jock (1917–94) 68, 78, 158, 168, 171, 179, 217
Kinsman, Rodney 252
Knox, Graham 170
Koren, Vilhelm 115
Lamble, Kenneth 163, 168, 175
McCrum, J P 'Joe' 106, 124, 149, 150
Mellor, David (1930–2009) 159
Miles, Ellis 158, 168, 172, 246
Newell & Sorrell 221, 223
Noël Haring & Associates 244
OMK Design 252
Peartree Design 249
Pentagram 189
Reeves, Angela 174
Reid, John (1925–92) 159
Reid, Sylvia (1925–) 159
Robertshaw, John 230
Rodber, Michael 235, 246, 250
Roundel Design 221, 248, 250
Rowlands, Martyn (1923–2004) 208
Russell, R D (1903–81) 105, 115
Sadler, Kenneth J 122, 123, 134
Sayer, Malcolm (1916–70) 146
Schreiber, Gaby (1916–91) 159
Sorrell, Frances 226
Spencer, Herbert (1924–2002) 174, 178, 228, 229
Stanier, Sir William 192
Straub, Marianne (1909–1994) 54, 121, 134, 169
Tilney Lumsden Shane 250
Tustin, Don 122, 130, 138
Tyrrell, Anne 227
Venture Design Consultants 249
Ward, Jack 106, 122, 123, 136, 161
Welch, Robert (1929–2000) 159, 160
Wilkes & Ashmore 105, 106, 109, 118, 122, 124, 126–7, 128, 130, 132, 133, 134, 135, 136, 137, 138, 139, 140, 142, 144, 145, 146, 148, 154, 155, 159, 161, 166, 168, 170, 171, 172, 186, 187, 192, 196, 204, 205
Wilkes & Ashmore: on liveries 141, 142, 144
Wilkes & Ashmore: on locomotive superstructures 149
Wilkes, E G M 106, 107, 109, 122, 123, 133, 136, 138, 142, 145, 187
Driving Van Trailer (DVT): Mark 3 224–5
Driving Van Trailer (DVT): Mark 4 224–5
Dutch Railways (NS - Nederlandse Spoorwegen) 248
Elliot, (Sir) John 67, 150
Ergonomics 142, 148, 188, 189
E-type Jaguar motor car 146
European design: influence of 111, 130, 171, 174
Eurostar 250, 252
Exhibition trains
   'The New Railways', 1964 166
   'European Conservation Year 1970' 187
Exhibitions
   'Britain Can Make It', London, 1946 149
   Festival of Britain, 1951 71, 106, 109, 122, 149

   'Modern Railway Travel', 1957 112–3
   'New Design for British Railways', London, 1963 166, 168
   'The new face of British Railways', London, 1965 174
   'The Next Train...', London, 1969 184, 185, 192
   'International Exhibition of Railway Rolling Stock', Moscow, 1971 148
   'Transpo 72', Washington DC, 1972 182
   'International Transport Exhibition', Hamburg, 1979 189
Fiennes, G F 136
Ford Motor Company 122, 148
Formica 73
Freight vehicles: liveries for 167, 174, 181
French Railways (SNCF) 246, 247, 250, 253
Furniture: for stations 69, 72
Ganz-MÁVAG, Hungary 201
Gatwick Express 222, 228
General Motors *Aerotrain* 197
German Federal Railways *E03* locomotive 146
German Federal Railways *V200* locomotive 150
Glasgow Suburban electrification scheme 130, 158, 159, 168
Gorb, Peter 184
Grand, K W C 150, 154
Green, Chris 228, 229, 240, 241
Hancock, Basil 198
Haresnape, Brian 144, 154, 160, 166, 246
Harrison, J F 185
Hayter, (Lord) George 187
High Speed Train
   (HST) 146, 184, 197, 224, 226
   (HST) class 252 194
   (HST) class 253 194
   (HST) class 253/254: liveries for 194
   (HST) class 254 194
   (HST) class 41 192–3
   (HST) class 41: interiors for 193
   (HST) class 41: liveries for 192
Hill, Sir Reginald 14
Hurcombe, (Lord) Cyril (1883–1975) 10, 11, 14
Ikarus bus manufacturer, Hungary 201
Imperial Chemical Industries (ICI) 108, 158
Imperial College (London) 193
Industrial design for transport:
   aesthetic considerations 110–11, 122, 139, 145
   processes 110, 122
   purpose of 108, 122
Inter-City 'Monica' advertising campaign 210
InterCity: branding 223
Ivatt, George (1886–1976) 54
J Walter Thompson 230
Japanese National Railways *Shinkansen* train 187
Johnson, (Sir) Henry 184
Jones, Dr Sydney 186
Kaye, Tony 223
Koratron 182
Le Shuttle 224, 250, 251
Letter forms: Gill Sans 12, 13, 16, 65, 66 ,67, 68, 128
Letter forms
   Helvetica (Neue Haas Grotesk) 171
   Joanna 241
   Johnston/Underground 11
   Rail Alphabet 171, 177, 217
   Transport 68, 78, 158, 159, 171
Leyland Experimental Vehicle 198
Leyland *National* bus 198, 199, 202
Leyland *National* bus Mk 2 198
Leyland *Titan* bus 202

Limpet magnetic levitation train 187
Locomotive design: north American practice 54
Locomotives for the 1970s 185
Locomotives
   10000 (LMS) 54
   10001 (LMS) 54
   10201 (SR) 54
   10202 (SR) 54, 55
   10203 (SR) 54
   10800 (LMS) 54
   18100 (GWR) 54, 55
   CC1–CC3 41
   class 08 113, 115
   class 29 150
   class 50 (D400 series) 145
   class 56 186, 196
   class 58 246, 247
   class 60 246, 247
   class 86 155, 192
   class 87 186, 196
   class 89 'Avocet' 224
   class 9/class 9000 224, 250–1
   class 90 225
   class 91 'Electra' 224–5
   class 92 247
   class AL1/81 series 149, 155
   class AL2/82 series 149, 155
   class AL3/83 series 149, 155
   class AL4/84 series 149, 155
   class AL5/85 series 149, 155
   Coronation class 192
   D0260 *Lion* 124, 139, 140, 141, 144, 148
   D0280 *Falcon* 124, 139, 140, 144
   D1 series (class 44) 54, 116, 117
   D1000 series (class 52) 'Western' 106, 111, 149, 150, 152–3, 154, 166, 171, 185
   D11 series (class 45) 116, 117
   D138 series (class 46) 116
   D1500 series (class 47) 124, 139, 142, 143, 144, 146, 148, 168–9, 185, 246
   D200 series (class 40) 54
   D5000 series (class 24) 126, 128
   D5151 series (class 25) 126, 127
   D5300 series (class 26) 125, 127, 128–9
   D5347 series (class 27) 129
   D5500 series (class 30/31) 124, 125, 139, 144
   D5700 series (class 28) 116, 117
   D5900 series (class 23) 54
   D600 series (class 41) 'Warship' 149
   D6100 series (class 21) 149, 150
   D6300 series (class 22) 149, 150
   D6500 series (class 33) 125, 128
   D6700 series (class 37) 54, 144, 145
   D7000 series (class 35) 11, 124, 138, 139, 144, 166
   D800 series (class 42/class 43) 'Warship' 106, 139, 149, 150, 171
   D8000 series (class 20) 113, 114, 246
   D8200 series (class 15) 115
   D8400 series (class 16) 54
   D8500 series (class 17) 116, 117
   D9000 series (class 55) 'Deltic' 20, 113, 136–7, 145, 146, 185
   D9500 series (class 14) 116
   DP2 (Deltic Prototype 2) 139, 145
   E1000/E2001 55
   E5000 series (class HA/71) 149, 151, 155
   E6000 series (class JA/73) 151
   Heavy Freight Locomotive 185
   Kestrel 146, 147, 148
   liveries for 38, 39, 55, 124, 125, 126, 128, 136, 137, 138, 139, 140, 141, 144, 148, 150, 152–3, 154, 166, 167, 168–9, 171, 172, 180–1, 225, 230, 246, 248, 249, 250, 264
   liveries for: 'large logo' 246
   standard steam classes 36, 37
   superstructure design 54, 105, 106, 109, 110, 111, 114, 115, 116, 117, 122, 124–6, 128, 139, 142, 144, 149, 185, 224, 225,
   superstructure design: semi-streamlined 146, 148
Logotypes
   British Rail 176, 210
   British Rail regions 176
   InterCity and Swallow 223
   Seaspeed 176
London Business School: Design Management Unit 184
London Overground 84

London Transport 9, 11, 12, 62, 67, 69, 108, 133, 172, 184
London Underground 67, 81, 86, 118, 237
Lynes, Lionel 41
Main line railways
   Caledonian Railway 12
   Great Eastern Railway 12
   Great Western Railway (GWR) 10, 12, 36, 39, 40, 41, 42, 52, 54, 55, 60, 64, 66, 68, 95, 108, 118, 138, 150, 154, 164
   London and North Eastern Railway (LNER) 10, 11, 12, 13, 39, 40, 60
   London and South Western Railway 41
   London, Brighton and South Coast Railway 144
   London, Midland and Scottish Railway (LMS) 10, 36, 39, 40, 54, 60, 61, 62, 63, 67, 95, 116, 192
   Southern Railway (SR) 10, 39, 41, 54, 55, 58, 60, 67
Malayan Railways 201
Manchester Royal Exchange Theatre 239
Manchester University 187
Manufacturers
   ABB Transportation Systems 247
   William Alexander 242, 243
   Andrew Barclay & Sons 243
   Beyer Peacock 138
   Birmingham Railway Carriage & Wagon Company 49, 50, 113, 128, 140, 141
   British Leyland 197, 198–203, 244
   British Rail Engineering 196, 198, 200, 207, 224, 234, 243, 245, 246
   British Thomson-Houston 115
   Brush Traction 124, 125, 139, 140, 142, 146, 147, 148, 196, 224, 246, 247
   Clayton Equipment Company 143
   Cravens Limited 49, 113
   Edinburgh Weavers 134
   Electroputere 196
   English Electric 54, 136, 139
   English Electric: design of superstructures 136, 144, 145
   GEC 224
   Gloucester Railway Carriage & Wagon 49, 50
   Hawker Siddeley 146
   Hille and Company 113
   Hunslet Transportation Projects 245
   Metropolitan-Cammell (Metro-Cammell) 42, 46, 49, 50, 51, 118, 224, 244
   Metropolitan-Vickers 116
   Park Royal Vehicles 49, 50
   Pressed Steel 49, 130
   Robert Stephenson & Hawthorn 115
   Tamesa Fabrics 134
   Vulcan Foundry 115
   Warner Fabrics 121
   D Wickham of Ware 49, 198
Marine vessels: liveries for 180–1
Marples, (Baron) Ernest 105
Marsh, (Sir) Richard 184
Maxpax 208
McKenna, David 184
Midland Pullman 116, 118–21
Miller, T C B 'Terry' 185
Ministry of Transport 158
Modernisation Plan 40, 54, 105, 108, 115
Modernisation Plan Pilot Scheme 54, 128, 136, 138, 149, 150, 185
Monotype Corporation 11
Moquette 45, 46, 244
Motorway service areas 76
Multiple-unit
   4REP (class 432) 134
   Advanced Passenger Train (*APT*) 146, 182, 184, 185, 186, 187, 192, 194, 197, 208, 222
   Advanced Suburban Train 236
   semi-streamlined 146
Multiple-unit: diesel
   3D (class 207) 135
   3H (class 205) 48
   5L (class 203) 48, 113
   6L (class 202) 48, 113
   'Blue Pullman' high-speed train 118–121, 155, 157, 160
   class 100 49, 50

class 101/102 49, 50, 51
class 103 49, 50
class 104 49, 50
class 107 49
class 108 49, 50
class 110 49, 50
class 111 49
class 114 49
class 115 49
class 116 49
class 118 49
class 119 49, 50
class 120 52, 53
class 122 49
class 123 135
class 124 130, 131
class 125 49
class 126 52
class 127 49, 51
class 143/4 235
class 150 197
class 158 *Express Sprinter* 245
class 159 245
class 165 *Network Turbo* 232, 237
class 166 *Network Turbo* 237
class 210 197
'Derby Lightweight' 49
High Speed Train (HST) 146, 148, 184, 192–3, 197, 224, 226
High Speed Train (*HST*) class 252 194
High Speed Train (*HST*) class 253 194
High Speed Train (*HST*) class 254 194
High Speed Train (*HST*) class 41 19
Multiple-unit: electric
   2EPB (class 416/1) 42
   2EPB (class 416/2) 42, 48
   2HAP (class 414) 42
   2HAP (class 414/1) 42
   2PEP (class 446) 205
   4BEP (class 412) 45
   4CEP (class 411) 44, 45
   4CIG (class 421) 134, 135, 232
   4EPB (class 415/1) 42, 43
   4PEP (class 445) 204–5
   4SUB (class 405) 41, 42
   4VEP (class 423) 134
   Advanced Passenger Train (*APT-250*) 190
   Advanced Passenger Train (*APT-S*) 190
   Advanced Passenger Train (*APT-P*) (class 370) 190–1, 222
   Advanced Suburban Train 236
   AM2 (class 302) 42, 43, 46
   AM3 (class 303) 130–1
   AM4 (class 304) 46, 47
   AM5 (class 305) 46, 133
   AM7 (class 307) 42, 43
   AM8 (class 308) 46
   AM9 (class 309) 130, 133
   AM10 (class 310) 135
   class 313 206, 232
   class 314 206
   class 315 206
   class 317/1 197, 207
   class 317/2 207
   class 318 207
   class 319 232, 233, 234, 235
   class 321 232, 236
   class 322 236
   class 323 245
   class 341 237
   class 373 250, 251
   class 374 e320 250
   class 442 *Wessex Electrics* 235, 236
   class 445/446 206
   class 455/7 207
   class 455/8 197, 207
   class 455/9 207
   class 465 *Networker* 232, 236–7
   class 471 232, 237
   class 501 42, 43
   class 504 46
   class 507 206
   class 508 206
   Tyneside 42, 43
Multiple-unit: gas turbine
   Advanced Passenger Train (*APT-E*) 187, 188, 189, 190

Multiple-unit: high-density 204–5
Multiple-unit: high-density: interiors for 204
Multiple-unit: Highlands observation train 132
Multiple-unit: interiors for 133, 134, 204, 206
Multiple-unit: liveries for 132, 133, 134, 171, 188, 246, 264
Multiple-unit: XPT 196
National Bus Company 198
National Rail 253
National Railway Museum, York 188
National railway network: modernisation 10
National railway network: visual consistency 10
National Traction Plan 184
Nelson, John 240
Ness, James 130
Network SouthCentral 253
Network SouthEast
    branding 228–30
    liveries for 205, 230, 235, 236, 237
    privatisation of 253
'New Towns' 58, 62, 77
Nielsen, Jens 220
North America 9
Northern Ireland Railways 199
Norwegian State Railways (*Norges Statsbaner*) 171
O'Brien, Jim 219, 220
Ogilvy, Lady Virginia 234
Ottaway, E C 108
Paris *Metro* 239
Parker, (Sir) Peter 184
Parker, (Sir) Peter: on design for British Rail 184
Passenger Transport Executives 184, 197
    Greater Manchester 202
    Tyne & Wear 243
    West Yorkshire 200, 243
Passenger vehicles
    Autocoach 41
    Auto-trailer 41
    'Coach of the Future' 154, 159, 160–1, 166, 168
    interiors for 45, 46, 48, 113, 114, 118–21, 130, 159, 160, 168–9, 170, 188, 189, 190–1, 193, 199, 226, 234, 244
    liveries for 38, 39, 118, 121, 160, 166, 168–9, 170, 171, 180–1, 222, 223, 225, 228, 230, 235, 236, 237, 242, 244, 264
    Mark I coach 45, 48, 52, 54, 203, 232
    Mark II coach 54, 159, 168–9, 170, 193, 224, 232
    Mark 3 coach 184, 185, 193, 207, 224, 236
    Mark 3a coach 226
    Mark 3b coach 226
    Mark 4 coach 224, 226
Passenger vehicles:
    railbus 40, 197, 198–203
    class 140 199
    class 141 (R4) 199, 200–1
    class 142 (R5) 202, 203, 235
    class 142/1 202
    class 143 242, 243
    class 144 243
    class 150 *Sprinter* 243, 244
    class 150/2 *Sprinter* 243
    class 151 244
    class 153 244
    class 155 *Super Sprinter* 244
    class 156 244
    double-deck 203
    interiors for 198, 199, 200, 202
    international trials 201
    night coach' 203
    R1 198
    R3.01/LEV 1 198
    R3.02 199
    R3.03 199
    'USA' 199
Passenger vehicles: railcar 40, 41, 118
Passenger vehicles: Regional Railways: liveries for 244, 245
Passenger vehicles: 'xp64' 159, 168, 170
Paytrains 85
Pick, Frank (1878–1941) 108
Pilkington's Limited 80

Plastic laminate 45, 46, 69, 71, 72, 73, 113, 114, 168
Polish Air Force 248
Portsmouth Aviation 189
Prideaux, Dr John 220, 222, 223
Priestman, Dr Jane 221, 221, 223, 230, 232, 252
Publicity
    handbills 16, 30
    Holiday Guides 22–23
    Publicity: *Holiday Haunts* 22–23
    InterCity 228
    leaflets 210–3
    Network SouthEast 230–3
    printing techniques 28, 29, 30, 31
    timetables 17, 18, 20, 21, 177, 178, 216
    tourist resorts 24, 25, 31
Pullman 118, 170, 180, 222, 226
R.e.s 222, 250
R.e.s: privatisation of 253
Rail-Air Link 182, 183
Railway Executive Committee 10
Railway Technical Centre, Derby 186, 187
Railways Act, 1993 253
Railways: nationalisation of 10
Ratter, John 108
Raymond, (Sir) Stanley (1913–88) 184
Read, Herbert 155
Reid, Sir Bob (1934–) 220
Reid, Sir Robert (1921–93) 219
Rhodesian Railways 143, 148
Riddles, Robert A 'Robin' (1892–1983) 36, 42
Robertson, Sir Brian (1896–1974) 15
Rolling Stock Companies (ROSCOs) 253
Rootes Group 122
Royal College of Art (London) 106, 113, 114, 115
Royal Festival Hall 62
Royal Society of Arts 187
Russell, Sir Gordon 108
Saatchi & Saatchi 223
Scottish Design Centre 166
Seaspeed 176, 183
Shaw, Phoebe (an Inter-City 'Monica' model) 210, 211
Shell-Mex and B P 81
Sign Standards [design manual], 1948 65, 66
Signal box: power 101
Signs: new signs for stations 179
Skeggs, Tony 221
Society of Industrial Artists 149
South West Trains 253
Staff grades
    Driver 170
    Excess Luggage clerk 32, 33, 34, 35
    Foreman 32, 33, 34, 35
    Guard 32, 33, 34, 35, 170
    Inspector 32, 33, 163
    Porter (including Senior or Leading Porter) 32, 33, 34, 35, 163, 164
    Purserette 182, 183
    Rail-Air Link hostess 182, 183
    Secondman 170
    Senior Station Master 163, 165
    Signalwoman 33
    Station Master 32, 33, 34, 35, 163, 165
    Ticket Collector 32, 33, 34, 35, 163, 164, 165
    Yard Master 34, 35
Stansted Express 236
State Railway of Thailand 245
Stations
    Apsley (Hertfordshire) 60
    Banbury (Oxfordshire) 59
    Barking (London) 69
    Barrow-in-Furness (Cumbria) 69, 70
    Bedford (Bedfordshire) 100
    Belvedere (Kent) 96
    Birmingham New Street 47
    Birmingham New Street (West Midlands) 90, 91, 92, 101
    Bishop's Stortford (Hertfordshire) 100

Bishopstone (Sussex) 60, 61
Bletchley (Buckinghamshire) 83
Bootle New Strand (Merseyside) 62
Broad Street 238
Brondesbury Park 240
Brondesbury Park 240
Broxbourne (Hertfordshire) 74, 75
Burnage (Lancashire) 82
Camberley (Surrey) 98, 99
Cannon Street (London) 86
Charing Cross (London) 90
Chelford (Cheshire) 82
Chichester (West Sussex) 69, 70, 71
Colchester (Essex) 72, 73
Congleton (Cheshire) 83
Corrour (Inverness-shire) 66
Coventry (Warwickshire) 76, 78, 79
Dalston Junction (Greater London) 84
East Croydon (Surrey) 240
East Didsbury (Lancashire) 82, 83
Edinburgh Haymarket (Lothian) 65
Euston (London) 86, 87, 88, 89
Fenchurch Street (London) 86
Fleet (Hampshire) 94, 95
Folkestone Central (Kent) 74, 75
Forest Hill (London) 94
Gatley (Cheshire) 82
Gatwick Airport (West Sussex) 100
Glasgow Queen Street (Lanarkshire) 90, 91
Gleneagles (Perthshire) 66
Greenford (Middlesex) 60, 62
Hadley Wood (Greater London) 83, 84, 98
Handforth (Cheshire) 82, 83
Hanger Lane (Middlesex) 60
Harlow Town (Essex) 76, 77
Harpenden Central (Hertfordshire) 65
Heald Green (Cheshire) 82
Hemel Hempstead (Hertfordshire) 83
Holborn Viaduct (London) 86
Holmes Chapel (Cheshire) 82
Hoylake (Merseyside) 60, 61
Kidsgrove (Staffordshire) 83
Kings Cross (London) 73, 100
Leytonstone High Road (Essex) 83, 84
Liss (Hampshire) 98
Liverpool Street 238–9
Liverpool Street 72, 73, 238–9
Loughton (Essex) 60
Manchester Piccadilly (Lancashire) 80, 81
Marsh Lane and Strand Road (Merseyside) 62, 63
Mauldeth Road (Lancashire) 82
Maze Hill (London) 96–97, 98
Milton Keynes Central (Buckinghamshire) 101, 102–3
Mossley Hill (Merseyside) 82
New Cross (London) 98, 99
Oxford Road, Manchester (Lancashire) 78, 79
Perivale (Middlesex) 60
Potters Bar (Hertfordshire) 69, 70
Queens Park (Middlesex) 62
RA traditional building type (RAT) 240
Radlett (Hertfordshire) 100
Ruislip Gardens (Middlesex) 69
Rye House (Hertfordshire) 98
Sandbach (Cheshire) 82
Sawbridgeworth (Hertfordshire) 83, 84
Sheffield Victoria (South Yorkshire) 72, 73
South Kenton (Middlesex) 62
South Ruislip (Middlesex) 69
Southampton (Hampshire) 98
Southend on Sea Central (Essex) 73
St Pancras (London) 85
St. Helens Shaw Street (Lancashire) 80, 81
St. Pancras (London) 252
Stafford (Staffordshire) 83
Stone Crossing Halt (London) 66
Sunbury (Middlesex) 95
Sunderland (County Durham) 84, 85
Tamworth (Staffordshire) 83
Tolworth (Surrey) 60
Waterloo (London) 90
Waterloo International (London) 252
West Hampstead (Middlesex) 63
West Ruislip (Middlesex) 69
Winnersh 240
Wolverhampton High Level (Staffordshire) 83
Wood Street (London) 98, 99

Stations: 'air rights' over 85, 86
Stations: and urban development 85, 86
Stations: catering 72, 73, 88, 89, 90, 91–93
Stations: for InterCity 226
Stations: interiors 76, 78, 79, 81, 86, 87, 88, 89, 95
Stations: planning of 62, 74, 76, 86, 87, 88, 89, 95
Stations: redevelopment of 86, 87, 88, 89, 95
Structural Engineers: Anthony Hunt Associates 252
Summerson, T H 39, 108, 157, 159
Superloo (Euston, London, station) 89
Swedish Railways 163, 164
Symbols, brand marks and logos
    bar and circle 11
    British Railways crest 14, 33, 34, 35
    British Railways crest: on vehicles 15
    British Railways lion & crown 15, 163, 165, 170, 172
    British Railways lion & crown: on vehicles 15
    British Railways logotype 18, 20, 21, 26, 27, 28, 29
    British Road Services 15
    British Transport Waterways 14
    development for British Rail 172
    Docks and Inland Waterways Executive 14
    double arrow 173, 176, 217
    double arrow: on uniforms 208–9, 227
    Glasgow Suburban electrification scheme 158, 159
    lion & wheel 11, 172
    lion & wheel: British Railways 13
    lion & wheel: British Railways: on uniforms 32, 33, 34, 35
    lion & wheel: British Road Services 14
    lion & wheel: British Transport 14
    LNER lozenge 12
    Load Haul 249
    London Midland Railway 19, 20, 118

London Transport bar and circle 11, 14, 15, 172
Mainline Freight 249
Railfreight subsector marks 248–9
totem 11, 12, 14, 15, 65–7, 68, 172
totem: cessation of use 14, 15, 18
totem: colours for 12, 13, 19
totem: forms of 13, 19, 20
totem: on publicity 12, 14, 15, 16, 18, 19, 20, 21–27, 30
totem: on signs 12, 14, 65–7, 68
totem: on uniforms 32, 33, 34, 35
Transrail Freight 249
Western Railway 19, 20
Taylor Woodrow 86
Terylene 189
Thameslink 234–5
Thameslink 2000 228
Thameslink Express 237
The Reshaping of British Railways 158, 184
Thomas, Cecil Walter (1885–1976) 11
Tickets: design and production of 214–5
TOPS computer system 184
Train Operating Companies (TOCs) 253
Transport Act, 1947 10
Transport Act, 1953 15
Transport Act, 1953 10
Transport Act, 1962 105
Transport Act, 1968 184
Travelling Post Office 54
Uniform design: influence of European examples 163
Uniforms
    cap badge 14, 32, 33, 34, 35, 162, 163, 165, 170, 182
    cap badge (1978) 208 9

    cap badge (1988) 227
    design of 32, 162–5, 166, 170, 182
    design of (1978) 208–9
    design of (1988) 227
    design of (1991) 227
    insignia (1978) 208–9
    insignia (1988) 227
    InterCity (1991) 227
Vauxhall Cresta motor car 136
Vauxhall Motors 130, 136
Vauxhall Victor motor car 130, 136
Victoria and Albert Museum 149
Victoria line 172
Victorian Society 85
Vitrolite 81
Wansborough-Jones, Major-General Llewelyn 108
Warerite 71, 72, 73
Washington Metropolitan Area Transit Authority, USA 206
Wessex Electrics 235
Western Pullman 116, 118–21
White, A J 12, 13, 14, 65, 67
White, A J, and Railway Executive totem symbol 14
Wickens, Dr Alan 186
Williams, George (–1965) 106, 108, 109, 116, 122, 146, 146, 157, 158–159, 166, 172, 174, 187
Williams, George: on British Railways' public image 157, 168
Wisconsin Central 249
Worboys, (Sir) Walter 158
Your New Uniform [staff booklet] 182

Picture credits

Pictures are referenced by their vertical position on the page and then the column, for example: T(op), U(pper), U(pper) M(iddle), Lo(wer) M(iddle), B(ottom), Le(ft column), R(ight column), U(pper) M(iddle) Le(ft), and so on. T(op), M(iddle) and B(ottom) are used where there are two or three images on a page.

Alexander Donnis: 242 B. British Railways Board and British Railways Board/Ian Allan Library: 33 B; 36 UM, LoM, B; 37 UML, LMR, BR; 43 TL, BL; 44; 45 TLe, TR; 46 TL, BL; 48 LL; 56; 69 T; 72 all; 73 all; 75 TLe, BLe, TR; 76 all; 77 all; 79 M; 80 all; 81 B; 82 all; 83 all; 84 all; 85; 88 T; 90 all, 91 all, 92 all; 94 B; 96 7; 98 UM; 99 M, B; 100 B; 101; 102–3; 114; 115; 119 B; 133 M, B; 134 TLe, BLe, TR; 162; 164–5; 166 M, B; 168; 169 BLe, TR, BR; 173 LR; 175; 176; 177; 179 BLe, BR; 180; 181; 182 main; 183 all; 185 T, M; 186 B; 187 all; 189 TR, BR; 190; 191 all; 192 L; 193 M, By; 197 T; 198 B; 203 MLe; 204 BLe, MR; 207 BR; 208 all; 217 all; 220; 221; 225 TR; 226 all; 234 B; 238 B. Gerry Barney: 173 BLe. Ben Brooksbank: 98 T; 238 M. Collection David Burnicle: 197 B; 198 T; 199 TLe, MLe, BLe; 200 B; 201 all; 202 all; 203 T. David Christie: 120 B; 128 BR; 137 MR; 140 MR; 148; 150 B; 151 BR; 152–3; 154 B; 155 U. Ian Folland: 203 BR. Collection Chris Green: 218; 230 T; 231 TM, TR, BLe, BM; 235 all; 236 B; 237 TR; 238 B. Collection Anthony Hill: 146 T; 147 all. Atholl Hill: 188 Le, TR, MR; 189 TLe, MLe. Jack Howe: 119 T. Ian Allan Library: anonymous: 37 TLe, TR; 46 TR; 78; 79 T; 124 T, M; 135 M; 155 T; 159 M; 169 MLe; 170 all; 185 B; 192 U, L; 211; 224; 236 M; 252 Le; Harry Bedford: 46 MR; Paul A Biggs: 247 TLe; C P Boocock: 199 BR; Kyle F Bosworth: 151 TR; David Brown: 41; J Buckley: 36 T; John W Byrne: 237 BR; P Dark: 53; 145 R; R S Freeman: 48 ULe; 207 TLe; J G Glover: 98 U; P H Groom: 55 B; M Hale: 43 MLe; Brian Haresnape: 156; Peter Harris: 135 Le; Philip D Hawkins: 43 MR; M Hilbert: 246 M; Ian G Holt: 50 LMLe; John F Hughes: 136; C G Maggs: 179 TR; C J Marsden: 204 BR; Chris Metcalfe: 51 B; Chris Morrison: 47; 246 B; G R Mortimer: 50 TLe; T W Nicholls: 194; D Penney: 37 UMR; B Perryman: 51 T; John Robertson: 37 BLe; D Rodgers: 131 BR; P J Sharpe: 43 TR; 46 MLe; 50 UMLe, TR, UMR; 131 MR; Alec Swain: 52 Le; H Wheeler: 37 LoMLe. Nick Jardine, courtesy of Tabitha Bodin: 81 T. Brian Morrison: 193 T; 207 BL; 237 L; 245 B; 247 B; 250 B. Collection Michael Papps: 99 TR; 100 T; 240 M, Lo. Collection Jane Priestman: 228; 252 BR. Roger Jones: 247 MLe, TR, MR. Private collection: 67; 68 M, Lo. Collection Peter Raybould: 34-5. Collection Michael Walton: 22–3 all; 24–5 all; 27 LE; 31 all; 48 R; 52 TR, BR; 118 B; 220; 232 T. Wilkes & Ward/Jack Ward: 4; 104; 107 T; 109 T; 123; 125 T; 128 TLe, BLe, TR; 130 T; 131 T; 132 all; 133 T; 137 T, MLe; 138 T, M; 139; 140 Le, TR, BR; 142 T; 145 TLe; 146 M, B; 160 all; 161 all; 169 TLe; 186 T; 192 T; 204 TLe. Bill Wright: 38 U; 114 BLe, BR; 117 all; 126 B; 127 Le, BR; 131 BLe; 137 BLe; 138 B; 142 U, Lo; 144 all; 150 T, M; 155 B. Alan Young: 65 BR; 66 M, Lo.

All other images: collection David Lawrence.

The British Rail Double Arrow Trademark Number: 2107832, and associated logotype are reproduced by permission of the Department for Transport.

⇌ 272